THE DONNELLYS

*To the survivors and their offspring in the
hope that times have passed and peace has come.*

JOHN LITTLE

THE DONNELLYS

VOLUME II

MASSACRE, TRIAL AND AFTERMATH, 1880–1916

Published by ECW Press
665 Gerrard Street East
Toronto, Ontario, Canada M4M 1Y2
416-694-3348 / info@ecwpress.com

Cover design: David A. Gee
Map designs: Rhys Davies

LIBRARY AND ARCHIVES CANADA CATALOGUING
IN PUBLICATION

Title: The Donnellys / John Little.

Names: Little, John R., 1960- author.

Description: Contents: v. 2. Massacre, trial and
aftermath, 1880–1916.

Identifiers: Canadiana (print) 20210191104 | Canadiana
(ebook) 20210191120

ISBN 978-1-77041-620-8 (v. 2 ; softcover)
ISBN 978-1-77305-836-8 (v. 2 ; ePub)
ISBN 978-1-77305-837-5 (v. 2 ; PDF)
ISBN 978-1-77305-838-2 (v. 2 ; Kindle)

Subjects: LCSH: Donnelly family. | LCSH: Murder—
Ontario—Lucan. | LCSH: Criminals—Ontario—Lucan.

Classification: LCC HV6810.L8 L58 2021 | DDC
364.152/3092271325—dc23

This book is funded in part by the Government of Canada. *Ce livre est financé en partie par le gouvernement du Canada.*
We acknowledge the support of the Canada Council for the Arts. *Nous remercions le Conseil des arts du Canada de son
soutien.* We acknowledge the support of the Ontario Arts Council (OAC), an agency of the Government of Ontario, which
last year funded 1,965 individual artists and 1,152 organizations in 197 communities across Ontario for a total of $51.9
million. We also acknowledge the support of the Government of Ontario through Ontario Creates.

PRINTED AND BOUND IN CANADA   PRINTING: MARQUIS   5   4   3   2   1

Cover image by permission of Ray Fazakas, author *The Donnelly Album* and *In Search of the Donnellys.*

"I begged of him for God's sake to do something towards disbanding the Society, for I was sure it would end in murder. The world now knows how terribly my prophecy has been realized."

— WILLIAM DONNELLY

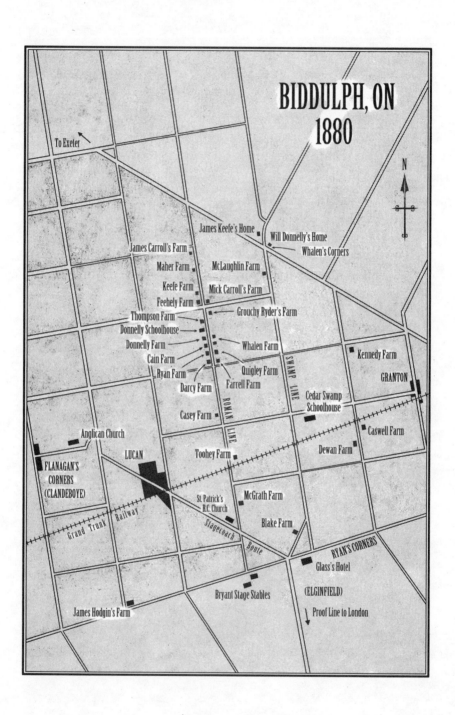

BIDDULPH, ON
1880

N

To Exeter

James Keefe's Home
Will Donnelly's Home
Whalen's Corners

James Carroll's Farm
Maher Farm   McLaughlin Farm
Keefe Farm
Feehely Farm   Mick Carroll's Farm

Thompson Farm   Grouchy Ryder's Farm
Donnelly Schoolhouse
Donnelly Farm   Whalen Farm
Cain Farm
Ryan Farm   Quigley Farm
Darcy Farm   Farrell Farm

Casey Farm

Kennedy Farm

GRANTON

SWAMP LINE

ROMAN LINE

Cedar Swamp
Schoolhouse

Caswell Farm

Anglican Church   Dewan Farm

LUCAN   Toohey Farm

FLANAGAN'S
CORNERS
(CLANDEBOYE)

St. Patrick's   McGrath Farm
R.C. Church

Grand Trunk Railway   Blake Farm

                        Stagecoach
                                  Route   RYAN'S CORNERS

                                     Glass's Hotel

                                     (ELGINFIELD)

James Hodgin's Farm   Bryant Stage Stables

                        Proof Line to London

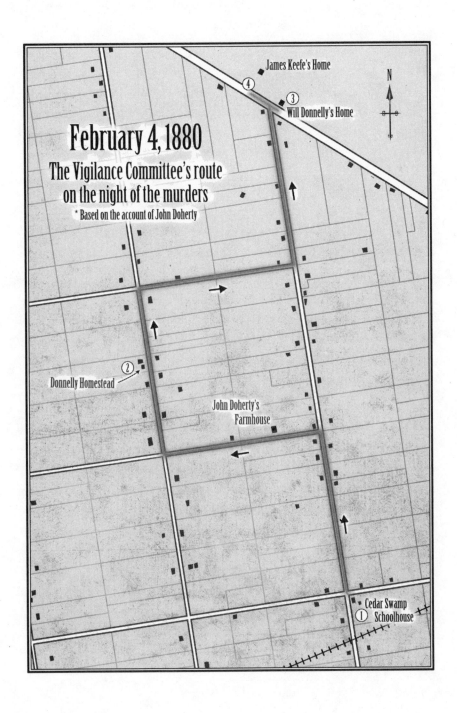

February 4, 1880
The Vigilance Committee's route
on the night of the murders
* Based on the account of John Doherty

James Keefe's Home

Will Donnelly's Home

Donnelly Homestead

John Doherty's
Farmhouse

Cedar Swamp
Schoolhouse

N

TABLE OF CONTENTS

PREFACE

A perfect storm of events, supposed, actual, communal and spiritual, combined to set the wheels in motion for the Donnelly family's destruction. (Artwork courtesy of Ben Little / Bob Donnelly image by permission of Ray Fazakas, author of *The Donnelly Album* and *In Search of the Donnellys*)

"The very ink with which all history is written," Mark Twain once said, "is merely fluid prejudice." While this adage from the Connecticut scribe is a certainly a cynical view of history, it proved to be true in regard to the Donnelly tragedy. When a physician friend of mine learned of the subject matter of this book during a recent conversation, he felt obliged to exclaim, "Ah, the *Black Donnellys*!" The fact that the family was never referred to by that appellation during their lifetime is lost on most people. Indeed, the only time anyone came close to using the term was when William Meredith, a lawyer and politician, told the jury of the first trial during his closing remarks that what they had heard were "incredible lies, from the *black heart* of William Donnelly!" While we don't know how black William Donnelly's heart was, we do know that, in time, the term became affixed to the Donnelly name. This shouldn't be surprising; after all, those who killed the family (and those who supported them both before and after the deed) far outnumbered the Donnellys who survived. And so, it was *their* version of the tale that would be told and retold for the better part of a century after the killings. It was *their* version of events that predominated in the press and in the first books written about the tragedy (one need only see the title of Thomas P. Kelley's *The Black Donnellys* for proof of this).

That the Donnellys were not a family of saints is clear — but what family in Biddulph township was? The problem, it seems, is that the Donnellys never sought the protection of a group; their number, and, thus, their strength, was firmly fixed to the number of their family members. This number had been sufficient to protect them when the boys of the family had grown into young men, but with the deaths of Jim and Mike, the imprisonment of Bob and the fact that Pat was living over a hundred miles away in the Niagara region, the remaining three brothers and their old father were no longer powerful enough to defend themselves. In short, this family of outsiders was vulnerable, which gave their adversaries the opening to put the Donnelly problem to bed once and for all.

It's important to note the people who murdered the Donnellys were not a fraternity of homicidal maniacs, but rather regular, hard-working farmers who slowly began to scapegoat a single family for all their community's problems, conflicts and tribulations. For this to happen several things needed to fall into place: the Donnellys' transgressions needed to be highlighted so as to define them, and other farmers' problems and misdeeds needed to be foisted on the Donnellys, rather than their accusers' own shortcomings. And, finally, the one source of solace and spiritual guidance in a small community — the Catholic parish of St. Patrick's Church — needed to paint the Donnellys as being every bit as evil as their enemies believed.

The amazing thing is that all of these things happened. It was a perfect storm. If any one of the above elements had been missing, the murders may never have occurred.

As it happened, the family's enemies had grown to fear a bogeyman of their own creation, and then sought security within a herd of like-minded individuals. They had allowed their resentment and fear of the Donnellys to distort their judgement so much that, in an attempt to justify the butchery, the Donnellys were painted as an evil family that simply received its comeuppance at the hands of an exasperated township. That they were murdered was unfortunate, yes, it was said, but those who killed them simply had no choice. The position of the community was that they were driven to commit the deed in an effort to save their farms, their town and their lives from a rabid family that was hellbent on destroying all of this. Even the matriarch of the family had to be centred out as being extraordinarily evil (this was necessary as the killing of women and children was particularly frowned upon from an ethical perspective), and so the rumour was spread that the mother of the family was deranged and insisted that each of her children had to kill a man.

This, with few exceptions, has been the tale that has been passed down to Canadians over the generations. As the reader now knows, it has turned out to be a myth, and consequently the township and those in proximity to it later thought it best not to talk of the matter at all. All of Lucan, London and Middlesex County became silent, and even the offspring of the Vigilance Committee members could recall no mention ever being made within their respective homes of the Donnellys, nor of their relatives' role in what was once the biggest news story in the Dominion. It was thought the matter might go away if it was never mentioned. And yet, 141 years later, the tale endures.

By contrast, outside of Middlesex County, the version of the story put forth by the Vigilance Committee never passed muster. And in those areas of the country that didn't depend upon the freedom of twenty to forty men for its success in commerce, tithing and survival, the killers received no such support or loyalty. Indeed, the bulk of Canada's sympathy landed on the side of the murdered family. Even a cursory inspection of the facts makes it clear that in the background of the drama pulling the strings were wealthy business and political interests that wanted the Donnellys gone by any means necessary. And then as now, all of the villagers followed the "golden rule" of power, i.e., those who had the gold made the rules. The Stanley brothers of Lucan certainly had the most gold and opposed any person or family that didn't fall in line with their wishes. And when a Catholic family, particularly one that had a satirist such as William Donnelly at its helm, was only too happy to publicly remind the Stanleys of their own crimes, the higher-ups had to take steps to ensure that such uppity farmers were put in their place. And so, it was done.

I must confess that as I began my research into the story, I half expected to discover that the Donnelly brothers had gone on a murderous rampage to avenge the deaths of their family members; that they would have burned down Maher's farm (where James Carroll and his brother were living), or that Carroll himself would have mysteriously disappeared (instead of living in town for a while longer, then moving out west where he would live into his sixties). But no such thing ever occurred. And the reason, simply, is that the Donnellys were not the fiends their enemies made them out to be; murder simply wasn't their way. There is no evidence that they killed anybody during their wild and woolly youth, and so there was no intrinsic impulse for them to kill afterwards. As before the murders, the Donnellys always settled their problems in the streets (à la John Donnelly's fistfight with Constable Hodgins, or Bob Donnelly's later attempts to draw James Carroll into a fight) or in the courts (under the stewardship of William Donnelly). And that was the way they decided to combat the grievous deaths of their beloved family members after the horrendous night of February 4, 1880.

— JOHN LITTLE, BRACEBRIDGE, ONTARIO, 2021

CHAPTER SEVENTEEN

THE MASSACRE

Donnelly author Ray Fazakas's painting of the Donnelly farmhouse as it would have appeared when James and Tom Donnelly, together with Johnny O'Connor, were arriving back from Lucan on the evening of February 3, shortly before the murders took place. (By permission of Ray Fazakas, author of *The Donnelly Album* and *In Search of the Donnellys*)

The skis of the horse-drawn sleigh cut deep grooves in the snow as James and Tom Donnelly, together with young Johnny O'Connor, travelled northward along the Roman Line. It was still light outside, but the darkness was closing in quickly. Eventually, Tom slowed the team to turn into the laneway of the Donnelly home and brought the horses to a stop beside the house. James Donnelly and Johnny O'Connor stepped down from the sleigh and hurried inside the house to warm up. Tom stayed outside, where he was soon joined by his brother John, and the pair detached the horses from their harnesses and walked them behind the farmhouse and into the stable. It was, O'Connor would later recall, "a very cold night."[1]

After securing and sheltering the horses, Tom and John hurried back to the warmth of the farmhouse. Once inside, they huddled around the stove in the kitchen. Johnny O'Connor was certainly no stranger to the Donnelly farmhouse, having spent the night there several times in the past. His most recent visit was five days previously, when, on Thursday, January 29, the Donnellys had travelled to Granton for their third appearance in court for the arson case. The Donnellys typically arranged with Johnny's parents to pick him up the night before they would be away. He would sleep over and then tend to their livestock — feeding the pigs and cattle — during the family's absence the next day. The routine was expected to be the same this time around. Johnny was sitting at the kitchen table, along with John, Tom and James Sr. and, after some small talk, the conversation shifted to coordinating the travel arrangements for the trip to Granton the next morning. John Donnelly volunteered to go to William's place that night to pick up the O'Connors' cutter. That was welcome news to Tom, who, despite indicating otherwise to William the day before, had no desire to head out to Whalen's Corners on such a cold night. After a quick dinner, John Donnelly headed out to the stable behind the house, saddled up a pony and, throwing the harness for the cutter around its neck, rode off from the property north along the Roman Line. Donnelly neighbour John Whalen would later recall seeing John riding away from the farm at approximately five o'clock.[2]

Not long after John had left, Tom Donnelly and Johnny O'Connor ventured out to the stable to tend to the evening chores. Tom wanted to make sure his horse would be warm, and had Johnny fetch a heavy blanket he could throw over the animal. He then gave the boy a small whip to use to keep the pigs away as he poured their evening meal of feed into the trough. After feeding the hogs, Tom climbed up into the hayloft of the barn and forked out some straw from the stack, which he and Johnny then fed to the horses. The livestock chores now complete for the night, the pair returned to the house and snacked on some apples from the Donnellys' root cellar.

One mile north of the Donnelly farm lies the township of Usborne, which borders on Middlesex County. It was here that long-time Donnelly friends James and Robert Keefe had their farm. Theirs was a good-sized property, one hundred acres, with portions yet uncleared. William Donnelly and James Keefe had been busy most of that afternoon splitting wood together. Two weeks earlier, the men had felled a maple tree, sixteen inches in diameter, that was still green — too small to be of much use for anything other than fuel for the cooking stove and, even then, it would need to be stored for a year in order to dry out sufficiently. But a good supply of firewood was never a bad thing to have around. The pair cut the tree into sections and then spent the afternoon chopping these sections into smaller pieces that would dry out more quickly. They drew the quartered lumber from the woods, taking some of it to Keefe's and the remainder up to William's house at Whalen's Corners, about three-quarters of a mile to the east.

Once at William's house, the two moved the wood out to the back of the house where they split it into smaller pieces and stacked it on the woodpile. When John Donnelly arrived at William's house, it was 5:20 p.m. He dismounted from his pony and led the animal to one of two stables on William's property. A large log stable contained William's stallion — his prized possession, and the animal upon which he had based his breeding business. Not wanting any problems with the stallion, John led his pony to the smaller stable that sat next to it, near the northern end of the house. He propped a stick up against the stable door to ensure that it would remain closed for the night.

William and Nora's house would be busy that evening, as next to arrive was thirty-six-year-old Martin Hogan, fresh from a threshing job in Biddulph. He had come from John Morkin's farm, which sat one mile south on the Eighth Concession. Hogan's plan was to visit with William and Nora, and then head back to Morkin's later that evening, where he would spend the night, as he was about to start a threshing job for the farmer the next morning. Shortly after Hogan arrived, the men finished stacking the wood and then came inside and had dinner. William and Nora were in good spirits: Nora was four months pregnant and, with William's horse breeding business slowly picking up, they were looking forward to the future. After dinner, Nora's father, John Kennedy Sr., dropped in for tea.

I n 2014, when I visited the site of the old Donnelly homestead, I was told by Robert Salts, the man who owned the property, that the Donnellys' original farmhouse was considered to be of standard size for the time. According to Salts, the home was comprised of two parts; a front room that measured eighteen by twenty-six feet, and a large kitchen area, that was added onto the back (or western portion) of the house in 1871.[3] The southwest corner of the kitchen was partitioned off and served as Tom's bedroom. Entrance to the dwelling was accomplished through two doors; a front door in the main room that faced east toward the Roman Line, and a rear door in the kitchen area that faced south onto the Donnellys' lane way. The kitchen door was situated just slightly east of Tom Donnelly's bedroom. The southern half of the front room of the house had also been partitioned off to accommodate two bedrooms. The northern half functioned as the family's living room.

James and Johannah slept in the room closest to the front door, while Bridget slept in the room nearest the kitchen. In James and Johannah's room sat a large four-poster bed, the posts of which reached almost to the ceiling. A valance typically hung down and around the bed for privacy, but it had been removed during Mike Donnelly's wake at the house and Johannah hadn't reattached it since. James and Johannah's room was separated from the adjacent bedroom by an inch-thick partition wall that didn't quite reach the ceiling. The front room of the house also contained a stairway along its northern wall that led up to a loft in the upper level of the house.

James Donnelly decided he and Johnny O'Connor would sleep in the big bed that night, while Bridget and Johannah would sleep in the guest room. Tom was willing to have Johnny sleep with him in his bed just off the kitchen, but he was overruled by his father on the matter. When John came back from William's house, he could bunk in with Tom. James Donnelly Sr. said his prayers, climbed into bed and rolled up his coat to make a pillow for Johnny, who crawled into bed with him shortly afterwards. The head of their bed faced east toward the front of the house and hugged the south wall. Johnny slept on the inside, next to the wall, with James sleeping on the outside closest to the bedroom door.

Tom, Bridget and Johannah Donnelly stayed up a little longer that evening, talking at the kitchen table. As they were talking, someone knocked on their kitchen door. It was James Feeheley. He'd seen the light on in the kitchen, he said, and had popped in to say hello. He wouldn't be staying long. Tom welcomed him in and pulled up a chair for their guest to join them at the table. But Feeheley wasn't paying a social visit, of course. He was there to gather intel on the family for the benefit of the Vigilance Committee, some of whom had already started to gather a little farther south on the Roman Line. Feeheley made small talk with the family members, asking innocent questions about who was in the home, where they would all be sleeping, and looking about to see where any weapons might be located.

Johnny O'Connor heard the voices coming from the kitchen, and then turned and buried his head deeply into James Donnelly's coat. A few minutes later he was fast asleep. Feeheley had no idea Johnny O'Connor was even in the house, as the boy had gone to bed prior to Feeheley's arrival in a room that was not visible from the kitchen. When either the women or Tom mentioned "Johnny" being in the house, Feeheley just assumed they were talking about

John Donnelly — not Johnny O'Connor.[4] After having taken the measure of the surroundings but staying and talking long enough to avoid raising any suspicion about his intent, James Feeheley said good night and departed from the Donnelly home. He headed south on the Roman Line to a place where James Carroll and James Maher were waiting for him. He told them who was in the house and what rooms they would be sleeping in that night. The men nodded and then Carroll sent Feeheley north to spy on William Donnelly's house at Whalen's Corners. He wanted to know who came in and out of the dwelling.[5] Feeheley was further instructed to wait outside William Donnelly's place until Carroll and other members of the Committee arrived there later that evening.

Unlike his parents' home on the Roman Line, the house within which William and Nora Donnelly lived was far more modest. A single story dwelling, the house originally had but two rooms. Over the years its owner, Edward Sutherby, had attached three additional rooms onto it, affixing a modest sized kitchen to the rear of the home, a workshop to the front, and a small woodshed off the southern end of the kitchen. The house was situated just east of Eighth Concession Road, which ran north and south, and Whalen Road, which ran east and west. Its location was just a handful of yards from where the two roads intersected. William and Nora's bedroom was within the northernmost of the two original rooms of the house. The southernmost of the two original rooms was now a guest room.

Gathered around the kitchen table that evening were William, Nora and John Donnelly, along with John Kennedy Sr., James Keefe and Martin Hogan. The main topic of discussion was the Ryder barn burning case, and how it was all a set-up by the Vigilance Committee. The next morning the Donnelly parents would make their move against Committee member Grouchy Ryder by filing their countersuit for malicious prosecution. John Kennedy Sr. was no fan of the Vigilance Committee, nor of his son John's involvement with it. He stood up from the table and announced that he was heading home. He wished William luck at his parents' court case, said his goodbyes and left the house. Nora's pregnancy, coupled with her work around the house that day, had left her tired, and, after putting another stick of wood in the stove at 9:30 p.m., she headed off to bed. The men stayed up talking for another hour or so, at which point James Keefe decided it was time for him to head home as well. The wood splitting had tired him out, and he knew the Donnelly brothers had to get up early the next morning in order to travel to Granton for their parents' trial. He said his goodbyes and left through the kitchen door, stepping out under a small, covered section where the roof projected out some six feet beyond the doorway. Unbeknownst to all, James Feeheley was watching from the shadows.

With Keefe's departure, Martin Hogan felt he should call it a night too. He stood up and put on his jacket and mitts, but John Donnelly told him to stay. "Morkin has a large family," he said. "They will all be in bed now, and you had better stay."[6]

John had decided to stay the night, and they could talk a bit, and the bed in William's guest room was big enough to accommodate both of them. Apparently, this persuaded Hogan to stick around. The three men continued talking until 12:30 a.m., and then William announced he was turning in for the night. He showed John and Martin to the guest room and bade them good night. There wasn't as much heat in the guest room as there had been in the kitchen, which caused Hogan to quip, "We'll have lots of *fresh air* in here!" William laughed. He put another stick of wood in the box stove, then wound the kitchen clock and entered his bedroom. He noticed right away that Nora was still awake, and lying on his side of the bed.

"Shove over," he said.

"No," Nora laughed. "I have got my side of the bed warm and I'm not going to warm yours!"

William chuckled and crawled over her to the inside of the bed next to the wall. It was cold outside, but the wood stove in the kitchen was throwing off sufficient heat to make the room, in his words, "comfortable that night. I was nice and warm when I went to bed." He didn't fall asleep right away. Despite the fact that the door separating his bedroom from the guest room was closed, he could still hear the muffled conversation of John and Martin going on. Nevertheless, by one o'clock that morning, everybody in the house was fast asleep.

A sudden disturbance in the bedroom woke Johnny O'Connor from his slumbers. Through sleepy eyes he saw James Donnelly Sr. was now out of bed and on his feet. The light of a candle flickered from just outside the bedroom door. James Donnelly's movements were casting shadows across the bedroom wall. He heard voices — raised voices — one of them being James Donnelly's. The other voice was familiar, but Johnny was too soon into consciousness to make the identification.

"Where's Jack?" the boy thought he heard the man ask.

"He isn't in!" snapped the old man.

"Well, where is he?" the voice from the darkness asked again.

"Didn't I tell you he wasn't in?"

The boy's senses were now at full acuity.

"Well, I'm arresting *you*, then," said the voice.

"What are you arresting me for *now*?" asked James Donnelly, a hint of desperation now colouring his discourse.

"I've got another charge against you," said the voice.

"Hold the light here till I've dressed myself," said the old man.

The flickering light moved closer to the doorway, illuminating more and more of the bedroom as it approached. Clearly someone was holding a candle, and when that person moved directly in front of the doorway to the room, the light from the candle reflected back at him from the bare walls and revealed his identity: it was James Carroll. Johnny knew Carroll was a constable, as he had seen him around Lucan. The boy could have sworn Carroll was staring right at him as he stood in the doorway. But with the old man moving around as he pulled on his pants and suspenders, he was casting shadows upon everything behind him, including young O'Connor lying in the bed next to the wall. The incandescence from the candle allowed Johnny to see Constable Carroll clearly: he saw that Carroll was wearing a soft felt hat, a black coat and grey flannel trousers. From the bedroom next door, he heard Johannah's voice telling Bridget to get up and start a fire in the kitchen stove. He next heard the sound of the womens' feet upon the floorboards as they made their way toward the kitchen. Soon light beamed into the front room from the kitchen as a candle was lit and the stove door was opened to allow Bridget to put some wood in and reignite the fire.

"Where's my coat?" asked James Donnelly loudly enough for his wife to hear him in the kitchen. He had forgotten for the moment that he had placed it in his bed as a makeshift pillow for O'Connor.

"I don't know where it is," answered Johannah.

The old man sighed and made his way to the kitchen to look for his coat. As he walked to the kitchen, Carroll remained behind in the front room, walking about with his candle exploring the contents within the room that would soon be lost to history. He looked at the cabinet and the clock, as well as some photographs and religious artefacts that were hung upon the walls. He began whistling a now forgotten tune as he walked about the room. Only he knew what was about to go down; the family never saw it coming.

Not finding his coat in the kitchen, James Donnelly returned to the bedroom. By now Johnny O'Connor was sitting up in the bed, his presence still unknown to Carroll as the constable meandered about the front room. When O'Connor had sat up in bed, he noticed the coat he had been using for a pillow. He picked it up and handed it up to the old man, who was squinting his eyes in an attempt to locate the garment.

"Here it is," O'Connor said.

James Donnelly took the coat from the boy and put it on. He fumbled around near the bed and found his spectacles, which he also put on, and then left the bedroom and headed back toward the kitchen. James Carroll and his candle followed him from behind.

Upon entering the kitchen, James Sr. was shocked to see his son Tom had already been handcuffed. Tom was livid. Evidently Carroll had snuck into the house, gone directly to Tom's bedroom and slipped the handcuffs on him while the young man was still asleep.

"Tom, are you handcuffed?" asked the old man.

Carroll now entered the kitchen.

"Yes, he thinks he's smart," Tom said. He looked at Carroll with contempt.

Carroll smirked with a confidence that was strangely out of place for a lamb in a lion's den.

James Donnelly wanted answers. "Jim," he said, turning to Carroll, "what have you got against me now?"

"I've got another charge against you."

"Read the warrant!" Tom demanded.

Carroll smiled again. "There's lots of time for that," he said.

An awkward silence followed. Carroll said nothing. He made no move. Tom looked to his father. There was something strange going on here.

Suddenly the kitchen door burst open and upwards of twenty men — armed with shillelaghs, sticks, axes and shovels — charged in and immediately began attacking the Donnellys. Blows rained down violently and incessantly upon the family members; the two old people were driven into the northwest corner of the kitchen by the bombardment of strikes they received. Tom Donnelly, still bound in handcuffs, fought back as best he could. Bridget shrieked and ran out of the kitchen, through the front room and toward the stairway that would deliver her to the loft where she mistakenly thought she would find sanctuary. Johnny O'Connor heard the violence coming from the kitchen (which he described as sounding like "hammering") and caught sight through the bedroom door of Bridget screaming for her life as she ran toward the stairs. Johnny immediately leapt from the bed and ran up the stairs after her. But once he reached the entrance to the loft, Bridget slammed the door behind her, leaving him alone at the top of the stairs. Johnny was now understandably terrified; he turned and ran back down the stairs and across the still-darkened front room back into the bedroom. Once inside the room he dove under the bed and pulled a laundry basket in front of him for additional cover. The basket was large, coming almost up to the bottom of the bed frame, but there was still enough space for him to see over the top of it. And while the boy couldn't see what was happening in the kitchen, he certainly heard all of it. Every sickening whack of a club on a human skull, arm or ribcage, every strike of a foot or a fist, or a shovel or an axe — and every word that was said or screamed. Reams of copy have been published on things claimed to have been said and done during the murders,[7] but most of this has been reported by people who weren't there when the crime was being committed, such as reporters looking for sensationalist copy and writers seeking to support a particular thesis. Johnny O'Connor, however, was there and would report unwaveringly in his testimony as to what he heard and saw that night. It was not an experience anyone could forget. In truth, nothing was said by the murderers during the commission of the act. Nothing needed to be. The crime had been premeditated. All the people involved in the murders knew what they were doing; there was nothing to say, only actions to be carried out.

Johannah Donnelly was beaten savagely as she tried to flee from the kitchen to the front room; she would make it only as far as the threshold separating the two rooms. There, as the weapons bit into her arms, legs and head, she stumbled and fell — and that's when the clubs of the mob finished her off.[8]

James Donnelly Sr., at almost sixty-five years of age, had no chance of fighting back. The numbers in the opposition were too great. Struck savagely and incessantly with hardwood clubs, he was overwhelmed and collapsed in the corner of the kitchen near the stove. Still the blows rained down upon him until his skull was smashed and his life extinguished.[9]

Tom Donnelly, believed to be the strongest of the brothers, had fought back hard, deflecting what blows he could with his hand-cuffed arms, and striking back when able. When James Toohey moved in on him, Tom struck him in the face, which blackened Toohey's eye,[10] and sent him sprawling backwards onto the floor. His fall had created an opening in the crowd, an exit path leading from the kitchen to the front room. If Tom could make it through the room to the front door, there was a chance he could get outside and away from the mob. At this point he would have to, literally, run for his life. It was the only chance he had. Tom bulled his way through the opening like a linebacker, absorbing blows from clubs as he ran from the kitchen through the front room directly to the front door, which he hit so hard with his shoulder that he almost broke it from its hinges. From his vantage point under the bed, Johnny O'Connor witnessed Tom's valiant attempt to escape. He recognized Tom's stocking feet run past the bedroom door, as well as numerous other pairs of booted feet that followed him in hot pursuit. O'Connor estimated there were at least twenty people in the house at the time, and the bulk of them were now after Tom.

Once outside the front door, Tom had started to run toward the Roman Line when he was intercepted by some of the Vigilance Committee members who had been stationed outside in the event of such an escape attempt. Tom absorbed more blows from their clubs as they encircled him and continued pounding on him until he hit the ground, at which point the mob now set upon their prey and more clubs began beating him unceasingly.[11] Johnny heard Tom cry out, "Oh! Oh! Oh!" as the Committee members continued their onslaught. Blood flowed freely from Tom's wounds and pooled beneath him. It seeped out into the snow, and more blood sprayed out with each additional swing from a club, causing him to twitch and turn in a futile effort to protect himself. His spasmodic movements left three pools of crimson in and around the area where he was lying.

Across the road, staring from behind the front fence of John Whalen's property, stood William Feeheley. He did nothing but look on as his old friend Tom Donnelly was being beaten to death. Feeheley looked up to the bedroom window of the Whalen home and saw John Whalen placidly watching the murder as well.[12] When Feeheley looked back, Tom Donnelly was now lying motionless on the ground, not twelve feet from his front door. But the Vigilance Committee couldn't leave his body lying outside the home; it had to be made to look like the Donnellys had been killed by an act of God — a fire, not butchered by a mob. Three of the men who had been beating Tom Donnelly — whom Feeheley had recognized as being James Toohey, Patrick Quigley and James Maher[13] — now picked up his body and carried it back inside, through the front door of the Donnellys' house. There they dropped him on the floor. Still William Feeheley looked on. He looked on from directly across the road where he could see inside the still-open front door of the Donnelly home, the same home where he had been taken in and fed many times over the years. He looked on as the men in the kitchen area stepped over the inert body of Johannah Donnelly and entered the front room. And he looked on as Tom Donnelly suddenly sat upright, his will to survive trying desperately, one last time, to assert itself. Donnelly opened his mouth as if to say something,[14] but one of the men yelled, "Hit that fellow with a spade — and break his skull open!" And he looked on as Patrick Quigley raised his spade and brought it crashing down on Tom Donnelly's skull.[15]

From his vantage point under the bed, Johnny O'Connor had seen Tom Donnelly's sock feet when the men had dropped his body right in front of the open bedroom door. He cringed as he heard the sound of Quigley's spade striking Tom's skull not once, but three or four times more. And then the youngest Donnelly brother stirred no more.

One of the men standing around his body called out, "Fetch the candle here!" A man with a candle then entered the front room from the kitchen. His arrival brought light into the room. At this point O'Connor saw faces that he recognized, as well as some of the weapons the Committee members had employed to great effect that evening. He saw a hand-hewn club in a man's hand, which O'Connor recognized as being "a cord wood stick, split fine, with three sides chopped at the end, and the handle whittled." Such a stick would not just bludgeon, but any one of its three distinct edges would dig into whatever it contacted, almost like an axe. Peeking out around the edge of the laundry basket, the boy could see some of the faces of the mob, but they were not easy to identify — one had his face darkened with grease, another was wearing a hat, still another had on a woman's dress.[16] Others that he could see clearly were strangers to him.

Of the men that now gathered around Tom Donnelly's body, O'Connor recognized John Purtell and Thomas Ryder, who were in the process of removing the handcuffs from Tom's wrists. This they had to do; there could be no evidence of his having been manacled prior to the fire being set, as steel handcuffs wouldn't melt in the blaze and their presence would reveal that a murder had occurred. As O'Connor recollected, "Purtell was dressed in black clothes; Ryder had on a peaked cap. Purtell and Ryder were standing up straight around where Tom's body was. I know Purtell and Ryder well, just as well as I did Carroll." As the mob stood gathered around Tom Donnelly's body, one of them noted they had overlooked somebody.

"Where's the girl?" he inquired.

"Upstairs!" declared another voice.

Immediately members of the mob rushed to ascend the stairs to the loft where Bridget Donnelly was hiding. O'Connor pressed himself farther under the bed until his legs were touching the wall. He heard no noise coming from upstairs. Shortly afterwards the group returned from upstairs. One of them was asked how it went with the girl. "She's all right," came the curt reply. The men left the front room and returned to the kitchen. Now was the time to enact "God's will." A coal oil lamp was taken from the kitchen table and a portion of its contents poured onto Tom Donnelly's bed. A match was struck and tossed onto the sheets, and the bed caught fire. To ensure that the entire structure would be destroyed, a fire needed to be set in the front room of the house as well. The lamp was brought into the room where Johnny O'Connor was hiding, and the remainder of its flammable liquid was emptied onto the bedsheets above his head. The feet of the man holding the lamp were only inches away from the boy. If O'Connor made a sound, he knew the mob would discover him and beat him to death as they had the others. He held his breath and remained motionless. He could now smell the odour of coal oil in the room as it soaked down into the blankets.

"The coal oil will burn off and won't set fire to the beds at all," said a voice that came from outside the room. O'Connor watched as the man in the room walked over to the small window on the east wall of the bedroom and placed the lamp on the sill. Next, he heard the sound of a match being struck, followed by the sound of flame consuming fabric. The sheets burned first, then the mattress, but before the flames could drop any lower through the bed, the man turned and left the room. O'Connor now heard the sound of many pairs of boots upon the wooden floor in the kitchen, and then the sound of people tromping through the snow as they passed beside his bedroom window and onward toward the road. But for the corpses, the house was now empty.

The boy knew that, despite the proximity of the mob outside, if he didn't make his move to escape now he would be burned alive. He quickly scrambled out from under the bed. By now the room was completely illuminated from the flames of the burning bed. He spotted his coat lying on the floor and picked it up. Turning, he saw that the fire had already burned through the blankets and the feather tick, and was now devouring the straw mattress beneath. He impulsively struck out at the flames with his jacket, but to no avail; the fire had now extended to the north wall of the bedroom. The levels of smoke and the heat within the house were rising and growing hard to withstand. Looking out through watery eyes, the boy groped for the doorway and made his way haltingly out of the bedroom. Tom Donnelly's bed in the kitchen was totally consumed by flame, which was now eating away at the partition that separated the kitchen from the front room. The smoke was making it hard for O'Connor to breathe. He turned to his right, toward the front door of the house, but Tom Donnelly's broken and bloodied body blocked his way. Looking down, O'Connor could see that Tom Donnelly, unbelievably, was still breathing. The boy paused. He had no way of knowing that Tom was beyond help, but he did know that the fire was rapidly sealing off all avenues of escape. Self-preservation kicked in. If he could get out, he could get help — but he had to get out fast.

Turning to his left, O'Connor made his way toward the kitchen, where he hoped he could exit through the rear door of the house. On his way, and with smoke still burning his eyes, he accidentally stepped on the body of Mrs. Donnelly. Incredibly, she let out a soft moan — she, too, was still alive. Through the smoke he spotted the kitchen door; it had been left ajar by the mob upon their exit. He cut hard to his left and forced his way through it to the outside of the house. The frigid air hit his lungs — hard. Gasping, and in his bare feet on one of the coldest nights of the year, he stumbled south from the house, and then east to the Roman Line. Once on the concession road, he could make out the vague shape of a mob of people heading north. Panicking, the boy started in the opposite direction, running south some fifty yards toward the farmhouse of Patrick Whalen. In so doing he was observed by John Whalen, who was still silently watching everything from his upper-level window.

A t approximately 2:15 a.m., John Donnelly was jolted from his sleep. He was certain he'd heard a noise. Less than ten seconds later he heard somebody pounding on the kitchen door of William's house.

"Fire! Fire!" called a voice from outside in the darkness.

The pounding on the door resumed.

John reflexively was out of bed and on his feet. The calls came again, but this time from a different voice.

"Fire! Fire!"

"Open the door!"

The rapping on the door intensified. John decided to investigate the commotion, waking Martin Hogan as he jumped off the bed and walked across the bedroom floor of the guest room and through the door that led into William Donnelly's bedroom. As it had been cold in the guest room, John still had his clothes on. His entry into the bedroom awakened his brother William, who now also heard the pounding on the door and sat up in his bed. As John walked into William's room, he looked at his brother and asked, "Who's hollering 'fire' and rapping at the door?" William watched as his brother turned to his right and opened the door that led into the kitchen.

Again, the voices came.

"Fire! Fire!"

"Will! Open the door!"

Having reached the kitchen door, John Donnelly now threw it open.

"Who's there?" he asked.

In reply came a blast from a shotgun, augmented by the simultaneous discharge of a rifle. Thirty pieces of shot ripped through John's upper torso, snapping ribs and shattering his collarbone in the process. The bullet from the rifle tore through his groin in an upward trajectory, ripping through his flesh front and back, and ultimately lodging itself in the window frame at the north end of the kitchen. The impact of the shots lifted John off the floor and sent him hurtling backwards several feet, where he hit the door frame to William and Nora's room and then fell onto his back, his head coming to rest against the door jamb. A wad of paper from the shotgun blast slowly floated in from the open door and came to rest upon the kitchen floor. Everyone in the house was now awake.

"Will! Will! I'm shot!" John gasped. His breathing became laboured as he felt his life begin to ebb from his body. He then offered up a short and raspy prayer before the darkness descended upon him. "And may the Lord have mercy on my soul!"

Panic now spread among the occupants of the house.

"Martin! Get up!" William yelled. "John's been shot!"

Hogan, still within the guest room, replied, but only loud enough for William to hear: "Will! Be quiet or *we'll all be killed*!" After a brief pause he added, "It's *you* they want."

Suddenly, seven shots from multiple revolvers rang out from in the front of the house. William and Nora instinctively flattened themselves upon their bed. For a short time, nobody said a word. The only noise in the room was the pitiful sound of John Donnelly's gurgling as blood began to fill his lungs, slowly drowning him.

In time, the noises from outside the home ceased. William sat up and lifted the corner of the blind that covered the glass window next to his bed. Peering out, he saw his brother-in-law, John Kennedy Jr., not nine feet away from the window.

Beyond him, standing several feet farther west, stood James Carroll. Both men were close enough that William could tell what they were wearing — Carroll had on a dark coat and a black hat;

Kennedy was wearing a heavy black cap and an overcoat and was carrying a stick of some sort. William pressed his ear to the window. He heard Kennedy say to Carroll, "Brother-in-law is easy at last." Carroll nodded in the affirmative and replied, "What next?" At least, that was how it sounded to William Donnelly's ear. Beyond Carroll, on the other side of the picket fence at the front of the property, stood several other men whom William thought he recognized — William Carroll, the twenty-year-old brother of James Carroll; Patrick Ryder Jr., the son and namesake of his parents' neighbour on the Roman Line; and twenty-four-year-old Michael Heenan, a farmer from the community. He could make out the sound of other voices, but they were too far away for him to discern the content of their discourse.

John Donnelly suddenly wheezed, which snapped Nora out of her fear of the men outside and drew her attention to the fact that her brother-in-law was dying just a few feet away from her. Her compassion trumped her better judgement. She suddenly leapt out of bed.

"If he's shot, I'm going to him!" she announced.

John was now in his final death throes: the blood in his lungs was causing him to choke; it had backed up in his throat and the overflow was pouring forth from his mouth.

Nora lit the lamp in the bedroom, which caused William to immediately release his hold of the blind. He did not want whoever was outside to see into the house. Nora walked into the kitchen with the lamp and closed the kitchen door, which had remained open since John had been shot. Setting down the candle, she tried to pull John toward the bedroom. "Oh, Lord, he's dying!" she called to William. She tried again to move him, but he was too heavy.

William saw Martin Hogan crawling on his hands and knees toward the kitchen door. "Pull him in!" William called out. Hogan crawled to where Nora was, hooked his arm under John's, and successfully dragged the dying man into William's bedroom. A bloody trail followed the body. Nora ran to get a piece of blessed candle and placed it in John's hands. Hogan had by this point crawled under William's bed and, reaching out, he clasped his hands around John's to ensure that the candle stayed upright. John Donnelly stopped breathing a few minutes later.

"He's dead," Nora said.

William asked his wife what time it was; he wanted to know the exact minute that John had expired. It was a little after 2:30 a.m. Leaving the lamp on the floor, Nora stood up and walked to the kitchen, where she put another piece of wood in the stove. It was all surreal to her; she was clearly in shock. Nora walked through her bedroom to the guest room and brought Hogan's boots and socks to him. Then she began to pace about the house, periodically looking out through the windows to discern if John's killers were still outside. For his part, William was racking his brain trying to identify the voices he had heard calling out his name just prior to the shooting. Beneath his bed he could hear Martin Hogan shaking; the cold floor combined with the terror of what had occurred had left him a nervous wreck. He was still holding the dead man's hands. "Come up onto the bed," William said. Hogan declined; he felt safer being next to the ground.

After a few minutes he heard Hogan lament, "Oh, good God! I always thought they would do this!"

CHAPTER EIGHTEEN

AFTERSHOCK

Johnny O'Connor dressed in the clothes he wore when he ran from the
Donnellys' burning house. The photo was taken a mere several hours
after the murders. (By permission of Ray Fazakas, author of
The Donnelly Album and *In Search of the Donnellys*)

"**W**ho is it?"[1] asked seventy-year-old Ann Whalen as she
shuffled toward her front door. It was 1:30 a.m., far too
late for any of her neighbours to come calling. Johnny O'Connor
had only been waiting a minute or two, but it seemed like an hour
had passed since he had first arrived and pounded on the Whalens'
front door. He was crying, terrified and frozen. Old Ann was taking
far too long to respond to his repeated knocking, and so O'Connor
tried the door and, discovering that it was unlocked, he pushed it
open and stepped inside.

"Who are you?" asked Ann Whalen.

"I'm Mr. O'Connor's boy," he replied in between sobs. His teeth were chattering. Ann Whalen looked down at the boy's feet; he wasn't wearing any shoes or socks. Images of the horror that had just occurred were now running through the boy's mind so rapidly that he couldn't organize or articulate them. When the words came they did so in frenetic bursts.

"A lot of men had come in women's clothes! They hunted the Donnellys out!" he exclaimed, before adding, "and they set the bed on fire!"

Ann Whalen was understandably bewildered by the statements.

Johnny O'Connor suddenly remembered that both Johannah and Tom Donnelly had still been breathing when he left. In his young mind, he didn't comprehend they were dying and their bodies' autonomic nervous systems were simply shutting down slowly. He just knew they appeared to be alive when he left their house and therefore still might be saved.

"Call up the old man!" he cried, in reference to old Patrick Whalen, Ann's husband, who, at sixty-four years of age, was actually younger than his wife. Patrick, however, having heard the pounding on the door and the frantic pronouncements from the boy in the hallway, was already up. He pulled on his pants and walked into the main room of the farmhouse. He opened the stove and motioned for the boy to put his feet up on its hearth to warm himself. After several minutes, Johnny O'Connor was warm and had seemed to calm down somewhat.

"What's brought you out at this time of night, boy?" asked Whalen.

Once again O'Connor said his piece about the group of men who had attacked the Donnellys. He then added, "The house is on fire — call up the boys to go over and quench it!" The boys he was referencing were Patrick Whalen's sons, William and Joseph, who lived at home with their parents but were presently asleep upstairs in the house. Intrigued by the boy's story, Patrick Whalen walked to his window and looked out toward the Donnelly farmhouse. He could see a light in the south window of the home, but to the old man it looked like a lamp on a windowsill. Certainly, there was nothing ominous about it. He turned from the window and looked at O'Connor.

"You must be foolish," Whalen said, "there is no fire there."

O'Connor, however, was adamant. "There is! Call up the boys!"

Whalen snorted derisively. He looked out from his window again and it looked to him now as though the lamp was now out. There was no light in the window. "You are foolish telling such a story as that. You must be dreaming! Are you in the habit of getting up in the night in this way?"

"No, I'm not!" O'Connor exclaimed. "For Mrs. Donnelly is killed!"

"How do you know?"

"I heard them moaning."

Patrick Whalen decided he had better take one more look out his window at the Donnelly farmhouse. When he looked this time, however, he saw flames poking out of the southern portion of the house.

"It's a fire!" exclaimed Whalen. He quickly put on his boots and jacket and left the house, hurrying south along the Roman Line. As he approached the Donnelly farmhouse, he saw his son, John, standing in the doorway of his home, directly across the road from the spectacle. He, too, was watching the flames. Patrick had no idea his son had witnessed the murders occurring from his upstairs window only minutes before, and had only now ventured outside.

"Donnelly's house is all on fire!" yelled the senior Whelan to his son.

"I see it!" John replied. Both men could also see that the back of the Donnelly house, the kitchen area, was now completely engulfed by flames. Patrick ventured onto the Donnelly property and tried to peer in through the front window of the home but all he could see was smoke. Suddenly the gunpowder ignited from the ammunition within the guns that James Donnelly had stored in the corner of his bedroom. The explosion blew out both the front door and window of the house. Fragments of flying glass narrowly missed Whalen's face.

After recovering from the explosion, Whalen walked west to the rear of the building in the hope of obtaining a better view inside. He looked in through the semi-open kitchen door and thought he could make out the shape of what appeared to be a body lying between the kitchen and the front room. The light from the fire had illuminated not only the interior of the house, but also the ground around the structure. Looking down, Whalen noticed that there were many sets of footprints in the snow, which, in his opinion, were "more than I would expect to see." When he returned to the front of the house, he spotted three distinct patches of blood on the ground. The heat from the fire had melted the snow around where the blood was, so there was no longer any evidence of footprints, or any sign of a struggle, that might have led to such a bloodletting.

Back inside the Whalen home, seventeen-year-old Joseph Whalen, the youngest son of the Whalen family, now came downstairs to see what the commotion was about. Upon learning there was a fire at the Donnelly farmhouse, he decided he wanted to investigate. Johnny O'Connor said he would go with him, and, borrowing a pair of socks and boots from Ann Whalen, he returned to the Donnelly property with Joseph. Upon their arrival, Patrick and John Whalen were surveying the fire from a safe distance. The quartet would later recall the experience:

> John Whalen: There was a great deal of black smoke
> coming out of the front of the house. I did not detect
> any unusual smell. I could not say whether the
> smoke was from burning wood or not. The wind was
> blowing from the back toward the front of the house.[2]

Joseph Whalen: I went to the kitchen [area] — the whole house was on fire, back and front. I saw the remains of four bodies. I saw blood outside the front door; about six or seven feet from the door. The fire was too hot to enter the house when I got there. I saw tracks, a good few of them about there, that appeared to be going north.[3]

Johnny O'Connor: We went to the front door and seen a whole lot of blood outside. [There was] too much heat and smoke; we could not get up to the front door.[4]

Patrick Whalen: The only persons who came to the fire was my two sons and Connors; after the fire burned down, I could distinguish what appeared to be the remains of four persons. I could not recognize any of the bodies.[5]

Perhaps out of concern for his sons' safety, perhaps to spare them and young O'Connor from viewing the grisly sight of human bodies being roasted into chunks of charcoal or perhaps because the thickness of the smoke pouring out from the house made visibility useless and any further action impossible, Patrick Whalen decided to take Joseph and Johnny O'Connor back to his house. His son John also departed the scene, walking back across the road to his home, where he would stay for the remainder of the night. Upon arriving back at the Whalen homestead, Patrick Whalen asked Johnny O'Connor a question.

"Did John Donnelly come home? I saw him going down the road earlier."

"I couldn't tell you," replied O'Connor.

"Where did he go?" asked Whalen.

"He went to James Keefe's for a cutter to go to the law tomorrow."

While it was true that John Donnelly had left to pick up a cutter, he had gone to his brother William's house to get it — not James Keefe's. Nevertheless, the belief that John might have gone to Keefe's that night could explain what William Donnelly would observe at some point during the hours that followed, which we will touch upon shortly.

Ann Whalen told her son Joseph and Johnny O'Connor to go to bed in Joseph's bedroom upstairs. But Johnny was still running on adrenalin and wanted to let Ann know more about what he had witnessed at the Donnelly house that night. He told her he thought Mrs. Donnelly had been killed, and Tom as well. He told her that he had been awakened by the noise of the family being bludgeoned, that he had hidden under the bed when the killing started — and that he had observed James Carroll front and centre of it all. This last name served to spook Mrs. Whalen; after all, only a week earlier she had refused to testify on his behalf during the Ryder arson trial, and her husband had chased him from their property with an axe. For all she knew, Carroll and his crew could now be on a rampage, settling scores with those he believed had wronged him.

"How do you know it was Carroll?" she asked.

"I knew by his talk," said O'Connor.

"Don't say anything about it!" replied Ann Whalen, somewhat testily. "I don't want to be brought into this."

O'Connor said nothing more about what he saw.

Patrick Whalen was downstairs during O'Connor's conversation with Ann but, as it was a small house, he clearly heard every word of the discussion. Moreover, he was still fretting over his own conversation with the boy — where was John Donnelly? If he had picked up a cutter and returned home, then the cutter should be somewhere on the Donnelly property. Once again, Patrick Whalen left his house and returned to the Donnelly homestead. The mob had not burned the stables or any other structure on the property; to do so would have made it obvious that the fire was the result of arson, rather than a random act of God. Consequently, the fire had been confined only to the family home. Whalen went to the Donnelly stables and noted that the pony that he saw John Donnelly riding earlier was not there. He looked in at other points around the property and saw no evidence of the cutter John Donnelly was said to have retrieved. He then walked back to the burning building and took another look inside, straining his eyes through the smoke and fire to discern the identity of the corpses. He hadn't been looking long when the kitchen area collapsed in flames. His eyes now focused on what he took to be the body of Johannah Donnelly. "I recognized her," he recalled, "as the flesh was not then all burnt, and I guessed it was her by the size." Whalen would estimate he had been there for about an hour when the roof fell in, sending a shower of sparks skyward:

> There was no big blaze until the roof fell in; I saw
> a body in the front room, but could not be sure
> whose body it was, but thought it was Thomas, as I
> got a good view of it before it was much burnt. The
> body was on the floor between the front door and
> the kitchen door, his head was toward me; he was a
> little north of the door. I could not see distinctly, but
> I think he was on his back. I did not notice anything
> peculiar about his head. When I saw Tom Donnelly's
> body the fire was all about it, and the draught of
> the doors made it worse. What I thought was a coat
> might have been the smoke around the body. I saw
> the fire through all the back kitchen.[6]

Unbeknownst to Patrick Whalen, several things occurred when the roof collapsed. First, what had been concealing the brightness of the flames had now been removed, with the result that the light from the conflagration now shot up into the sky like a searchlight. As this was farming country, the land was predominantly flat, resulting in the fire producing an eerie glow upon the horizon that could be seen for miles. Indeed, William Blackwell, who lived some three miles away to the northeast, claimed, "I went to the window. I saw the reflection of a fire in the direction of the old Donnelly homestead."[7] The second thing that occurred with the structural collapse was that it took out the wall that divided the kitchen from the front room of the house. This wall also served as the primary support for the loft, so when it gave way, the southern portion of the garret dropped down like a trap door, rolling its contents, including the lifeless body of Bridget Donnelly, down into the kitchen. Her body landed beside that of her uncle, James Donnelly, next to the stove. And, finally, the shelter the roof had provided against the cold air had now been ripped away, allowing wind to blow in from the west, which served to magnify the heat and intensify the potency of the flames that continued to move throughout the dwelling. The flames devoured everything in their path, including the bodies of the Donnelly family, destroying their clothing, flesh and sinews, until their charred skulls cracked from the heat and their limbs separated from their torsos. The time was approximately 3 a.m.

It was 4 a.m. when William Donnelly next lifted the blind and looked outside his bedroom window. It was snowing — and dark. The last time he had looked outside, an hour and a half earlier, it was snowing as well, but it seemed to him to have been brighter outside at that point. He was right: the brightness had been due to the glow from the fire that by then had been consuming his parents' home.[8] By 4 a.m., however, the flames had died down considerably, allowing darkness to return. William, Nora and Martin Hogan were all still in the bedroom. John Donnelly's corpse lay at the foot of the bed, its head toward the road and its feet near the guest room.

"This is a terrible thing," William said, more to himself than to anybody else.

"Don't be talking!" said Hogan in a harsh whisper, still paranoid that the killers were lurking just outside the house.

"Did you see anybody?" Donnelly asked.

"Don't talk to me about it," snapped Hogan. "Keep to yourself what you know and I will do the same!"

Nora now lifted the blind to the bedroom window and looked outside. She knew that William had seen people standing outside the window when he had looked out immediately after John had been shot. "Who in the world did it?" she asked.

Thinking that Nora was planning on going outside, Hogan's voice again was heard coming from underneath the bed: "Don't go out!"

William's mind was racing; John was dead. He had to tell his parents and siblings, and he knew the news would absolutely destroy them. And if he told Nora he had seen her brother John Kennedy Jr. standing outside his window after the shooting, it would destroy her as well. He couldn't bring himself to do that. Not yet anyway.

"Hold your tongue," William cautioned, before adding by way of answer, "I know some of them."

He said nothing else and Nora didn't pursue the matter. Later she said, "I have been married to my husband for over five years, and know his peculiarities, and I know that if he didn't want to tell me anything there would be no use asking him, and from what he said, I judge that he didn't want to tell me."[9]

A light now came on in the house of their neighbour Joseph Morley. To William, this was a fair indication the killers had left. Like all mice, they would scurry away at the first sign of light. He got out of bed and walked to the body of his late brother:

> I examined John's breast when I got out of bed;
> I counted twenty-nine holes. His collar bone was
> broken and a piece of it sticking out. Most of the

wounds were lower into the lung; there was a little
mark above his forehead, on the right side of his
forehead. I thought he had fallen on this place . . .
he was quite dead.[10]

While William was examining his brother, Nora walked into the
kitchen and noted the wadding of newspaper that had drifted into
that room from when the shotgun had been discharged.

"Here is a lot of paper!" Nora called out.

"Bring it in," William replied. She returned to the bedroom and
handed the paper to her husband. William recalled that

[i]t was in different pieces but, if put together, would
be larger than my hand. There was blood on it and
shot holes through it, and was blackened as if with
powder. I account for the blood being there from
its being found near to where John was lying. The
blood was fresh. I could tell from the reading and
the shape of the print that it was the *Catholic Record*
[newspaper]. I told the missus to put it in a glass.[11]

William was already thinking like a lawyer; he was attempting now
to collect and preserve evidence from the scene of the crime. The
Vigilance Committee would be made to pay for this killing, and
William's weapon of choice was always the courts. He found a
patched quilt and placed it over the body of his late brother and
then began looking for any additional evidence that would bolster
his case. He lit a lantern and walked through the kitchen to the
door. Upon opening it he was struck by the fact there were footprints in the snow outside. This was where the killers had stood
when they had shot his brother. His nearest neighbour was William
Blackwell, whose home was twenty feet directly south of the
Donnellys' kitchen door. Blackwell must have seen somebody, or at

least heard the shots. William Donnelly walked over to his neighbour's and knocked upon his door. His assumption was correct; Blackwell had been up since hearing the gunshots two and a half hours earlier; it was now 5 a.m. When he opened his door, he saw William Donnelly looking grim.

"They shot Jack," he said.

"Who did it?" asked Blackwell.

"They done it," William replied. "Did you hear the shots?"

"I did," said Blackwell. The pair were now joined by Blackwell's wife. The three then walked back to William Donnelly's house and entered through the kitchen door. William Blackwell went into Donnelly's bedroom and looked at the body of John Donnelly. When he returned to the kitchen, William was digging a bullet out of the wall opposite the kitchen door that had evidently travelled through John's body and lodged there. William Donnelly would recall:

> I saw where the bullet went through the wall on
> the inside, through the wainscoting under the north
> window in the kitchen. My wife and I think Mrs.
> Blackwell was there when I was searching for the
> bullet. One of them put a little rod of iron through
> the hole striking the boards on the outside of the
> house so that I could cut opposite the hole; I found
> the bullet lying on the sill.[12]

William placed the bullet in an envelope with the idea of giving it to the police in due course. A horrific thought now came to him. He quickly looked out the window toward his stable.

"The bar of the stable door is down," he said. "I bet they have killed the stallion!"

As he walked toward the door of the house closest to the stable, Blackwell tried to stop him. "Don't go till daylight! You don't know who might be there!"

Donnelly ignored the warning and went outside. Hesitantly, Blackwell followed. Donnelly saw the iron bar that went across the latch of the stallion's stall had been taken down and left propped against the door. The fork had also been taken from his grey mare's stable door and thrown on the dung pile. John's pony was in the smaller stable, and there were no footprints leading in that direction. When William entered the stable, he was relieved to discover the stallion was fine, although he was still frightened and would not let William get near him. He secured the door to the stable and turned toward Blackwell. It was then that both men noticed the number of footprints that ran throughout the property. "There were tracks all through Mr. Walker's garden," William recalled, referring to his neighbour. "There were tracks to all the windows in my house except the one opposite to the door that John was shot at. It appeared as if there were a great many people there. It was trampled down all around my place and around Mr. Blackwell's house."[13]

According to Blackwell, "I observed tracks about the place, a good few: I saw tracks up to William's bedroom window, the tracks to all the windows. . . . The snow was trampled quite a bit back of the wood shop. I supposed from the tracks there were such as fifteen or twenty men might make."[14]

William mentioned that he had to go and tell his father that John was dead. It was then that Blackwell shared with William some disturbing news: "Blackwell showed me the direction in which he had observed a fire during the night . . ." William said, "and when Blackwell showed me the direction, I was satisfied that the fire was at my father's."[15]

A wave of despair washed over William Donnelly at this point. The last time there had been an arson at the Donnelly farm had been when the family's barn had been torched by their enemies in December 1870. Were his parents safe, or had they been in the house as it had burned down around them? And what of his brother

Tom and cousin Bridget? His mind was racing now. He needed to sit down and catch his breath. He needed to think clearly. He didn't believe Blackwell or Hogan would be of any help; neither wanted any part of the mob. And Nora, well, he couldn't tell her yet that her brother and the group of which he was a charter member had killed his brother John (and who knew who else?) a few hours ago. She'd been through enough already. He needed to speak with someone he could trust, and the only name that came to his mind was that of his old friend James Keefe. William saddled up John's pony and rode west toward Usborne. As he rode, William continued to observe the footprints that led away from his house. He tracked them to where the town lines of Usborne, Blanchard and Biddulph met. At this point, two sets of tracks headed north in the direction of James Maher's farm, while the bulk of the footprints turned on the town line of Usborne and Blanchard, and led along the First Concession road toward Keefe's place. Did the Committee members pay Keefe a visit as well?

He later recalled:

> [The tracks] went about ten or twelve rods down the
> concession line leading to Keefe's house, and then
> they stopped. There appeared to be a great number
> of tracks up to where they stopped . . . nearly half
> a mile from Keefe's house. After this, the tracks
> stopped, you couldn't tell where they led to. There
> was one track leading to Keefe's; it was more covered
> up with snow than the others.[16]

This solitary set of tracks were most likely made by James Keefe himself when he'd walked home from William Donnelly's the night before. It dawned on William from observing the tracks that the mob had left his house and then had headed straight for Keefe's place. Perhaps they had intended to kill him as well, or thought, as Johnny O'Connor evidently believed, that John Donnelly was staying at Keefe's that night. If so, then their intent in going to Keefe's would have been to finish off all the Donnellys that evening in one fell swoop. But then, for some reason (perhaps their blood-lust already having been sated), the mob had stopped and didn't follow through with their plan. Unlike the Committee members, however, William Donnelly continued on until he reached the Keefe farmhouse. It was now 7 a.m.

James Keefe was still in bed when William arrived. He was roused from his slumbers and given the news:

> I told him what happened. He told me not to speak
> about it till I went and got [London detectives
> Harry] Phair and [Enoch] Murphy first thing. I gave
> Keefe no particular instruction. I stayed at Keefe's
> about ten minutes, a short time. I told him to come
> right up to my house. He came there; I rode upon
> the pony, he walked up.[17]

Upon his return to Whalen's Corners, William Donnelly stopped in at the home of another neighbour, John Walker. Walker was a blacksmith by trade, who also did the odd labour job, most recently for the Keefes. The thought that his parents might be dead was still weighing heavily on William's mind, but he could not bring himself to go to his parents' farm. He was truly fearful of what he might discover there — and he simply wasn't up to it: "I asked Mr. Walker if he would drive over [to the Donnelly farm-house] and see if anything was the matter. And, if not, to tell them that John was dead. He took John's pony and my cutter and went over. I did not go with him."[18]

While he waited for James Keefe to arrive, William mulled over in his mind the evidence he had collected about his property that morning. Again, he recalled the voices he had heard outside his kitchen door that had called for him to come outside prior to John being shot. He was certain now he recognized them:

> I knew the voices; they were Martin McLaughlin
> and James Ryder. I am positive it was their voices.
> I have known Martin McLaughlin as long as I
> have known anybody. He was raised on the second
> next farm to my father's. I was well acquainted
> with James Ryder's voice. I have known him since
> he was born [and] knew his father before he was
> married. It was Ryder that spoke the second time
> [calling out "Will! Open the door!"]. It was by
> his speaking my name that I recognized his voice
> more than anything else. I would have recognized
> his voice whether he had said "Will" or not. Ryder
> generally called me "Will" when we were on
> speaking terms.[19]

As there had only been two sets of footprints in the snow outside the kitchen door, and as James "Young Grouch" Ryder and Martin McLaughlin had been the ones whose voices William now recognized as belonging to the ones calling for him to come outside, it had to have been these two men who had shot his brother. At least, that's what the evidence suggested. Soon James Keefe arrived at William's house. William told him the names of the people he had heard and seen; he also showed him the footprints that surrounded his house. Keefe repeated his earlier statement that William should not tell anyone else about the murder just yet. William shared with his friend his fear about his parents' well-being and that, depending upon Walker's report, he might need Keefe to head to the telegraph office in Lucan to send telegrams of the tragic news to both his brother Patrick and sister Jennie. Since his brother Bob lived near Jennie, she could relay the information to him.

John Walker finally returned, and the news he brought confirmed William's worst fears — his parents, as well as his youngest brother Tom and cousin Bridget — had all died in a fire that had burned the family homestead to the ground. His wife Nora and friend James Keefe were almost as devastated as William was. Still, there was work to be done. William wrote out the content of the telegrams to be sent to his brother and sister. Keefe saddled up and rode toward Lucan. It was 9 a.m.

Johnny O'Connor was still sleeping in the upstairs bedroom when Patrick Whalen hitched up his cutter and started out toward Granton to meet with James Carroll. Whalen had apparently come to some sort of settlement arrangement with regard to the charges brought against him by the constable for having chased him from his property with an axe the previous week. For reasons that were never revealed (since Carroll had normally stayed at the house of his uncle James Maher, but evidently had spent the night of the murders at William and Mary Thompson's farmhouse, either of which was within minutes of Whalen's house),[20] the two had evidently agreed to meet in a bar in Granton that morning to conclude the matter.[21] Whalen, running on about two and a half hours of sleep by this point, had left his house shortly after 6 a.m.[22] He told almost everyone he encountered between there and Granton about the Donnelly tragedy. He first met local farmer James Hobbins and informed him about the fire at the Donnellys', and how he had seen two bodies in the ruins of their house.[23] He next encountered the Vigilance Committee magistrate, William Casey (who lived directly across the road from Hobbins) and told him the same story[24] — although Casey would later deny that Whalen had mentioned seeing the dead bodies in the house.[25]

Whalen then put in at Richard Curtain's farmhouse, where he had breakfast with Curtain and informed him not only of the fire and the two dead bodies he had seen, but also about the boy who had run to his home directly from the fire.[26] Whalen then continued on his way southeast to Granton. Magistrate Casey, likewise, was heading to Granton that morning, but rather surprisingly, given how cold it was, along with the fact that Granton was four and three-quarter miles away, he had decided to walk there.[27] About this time, William Thompson Jr. happened to look out the window of his kitchen, which faced south toward the Donnelly homestead. Only 440 yards separated the two farmhouses, and so he could clearly see "the smoke through the window of the Donnellys' house. I saw that the house was burned."[28] He called for his wife, Mary, and his two house guests, James Carroll and his younger brother William, to come and have a look. Mary came into the kitchen, looked out the window, saw that the Donnelly home was "blazing some"[29] and then promptly went back to bed. The two Carrolls then sauntered down the stairs and looked out the window. James stared out at the smoke coming from the Donnelly home for a while and then, with an almost yawning indifference, said, "It's kind of hard on a stormy morning like this to have no house to go into."[30] William Carroll looked at his older brother and commented, "It's a hard morning for the Donnellys to go to Granton."[31] None bothered to venture over to the Donnelly farm to investigate the matter further. Mary Thompson later returned to the kitchen and the four sat down to breakfast.

Farther south along the east side of the Roman Line, Ann and Joseph Whalen, joined this morning by the Whalens' eighteen-year-old daughter Theresa and their house guest Johnny O'Connor, were likewise sitting down to breakfast. During the meal, O'Connor again brought up the fact that he had seen James Carroll at the murder scene: "I was not afraid to mention Carroll's name; it was for the purpose of having Carroll punished. I wanted them all punished. I was afraid to tell about Purtell and Ryder, but not Carroll."[32]

Ann Whalen, as she had several hours before, tried to shut him down. "You'll be hauled up as a witness!"[33] she said ominously. O'Connor, not really understanding the law in such matters, assumed that she meant that he could be arrested for having been at the property when the crime had been committed. He decided he'd better not say anything else.[34] As Theresa hadn't seen the site of the fire, it was then decided that she and O'Connor would head over to take a look at the damage in the daylight. According to Theresa: "I went to the fire next day between eight and nine; I saw a knife near the body of what I thought was old Mr. Donnelly. I saw a watch chain afterwards, which was picked up. It was Catherine Toohey who picked up the watch chain."[35]

Theresa and Johnny were joined at the ruins by John Whalen. And while Patrick Whalen had been certain that he'd seen only two bodies in the debris when he had ridden past the Donnelly property earlier that morning,[36] John Whalen claimed that he had seen four.[37] So too, did Johnny O'Connor.[38] By this point in time the flames had long since burned out, replaced by a dense smoke that now emanated from the embers. The four bodies were unrecognizable as anything other than charred lumps. Bridget and James's corpses lay side by side next to the iron stove, which jutted out from among the ash. Johannah's remains lay between what had been the kitchen and the front room. A melted ball of glass and wire was all that remained of her spectacles, which lay beside her broken and brittle skull. James Donnelly Sr.'s skull was also charred and brittle. A large hole was visible on it from where a Committee member's club had unleashed its havoc. The wire rims of his broken spectacles, a pocket knife, an axe head, the metal buttons from his coat, and whatever change he had in his coat pocket — in the event, a quarter, a dime and a penny — lay next to his body.[39]

Thomas Donnelly's corpse had fallen into the root cellar once the fire had burned through the wooden flooring and was now lying on its back atop a pile of scorched apples and potatoes. Like his parents', Tom's skull had been fractured, and the blade of the spade that had caused the wound lay beneath his body, its wooden handle having burned away. On top of what was left of his body were buckles from his suspenders and buttons from what had been his jacket. Until Catherine Toohey had shown up, his pocket watch and chain lay next to his body.

People now started arriving at the site. Some had seen the glow in the sky from the night before and were simply curious to discover its source; others were looking to pillage from the debris. Still others, members of the Committee, had come by to see the results of their handiwork from the night before.

James Carroll, after having finished his breakfast with the Thompsons, saddled up a horse and started off in the direction of Granton, where his arson trial against the Donnelly parents was set to resume that afternoon. Carroll would have had to ride south past the Donnelly ruins on his way to the east sideroad that would deliver him to Granton. Somewhere along the Roman Line or the Granton sideroad Carroll happened upon fellow Vigilance Committee member William Casey, who would be one of the three magistrates presiding over the Donnelly trial that afternoon. While both men already knew (and had a direct hand in) what had befallen the Donnellys, when they told their stories later before a jury, they naturally assumed a pose of shock and innocence. According to Casey's version, he had questions for Carroll.

"What about this fire?" he asked.

"Somebody told me that there were four bodies in the fire," Carroll was said to have replied. How the constable came into this bit of information is unclear, however, as Mary Thompson would claim that Carroll never went to the Donnelly ruins to investigate.

"It is a very strange-looking affair," Casey mused.

Carroll nodded. "It is a very strange thing."[40]

Casey would later testify that it struck him that Carroll seemed quite surprised by the news.[41] Be that as it may, even if they had not been directly involved with the tragedy it was odd that it didn't occur to either man to head over to investigate the smoked-out ruins of the Donnelly home. If the report that Carroll had heard was true, then the Donnellys were dead, which would have had quite an impact on the trial that both men were to be involved in that very afternoon. And yet, both the constable and the magistrate continued on toward Granton, Casey on foot and Carroll on his horse.

Patrick Whalen arrived in Granton at 9 a.m. and went to Thomas Culbert's tavern to await the arrival of James Carroll so they could settle their legal business before their trial was to take place later that morning. When he entered the barroom, several people were already talking about a fire they suspected had broken out on the Roman Line some time during the night. They had seen the light in the dark sky and, recognizing Whalen as living in that area, some of the bar's patrons felt obliged to ask him what he knew about it. Whalen proved a veritable fount of information in this regard; he told them of the fire and of the dead bodies he saw. He may also have mentioned the boy who ran to his house to tell him what he had seen and heard. "I did not tell them about the boy telling Carroll's name,"[42] he would later recall.

His prudence was timely as, just after enlightening the taverners with his personal insights regarding the tragedy, into the bar walked James Carroll. The constable, ignoring the conversation that was going on around him, greeted Whalen, and the two men bellied up to the bar and threw down a shot of whiskey apiece. Whalen then produced the money necessary to cover both men's court costs for the day, and Carroll agreed to drop the charge against him. Neither man, according to Whalen, spoke of the Donnellys. Shortly after concluding their transaction, however, John Kennedy Jr.

entered the tavern and pulled Carroll aside. The pair entered into an animated if hushed conversation. One patron in the barroom noticed that their conversation was lengthy and that something appeared to be troubling the two men.[43]

As Patrick Whalen's business in Granton was now complete, he left the tavern and poked around the village a bit. While doing so, he again encountered Magistrate William Casey. He had hoped that Casey would have been present for his settlement with Carroll, and, indeed, had asked him to attend the meeting in order to "see that there were not too much costs put on me."[44] But despite leaving early enough, William Casey hadn't made it to town on time. Whalen was upset and felt obliged to point out to the magistrate that he had settled the matter with Carroll on his own, and that Casey had not come in early as he had promised he would.[45] The magistrate, however, was more interested in pressing Whalen for details on a rumour he had heard that there was a boy who had been to the farmer's house in the night. He wanted to know who the boy was and what he told him about the Donnelly murders — but Whalen refused to tell him.[46]

Casey became irate. After he had spoken with Whalen on the Roman Line on his way into Granton that morning, he had encountered the farmer Richard Curtain, the man with whom Whalen had shared breakfast. From Curtain he learned the startling news that Whalen had told the farmer a boy had been to his house the night before who had witnessed the murders.[47] Casey knew this bit of news immediately blew the lid off any attempt by the Vigilance Committee to paint the killings as an Act of God. The magistrate needed to know what the boy had witnessed in order to know what steps the Committee would need to take to protect themselves from any legal repercussions. He tried to browbeat Whalen. "Curtain told me that the boy escaped from the fire! Why didn't you give me the information about the boy when you were giving it to other people on the road?" demanded Casey.[48]

Whalen wasn't intimidated and refused to disclose anything to the magistrate.[49] The two parted ways, leaving Casey to fret over the Committee's next move.

Meanwhile, the object of the Vigilance Committee's consternation, Johnny O'Connor, had borrowed a horse and was on his way home to Lucan. It was bitterly cold that morning and the Whalens had loaned him some clothing to keep him warm on his ride back to town. He had borrowed a coat and hat of Theresa Whalen's, the latter of which was oversized and floppy. As he rode onto his family's property, he was spotted by his two brothers who immediately came out to put up the horse for him. Johnny dismounted and walked into his home. His mother, father and sister entered the front room of the house to greet him, and to inquire as to why he was back from the Donnellys' so soon. They had expected him to be at James and Johannah's home during their trial that afternoon, which was still several hours from taking place.

Johnny's mother, Mary O'Connor, burst out laughing when she saw her son wearing an outrageous hat. But then she detected that something was terribly wrong.

"Where's your coat?" she asked.[50]

Tears now began streaming from her son's eyes. "Ma," he finally said, his voice halting, "it is burnt in the fire."

"Good God!" his mother exclaimed, assuming that a simple accident had occurred, "is the stable burned?"

"No," replied Johnny, "the house is burned!" Then came the bombshell: "The old woman and Bridget is *burned*, Tom and the old man and all were killed — *they are all dead and burned*!"

Johnny's parents now looked at each other in shock. Mary started shaking and a wave of fear washed over her. Johnny clearly didn't want to talk about what he had been through. After he had calmed down a bit, he told his father the news. Michael O'Connor took Johnny into town with him as he had some errands to run. On the way uptown, Michael had told his son not to say anything about what he knew. Not yet anyway. They were able to keep silent until James Keefe arrived in town.

Keefe had ridden past the Donnelly property on his way to Lucan that morning and, along with the news of John's murder, he now could confirm John Walker's earlier report that the Donnelly family had died in a fire on their property. He delivered the news of the deaths to coroner Thomas Hossack, who immediately set about arranging an inquest into the matter. Keefe than proceeded to the post office where he conferred with postmaster William Porte regarding the telegrams he had received from William Donnelly that needed to be sent to the surviving family members. Word travelled fast throughout the town. Indeed, by the time Michael O'Connor and Johnny had arrived at Bernard Stanley's hardware store, Bernard's brother William, a local justice of the peace, approached them. He had already heard about the murders and also knew that Johnny O'Connor had been in the house when the killings went down. He asked the boy directly if he could identify any of the killers. Johnny lied and said that he didn't know any of them. While his father stayed in town to talk, Johnny walked back to his house.

Mary O'Connor was still mortified by what her son had told her. So many emotions came into play — gratitude that her son was alive, fear that persons unknown had exposed him to the horror of their acts, anger at these same people for having done so, shame that she had allowed her son to enter such a hostile environment, a gnawing anxiety as to how this tragedy occurred and if her son was in any present danger as a result — to name but a few. Consequently, by the time Johnny returned to his house Mary O'Connor had some specific questions that, as a mother, she wanted answers to. Her first question concerned whether there was any near and present danger to her son — specifically, could he identify who had killed the Donnellys?

At first Johnny said nothing. He was still labouring under the misapprehension that he might at any minute be arrested for having been present when the crime went down. However, he could not keep a secret of this magnitude from his mother. And as he began to speak, it all came flooding out. He told her that he had seen James Carroll standing in the bedroom doorway with a candle in his hand, and that he had also seen Thomas Ryder and John Purtell standing over the body of Tom Donnelly. He told of the mob rushing into the Donnellys' house, and of Tom Donnelly's brutal fate. How he had hidden under the bed to avoid detection and that the gang then poured coal oil on the bed and set the Donnellys' house on fire.

"Did they see you under the bed?" his mother asked.

Johnny shook his head. "If they did, I'm sure I'd have been killed!"

A t two o'clock that afternoon, Michael O'Connor was visiting with William Porte inside the Lucan post office, filling him in on what his son had told him about the tragedy, when he was approached by two county constables, Charles Pope and William Hodge, who had been dispatched by Coroner Hossack to round up witnesses for his inquest into the murders. Hodge addressed him directly.

"Are you the father of the boy O'Connor who was at the Donnellys' house on the night of the murder?"[51]

"I am," replied Michael O'Connor.

"Can I see the boy?" asked Hodge.

Since he recognized the two men as being officers of the law, it was clear to O'Connor that his son's involvement in the affair was now a matter of public knowledge. The ball had already started rolling toward a murder trial, and his son's future welfare would depend upon his cooperation with such agents of law enforcement.

He looked to William Porte, who only nodded that he should oblige the constables' request.

"He's over at the house," replied O'Connor.

The three men then proceeded to the O'Connor home. According to Constable Hodge: "O'Connor and Pope and I went to the house and saw the boy. He seemed scared and didn't want to talk to anyone. We saw him in the house. I told him who I was, and I took the boy on my knee. His father told him to tell all he knew about it, so he commenced from the first and told me."[52] Michael and Mary O'Connor listened as Johnny revealed all the events that had occurred, starting the day before when he had been picked up in Lucan by James Sr. and Tom Donnelly and ending with him running for his life from the burning farmhouse. Constable Hodge recognized that if what the boy had told him was true, then Johnny O'Connor was now the star witness in a murder investigation, and that there would be plenty of interested parties who were connected to the crimes who would want him dead. For the boy's own safety Constable Hodge told him "not to tell anyone who came to ask him about it. His father said he would keep him upstairs, out of the way."[53]

By now the entire town of Lucan was abuzz with the news of the Donnelly murders, and how a young boy had witnessed the horrid event and had lived to tell the tale. The local press had also caught wind of the killings by now, and sent reporters to the crime scenes to ferret out material that would be of interest to their readers' growing intrigue and morbid curiosity. The city of London's police force were quickly brought up to speed on the details of the massacre and, under the direction of their police chief, William Thomas Trounce Williams, detectives were dispatched to Biddulph in order to gather information on the crimes.

Farther northwest, in Granton, at two o'clock sharp, magistrate William Casey, along with fellow magistrates James Grant and

Philip Mowbray, permanently adjourned the arson case against James and Johannah Donnelly.[54]

Constable James Carroll was present for the dismissal — at least physically. His mind was still reeling, not only from the news that there had been a witness to the murder of the Donnelly family, but also upon learning that the vigilante gunmen had missed their intended mark the night before when John Donnelly was shot instead of William. Carroll was terrified. Had he been spotted at the crime scenes? Did William Donnelly know of his involvement? The constable immediately sent a boy northwest to Whalen's Corners to observe William and Nora's house to see if William Donnelly was alive. When the boy caught sight of William, he returned and gave Carroll the news. The constable quickly sped off to share the report with fellow members of the Vigilance Committee.[55] That William Donnelly was still alive caused panic to spread among the Committee members. Any time propaganda is fabricated to make an enemy appear more dangerous and more evil than he really is, it becomes easy to mistake the construct as the reality. Having thus imbued William Donnelly with such evil and powerful attributes — which had been necessary to help the Committee members override any sense of moral propriety that might have prevented their attempt to kill him — the group feared that the surviving Donnelly family member would now be motivated to wield his powers of darkness against them. An immediate meeting of the inner circle of the Vigilance Committee was convened, and options discussed.

By four o'clock, London police chief Williams was in Lucan. There, he had procured a horse and buggy and headed out to investigate what was left of the Donnelly homestead. As he recalled:

> I went from Lucan to the Donnelly farm; the bodies
> were there at that time, apparently four: one near
> the front door and three in the kitchen; I looked
> about the place to a considerable extent. We looked

for skulls; there was apparently only one. I took that in my hand and it crumbled. The bodies were all burned. I found nothing about the place but a pool of blood about six-feet from the front door; there were three small pools nearly together.[56]

In the meantime, William Donnelly was busying himself jotting down the facts he would need to present to Chief Williams during his interview with the chief that was due to take place in Lucan later that evening. He also had to make preparations for the wakes and interments of his murdered family members. To this end, the O'Connor family had graciously offered William the use of their home to host the wake. As William's house was still being investigated by the authorities as a crime scene, and as the Donnelly farmhouse was now nothing more than cinders, William was out of options and both relieved and grateful for the O'Connors' offer.

At approximately five o'clock, two Lucan constables, Silas Gilbert Moore and Alfred Brown, arrived by wagon at William and Nora Donnelly's house. They were there to collect the body of John Donnelly for autopsy back in Lucan, and had brought with them a casket within which they placed the corpse. As William recalled, "John was put in the coffin just as he was. The constables took the body to Lucan. I went with the body to Lucan. The body was taken to Mr. O'Connor's."[57]

Coroner Hossack had already empanelled a jury of fifteen men to participate in the official inquest. His jury consisted of John McGuire, William Henry, J.W. Orme, John Bawden, James Mayo, George Kerrick, William Pratt, William Quigley, William Benn, Edward Roberts Hodgins, Jacob Palmer, Thomas Robinson, John Judge, Thomas Cubbins, and Henry Wilson.[58]

These were interesting choices to be certain; John McGuire, who had been selected as foreman of the jury, had testified against the Donnelly boys during their trial for the arson of their stagecoach rival Patrick Flanagan's stables. John Bawden was a constable who had been involved in the melee with the Donnelly brothers at the Ryder wedding reception. James Mayo, George Kerrick, Thomas Cubbins and Edward Roberts Hodgins were all employees of William Stanley at his mill (and Stanley, as a Lucan business owner, was no fan of the Donnellys) and Hodgins had also been tasked by Constable Samuel Everett to spy on Bob Donnelly during the latter's trial for allegedly shooting at the constable. Jacob Palmer had been one of the men who had tortured the Donnellys' friend William Atkinson and who had similarly been asked to spy on Bob Donnelly. Thomas Robinson had testified against William Donnelly in a perjury case.

All in all, the panel did not seem like it would be particularly sympathetic to the Donnellys' cause in the matter.

After being sworn in, the jury gathered at the Central (McLean's) Hotel, which was where Chief Williams had set up his satellite office of the London police force while conducting his investigation of the murders. From the hotel, the jury was taken by sleigh to view the smoked-out ruins of the Donnelly homestead and the human remains that were still inside it. From there, the jury was delivered to the O'Connor home to examine the corpse of John Donnelly. Finally, they were brought to the Town Hall in Lucan, which was actually the third floor of the Lucan Public School, where Coroner Hossack would shortly bring in three members of the Whalen family — Patrick, John and Joseph — to testify about the fire they had witnessed at the Donnelly homestead earlier that morning.

Chief Williams in the meantime had instructed one of the constables under his charge to get a wooden box and head out to the Donnelly ruins the next morning. His job would be to scrape up the remains of the Donnelly family members and bring them to Hossack for examination. Williams then walked over to the Town Hall to attend the opening of the coroner's inquest and listen to the Whalens' testimony. After the Whalens had presented their recollections of the fire and their experience with Johnny O'Connor, Hossack announced that he would adjourn the jury for one week to allow for postmortem examinations to be conducted on the bodies.

Chief Williams conferred briefly with Coroner Hossack and then walked to the Central Hotel, where William Donnelly was waiting to speak with him. The two men sat down and William related his account of how his brother John had been murdered. According to Williams:

> I had a long conversation with him. He told me what had occurred at his house about the death of his brother. I asked him if he had any idea how it had come about. He said there were two parties in it; that one party had gone to his father's and one to his. I asked him if he knew any of the fellows who were at his house. He told me he could swear to four. I asked who they were. He told me he could swear to [John] Kennedy, Jim Ryder, Martin McLaughlin and Carroll the constable. He said that McLaughlin and Ryder were the men that shot his brother.[59]

Having collected his information from Donnelly, Chief Williams informed William that he was now going to take one of his detectives with him and head over to the O'Connors' house to speak with the boy. William Donnelly told the chief that he would accompany him as he was heading to the O'Connors' home himself; the coroner had informed him that John was to be autopsied there that evening, and Pat Donnelly was due to arrive there from Thorold later that evening as well. Donnelly, the chief and his detective then proceeded to the O'Connor home. Upon arriving, William Donnelly went into the main room to be with the body of his late brother, while Williams and his detective waited at the front door for Mary O'Connor. As Chief Williams would recall:

I asked for the boy O'Connor. His mother refused
to let me see him. And I got the father and he called
the boy to the door. I said I wanted to ask him some
questions. O'Connor's father said that Hodge and
Pope had told him not to answer any questions and
that he didn't think it would be any use asking him
any. I asked Hodge if it was so [and] he said it was
so. I didn't ask the boy any questions. I only heard
the boy's story from Hodge and Pope.[60]

Based on what he heard from Hodge and Pope, together with what
he had learned from William Donnelly, Chief Williams believed he
had sufficient evidence to charge James Carroll, John Kennedy Jr.,
John Purtell, James Ryder and Martin McLaughlin with the murder
of the Donnelly family.

CHAPTER NINETEEN

DEALING WITH THE DEAD

A single button fused onto melted glass, which was discovered within the ruins of the Donnelly farmhouse after the fire. (By permission of Ray Fazakas, author of *The Donnelly Album* and *In Search of the Donnellys*)

The wake for the murdered family was to start on the evening of Wednesday, February 4, and run through until the bodies would be buried on Friday morning. However, the surviving family members were at the mercy of the local coroner, Dr. Thomas Hossack, who needed to have the remains autopsied prior to releasing them to the family for the wake.

Hossack, however, had decided that his limited time and resources were best employed in the running of the inquest, and so had prevailed upon his colleague, Dr. Christopher William Flock, to perform the postmortem procedures. Dr. Flock was a knowledge-able and experienced physician in Lucan, having practised medicine for some twenty-nine years since graduating from Rolph's Medical School (now the University of Toronto Faculty of Medicine) in 1851.[1] Hossack had asked permission from the O'Connors, for the sake of expediency, to perform the autopsies at their house. After all, John Donnelly's body was already in their home, while the remains of James, Johannah, Tom and Bridget were to be brought there the next day. The O'Connors gave their consent and Hossack notified Flock, who agreed to go to the O'Connors' house later that evening to perform the postmortem on John Donnelly's body. The news came as something of a shock to William Donnelly when he had first learned of it shortly after the conclusion of the inquest that night, but as the wake couldn't start until after the autopsies had been performed on John and the remainder of his late family members, he really didn't have any say in the matter. William had many questions that he wanted to ask Johnny O'Connor about what and whom he had seen on the night of the murders, but given the boy's reticence to speak about it with the police chief, and with the autopsy soon to take place, and his brother Pat arriving, clearly now was not the time.[2]

William certainly wouldn't be wanting for company this evening. The reporter John Lambert Payne appeared at the O'Connors' house to cover the autopsy for the benefit of the readers of the *London Free Press*.[3] Dr. Flock arrived a little after nine o'clock in the evening, and immediately set to work on the corpse of John Donnelly. He first examined the body for any signs of trauma. Apart from the gunshot wounds, he could find none. Next he opened the body and probed the internal organs as well as the chest and abdominal cavities. Within the lungs he found several pellets, such as might have been expelled from a shotgun. His conclusion was the obvious one: John Donnelly died from bleeding out as a result of gunshot wounds.[4]

How William Donnelly was able to witness this is beyond the author's comprehension, but he did, later commenting:

I was there when Dr. Flock examined him; I saw the
doctor open his breast and take out a lung; his lung
was full of holes; the shot the doctor took out were
pretty large shot, smaller than buckshot. The doctor
couldn't find all the shot. His ribs were broken
on the right side. I saw the doctor probe the body
where the bullet went through him; it went in on the
front of the right side and passed through on a little
inward slant and passed out the back. The doctor
opened his body and found the hole right through.[5]

William had been able to maintain a calm and almost detached
demeanour — until Dr. Flock opened John's chest completely and
made the comment that he "had never seen a man with so large a
heart." At this point William's legs threatened to give out beneath
him. "'Tis more than flesh and blood can endure!" he exclaimed.
"My only sincere wish now is that I was lying there along with
him!"[6] Some others in attendance led him away from the room for
a few minutes until he was able to regain his composure.

The postmortem now over, John Donnelly's body was put back
together, cleaned with holy water (so that all traces of blood upon
his face was removed) and then wrapped in white linen so only his
face was exposed. He was placed back into the coffin and rosary
beads were wound around his hands and a crucifix placed upon his
chest in preparation for the wake that would take place the next day.

At ten o'clock, Patrick Donnelly arrived from Thorold. Like his
older brother William, Patrick was stoic, despite the magnitude of
the tragedy being on an order that would have emotionally devastated most people. The two brothers' lack of emotion no doubt was
a combination of shock and not wanting to display weakness in
the face of their adversaries who, after all, were still at large. Their
demeanour impressed reporter Payne, who wrote:

It is remarked on all sides the remarkable stoicism
of the two living brothers now here. Men of vast
experience in such matters say they are utterly
astonished at the cool shrewdness exhibited by the
brothers in the trying ordeal through which they are
passing. One of them was heard to remark, "The
time has gone by for crying. I might cry for one, but
no tears can do justice in this case. Action, not tears,
is the watchword."[7]

By the next morning, February 5, Chief Williams had already
issued his warrants and instructions, and, together with his
constables, made sure to get off to an early start. It was going to
be another busy day.[8] Constables Alfred Brown and Silas Gilbert
Moore travelled together by sleigh to the Donnelly ruins. Their job
was to bring in the remains of the victims from the fire. According
to Brown:

We found four bodies. . . . I collected the remains
of each of them separately, and kept them separated
by paper, and put them into a coffin and brought
them to Lucan, to Michael [O'Connor's home], and
kept charge of them until they were examined by
Dr. Flock, and then given over to their friends.[9]

The coffin that Constable Brown referenced was actually a small
wooden box, and the remains of the four victims were so scant they
all fit within its narrow confines. The constables placed the box in
their sleigh and proceeded to the O'Connor home in Lucan, where
it was then placed beside the casket containing the corpse of John
Donnelly.[10] Dr. Flock was once again summoned to examine the

remains, doing his best to form an opinion as to the cause of death of the four victims:

On Thursday, 5 February, 1880, at the residence of Mr. Michael O'Connors [sic], Lucan, I made a post-mortem examination of the remains of the bodies represented to me as those of the late James, Julia [Johannah], Thomas and Bridget Donnelly, of Biddulph. All these bodies had been very much burned by fire, many of the bones disarticulated, and only portions of some of them remaining, the rest having been destroyed. Most of the internal organs were so much charred that I could not distinguish them, some portions I could. There were no complete skulls to any of them, only a very few pieces. There were portions of vertical columns, ribs, femurs, etc., many disarticulated. Fire had made great havoc on all of them, the burning had been so destructive that I could not distinguish male from female. There were sufficient however of the remains to enable me to know that they were of four human beings. I cannot say positively what was the cause of death; death may have been caused by burning alone, or they may have been dead or injured previous to being burnt. There are no means by which I can determine. There was no evidence in the remains by which I could say that other than fire produced it.[11]

Dr. Flock's postmortem examination now complete, at least to what extent it was possible, Coroner Hossack issued his order for the interment of the remains, which he set for the next morning, Friday, February 6, at 9:30 a.m.[12]

The local newspapers had been quick to pick up on the story, but no one could have anticipated how quickly it would spread. Almost immediately it had appeared in newspapers across the Dominion and throughout the United States. Indeed, newspapers from as far away as Oakland, California, had actually run the story on the very day that the murders had occurred.[13] Within twenty-four hours, it appeared within the pages of the *New York Times* under the headline:

LYNCHERS' HORRIBLE WORK:
FIVE PERSONS MURDERED UPON SUSPICION
OF CRIME — THEIR HOUSE SET ON FIRE.[14]

Most of the newspaper stories reflected the shock and horror that most people felt about such a wanton slaughter and served to rouse sympathy for the murdered family. Sensing this, the Vigilance Committee felt they could not let public opinion be shaped against them this early in the proceedings. They sent out their own representatives to speak with the press and encouraged the papers to interview those who would be sympathetic to their cause. One of the first interviews granted by a member of the pro–Vigilance Committee side was believed to be the Lucan businessman and magistrate William Stanley:[15]

> A reporter of the *Advertiser* chanced to meet with
> a gentleman, well known in Lucan and Biddulph,
> who occupies a high position, and who is universally
> respected. A series of questions revealed the feeling
> of the gentleman spoken of, and as he is in a sense a
> representative man, what he says may be taken as a
> very fair reflex of general opinion, in a way. He gave
> what may be called the anti-Donnelly view of the
> tragedy, and his opinions, calmly expressed, reveal a

curious state of affairs. He said that he had no doubt the murderers were well-known to many.

"Can that be proven?" asked the reporter.

"No, I think not. There is no doubt in my mind that the Vigilance Committee is in the secret, but they will keep it. Moreover, the people of the neighbourhood are under a debt of gratitude to them for their action to rid the place of the Donnellys, and no one will testify against the Committee."

"But how do they justify such a course?"

"Well, it was necessary. Our barns were burnt, our horses' tongues cut out, our cattle disemboweled, and no one was safe whoever said a word against the Donnellys."

REPORTER: "But I suppose that the people who could plan and deliberately execute such a horrible crime would be as bad as the Donnellys ever were."

LUCANITE: "No siree! If the truth were known, it will be found that the murderers are the most respectable people in the township — good farmers and honest men. But they had to do it. There was no other way."

REPORTER: "Was there no law?"

LUCANITE: "Law! Well, I'll be — where did anybody ever get the best of the Donnellys in law! Why, we never saw them up and get their deserts. If they happened to be found guilty, the sentence was ridiculously light. Look at the two years for shooting at [Constable] Everett!"

REPORTER: "How do the people regard it?"

LUCANITE: "Well, they felt that it had to be. There was no other course. The Donnellys had to be killed. Perhaps it was a mistake that Bill was not killed, but that can't be helped. They were a bad family, and the only difference between them and a dog was in the shape."

REPORTER: "Then you think the murderers won't be found guilty?"

LUCANITE: "Why, they can't be. There will be any amount of money at their back, the best counsel will be procured, and nothing will be left undone. The murderers, as you call them, are respectable men who would not harm a fly, but they had to kill the Donnellys, just as they would a mad dog. People cannot live in a state of terror forever."

REPORTER: "But the women!"

LUCANITE: "There need be no sympathy for Mrs. Donnelly. She was kind-hearted and did lots of little acts of kindness, but she had a wicked mind. Why, it is said that she prayed on her knees that the souls of her sons might forever and ever frizzle in hell if they ever forgave an enemy or failed to take revenge."

REPORTER: "But still all that does not alter the legal liability of the murderers."

LUCANITE (with a shrug): "Well, perhaps not — but they ain't caught yet."[16]

Several parties within the community that were clearly still hostile to the Donnellys had put forth the rumour that the bodies of the family had been denied burial in St. Patrick's cemetery and would have to be interred in the Church of England's graveyard. Upon investigating the report, reporter Payne discovered that it wasn't true.[17] However, as the Donnellys had been members of St. Patrick's congregation (even if William and his brothers had boycotted the parish), the local reporters sought to interview Father John

Connolly about the murdered family, in addition to investigating some rumblings they'd heard about an anti-crime society the priest had formed and had championed from his pulpit within his church. The Father graciously consented to the interview requests during the afternoon of February 5. His comments would appear in the local papers the next day.

Payne would later recall that "Father Connolly was a gentle old soul, and he told me his sole objective was to create a local protective body for the purpose of checking lawlessness and bringing the guilty parties to justice."[18] That was certainly true, but only half the story. The priest had been a major player in making a pariah of the Donnelly family in the Roman Catholic community; he had lambasted them from his pulpit and shouted at various family members during their trials. He had contributed to whipping many of his parishioners into an emotional lather that had ultimately culminated in the deaths of five people. And, like several of the Vigilance Committee members, Father Connolly was now terrified of what the surviving Donnellys might do to him. When Charles Albert Matthews of the *London Advertiser* went to interview him for the newspaper,[19] the priest twice mentioned that he expected to be arrested, and to suffer William Donnelly's wrath.[20]

Father Connolly's interview with the reporter from the *London Advertiser* was a revealing one in many respects. He stated that the Donnellys were thieves who intimidated people through threats of personal violence into assisting them in their crimes.[21] The priest further revealed that he had been aware of the Vigilance Committee's existence — but had attempted to distance himself from it:

> It afterwards came to my knowledge that a number
> of the Vigilance Committee which I had formed
> banded together, without my knowledge or consent,
> and formed a Committee of their own. The members,

although not taking an oath in a theological sense,
making a solemn declaration, and, without using
the form "So help me God," kissed the book. The
meetings of this committee cannot be said to have
been secret, but they were, of course, private among
themselves, as they had no inclination to let everyone
hear what their business was. This Committee, so far
as I can learn, had no officers, and met only at the
call of the member who had been victimized. . . . So
far as I am concerned I am perfectly innocent of any
connection with, or knowledge of, the movements of
the second Vigilance Committee.[22]

And, finally, Father Connolly indicated that he had not banned
the Donnelly family from the church.[23] This was technically true;
he had never overtly decreed that the Donnelly family had been
banned. However, the Father had confronted some of his parishioners, such as James Keefe Sr. and John Kennedy Sr., and told
them not to give the senior Donnellys any transport to or from the
church, or otherwise associate with them.

Despite his consternation, the priest had no need to fear any of
the Donnelly survivors, and this was particularly true with regard
to William Donnelly, who was now focused primarily on burying
his murdered family members. Indeed, when reporter Matthews
approached him to confirm or deny Father Connolly's statement
that William intended to have the priest arrested, the local scribe was
surprised to learn that the original report was without foundation:

Whatever the faults of the Donnelly family were, and
no doubt they were legion, in this instance the man
William deserves credit. It has been conceded that
Father Connolly's object in organizing the Committee
he did was for the purpose of maintaining law and

order in the settlement where it originated; that his written instructions were to commit no aggressive act of any kind, and these facts were well known in the surrounding vicinity. Nevertheless, to the disgrace of one or two parties, they used all the influence they were possessed of in order to induce the man William Donnelly to have a warrant issued for the apprehension of the reverend gentleman. To his credit be it here stated that he steadfastly refused to commit himself to any overact [sic] of the kind, giving as his reasons for so doing that he was fully convinced that Father Connolly's views were sound and wholesome ones in forming this Committee, and that although he had heard that his reverence hourly expected such a result, from reports he received of the inveterate enmity which Donnelly bore toward him, still it never was his intention to do any such thing. He (Donnelly) furthermore stated that it was his firm belief, if the Committee had been guided by Father Connolly's precepts, his relatives tonight would be alive and well, and the Township of Biddulph would be free from a stain which will not be wiped out for generations to come. Those are the sentiments expressed by William Donnelly, and they were delivered in all sincerity.[24]

Throughout the evening of February 4 and into the early morning, Chief Williams had prepared several arrest warrants based upon the testimony he had heard first-hand from William Donnelly, and second-hand from Constable William Hodge, regarding the contents of his interview with young Johnny O'Connor. Warrants for the apprehension of Martin McLaughlin, James Ryder, John

Purtell, Thomas Ryder, John Kennedy Jr., James Maher Sr., James Maher Jr. and James Carroll were on the chief's desk when constables Charles Pope and William Hodge arrived the morning of February 5 in Lucan. Williams handed the warrant to arrest James Carroll to constables Charles Pope and William Hodge.[25]

As Carroll had been identified by both Johnny O'Connor and William Donnelly as having been present at the two murder scenes, he was the big fish that Williams wanted most to catch.

The constables had some experience with Carroll in the past; they had arrested him once before on the charge of pointing a revolver at Johannah Donnelly. That arrest had been made at the home of Carroll's uncle, James Maher, and it was their belief they would find him there again on this day. They also knew he would most likely be in the company of his relatives, the Mahers, and if the reports about them having committed multiple murders against the Donnelly family were true, it could be assumed these same three men would have no compunction against killing again to avoid capture. The constables would have to use finesse on this one. As the chief had wanted them to bring Carroll "quietly to Lucan," it was decided their best course of action would be to mislead Carroll into thinking Chief Williams needed him back in Lucan to help investigate the Donnelly murders. He was a constable, after all, so the request wouldn't seem suspicious or inappropriate.[26] They could thus lure him away from the protection of the Mahers and bring him into town alone, at which point they would officially arrest him. Then, having reduced their opponents' strength in numbers, they could pick off the Mahers and the other alleged killers individually once Carroll was safely behind bars. With their plan now in place, the constables climbed into their large double sleigh and headed off in the direction of the Roman Line.

A little over five and a half miles out of Lucan, and heading north along the Roman Line, the constables saw a lone man walking along the east side of the road. The man had already walked past the Donnelly ruins and was within a quarter-mile of the Maher farmhouse. Based on the clothes he wore and the manner in which he walked, both men suspected that this person was James Carroll.[27] The man was wearing a pair of dark grey tweed pants tucked into a pair of long boots. He had on a long brown overcoat, which he wore over a homemade flannel shirt. As the constables drew closer they were able to confirm that the man was, indeed, James Carroll. They pulled their sleigh alongside him and brought it to a stop.

"Jim," called out Constable Hodge, "the chief wants you up at Lucan."

Carroll suddenly became agitated; Constable Pope thought that his colour changed. Certainly, his suspicion had been aroused. "What for?" Carroll asked.

Hodge mentioned the Donnelly murders.

"This is an awful affair, Jim," Hodge said.

"It is," nodded Carroll.

"We want you to help us work on this being as you're a constable," Hodge continued. "Jim, you are just the man to work up the case." The request appealed both to Carroll's ego and also to his sense of self-preservation. After all, if he was going to be the one to work up the case for the prosecution, then he could ensure neither he nor the members of the Vigilance Committee would be in any danger of being arrested for the crime.

"All right," Carroll replied. "If you would go over to the house with me," he said, pointing up the road to Maher's, "I'll go up with you."

"What do you need to go to the house for?" asked Hodge.

"I want to change my clothes," Carroll replied. "I want to go to Lucan looking respectable." The men nodded and Carroll climbed aboard their sleigh. Pope, with a light snap of the reins, started the horses off, pulling the sleigh north along the Roman Line. The trio arrived at the Maher farmhouse a few minutes later. Constable

Pope and James Carroll exited the conveyance and went inside, leaving Hodge outside in the sleigh. Once inside, Pope waited in the main room while Carroll went upstairs to change his clothes, which evidently consisted of merely putting on a white shirt. This accomplished, Carroll and Pope left the farmhouse and returned to the sleigh, with Carroll sitting in the back seat with Hodge and Pope sitting up front driving the team. Looking over his shoulder at Carroll, Pope asked, "Do you have your handcuffs with you?"

"I do," replied Carroll.

As they headed south along the Roman Line the trio soon passed the ruins of the Donnelly house. "Look at that," said Pope, pointing to the charred debris that had once been the family's home. Carroll refused to look.

"When did you hear about this?" Pope asked.

"The next afternoon," said Carroll, still not looking at the ruins.

"Jim, this is a pretty bad affair. I wonder who it could have been that done it?"

"It's a kind of mysterious affair to me," replied Carroll.

Hodge now turned toward Carroll. "Where did you sleep the night of the murders?" he asked.

"Me and my brother slept at Thompsons'," said Carroll, now getting somewhat uncomfortable with the questions he was being asked.

As the sleigh turned west along the road that led toward Lucan, the trio encountered Vigilance Committee member William Feeheley, who was walking toward town with a friend. The constables stopped and offered them a lift, which the pair readily accepted. They climbed into the front seat of the sleigh next to Charles Pope. The presence of the new arrivals (particularly when one of them was a fellow Committee member) brought some momentary relief to James Carroll, as the conversation now shifted away from him and onto general small talk for the duration of the journey into town.

The sleigh came to a stop in front of the Central Hotel, where Police Chief Williams and the detectives and constables who were working the Donnelly murder case were now headquartered. Hodge and Carroll entered the hotel and went to the sitting room at the bar, where they were joined by Constable John Larkin. Pope said he would look for Chief Williams and left the room. Pope then took Hodge aside and said, "We had better do our little business." The pair re-entered the sitting room and Hodge walked up to Carroll and announced that he was under arrest for the murder of the Donnellys. According to Pope, "Hodge told him what he wanted with him and what he was arresting him for. He [Carroll] said 'all right' and dropped his head and held out his hands for the cuffs. He seemed frightened and said nothing, like as if a shock had come over him. He gave up quietly."

The constables led Carroll outside and walked him along the sidewalk toward the Lucan jail. On their way, they passed James Keefe, William Donnelly's good friend. Recalling that Carroll had drawn a pistol on both John and Tom Donnelly on two prior occasions, Keefe commented, "Search him for a revolver!" Keefe followed the men along the sidewalk and into the jailhouse. As Hodge would later recall:

> I think James Keefe followed right along to the
> lock-up. I think he stepped inside the door. I think
> he was present at the search. Someone spoke about
> the handcuffs, and to the best of my knowledge it
> was James Keefe. Whoever it was said, "Has he got
> his cuffs or revolver?" Whoever it was, appeared
> to know that he had a pair of handcuffs. Pope was
> there when I found that he didn't have his handcuffs.
> I didn't say anything to Carroll; I didn't remind
> him that he had told me on the road that he had his

cuffs. We searched him then; he had nothing with him. He had no handcuffs with him. We then locked him up in the lockup.

Shortly after Carroll had been incarcerated, county constables Alfred Brown and Silas Gilbert Moore arrested sixty-one-year-old local farmer John Darcy Sr. on the charge of being an accessory to murder. He was said to have quietly submitted to the arrest.[28] An hour later, constables Hodge and Pope spotted James Maher Sr. and James Maher Jr. in Lucan, and promptly arrested both of them on the same charge. The senior Maher muttered, "I expected it."[29]

Police Chief Williams, together with Constables Phair and Murphy, then went on the hunt for John Kennedy Jr. They went to his father's house but were told that he was not at home. John Kennedy Sr., however, stepped forth and pointed out to the chief and his constables that there were some footprints in the snow, and said that he believed his son had fled across the field. The police followed these until they came to the home of farmer Anthony Heenan on the Ninth Concession. Inside the house they found John Kennedy Jr.[30] Kennedy submitted to the authorities peacefully and expressed his sorrow over the death of an innocent girl. However, he then felt obliged to mention that there was "something manly about shooting a man dead as in the case of John Donnelly."[31]

The next Vigilance Committee member to be arrested was Martin McLaughlin, one of the two men believed by William Donnelly to have shot his brother. According to the *London Advertiser*'s report:

Detectives Phair and Murphy arrested McLaughlin, and upon searching the house, Murphy found a seven-chambered repeating rifle nearly new. The rifle is a

large bore, and a most dangerous looking weapon,
carrying a large cartridge. Four of the chambers were
loaded, whilst another chamber had the appearance
of being recently discharged. Murphy retained the
rifle. The bullets found in the cartridges in the weapon
are similar in size and weight to that which was
shot at and passed through John Donnelly, and was
afterwards found embedded in one wall.[32]

And the arrests continued. Upon arriving at the home of Patrick "Grouchy" Ryder, the chief and his constables produced warrants for the arrest of Patrick and two of his sons, Patrick Jr. and James. However, the trio were given the runaround by members of the Ryder family as to where the father and sons were. It was said that Patrick Sr. was at a neighbour's, then it was said that he had gone to Lucan. However, when the men left the Ryder home they fortuitously encountered Patrick Sr. walking along the Roman Line and immediately placed him under arrest. The old man then led Constable Phair into the bush where his sons, James and Patrick Jr., along with two others, were chopping wood. The two Ryder boys offered no resistance when Phair arrested them and, together with their father, they were then delivered to the town jail in Lucan.[33]

John Lambert Payne, in his continued pursuit of any developments in the story, dropped into the Lucan lock-up and observed that

[a]fter these nine prisoners had been incarcerated
in the lock-up — an institution which serves the
additional purpose of being the fire station — four
constables were detailed to keep guard and prevent
the men from conversing together. McLaughlin sang
and another danced, but the majority were very
much downcast and anxious-looking.[34]

All the arrests had occurred throughout the morning and afternoon of February 5. By ten o'clock that evening the prisoners had been transferred south to the London jail by train and sleigh.[35] A large crowd stood waiting for the prisoners' train to arrive at the Great Western Station in London. Then, like today, people were intrigued by those who saw themselves as being above the laws that governed others. What did the murderers look like? People elbowed one another for a better vantage point to view the spectacle unfolding before them at the train station. First out of the railway car was Constable Enoch Murphy. Once he sensed that the coast was clear, he motioned to the first four prisoners to exit the train. The prisoners, handcuffed two-by-two, shuffled off the train and onto the platform. Next off the train was Constable John Larkin with two other prisoners. Constable Charles Pope, baton in hand, walked behind the group, while Murphy led the way, carrying the rifle the constables had seized as evidence from Martin McLaughlin's home.[36] Also brought from the train were an assortment of spades, shovels, picks and other makeshift weapons that had been collected from the Donnelly property.[37] The crowd followed the penal procession out of the train station, and along Richmond Street to the London Police Station. Upon entering the station, the doors were closed behind them, leaving the gawking masses behind to speculate on what would happen next. A reporter from the *London Advertiser* was admitted inside the station and jotted down some brief character profiles of the prisoners:

- John Kennedy was the first to stand forward. He is a very large and powerful-looking man, with dark beard and whiskers. He gave his age as thirty-five, and said he was born in Canada.
- James Maher is quite an old man, and does not bear any of the distinguishing marks of a villain. He was born in Ireland and is fifty-two years of age.

- Martin McLaughlin stood forward in a hesitating kind of way and gave his age as forty-two. He was born in Ireland.
- James Ryder was, however, of all the party the most uneasy-looking. He is a short, thick-set young man of twenty-three, and looks as if he was very much afraid of something dreadful happening.
- Patrick Ryder, father of the above, is fifty-three years of age. He has short, grey whiskers, and bears a very respectable appearance.
- Constable Jim Carroll is a very powerful-looking young man, and is considered to be the most dangerous of the party. He is about twenty-eight years of age.[38]

Before the prisoners were shown to their cells, a sleigh containing eighteen-year-old James Maher Jr., together with constables Hodge and Brown, arrived from Lucan. Then came the arrival of prisoner John Darcy, who was brought into the jail by Constable Silas Gilbert Moore. And, finally, twenty-three-year-old Patrick Ryder Jr. was delivered to the jailhouse by Chief Williams and Detective Phair.[39]

While the prisoners were in London dealing with the consequences of their sins, back in Lucan the surviving Donnelly family members were dealing with the enormity of their loss. The wake for the murdered family members was coming to the end of its first long day on February 5, with William and Patrick being the only family members present to stand watch over their family's mortal remains. Their sister, Jennie Currie, now the only living female of the family, would be an important presence; she was expected to arrive from St. Thomas later that evening, as was the

Donnellys' youngest surviving son, Bob Donnelly, who would be making the trip in from Glencoe.

A wake is an interesting tradition among the Irish; it forces the reality of mortality upon us, when almost every other thing we do in our lives serves to smokescreen it. We like security and predictability; we want things to stay the same. But that's not the way it is; things never stay the same, and, therefore, predictability and security are illusory and impermanent. Confronting death directly reminds us that we ultimately have little control or efficacy in our brief span upon this earth. The Irish know this — they see through the veil of illusion behind which most of us live our lives, recognizing it as being nothing more than the window dressing that it is. They also know the freakishly high odds against any one of us being here and, consequently, they celebrate births and deaths — the only two realities of life — as the only true milestones of existence worthy of acknowledgement.

The Donnellys were certainly no strangers to wakes, having hosted no fewer than three of them in their parents' home over the past three years. The wake, to them, would be a benediction; the barrel of emotion would be drained to its dregs, and all sadness would be fully tapped out of them. In keeping with the tradition, a room within the O'Connors' home had been prepared to display John's corpse within its casket.[40] Here William and Patrick would remain. Next to John's casket was placed the wooden box containing what was left of the other murdered family members. Candles would have been lit at the head and foot of the caskets. A window would be opened in the room to allow the safe transition of the spirits of the deceased from their earthly vessels to heaven. After a few hours, the window would be closed and the curtains drawn so the souls of the departed would not return. All mirrors within the home would have been turned around to face the wall and covered with a linen cloth to conceal the physical remains of the departed from their departing souls and thus to no longer bind them to this earth. The caskets would never be left unattended until they were buried, a tradition, needless in this case, to ensure that the deceased did not "wake" and were truly dead.

Then would come the keening; the wailing and lamentations for the dead. This, too, was a tradition. It was a task usually performed by women, one of whom would be the lead keener, whose job it was to be the first to weep over the deceased's bodies. She would often recite poetry of special significance. At this point, the lead keener would be joined by other women and they would openly wail together. After all this had occurred, the friends and neighbours would be allowed in to pay their respects and offer their sympathy to the family. This marked the end of the formalities, if not the bereavement. Pipes and tobacco would be brought out, tea, sandwiches, homemade buns and cakes would be served (often brought by the guests) and generous quantities of beer or homemade alcohol (such as "potheen," a bootleg alcohol distilled from potatoes) would be available, which served to loosen tongues to tell tales of humour and affection regarding the departed. Laughter pushed the pendulum of emotion to the opposite end of the spectrum, affording a welcome repose from the weight of grief. And this would carry on throughout the night, until the time for burial the next morning. When dawn arrived, the bodies of the deceased would be conveyed to the church where they would be received by the priest.

John Lambert Payne took note of the proceedings: "During the entire night large parties, mostly friends of the deceased, and others, from mere curiosity, were continually going to and from the corpse-house, which kept the house full to overflowing."[41]

Of course, Payne wasn't the only member from the press to attend. The Donnelly tragedy and its ongoing development were big news. Special publications about the murder were in the works, as newspaper readership had expanded, and ad revenue was soaring. Comments about John Donnelly's appearance and anecdotes that were overhead about his character were reported: "He is a man not at all ill-featured, and, in the countenance, he somewhat resembled his mother. He was tolerably well-educated, and of genial disposition";[42] "quietest of the whole family";[43] "it is said that he would take a blow without resenting it, in order to avoid a disturbance";[44] "he was a fine built fellow, his physical development being complete. In death he wore the same smile that usually played about his face in life. He was, for some time, a strict temperance man. The medical gentleman who made the postmortem said that he had never seen a man with so large a heart."[45]

The reporters finally got the drama they'd craved for their readers when Jennie Currie arrived the evening of February 5. The *London Advertiser* reported, "A heartrending scene was witnessed when the only daughter of the family arrived. Upon being shown the bodies she went into violent hysterics, which continued nearly all night. She is the youngest of the family, being twenty-two years of age. She is married and has three children. Her residence is in St. Thomas."[46] The *Montreal Star* added, "Jennie Donnelly is the observed of all observers. Her screams are wafted out on the night air, and yet she knows nothing of the incidents connected with the tragedy. She knows or sees only one dear object before her, the charred remains of those most near and dear to her."[47]

The only first-hand testimony we have from Jennie Currie on her grief during this period is to be found within a letter that she penned from her home in St. Thomas to her brothers three days after the funeral:

St. Thomas, Feb. 9, 1880.

My Dear Brothers, William, Patrick, Robert,
    You will find enclosed the pictures of my loving
mother and my poor dead brother, Tom, who are
now before their God. I may say I did not receive

the message in time to mail yesterday, as the message boy could not find the house until just now. Dear brothers, I do not send these pictures for any other purpose but for you to procure *facsimiles* therefrom, and you will kindly preserve and return them when any of you come here. Oh, God! When I think of my poor mother, and the way she was so cruelly murdered, I feel like dropping down dead, and that my happiness in this life is blasted forever.

James [Jennie's husband, James Currie] tells me that William has preserved one of the bones of my poor mother's arm, and if so, when he comes to St. Thomas, let him bring it with him, so that I may kiss the loving arm that never failed to throw its protection around and provide for all of us in the darkest days of our need. If my father's little pet dog that he got from Harry Phair is alive, I trust you will send him to me, and I will keep him till he dies of old age.[48]

Oh! My dear brothers, I feel so lonely and heart-broken. I trust you will try, or some of you, or all of you, to pay me a visit at as early a day as possible; for the God above knows that in this trying hour I yearn to have you with me — all that is left of my poor brothers.

I sincerely hope and pray that you may be successful in bringing to justice those parties who have left me so lonely by their cruel and bloody deed.

Your loving sister,
Jennie Currie.[49]

At 2 a.m. on Friday morning, Bob Donnelly arrived at the O'Connor home.[50] He was greeted warmly by his siblings and then moved on to view the bodies of his murdered family members. And that was when his composure left him. Looking upon his late brother John in his casket, "his nerves collapsed, and he fell to the floor in a fit."[51] Overcome by grief, he forced himself to open the wooden box containing what was left of his parents, younger brother and cousin. A writer for the Toronto *Globe* later reported, "After gazing intently at them for some time, he picked up the burned heart of his father and kissed it tenderly. He then performed the same act on the liver of his brother Thomas."[52]

William approached his younger brother, and placing a fraternal hand on his shoulder, gently admonished him by altering the old proverb about spilt milk: "No use crying over burnt bodies," he said.[53] With that, the two brothers returned to Patrick and Jennie, and remained at the wake throughout the remainder of the night.

Not long after the sun rose on the morning of February 6, a reporter for the *London Advertiser* arrived at the O'Connor house in the company of John Thorn, a photographer from Lucan. The Donnelly siblings were still present when the lensman positioned himself over John Donnelly's casket and snapped his photo. Once again, Bob Donnelly broke down, "completely overcome and wept bitterly."[54] The two eldest brothers, William and Patrick, the reporter noted, "with the exception of a momentary falter of the voice or a stray tear, were firm as rocks, but the settled determination to discover the perpetrators of the deed was plainly to be read in their faces." Patrick walked to John's casket and examined the inscription on the coffin nameplate, which stated:

John Donnelly: Died February 4th, 1880. Aged
32-years and 11 months.[55]

Reading the engraving, Patrick Donnelly bristled, "Poor fellow. *Died*? It should have been *murdered*."[56]

At approximately the same time Thorn was busy snapping his photograph of John Donnelly's corpse in Lucan, seventeen miles away in London a large crowd gathered in front of London's Central Police Station. They were hoping to see the prisoners who had been arrested the day before and who were due to be arraigned this morning for their alleged crimes before Police Magistrate Lawrence Lawrason. The courthouse was on the upper level of the police station, and when the doors opened to the auditorium of the courthouse, the crowd rushed in. Unfortunately, the prisoners were not taken to the courtroom, but had simply been taken upstairs from their cells below to the office of Chief William T. Williams. There would be no courtroom activity this morning on the Donnelly case. As the prisoners and a squad of armed guards formed a semi-circle around the chief's desk, in walked Police Magistrate Lawrason to preside over the arraignment.

Representing the prisoners was Hugh MacMahon, Queen's Counsel, who turned to Chief Williams and asked that the warrants be read into the record. The chief replied that individuals John Kennedy Jr., Martin McLaughlin and James Ryder Jr. were under arrest on a warrant alleging "that in the Township of Biddulph, and County of Middlesex, on the Fourth day of February, 1880, they did feloniously, willfully, and of their malice aforethought, kill and murder James Donnelly, Judith Donnelly, Thomas Donnelly, Bridget Donnelly and John Donnelly."[57]

"On what warrant are the other prisoners arrested?" asked MacMahon.

"They are charged with being accessories to the fact. However, I intend to amend the first information, and adding the names of

Patrick Ryder Sr. and James Carroll as principals," replied Chief Williams.

"And when will the trial come on?" inquired MacMahon.

Turning to Magistrate Lawrason, Chief Williams answered, "I will ask for a remand of one week." Lawrason granted the request, stating that the trial could not proceed until after the coroner's inquest had been concluded.

"Can bail be taken in the meantime?" inquired MacMahon.

"Certainly not!" snapped Lawrason. "The charge is altogether too serious to admit of such a thing. The prisoners will have to be kept here in custody pending the order of the coroner and future developments. As soon as the coroner's inquest is concluded we will know better what to do about this dreadful business. I will make out a remand for eight days in the meantime, but if the prisoners can be brought up in the meantime I will be perfectly willing." The defence counsellor now conversed with the prisoners, who evidently were satisfied with the magistrate's decision on the matter. MacMahon then entered a plea of innocence on their behalf. Their collective plea now having been dutifully entered into the record, the prisoners were then returned to their cells.[58]

A crowd composed of farmers, friends and townspeople had begun to form at nine o'clock on the morning of Friday, February 6, in front of the O'Connors' house. The crowd continued to swell until 11 a.m., when six pallbearers emerged from the dwelling carrying the body of John Donnelly within a glass-topped rosewood coffin. Trailing behind came men carrying the wooden box, devoid of handles or ornamentation, containing the charred fragments of the other four victims. A lid had been nailed onto the box. John Donnelly's casket was taken to a hearse; the wooden box was placed into the back of a rough sleigh. It was reported that "there was an immense concourse of people on the road and all the avenues leading to the house,"[59] and that the funeral procession that lined the road consisted of one hundred sleighs and cutters and extended for over half a mile. The conveyance containing the surviving Donnelly family members was foremost in the procession, containing William and Nora Donnelly, Jennie and her husband James Currie, as well as Patrick and Bob Donnelly. It was said that "only William was stoic and calm." The procession slowly headed southeast for the better part of two miles along what is now Richmond Street, before turning north a short distance along the Roman Line, where it came to stop in front of St. Patrick's Church. There the family was met at the church doors by Father John Connolly and six acolytes.

The two coffins were carried into the church and placed in the centre aisle, while the mourners and pallbearers took their seats within the pews on either side. Every seat in the church was occupied, and the overflow of spectators were forced to stand at the rear of the church. All newspaper accounts placed the attendance that morning at five hundred people. Father Connolly led the funeral Mass and the church choir sang the Mass for the repose of the souls. Then Father Connolly addressed his congregation. A newspaper report stated its surprise that the priest did not condemn the Donnellys:

> Father Connolly preached the sermon. His remarks, which were strongly condemnatory of the assassins, have created almost as great astonishment as the tragedy. Prior to these remarks it was generally supposed that Father Connolly was a bitter enemy of the Donnellys, and ugly rumours were circulated concerning his connection with the Vigilance Committee. A feeling of relief is now experienced, and it is quite probable that the explanation of the Priest exonerating the Donnellys will go a great way

to restore confidence and materially aid in making
peace between the opposing parties.[60]

While the above passage made for a feel-good moment in the newspaper and in the community, it wasn't entirely accurate. Father
Connolly's address to his congregation at the conclusion of High
Mass had not been without its fireworks, although it had begun
innocently enough: "Dear friends, you are in the presence of one
of the most solemn scenes which I have ever witnessed. And I have
witnessed many a solemn scene — but never any like this. I am
heartbroken . . ."[61] This was as far along as he got. The priest
suddenly turned away from the congregation and burst into tears.
His body shook and he shifted his weight from foot to foot. This
awkward interlude continued for a solid five minutes[62] before he
was able to proceed:

> I never expected that such a scene as this would be
> enacted. In coming to Biddulph, I left a quiet place —
> a Christian place — and a place where the laws of
> God and man were observed and respected. I came
> to a district where neither the laws of God or man
> have been observed, and, hence, the consequence,
> terrible and fatal, which we see before us today.

Father Connolly then proceeded to introduce into his address
some of his old prejudices. Without naming them, he called out
the magistrates (who had come under his wrath on prior occasions
when they did not punish the Donnellys to his satisfaction):

> Yes, dear friends, the laws of the land, founded
> upon the eternal laws of God, have not been
> observed in this county and district. And those
> who have been entrusted with the execution of

those laws have neglected to carry them out, and they will have to answer for the lives of these five people at another place. Before I came here I did not know of the fires and terrible destructions which had taken place here, and I could not believe that there was an Irish Catholic in Biddulph that would bring such disgrace upon himself and upon his church by committing these scenes of blood, which would not have disgraced the community had the law been properly enforced. There are two things which must be observed in every society, no matter of what religion that society may be composed. Men may have their opinion upon the Gospel, and their individual opinion of its teachings, but there can be no second opinion that in the interests of Christianity — of society — all should endeavour to observe that law, and have it enforced. That has not always been done in Lucan and Biddulph, and those entrusted with the administration of our laws have not fulfilled their duty, and have prostituted it; and it is owing to this prostitution that we are called together on this solemn occasion.

At this point the surviving Donnelly family members may well have wondered where Father Connolly was heading with his sermon — was he implying that the murders of five of their beloved family members were the result of the local magistrates not having sent Tom or John Donnelly to jail? But Father Connolly had to walk a very narrow rope, on one side of which sat the nation's press, looking for answers as to how members of his congregation had become emboldened enough to commit mass murder; on the other side sat his parishioners, who had spent the better part of twelve months listening to their priest condemn the late family from his pulpit and from within courtrooms. The eyes of the world were quite literally now trained on the good Father to see how he would (or could) justify his prejudice against the late family, while simultaneously throwing a blanket of protection over those who, under his spiritual guidance, now stood accused of the most heinous crime in Canadian history. Father Connolly continued, now taking aim at the Donnelly family:

> The guilty men who have imbued their hands in innocent blood will have to answer before their God for the awful crime. . . . I feel deeply sorry for the afflicted family before me, but they are to a certain extent blameable for the events of the past few days. The old woman and I were good friends. The last time I spoke to her was at confession. The younger portion of the family bore bad names, but the old woman thought in time her sons would ultimately be brought back to the Church. On her last visit she informed me they were going to London for confession. The boys, as I have before said, were wild, and were accredited with many inhuman acts towards their neighbours. . . . The Donnelly boys were said to have committed many vicious offences, such as killing neighbours' animals, and as they did not respect themselves nor man nor God, how could they expect to secure the good-will of others? I would have been delighted to have become better acquainted with the boys, but they seemed to shun me, and I had none of them to speak to. The old man and old woman I knew best, and I considered Mrs. Donnelly to be a sensible woman. The father I believed could be easily carried away with excitement. Had Pat Donnelly been at home I think

this affair would not have taken place, as he was known to be a young man of good sense, and would, no doubt, have given his relatives sound counsel.[63]

The Donnelly survivors were nonplussed. The priest's words had offered them no comfort whatsoever. Instead he had just told the world that they were "to a certain extent" to be blamed for the murders; that they were "vicious," "wild," and did not respect God; that their late father had been "easily carried away with excitement," and that had the courts done their job and sent certain members of their family to prison, or if Pat Donnelly had only intervened, then these murders might not have occurred. Indeed, his words made it clear that the magistrates and the Donnellys had brought the murders on themselves. Jennie had been away too long; she didn't know all the details of the incidents to which the priest alluded. William did, however, and may well have crossed intellectual swords with the priest right then and there, had not Patrick Donnelly suddenly leapt to his feet and, in front of the priest and the entire congregation, demanded an explanation.

"Father Connolly, I wish *you* to give a detailed account!"

A hush fell over the church. Did Patrick Donnelly just challenge the priest to justify himself? Father Connolly slowly turned around to face Patrick. "What do you ask me, Mr. Donnelly?"

"I would like you to tell the *whole matter*," Patrick replied, "giving particulars more fully." Patrick was now speaking on behalf of the Donnellys who had gathered here on this day; he wanted the priest to justify his prejudice against his family, and also to justify how Father Connolly could have spawned a group that felt itself justified in breaking the Fifth Commandment — by a multiple of five. If the priest wanted to calm the waters between him and the family, now was the time. If he wished the family's respect, he couldn't simply assume it; he would have to earn it through the honesty of his answers. There was no doubt in anyone's mind that a gauntlet of sorts had just now been thrown down at Father Connolly's feet in front of a large audience. The children of James and Johannah Donnelly had walked into his church and, rather than weeping and nodding their heads regarding the sins he alleged they had committed, they instead had risen up and, without any trepidation, challenged him to defend his actions. The priest was now left with no alternative but to comply. "Well, perhaps it will be better for me to tell," he began:

> The only trouble I ever had with the family was that
> I thought they had not sufficient respect for their
> own character. When there was any hostile feeling
> displayed, it was always supposed that it came from
> the younger members of the family, and any trouble
> I ever had with them was not worth speaking of.
> It was the taking out of a horse from Kelly's that I
> first had trouble with them about. I met the boy and
> wanted to speak to him as a priest, and after this
> Mr. William Donnelly sent me a sharp, incisive letter,
> which might be a good one to write to a politician
> or businessman. He was naturally a talented young
> man, and capable of writing a good letter; if he were
> a newspaper editor it would be a good reply, but it
> was not a good letter for a priest. I did not make
> any mention of this letter to anyone until I heard
> that William talked, and said he was going to drive
> me from the country. Another thing was the Ryan
> threshing. Ryan came to me and wanted to get
> me to influence the young men to allow this
> threshing. I used my endeavours with a friend of
> mine at Quebec, a Minister, to get the young man
> [Bob Donnelly] out of Kingston. With regard to the
> old people, I never had any hard feeling. In fact, I

> never had with any of the family — but the boys had
> a hard character. These are the only troubles I have
> had in the world with these two men.

Father Connolly may have been trying to put his best foot forward, but he certainly wasn't honouring Pat Donnelly's request to "tell the whole matter." He had, for example, neglected to mention how he had called William Donnelly a "cripple and a devil" and had twice denied William's request for a meeting to discuss their differences. He also neglected to mention that he had denied confession to John Donnelly, and how he had chastised parishioners such as John Kennedy Sr. and James Keefe Sr. simply for associating with the Donnellys. And as for never having any "hard feeling" for the old people, hadn't the priest told the schoolteacher, James Patton, that "Johannah Donnelly wasn't worthy to receive the blessed sacrament and that she would die in a ditch"? And then, when Patton's wife protested that James Donnelly Sr. was too old to have attempted to burn Ryder's barn, he had answered that "James Donnelly is capable of doing anything." And he wasn't even being honest about his interaction with "the boy" whom he had accused of stealing James Kelly's horse. He hadn't once attempted to "speak to him as a priest," but instead had gone to Kelly's farm and demanded that "the boy" (Tom Ryan) be fired, kicked out of Kelly's home and run out of town. Having attempted to whitewash his animosity toward the Donnelly family, Father Connolly now moved on to attempt to distance himself from the Vigilance Committee, a group comprised largely of members of his congregation that had orchestrated the murder of the Donnelly family members:

> A Vigilance Committee was formed among the
> farmers long before I came to this place. I need not
> say I am not a member of it, neither have I incited
> any of its members to act in any other than a

law-abiding manner. I know many of the members, and had the greatest confidence in them. My beloved brethren, I trust those whom I know as members of the Committee are incapable of such acts of murder, and it must have taken place outside of the Society.[64]

William Donnelly, of course, knew first-hand this was not the case. The look in his eye caused Father Connolly to change tack, for he now decided to compliment the family members:

As far as the old people were concerned, I esteemed them as much as any people in the parish. Since the death of Mike Donnelly, they have been to communion. I never dreamed of an occurrence like this. I thought that the whole thing would wear away. The driving away of horses, and the shaving of horses' tails, were things which people did not like. It is a failing with all Irishmen that they have no faith. No man is anything without a character, but with it he is everything — and if he doesn't respect that character, we have no peace whatever. I have been delighted, and especially since I became acquainted with Patrick Donnelly, who I have found to be an honest, respectable young man, to have had him to speak to and consult with. And perhaps had he been here things would have been different. The old woman was a sensible sort of a woman whom I could talk to and consult, but the old man, although a good old man whom I liked, was not the sensible sort of a man that I could talk to like I could to the old woman. The last words I had with the old woman she said, "Father Connolly, I have been trying to get the boys to be good."

Again, the priest looked down at the two coffins; and, again, his voice failed him. However, he regained his composure and continued:

> I cannot understand how this has taken place. I did not believe that there was a man capable of doing anything like that in Biddulph. I believed that there were men who would give a man a clout when half drunk, or waylay him upon the road, but I never thought that they could make such a butchery as this. It is a disgrace to Biddulph and everyone who lives here. However, my beloved brethren, all that remains for us now, and for the family, is to pray for those that are gone, and those who are left must reform. For, no matter whether by the hand of God or by the wicked hand of man, we must all stand before a Living God, and the hour and time we know not of.

Father Connolly next pointed out that the Donnellys' deceased family members had not received the last rites; they had not been absolved; they had died in sin. Again, he gestured toward the two caskets:

> Think, then, of those unfortunate people who have been called without a moment in which to pray, to appear before God and answer for their sins. It is an awful thing for these people. Man is but a shadow. He has but a few years here. What will your position be after they have gone by? Will your society be that of thieves, reprobates and murderers — or will your society be that of the Son of the Living God? Had it been possible, I would have given my own life in order to save the souls of these five poor people,

who had not time to utter a prayer to God for mercy upon their souls.

Finally, Father Donnelly felt the need to end the matter on a positive note; he assured the family that John Donnelly (at least) was in heaven:

> I feel very much obliged to Patrick Donnelly,
> because I thought there might have been a hard
> feeling against me, but such I find is not the case.
> When people have a hard name, as a priest having
> the charge of souls I must set my face against their
> deeds. If Mr. Patrick Donnelly had been here I feel
> that I should have had a sound thinking person, and
> I might have counselled with him and had a better
> understanding. With regard to John, who died with
> a prayer upon his lips, he is now before his God, and
> his sins are forgiven.

All in all, it hadn't been a particularly comforting report. With nothing more to say, Father Connolly came down from the altar to pronounce benediction over the two caskets, an act that concluded the service. The congregation then proceeded outside to the cemetery and watched as the two caskets were interred. After the graves had been filled in, Martin Collisson, a friend of the Donnellys, asked William if he was afraid to go into the rectory and talk to the priest.

"No, I've never been afraid to talk to him,"[65] William replied. He then turned and headed toward the little brick parsonage behind the church that was home to Father Connolly. Upon his arrival, William noted that his brothers and sister were already sitting with the priest. William entered and, ensuring that he followed the proper protocol (that his wife apparently had not upon her first meeting with Father Connolly), he dropped to his knees.

"I'm prepared to beg your pardon if I have done anything wrong," William said. "But I consider that I have not, but was simply vindicating myself and my family in a proper way. I think you now have plenty of proof that I was right; that the letters I sent to the Bishop and to you were full of truth as to the characters of the Vigilance Committee."[66] William then rose to his feet.

"May God bless you," said Father Connolly.

Tea was poured and the two began a dialogue. "The worst thing I ever blamed you for was for calling me a cripple," William said.

"Oh, yes. It's too bad," the priest replied. "From the stories I had heard I thought that you were a desperate character, and would waylay me at some time."

"No," William Donnelly assured him, "I have more respect for myself than that and am a better Catholic than those who carried you such stories."[67]

The discussion between the priest and the family members continued on amicably for a little while longer. The Donnellys then left to grieve amongst themselves, while Father Connolly received a reporter from the Toronto press. Right away the journalist pressed the priest for more information about what he knew about the formation of the Vigilance Committee.

"The Vigilance Committee you mentioned in your address today was formed *before* your arrival in this district?"

Connolly easily deflected the question.

Yes, it was organized in 1876. At that time, as far as I can learn, it was necessary that some such society should be organized. Barns were continually being burned, horses stolen from stables and ridden to death, and other depredations of that kind were of nightly occurrence. The neighbouring farmers, the better to protect themselves from the perpetrators of these outrages, banded themselves together. The law appeared powerless, and at that time it was said that terror was the reigning king.[68]

Then, recognizing that the report would be printed in Toronto, the second-largest city in the Dominion (after Montreal), and that the prisoners and their families made up a significant portion of his congregation, he made it clear that the Donnellys were the architects of their own misfortune. He now went on the offensive and renewed his attack upon the late family.

> The Donnellys were the acknowledged ringleaders, and with their associates openly flaunted their defiance of the law. Their arrests were made, to be sure, but the local magistracy were either afraid to commit, or were incapable of impartially filling their office. Why, since I came here, I had occasion to speak to one of my parishioners, a friend of William Donnelly, about some wrongdoing charged to him. I was afterwards told that William Donnelly had openly boasted that it would only cost six cents to get rid of me. That was the exact sum it had cost to get my predecessor out of this district.

"How was the money to be expended to procure the result?" the reporter asked.

"Well, I supposed he referred to the cost of two three-cent postage stamps. Threatening letters were nothing unusual; but such epistles would not intimidate me."

His interviewer's next question caught the Father somewhat off guard: "It was rumoured in the village yesterday that you were going to be arrested as one of the members of the Vigilance Committee?"

The question attached the priest to the murderers by association. This had to be squelched, not only for the benefit of Father Connolly, but to protect the Church from any implication in the matter.

> Yes, I heard such a statement was being circulated; in fact, I see one of your reporters [has] despatched the news to your paper. I think it very wrong to publish any rumour of that kind, and you would do me a great favour by saying I have no fear of arrest, for I have done nothing to make myself amenable to the laws of the country.

While the coroner's inquest into the matter had not yet begun, the priest then felt obliged to reiterate that the murderers could not have come from his congregation and advanced an alternative hypothesis.

> From what I know of the members of that Committee I feel quite convinced in saying that they were utterly incapable of taking hand or part in such horrible tragedies. The murders were committed by persons outside the society. . . . It's a bad, shocking state of affairs. Such scenes would astonish even the residents of Texas or the South-Western States. In Canada, the deed stands without a parallel, and as a disgrace to the whole country; but more especially this particular neighbourhood. The old feuds had a horrible ending, for which the Donnellys alone were responsible.

When the newspaper report appeared, William Donnelly wasted no time in returning to the rectory and confronting Father Connolly about its contents. According to William, Father Connolly almost broke down again: "He felt entirely overcome, and admitted that he had been misled as to our family's character, and that the Society had taken advantage of him."[69]

And while William would state for the record that he "had no hard feelings toward his reverence," he was also quick to add that he would "leave the world to judge whether he or I were in the wrong from beginning to end."[70] William further sought out the Toronto reporter who had interviewed Father Connolly and adamantly denied that he was seeking to have the priest arrested. However, he concluded by saying, "I am not at all eager for his arrest, unless it can be shown he has taken some part in the affair. I feel assured he has not; but if he had, I would just as soon see him under arrest as I would a layman."[71]

CHAPTER TWENTY

THE CIRCUS COMES TO TOWN

Front page of the *Toronto Mail*, February 6, 1880.
Newspapers all across Canada, as well as certain newspapers
within the United States, carried the story.

The murder of the Donnelly family was now the biggest news to hit Canada since it had become a Dominion thirteen years previously. Within one month of the murders the Lucan telegraph operator, William Porte, would file 90,937 words of telegraph copy about the story for news reporters.[1]

The scope and brutality of the crime had put Canada on the international map in a most unflattering way. Until February 4, 1880, Canada had basked in the glow of being considered perhaps the most civilized of all the British Empire's self-governing bodies — far more so than, say, South Africa or Australia (at least from Canada's perspective), but the barbarousness of the massacre had changed that status overnight. Newspapers from within and without Canada felt compelled to comment on this:

> Toronto *Globe*: Yesterday before this dark deed became known no one would have believed such an occurrence as wholesale lynch murder by a vigilant committee possible; today the community is brought face to face with the humiliating fact that an event, for a parallel to which one must go to the annals of Texas or California, has taken place in a populous agricultural district only a few miles from the city of London, in this Province.[2]

> *Hamilton Spectator*: It is humiliating and shocking to think that such a deed of blood as this could be perpetrated in any part of Canada, and that, too, within fifteen miles of a populous city, well furnished with the crime-detecting agencies of the law, and in a well settled part of the country. Such crimes are at least comprehensible in the western wilds, where the organized tribunals of society have not yet taken root, and where the law of self-defence knows no legal forms; but we had all supposed that every part of Canada had long ago passed beyond the possibility of such deeds.[3]

> *Hamilton Times*: Such crimes as this we have been accustomed to look for in the wilds of Texas or Virginia, but certainly not in the order-loving communities of Canada.[4]

> *Listowel Banner*: The late massacre of the Donnelly family, in the township of Biddulph, by an armed

mob, is a crime which has no parallel in the history of Canada.[5]

Petrolia Topic: The tragedy enacted in the township of Biddulph . . . casts a foul blot on our fair name as a law-abiding and God-fearing people.[6]

Detroit News: The event is so unlike anything we are accustomed to, not even in degree, but in nature, that comment is silent because it is dumb with astonishment.[7]

While the news had certainly added a black eye to Canada's image upon the world stage, it was also exposure — and this represented a boon to commerce in the area. The hotels were filling up with press people, the taverns were doing a brisk business in alcohol and food and the newspapers were pumping out special editions: "Full particulars of the tragedy which has thrilled the whole Dominion," screamed the *Stratford Weekly Herald*. "We are satisfied to know that our advertisers will get the benefit of our increased circulation."[8]

People from as far away as Evansville, Indiana,[9] and Oakland, California, were now reading about the Donnelly murders in their local newspapers.[10] And while the world was reading about the tragedy, those who had survived it were busy tying up loose ends connected to their parents' estate. The remaining siblings pooled their resources and Pat Donnelly went into Lucan to square whatever debts were owed by his late parents.[11]

Of all the brothers, Pat was the only one against whom, for the most part, nobody seemed to hold a grudge — including the enemies of the family.[12] Father John Connolly had singled him out for praise during his funeral address,[13] local farmers told the press they would rebuild the Donnelly home at no charge if Patrick would live there (they also made it a point to say their offer applied to no other surviving family members)[14] and Donnelly author James Reaney uncovered information that no less a family adversary than Grouchy Ryder was Patrick Donnelly's godparent.[15] Like the remainder of his siblings, however, Pat was interested in justice — not reconciliation.

On February 6, the day of the Donnelly funeral, the London detectives arrested John Purtell and Michael Heenan. Purtell had been seen by Johnny O'Connor standing over the body of Tom Donnelly, while Heenan was observed to be among those who had visited William Donnelly's house on the night of John's murder. Purtell was terrified, and was heard to cry out in jail, "Lord have mercy on my soul for what I have done!"[16] What he had done was rather extensive, as it turned out. Purtell had a violent criminal background: in 1877 he, together with one of the Mahers, had attacked a group of German immigrants in Ellice Township. The immigrants were savagely beaten and stabbed to the point where one of them nearly died. Both Purtell and Maher would serve six months in Toronto's Central Prison for their role the affair, which revealed that gang brutality was by no means foreign to these two members of the Vigilance Committee.[17]

In the early morning hours of Saturday, February 7, Bob Donnelly found himself standing outside, staring at a large patch of white snow that lay mixed with black ashes. The odd charred artefact peeked out at him from within the greyness. He had last visited this place two weeks previously when it had been his parents' home. Now all that remained were two logs that had once been the steps to the front door.[18] He had learned that Johnny O'Connor had been at his parents' home on the night of the murders, and so he had approached the boy after the funeral. He wanted Johnny to accompany him to the site of the tragedy[19] — and to tell him exactly what happened. Hearing about it in court would be one thing, but Bob

Donnelly needed to experience his family's last hours directly. The broken and barbecued bones he had seen in that wooden box on Friday morning weren't his parents. He could only experience their presence once again on the Roman Line — in looking out upon the fields they had cultivated, in the barn and outbuildings they had built, and among the ruins of their house. He also wanted to see for himself exactly where his parents had drawn their last breath, and where his youngest brother had fallen to the mob just outside the front door. "I just went down to see where they were burned," he would later recollect.[20]

In time, Joseph Whalen spotted the pair walking about the property and ventured across the road to join them.[21] But two was company and three was a crowd; Bob Donnelly and Johnny left shortly thereafter. For the moment, Bob Donnelly had seen all that he needed to.

Later that same day William Carroll (James Carroll's younger brother) was arrested, along with Thomas Ryder (Patrick Ryder's younger brother),[22] and brought to the Central Hotel, in Lucan. It was the last stopping point prior to the prisoners being transported to the Middlesex County Gaol. The prisoners were handcuffed and made to sit at one of the tables in the bar of the hotel where they were watched over by members of the London constabulary until they would be taken to Clandeboye, where a train would arrive to take them to the city later that evening.

To the prisoners' surprise, seated at a table across from them in the bar was Bob Donnelly. He wanted to be present when his parents' killers were brought into town. While he knew Thomas Ryder, he'd never laid eyes on William Carroll before. It didn't matter; the fact that both these men now stood accused of murdering his family members was enough for Bob to hate them both beyond measure. He read their faces and noticed that William Carroll had a nervous twitch in his eyes, which, as a man fresh out of prison, Donnelly read as being signs of fear and weakness. "Boys, keep up your courage," he called out sarcastically, "there is lots of time ahead of you to do the crying."

Carroll's face turned red. "All but the cry," he said by way of comeback.

Thomas Ryder now looked toward Donnelly. "Don't fret, Bob," he said, "there won't be many tears dropped over the matter."[23] Donnelly simply stared through both men.

The pair remained at the hotel until 8:30 p.m., when, accompanied by Chief Williams and Detectives Phair and Murphy, they headed off to the Clandeboye train station and boarded the London, Huron and Bruce train bound for London. The London jail now contained thirteen suspects in the murder of the Donnelly family, each listing his occupation as "farmer":

Name of Prisoner:	Age:
John Kennedy Jr.	35
James Maher Sr.	52
Martin McLaughlin	48
James Ryder	22
Patrick Ryder Sr.	55
James Carroll	28
James Maher Jr.	19
John Darcy	60
Patrick Ryder Jr.	20
Michael Heenan	24
John Purtell	23
William Carroll	20
Thomas Ryder	30[24]

The Vigilance Committee now busied itself in efforts to support those of its members who had been arrested. A defence fund to pay the prisoners' legal expenses was set up,[25] and an intimidation campaign was coordinated and put into effect against those who might be considering coming forth to testify against the accused. To this end, Committee sympathizers visited farmers in the region who might have seen something untoward in the early morning hours of February 4, and instructed them to keep their mouths shut.[26] A letter-writing campaign was launched against the Committee's adversaries: Police Chief Williams was told to stay out of Biddulph,[27] while Johnny O'Connor's father, Michael, was informed that he and his family would be burned out of house and home if he allowed his son to testify (he received three such letters in one day). One missive warned, "You will be used the same as the Donnellys if you do not leave the place."[28] And, of course, William Donnelly was held in a position of special contempt, and so he received letters of a particularly revolting and threatening nature:

Port Huron, Michigan
February 11, 1880

William Donnelly — You and your relatives have
been a disgrace and a curse to our country. Your
chances are favourable to leave now. If you delay
our friends will assist you, so take warning. If your
brother Patrick remains at Lucan he will take his
chances with our friends for assistance when we
think proper.

Yours truly,
ONE WHO SAW YOUR
MOTHER AND FATHER FALL[29]

Mulmur, February 8, 1880
Wm. Donnelly, Lucan

Sir,

You know well enough whom the slugs were
intended for that took effect in your brother John.
It was a slight miscarriage but it was as well to get
Jack out of the way. There may be a slug or two left
for you if you don't be careful. I am not a man that
does anything by halves. My motto is "root and
branch" when a family has to be exterminated by
reason of their depredatory and incendiary acts, and
I believe you are a member of such a family.

Yours warningly,
ONE WHO KNOWS WHAT HE KNOWS[30]

Another letter came addressed to William and Bob Donnelly
that, while bereft of syntax, nevertheless clearly put its author's
point across:

This is to notify you that the Honest and
Law-abiding People of Lucan wishes you to remove
from this villeg at once, or you May be Moved
some knight & your colegs will be remembered.
Your Brother Jim was shot here by our police man
in 1877 in the act of incendrey cans, your rowdey
ism in our streets waylaying & robbery, burnings,
cutting our horses throats, Murdering. Dan Clark's
murder is not forgotten. Deluding our females,
robbing them of character & other bad acts.

A Friend To Lucan An Sitizen[31]

William Donnelly took the threats seriously (how could he not?) and refused to sleep more than two nights under the same roof throughout the duration of the coroner's inquest and preliminary hearings. His wife Nora was now five months into her pregnancy and, worried for her and their unborn child's safety, he sent Nora to live with her father for the time being.[32]

Since the press had descended upon the township, the Committee encouraged their supporters to go forth and speak to the newspapers in an effort to help shape public opinion to their favour. People such as Joseph Carswell, who had long nursed a grudge against the Donnellys and had longed to find an ear willing to listen to his screed, were quick to snap up the invitation, and Carswell told the press that "a workman earns his wages, and they got their just dues. . . . They burned and cut, and were cut and burned. . . . They brought it on themselves and deserved their end, and I'm not afraid to say so."[33] While he may not have been afraid to say so, he was certainly afraid of having his name appear in the newspaper as having said so. He told the reporter that he would prefer to remain anonymous.[34] Other anti-Donnelly sentiments found their way into the press at this time, ranging from simple vitriol ("Donnelly souls are roasting in hell now"[35]) to ones defending the character of certain prisoners ("What on earth did they arrest Maher for? He couldn't cut the ears off a cat"[36]). When postmaster William Porte was interviewed, he offered a far more balanced perspective on the situation:

> I tell you, the boys were bad enough, but there's two
> sides to this story. Anyone who has witnessed the
> manner in which they have been hounded about
> through the past eight or ten years, cannot wonder
> that the young men were revengeful. Thousands of
> dollars of their hard-earned money were expended in
> fines, costs and lawsuits. . . . A few quarrels among
> young men, as full of life as themselves, soon gained

for them enemies, and the people in this district being clannish, both sides had friends. All these men now charged with this murder were then their warmest supporters, and while some dropped off from time to time, owing to supposed injury to relatives, etc., others turned against them through pure jealousy. When the opposers became more numerous than the other party . . . then the persecution began.[37]

But Porte was speaking for a minority. Father Connolly then reinserted himself into the proceedings by writing an open letter to the press in which he declared that the incarcerated Vigilance Committee members were innocent.[38] This was a call to arms for every red-blooded Roman Catholic in Biddulph and Lucan to fall in line behind him in a show of solidarity. Any goodwill that may have been engendered between the priest and the surviving Donnelly members after the funeral was now in tatters. But what did it matter? There was, as William Donnelly had rightfully pointed out to his brother, no sense crying over burnt bodies. The family had to keep its focus on the future.

The bulk of the Donnelly family were dead by this point, and, thus, no longer wielded any power in the community. The Vigilance Committee members, by contrast, were still very much alive and, given that there is strength in numbers, the people of Biddulph wanted to be on the side of the big battalions. Besides, those Committee members who were in jail had friends and family within the community. It was *their* lives that were now at stake. If some of the townspeople opted to act with their conscience and proceed to bring evidence against them, no fewer (and probably more) than thirteen Roman Catholic families would be torn apart when the prisoners faced the gallows. If, however, these same people chose not to testify, they would be saving Roman Catholic lives, all the while thumbing their collective noses at the British law courts. They would be viewed as patriots (of a sort, at any rate). Given what was at stake for the community, it was quite simply a no-brainer to the citizenry of Biddulph and Lucan: the pragmatic (and safest) option was to close around their own and protect the prisoners. As Carswell would prophetically tell one of the reporters: "It will be hard to get anyone to swear against the prisoners, except the Donnellys. I never met an Irishman yet who would act as informer. If even an enemy of the men saw them committing the murder they'll not tell."[39]

This was certainly true. A Roman Line denizen dismissed the coroner's inquest with the statement "I'm no tell-tale."[40] The writing was on the wall. Even Crown attorney Charles Hutchinson, who would be prosecuting the Vigilance Committee members, was pessimistic: "There is little or no prospect of admissions or confessions. I question whether there is another township in Canada to correspond with Biddulph."[41]

Meanwhile, behind closed doors and among themselves, those who had taken part in the massacre posed the one question upon which the entire trial would hinge:

We did murder them — but can they *prove* it?[42]

Indeed. All the prosecution had for witnesses were William Donnelly and Johnny O'Connor — and both witnesses were problematic. The problem wasn't that either of them was untruthful in their recollection of what they had witnessed on the night of the murders, but rather lay in the fact that the former had a well-known animus against the men he claimed to have seen outside his bedroom window, while the latter had seen little beyond the bedroom door in a darkened Donnelly home — and from behind a laundry basket at that. This was weak evidence indeed to place in the balance against the lives of (at least) six men.

Charles Hutchinson knew what he was up against and dug in to make the best of a bad situation. He wanted the prisoners kept in jail, as he believed that their prolonged separation from the outside world would eventually cause a crack to form in the plaster of their non-compliance: "The persons who may be committed for trial should be detained in close custody, there is always the chance of one or more breaking down during a long imprisonment."[43]

The confession of just one of the prisoners was worth infinitely more to the prosecution's chances for securing a conviction than O'Connor and Donnelly's testimony combined.

Hutchinson had his reasons for believing that he was on to a good strategy. After all, the prisoner John Purtell had been in tears when he was arrested and looked close to confessing then. Even James Carroll had seemed to be almost expecting his arrest, and had willingly held forth his hands to be cuffed and taken to jail. The Crown attorney believed that it would pay dividends to watch these two prisoners closely. One of them was sure to break.

While Hutchinson had confidence in the above strategy coming to fruition, for the moment he had to focus on what he had in hand, namely, the testimony of William Donnelly and Johnny O'Connor. Given the recent spate of threats made by the supporters of the prisoners, he had grown fearful for the safety of his star witnesses. William Donnelly was less likely to be attacked as, despite the slaughter of half of his family, he still had Patrick and Bob, and three Donnelly brothers were still enough to give their adversaries pause. Moreover, despite local antipathy, the Donnelly survivors had the collective sympathy of the nation on their side. To add further tragedy to the family now would make it almost impossible to defend the prisoners.

Johnny O'Connor, however, was a sitting duck. The Vigilance Committee were, in Hutchinson's words, "a desperate and unscrupulous party,"[44] and it would not be beneath them to cause something untoward to happen to the boy. To keep O'Connor safe, and with the O'Connor family's blessing, Hutchinson had instructed Chief Williams to spirit the boy away from his home in

Lucan under the cover of darkness. Williams concealed Johnny in a rug that he had placed in the back of his sleigh, and then drove along a road that led south toward London and past the observing eyes of two Committee members who had been posted as sentinels on the outside of town.[45] O'Connor was secreted in a boarding house that was located close to the Middlesex County Courthouse. Once he was safely within its confines, his mother Mary moved in with him.[46] Both Mary and Johnny were then guarded by Constable Charles Pope. Michael O'Connor remained behind in Lucan with Johnny's siblings, despite the threats made by the Committee to burn him out of house and home.

The coroner's inquest resumed on February 11, 1880, and right away those who were allied with the Vigilance Committee did what they could to sabotage the proceedings. Despite having used the Town Hall for the first session of the inquest the week before, when the officials arrived at the building to resume the formal inquiry they discovered it was locked down. The use of the Town Hall evidently required a unanimous vote of approval from the members of the school board. This was provided, save for the vote of one Bernard Stanley, which made unanimity in the matter impossible. With the coroner, the jury, the constables and the inquest officials all required to attend, the use of the town's largest building was expected and necessary. However, Stanley wouldn't budge on the matter and the inquest was forced to continue within a twenty-by-thirty-foot room above the town jail, which had barely space enough to accommodate half the number of people required to be present.[47]

Members of the press and those seeking to witness the inquest attempted to push their way inside. Hundreds more were turned away. More misfortune followed when London Police Chief Williams's buggy broke down while he was driving to the inquest, which caused him to arrive late to the proceedings.[48] The excitement of the crowd outside was ratcheted up a notch when Johnny O'Connor, surrounded by a group of constables, arrived to present his testimony. Until this point, neither the defence counsel nor the Vigilance Committee knew precisely what O'Connor had seen or heard on the night of the murders and they needed this information in order to defend against it. When O'Connor was called to the witness stand his testimony was direct and implacable. He specifically named James Carroll, Thomas Ryder and John Purtell as being among the men who had murdered the Donnelly family. His evidence was strongly suggestive that Carroll had entered the Donnelly home in the dark of night and handcuffed Tom Donnelly while the latter had been asleep, thus rendering him defenceless when the murderers stormed the house. To the anti-Donnelly faction, such an act was perceived as being a clever precautionary strategy, but to the Donnelly survivors, as well as to those who would later research the subject of the Donnelly murders, it was viewed as a decidedly cowardly tactic.[49] Defence counsellor MacMahon had no success in poking holes in the boy's testimony and word travelled quickly back to the Cedar Swamp schoolhouse about what O'Connor had said. Word also travelled south to the Middlesex County Gaol, where James Carroll was heard to muse, "The boy goes pretty strong for me."[50] The inquest was then adjourned for another week.

Immediately the Committee supporters plied the newspapers with their spin on the testimony. O'Connor was not to be believed, they said, because he had clearly been told what to say ahead of time.[51] "O'Connor would swear the head of a ghost," said Mrs. James Maher.[52]

On Thursday, February 12, Bob Donnelly returned to the family property. Something had to be done with James and Johannah's livestock, and Bob had arranged for James Keefe to look after some of their cattle for the time being. As he drove the cows north toward Keefe's farm, he happened to notice something lying on the ground that seemed strangely out of place. Examining the object, he noticed that it was a bloodied club. As he rolled the elm weapon over in his hand, the bloodstains told its story; it had seen service in ending the life of one or more of his late family members. This realization hit him like a punch in the solar plexus. He laid the weapon down against his late father's woodpile and resumed his role of drover, herding the cows north along the Roman Line to Keefe's farm. Upon his return later that day, he retrieved the club and brought it with him to Lucan, where he handed it over to his brother William. William, in turn, gave it to Chief Williams for evidence.[53] William Donnelly, now the oldest surviving child of his late parents, was the one the Donnelly siblings naturally looked to for direction. It had always been that way in the Donnelly family. William was the cerebral one; he would know what to do. The gallows were what William envisioned for James Carroll, John Kennedy Jr. and his Vigilance Committee cohorts — and the path to the hangman led through the courts.

When William Donnelly came to London for the inquest, the members of the press were fascinated. Here was one of the notorious Donnelly family in the flesh, and he was nothing at all like they had been led to believe from the interviews they had conducted with the enemies of his family. To begin with, he was not a monstrous-looking fellow: William was of average height, and wore his dark hair long; it cascaded down to his shoulders in wavy ringlets.[54] With his long hair and goatee[55] he looked like Wild Bill Hickok but, unlike the gunslinger, he was erudite, and spoke with the folksy and well-honed wit of a Mark Twain.

When asked for his comment on the fact that approximately one hundred supporters of the Vigilance Committee had turned out to rebuild Grouchy Ryder's barns, William replied, "I do not wonder . . . there being nearly this number in the Vigilance Committee, none of whom are particular whether they work a few hours in the night or not."[56] This clearly was a double entendre, aimed at the Committee members who had not only joined together to rebuild Ryder's barn, but who had likewise joined together during the span of a few hours in the dark of night to murder his family. He was aware of the Vigilance Committee's attempts to paint his family as being solely responsible for the "reign of terror" that swept through Lucan in 1877, and used his encounters with the press to quash that spin by pointing out that "there's just as much 'reign of terror' in the township as ever there was. . . . It is well-known that many thefts and offences have been committed of late in the township, which the friends of the prisoners do their best to keep from getting published. . . . Since the Donnellys are gone, and cannot be blamed for offences such as described, it is not prudent to let the public know that even a concession line fight ever disturbs the quiet of life in Biddulph now."[57]

A letter written by a Vigilance Committee member to the editor of a London newspaper contained the allegation that the Donnelly family was responsible for all of the depredations the community had suffered over the years. This drew a letter to the editor in response from William, in which he presented a litany of crimes committed throughout Biddulph, dating back to 1845, that his family had nothing to do with. He then drove home the point that since the massacre of his family, the crimes had continued:

> I will pass on to the 4th of February last, at which
> time your special correspondent intimates the doers of
> all evils were removed from this earth, and that peace
> and quietness have returned after years of turmoil;
> but, dear sir, who committed all the above-mentioned
> crimes that have no equal in the history of Canada,

or who have committed the crimes that have been done since the memorable 4th of February? In about a month after that date Mr. Carter's grain store in Granton was set on fire and consumed, together with the contents, and a few nights after Mr. Timothy Collisson's barn and contents were reduced to ashes. Mr. Collisson has always been a good friend to our family, and surely my father's and mother's roasted bones did not go across from the churchyard and destroy his property.[58]

He concluded his missive with typical Donnelly flourish and pride:

As this history of crime is composed of facts that cannot be contradicted, I trust that you will give it a place in your valuable paper, and give the outer world an idea how long and deep the hands of Biddulphers (outside the Donnellys) have been steeped in crime. I also trust you will excuse my grammar and spelling. I have no big words to give you, but will use my own name and defy contradiction.[59]

The press was fascinated by his defiance in the face of adversity. He shrugged, and told them, "My father always taught me to say to a man's face what I would say behind his back."[60] William continued to work the press like a puppet; he ripped the lid of secrecy and clannishness from the Biddulph community for all the world to see, drawing a comparison between the way the Roman Catholic community had been rallying behind the murderers of his family and the way it had previously rallied around the murderers Grouchy Ryder and William Casey when they had killed the Englishman Richard Brimmacombe in 1857, stating "they of course got clear, the Key of Heaven having been chewed to pieces by the Roman Liners."[61] He openly mocked the Vigilance Committee members, who, like himself, hailed from humble Irish stock, but who believed they stood superior to his family.

His message having been delivered, William Donnelly now put his agile mind to work in the service of the prosecution. The man the Vigilance Committee had intended to kill on the evening of February 4 was now assisting the constables in gathering information that might yet see these same Committee members swing from a hangman's rope. While in Lucan, William stayed in a house that had been rented by his brother Bob from Michael O'Connor.[62] The house was next door to the O'Connors, and very close to Lucan's main street, which was convenient for the brothers to attend both the coroner's inquest and preliminary hearing.

The Committee supporters made sure to be on hand when the third hearing of the coroner's inquest took place on February 18. When the police sleighs from London arrived containing the three men whom O'Connor had named, the trio was met with raucous applause and cheering from the pro-Committee crowd. Such a show of enthusiasm and support emboldened the prisoners. Thomas Ryder spotted Michael O'Connor among the crowd and singled him out for a mock salute, before being taken into the Council Chamber above the Lucan lock-up.[63] The Crown attorney, Charles Hutchinson, together with defence attorney Hugh MacMahon, arrived at Clandeboye station by train from London, but thereupon learned that there would be no stages at the depot to transport them to Lucan. Consequently, the lawyers had to trek three miles by foot until they reached the jail-cum-council chamber on William Street.[64] Then, once everyone had squeezed into the room, it was announced that there would be no inquest that day as the coroner had taken ill and could not be present. The inquest was then put off until March 2. The three prisoners were led back outside to the police sleighs and, once again, were cheered jubilantly by the crowd. "You need not be vexed about us," Thomas Ryder yelled to his supporters, "we are as happy as kings!"[65] Patrick Donnelly witnessed the spectacle from the sidelines and mocked the crowd's partisanship by calling out to the constables in facetious indignation, "Don't go yet! Give the Vigilants a chance to shake hands with their friends!"[66]

Three days later, and before the coroner's inquest had resumed, the Crown initiated a magistrate's preliminary hearing against the six prisoners. The venue for the hearing was the Middlesex County Courthouse in London, which was considerably larger than the area above the Lucan lock-up and, thus, allowed for the Committee to stock it full with their supporters. The prisoners — James Carroll, Thomas Ryder, John Purtell, John Kennedy, James Ryder and Martin McLaughlin — were led handcuffed into court.[67] Unlike the coroner's inquest, which had heard testimony from only ten witnesses, the preliminary hearing was gearing up to receive testimony from no fewer than twenty-seven. Charles Hutchinson had added the Hamilton Queen's Counsel, Aemilius Irving, to his prosecution team,[68] while the Donnelly family had hired Edmund Meredith, a lawyer for Biddulph Township,[69] to assist Hutchinson and to look out for their interests in the case. Believing their evidence against the six prisoners to be the strongest, the Crown opted to let the remaining prisoners out on bail.

Meanwhile, the supporters of the prisoners had found a way to insinuate their influence into the London jail. The prisoners weren't made to subsist on prison food; instead, their friends brought them lavish fare from one of the London hotels.[70] "They give us six meals a day," one of the prisoners boasted.[71] Rather than being separated from the world outside, the world outside was allowed to come to them; friends and supporters of the six were allowed to visit whenever they wished and priests came in to offer their support from the London diocese,[72] while the prisoners amused themselves by reading about themselves in the local papers. Sounds of their singing and laughter could be heard echoing throughout the building.[73] Charles Hutchinson's belief that the hardships and privations of being in jail would gradually break down the prisoners simply wasn't materializing.

March 2 was the final day of the coroner's inquest and pandemonium reigned supreme. Once again, Chief Williams had sleigh problems, with the result that he now had to borrow a farmer's wagon to travel to Lucan. And once again, a great mob of supporters awaited the arrival of the prisoners.[74] Throughout the proceedings, members of the jury, the prisoners and their friends were permitted to walk about the room and talk freely among themselves — even when testimony was being delivered. Despite their best efforts to bring order to the room, the constables were unable to keep the interactions from occurring. And then things got worse; one of the members of the jury simply decided to leave the inquest while a witness was mid-testimony and went home. Apples and oranges were passed out to the prisoners during the proceedings.[75] At this point, Chief Williams had had enough:

> The Chief of Police stepped up to the Coroner's
> table and said, "I want to go home." "What!" said
> Mr. Hutchinson and the Coroner in one breath,
> "Are you sick?" The chief [replied], "I am not very
> well and want to be relieved of the responsibility of
> taking care of the prisoners. It is utterly impossible
> to look after both jurymen and prisoners with the
> staff I have here. The way things are going on now,
> with the jurymen and prisoners mixed up together,
> it would require a constable to each prisoner and
> juryman to look after them."[76]

Eventually, Chief Williams was convinced to stay and all the witnesses completed their testimony. The purpose of the coroner's inquest had been to determine if a crime had been committed, and if any person or persons could be implicated in the death of the Donnellys. At 11:15 a.m., the jury returned their verdict in the matter: a crime had most definitely been committed: the Donnellys had indeed been murdered and burned on the night of Tuesday, February 3, or early morning of Wednesday, February 4 — but by "some party or parties to the jury unknown."[77] This certainly had not been the result expected by the prosecution. Still, that verdict took care of the murder that Johnny O'Connor had witnessed. But there was still the matter of the murder of John Donnelly to be resolved. To this end, the jury was sequestered overnight and the prisoners were returned to their cells. The jury's decision was expected the next morning. It was a solemn and serious matter that they had been left to deliberate on, but you would never have known it based on a newspaper report of their behaviour that night:

> Complaints are made that the jury in the Donnelly
> inquest displayed a levity altogether unbecoming
> in the important questions which they had met to
> decide. It is said that although nominally locked
> up for the night, several of them were allowed to
> go around to hotels in the middle of the night. At
> 2 o'clock this morning they were carousing and
> singing, "We won't go home till morning." A pailful
> of beer was sent up to them by some person. This
> conduct might well become a tavern debating society,
> but is neither creditable or proper in a jury solemnly
> sworn to inquire into the causes of death of several
> murdered parties.[78]

Be that as it may, at 9:20 a.m. the next morning the jury were summoned to deliver their verdict on the death of John Donnelly: "That John Donnelly came to his death at the residence of William

Donnelly, on the morning of February 4th, by being shot by persons unknown."[79]

Only two of the fourteen jurors from Biddulph had wanted to commit the prisoners to stand trial. They were overruled.[80] The jury was then discharged.

Meanwhile, the preliminary hearing continued. Held before justices of the peace, the purpose of the preliminary hearing was to determine whether the charges brought against the prisoners warranted a formal trial before a judge and jury in the Superior Court at the next Assize. When the inquest had first been convened on February 4, a juror, having returned from seeing the four charred bodies within the ruins of the Donnelly homestead, had commented to William Donnelly, "This is a bad job, Bill." Donnelly had replied, "I guess I will live through the circus."[81] While his metaphor was apt, William Donnelly had no idea then that the circus had not yet begun. Much like at the coroner's inquest, a carnival-like atmosphere would pervade the preliminary hearings:

- Martin McLaughlin's wife brought the prisoners apples, which they ate in court during the testimony.[82]
- Spectators brought their dogs into the courtroom, resulting in the dogs fighting during witness testimony.[83]
- If the prosecution and defence attorneys clashed over a point of procedure, the crowd would boo, cheer and otherwise behave as though at a sporting event.[84]

Even the defence witnesses made a mockery of the proceedings. When Hutchinson discovered that the Donnellys' neighbour Patrick Whalen had attended several meetings of the Vigilance Committee, he put him on the stand in an effort to determine the anti-Donnelly bias of the group. When he asked Whalen what the Committee members did at their meetings, Whalen replied that they had done nothing.

"Did you sit there like a Quaker?" the attorney asked.

"I don't know how Quakers sit," replied Whalen.

"Quakers sit around without speaking until the spirit moves them. Did you do that?" queried the counsellor.

"Begorra!" answered Whalen, "I did not see any spirits there."[85]

And so it went until the preliminary hearings concluded on March 13, 1880. Unlike the result of the coroner's inquest, the two justices of the peace for the hearing, James Fisher and John Peters, concluded that the evidence brought before them was sufficient to commit the six prisoners to stand trial at the Middlesex Spring Assizes in April.[86] The prisoners were then returned to their cells, while the legal teams retired to prepare their respective cases.

Given the notoriety of the case, people now started coming out of the woodwork in an attempt to seek the spotlight of the moment. Detective Hugh McKinnon reappeared, reaching out to the London detectives to indicate his willingness and availability to assist them with the case (his services were declined).[87] Another man, detective George Walter Clay, brought forth lots of evidence to help the prosecution — all of it manufactured.[88] A lady named Kate Johnson became a groupie of sorts; she was impressed with the Donnelly brothers' reputation and showed up one day at the home Bob Donnelly had rented in Lucan. Somehow, she even managed to get herself invited to a get-together at the O'Connors' house. She ended up spending the night with Bob Donnelly and his wife, which immediately raised eyebrows in the neighbourhood.[89] The two London newspapers quickly realized the extent of public interest in the murder story and it didn't take long before they each released their own special booklets on the Donnelly murders in an effort to cash in on the public intrigue. An advertisement for the *London Free Press*'s booklet claimed that it was "[a] complete and

Graphic Narrative/of the Massacre of the Donnelly family/By their Neighbours in Disguise," while the front cover of the pamphlet put out by the *London Advertiser* depicted a handcuffed Tom Donnelly lying in front of the family home being beaten to death by the mob. Then, as now, sensationalism sells.

Oliver Mowat didn't hold the position of premier of Ontario for the better part of twenty-four years by accident.[90] He was an astute politician who knew how to play to his power base. While his Liberal party had traditionally been popular with Roman Catholics, the Conservatives had gained some influence as of late, as indicated by their recent success in the Middlesex North riding during the 1878 election. The Roman Catholic population within Canada was huge — even as early as 1867, they represented 45 percent of Canada's population. And, unlike the Protestant faith, which saw its adherents sharply delineated into various denominations, such as Presbyterian, Methodist, Anglican and Baptist, the Roman Catholics were a united block of 1,465,979 potential voters in a country with a total population of 3,278,575.[91] Any politician of ambition within the new Dominion recognized the singular importance of courting the Roman Catholic vote, and Mowat was an ambitious politician. But Mowat also recognized that he had a problem within the Catholic community because he was a Protestant (Presbyterian). Representing a party that courted the Roman Catholic vote, he did not want his office to do anything that might alienate his Roman Catholic constituency in the province.

Consequently, he had to walk a very narrow rope on the Donnelly matter. On the one hand, he had to be for justice; as the attorney general, that was his job. On the other hand, he could not be seen to be anti-Catholic — and the prosecution of a group of Catholics by a Protestant-led Liberal provincial government made that difficult. Initially, when the first reports of the murders had broken, the Donnellys had been seen as a Roman Catholic family, and so Mowat believed he would enjoy good political positioning in pushing hard for justice for this late Catholic family. However, the rumblings that were now coming out of Biddulph strongly suggested that the Donnellys had fallen out with their priest and with their fellow Roman Catholic parishioners. Thus, whatever sect or denomination the Donnellys belonged to didn't look as though it was Roman Catholic. They were clearly, with their family-first attitude, the smallest of possible minorities within the province; they had no lobby group that would speak for them or that carried sway in provincial offices. St. Patrick's Church, with its connection to the London diocese, was quite the opposite. And the church was clearly in support of the prisoners on this matter. Consequently, Oliver Mowat's actions would have to be tempered. He had to assure the public that his attorney general's office was strong and firmly against crime — and particularly the crime of murder — but he also could not risk coming across as being a Protestant premier on the hunt for Roman Catholic citizens. He was not prepared to use the power of his office to do anything that would risk his political standing within the Roman Catholic community, and this would prove to be an ongoing source of frustration for Crown attorney Charles Hutchinson throughout the months that followed.

To ensure that the matter never rose to a level that would impact him politically, Mowat personally appointed to the prosecution team a London lawyer by the name of James Magee. Magee was a man who was deeply loyal to Mowat's Liberal party and therefore would be able to keep the premier's office apprised of any of the prosecution's plans that might be potentially injurious to him politically.[92] Mowat's deputy John Scott had tried to whitewash Magee's appointment to Hutchinson, indicating that it was simply done "from the importance of the case and the public interest taken therein."[93] However, Hutchinson bristled at the imposition: "I have given no intimation to the government that I needed assistance, neither did the government inquire that I needed assistance."[94]

It didn't matter: James Magee was now part of the prosecution team. It was such a small world within which these various people were operating. Magee, for example, had run on the Liberal ticket in London during the previous provincial election and had lost out to a lawyer named William Ralph Meredith. Meredith was not only the brother of the Donnellys' lawyer, Edmund Meredith, but was also the current leader of the official Conservative opposition to Mowat.[95] Moreover, William Ralph Meredith had recently come on board to head the defence team for the prisoners, which would put him at odds with his brother Edmund.[96] Having lost to Mowat for the provincial leadership, William Ralph Meredith was always on the lookout for issues that might help turn the polls in his favour, and defending six Irish Roman Catholics against the persecution of Protestant Liberal leader Oliver Mowat's government struck Meredith as a good way to boost his stock among Ontario's largest minority group. The Donnelly case, then, could not avoid becoming deeply entwined with Canadian politics.[97]

In an effort to entice the reticent, Charles Hutchinson approached the attorney general with the suggestion that the government offer a financial reward to the general public for information that would lead to the conviction of any of the prisoners. It was a risky proposition, as any public declaration by the prosecution that they needed more evidence than they already had could be read as an indication that their case against the prisoners was weak. However, from Hutchinson's perspective, they weren't going to win the case with only Johnny O'Connor's and William Donnelly's testimony. He had hoped one of the prisoners might have flipped by now, but the incredible support of the Biddulph Roman Catholic community had actually fortified them. His belief now was if the reward was high enough, those who had witnessed something on the night of the murders might be willing to put aside their religious concerns about the forthcoming trial, as well as any loyalty they might entertain toward the Vigilance Committee, and bring forth evidence that would strengthen the prosecution's case, if not win it for them outright. He asked Oliver Mowat to provide $5,000 as a reward for such information.[98]

Mowat was apprehensive. Hutchinson, in an effort to conceal the weakness of the prosecution's case, indicated that the wording on the reward posters should suggest the government was looking for evidence to arrest not only those killers who were already in custody but also those who might still be at large.[99] While Mowat agreed with the idea of the reward in principle, he was very circumspect about how it would reflect on him politically. Wouldn't targeting those in the area who hadn't been caught yet be viewed as essentially putting a bounty on the heads of Roman Catholics? And Mowat's name would be attached to the bounty. It was a risk politically that the attorney general wasn't prepared to take. Instead, he offered a compromise: the amount of the reward would be reduced from $5,000 for any information, to $4,000 with stipulations that made such a reward almost impossible to collect:

D.A. MACDONALD
(Canada)
PROVINCE OF ONTARIO

Victoria, by the Grace of God, of the United
Kingdom of Great Britain and Ireland, Queen,
Defender of the Faith, &c., &c, &c.

PROCLAMATION
To all whom these presents shall come, or whom the
same may concern, — Greeting:

O. MOWAT, Attorney General} Whereas James Donnelly, Judith Donnelly, Thomas Donnelly, Bridget Donnelly, and John Donnelly, lately residents of the township of Biddulph, in the county of Middlesex, the 4th of February last, cruelly murdered by some person or persons unknown.

Now Know Ye that the sum of ($4,000) Four Thousand Dollars will be paid by the Province of Ontario, as a reward to such person or persons as shall hereafter give such information as will lead to the conviction of the murderers of the said James Donnelly, Judith Donnelly, Thomas Donnelly, Bridget Donnelly, and John Donnelly; Provided always, that in case the information given does not lead to the conviction of all the persons by whom the said murders were committed. Such proportion of the reward will be paid as may by the Lieutenant-Governor-in-Council be deemed just, and that in case more persons than one claim to be entitled to said reward, or to share therein, the decision of the Attorney-General of Ontario, as to the respective rights of the claimants shall be final and conclusive; and that all claims shall be filed in to the Provincial Secretary within such time as may be hereafter limited for that purpose, public notice thereof being given.

In testimony whereof, we have these, our letters, to be made patent and the great seal of our said Province of Ontario to be hereto affixed. Witness, the Honourable Donald Alexander Macdonald, Lieutenant-Governor of our Province of Ontario, at our Government House, in our City of Toronto, in our said Province, this eighteenth day of March, in

the year of our Lord, one thousand eight hundred
and eighty, and in the forty-third year of our reign.

By Command,
Arthur S. Hardy,
Secretary[100]

It was a document of political doublespeak. Such a compromise
actually hurt both Mowat and the prosecution; it still attached
Mowat's name to a Roman Catholic bounty in the eyes of the
public,[101] and it drew attention to the weakness of the prosecution's case.[102] It would have been better not to have offered a
reward at all.

FRIENDS IN LOW PLACES

Ontario premier and attorney general Oliver Mowat sought to distance
himself from the Donnelly prosecution almost from the outset.
(The British Library Collection, Wikipedia)

Both the coroner's inquest and the preliminary hearing had been
effectively sabotaged by the supporters of the prisoners. Fearing
a repeat of this should the forthcoming trial be held in either Lucan
or London, the prosecutors decided that their best hope for a fair
trial would be in a different venue. This would require an appeal
be made before the Superior Court of Justice in Toronto. If the trial
could be moved to a city such as Toronto, for example, it would be
free of the prejudice of the mob back in Biddulph.

To this end, Charles Hutchinson, with the blessing of his prosecution team of Aemilius Irving, Edmund Meredith and James
Magee, wrote to attorney general Oliver Mowat informing him of

their plan.[1] Mowat, perhaps predictably, blanched at the suggestion — Toronto was where his government offices were located, and he didn't want to be seen anywhere near the Donnelly prosecutions.[2] Still, Hutchinson received support and understanding for his proposed change from some of his legal colleagues, such as Magistrate Malcolm Colin Cameron, who wrote:

> You should obtain without delay a summons to
> change the venue from London to Toronto, Ottawa,
> or any other place you deem most suitable. The
> Biddulph inquests fully proved that no jury can be
> trusted, and no justice obtained, in Lucan, London, or
> any part of Middlesex. The further from these places
> that a jury is selected the better. There seems not a
> shadow of doubt that the parties arrested are guilty.[3]

The change of venue would be hugely helpful to the prosecution, particularly since the supporters of the Vigilance Committee had stepped up their attempts to intimidate potential witnesses. Their efforts had the desired effect on James Keefe, who had left the country. He had been counted on to corroborate William Donnelly's testimony that he had shared with him the names of the Committee members he had seen outside his bedroom window on the night of the murders.[4] In late March, Mary Kennedy, the mother of Nora Donnelly, passed away. The Donnelly boys, despite their feud with John Kennedy Jr., had remained on good terms with Nora's parents. William Donnelly knew it would be awkward for both Nora and her father if he attended the wake, and so, on March 27, Bob Donnelly took William's horse and buggy out to the Kennedy farm to pay his respects on behalf of the Donnelly family. The wake was attended by many of the members of the Vigilance Committee, however, and, according to the local newspapers, it didn't end well: "A dastardly case of malicious injury to property occurred in Biddulph on Saturday night. It appears that William Donnelly lent his brother Robert his horse and buggy to go over to the Kennedy homestead in relation to the death of Mrs. Kennedy, William Donnelly's mother-in-law. Robert Donnelly left the buggy some distance from the house when he went in, and upon his return found that the rig had been broken to pieces."[5]

The prosecution lawyers were growing more concerned by the day that plans were in the works by friends of the prisoners to get Johnny O'Connor out of the way.[6] It was abundantly clear that however much of a threat to public well-being the Donnellys may have once been believed to be, a far larger and more dangerous threat was now moving through Biddulph.

In a further attempt to infuse religion into the proceedings and, thus, cement public (and potential juror) support for the prisoners, James Carroll wrote a letter to one of the local newspapers in which he played the trial off as nothing more than an unwarranted attack against the community and its priest.[7] William Donnelly shared with the press a letter he had received, unsigned, that instructed him that if he wanted help paying the family's legal expenses, he could always "tramp among the Orangemen and Protestants of Biddulph and McGillivray."[8] During a dung bee that was held on the Roman Line by Pat Grace, a farmer who had remained friends with the Donnellys, his work crew was denied access to a water pump that sat on the property of Pat Darcy, a Vigilance Committee sympathizer. A sign placed on the pump stated: "No water for Blackfeet here. Go to old Donnelly's homestead and you will get all you want."[9] When asked what was meant by the term "Blackfeet" William Donnelly was nonplussed: "I don't know, unless it is to distinguish those who belong to the Vigilance Committee from those who don't, and whose sympathies and feelings are with us and on the side of law and order."[10] An anonymous letter then appeared in a London newspaper indicating that "there were two factions in Tipperary, the Cummins and the Darnaghs, who for half a generation maintained perpetual warfare on every occasion. They adopted or had given to them the names of 'Blackfeet' and 'Whitefeet.' The old man Donnelly belonged to the Blackfeet in his younger days, and Will must have known by tradition the origin of the term."[11] The debate in the press would continue into the next year, with one side saying there was never any factional warfare in Biddulph,[12] and the other side eventually capitulating that this was probably the case.[13]

Eighty-one years later, author Orlo Miller would take up the whole "Blackfeet vs Whitefeet" angle and make it the thesis of his book on the Donnelly murders, *The Donnellys Must Die* (Macmillan Company of Canada, 1962).[14] According to Miller, the Donnelly murders were the culmination of a feud that had originated many decades previously in Ireland between two factions — the Blackfeet (i.e., non-pure Catholics; persons who associated with Protestants) and the Whiteboys (pure Catholics who had no association with Protestants). Reams of copy, pro and con, have been written by Donnelly authors on this supposed long-standing religious/political feud.

However, the deeper one goes into this rabbit hole, the less certain Miller's thesis becomes. Apart from the fact that William Donnelly himself stated that he knew nothing of any such feud from the old country, it is evident that the person who posted the sign on the water pump was simply drawing a line in the sand indicating that the Donnellys were known associates of Protestants (as indicated in the contents of the letter written to William Donnelly cited above) and, therefore, unworthy of local Catholic support.[15] Nevertheless, the above suggests that the trial by this point had clearly taken a religious turn in the eyes of the Biddulph community; it was no longer simply a criminal matter.

And then came a heartrending letter from Ireland; Bridget Donnelly's brother, Michael, had just learned of the murders. He wrote to his cousin, William Donnelly, hoping the news wasn't true:

March 18, 1880

Dear William,

Would you be kind enough to let me know if it is true that your father and mother and two brothers and my poor sister Bridget were murdered? We saw a long account of it, but cannot believe it is true. I do not know whether my father wrote to you or not, but I am sure if the account we saw of the murder is true, it will be the breaking of my father's and mother's heart. As for myself, I cannot give you an idea of my feelings. When I think of the pleasure it gave to hear of Bridget going to my uncle, and he so many years without hearing from him, and compare that pleasure with the sorrowful tidings I have now, it almost drives me crazy.

Dear William, during the last year I have often thought I would sometime have the pleasure of seeing you all, but the sad news of the wholesale murder has disheartened me, and I know my comforts in this world are blasted forever. If the account be true, we have only to pray that their souls may be happy. The murderers may escape punishment in this world, but they cannot accuse themselves of the crime and expect to escape punishment in the world to come. I thought you were a bird born alone, until my mother wrote me you had two more brothers alive and also a sister.

Had I seen poor Bridget before she went to America, I would not feel so bad, but I am now living in Dublin eleven years, and have not had the pleasure of seeing her before she went. She wrote me a letter after arriving at your father's, telling me of your kindness to her. This was the last I heard from her, or ever will again on earth.

William, you will please write soon, and let me know all the particulars.

Your loving cousin,
Michael Donnelly[16]

What could William Donnelly offer in reply? The news that had travelled overseas to Dublin had been all too true. Bridget's family back in Dublin was devastatingly confused; what had she ever done to warrant such a fate?

There was talk for a time that the surviving Donnelly brothers would fold up their tents and move away — Toronto was mentioned as a likely destination.[17] But that was only speculation that came from outside of the family. The Donnellys weren't going anywhere. Indeed, in order to offset some of their legal expenses for the forthcoming trial, the siblings had temporarily leased their parents' farmland to the Feeheley family,[18] still ignorant of the roles the two Feeheley brothers had played in the murder of their family members. Rather than even considering moving away, the Donnellys instead were sinking their roots even deeper into the Biddulph soil. They had spoken among themselves of rebuilding the family home and Bob Donnelly had already spent considerable time replacing the fence that lined the front of his late parents' property.[19]

Then came the Spring Assizes for the County of Middlesex, on Monday, April 12, 1880. The presiding magistrate was the same one who had sentenced Bob Donnelly to Kingston two years previously: Justice Adam Wilson. The Middlesex County Courthouse, which sat upon the intersection of Dundas and Ridout streets, along the banks of the Thames River, was full to capacity. The prosecution team now put forward their formal request for a change of venue, not believing that a fair trial could be had in either London or Lucan. Justice Wilson contemplated the matter overnight and then denied the prosecution's request the next day.

The prosecution announced that it would appeal the decision and, to allow time for this, Justice Wilson put the trial over until the Fall Assizes. The resolve of the prisoners, now looking at the prospect of another several months in jail, finally started to wane. James Carroll in particular was showing signs that he was not bearing up well. In early April he'd had a seizure of sorts and passed out in his cell. A doctor was summoned to tend to him, but Carroll was still reported as appearing pale and nervous, and only sporadically able to sleep.[20] Whatever he was suffering from — whether a virus, his conscience or a combination thereof — it apparently began to affect some of the other prisoners, who likewise started to display some of his symptoms. Their singing and joking had now ceased.[21] And so, perhaps in an attempt to alleviate their suffering and bring the whole troubled affair to an end, the supporters of the Vigilance Committee decided to take their intimidation efforts to a whole new level.

When Michael O'Connor and his sixteen-year-old daughter, Mary Ellen, had left for London on Tuesday, April 13, to visit with his wife and son, he had sincerely believed that his family back in Lucan was safe. After all, his oldest son, Thomas, was living in the house, and lots of family friends had agreed to drop in during his absence to make sure the O'Connor children wanted for nothing. And if that wasn't security enough, Bob Donnelly and his wife, Annie, lived right next door, not fifty feet away, in a house they had rented from Michael O'Connor. That is to say, there were lots of eyes upon the O'Connor home during his absence.

But that was the problem. Among those eyes watching the property were adversarial ones: those belonging to people who were worried by the threat Johnny O'Connor's testimony represented. These eyes had been watching the O'Connor property for some time, looking for an opportunity to send a final, and quite possibly lethal, message.

Charles Hutchinson had feared for some time that the Committee and its supporters would make a move to either kidnap or kill the boy,[22] which was precisely why he had him under police protection in London. However, neither the father nor the prosecutors had considered that a move might be made against the remaining O'Connor children. Whether they threatened Johnny or Thomas, or Bridget, or Patrick, or Mary Ellen, the net result would be the same: the life of an O'Connor child would be at risk. And a serious threat made against the life of any of the O'Connor children might just cause the parents to withdraw Johnny from the court case. After all, no parent would willingly opt to gamble a child's life in order to score legal points in a courtroom.

On Tuesday evening, several hours after Michael and Mary Ellen had left for London, several people dropped by to look in on the O'Connor children. The first to arrive was Kate Johnson, whom the reader will recall as being (at least as far as the author can ascertain) something of a Donnelly groupie. Johnson is a mystery figure in our story;[23] indeed, were it not for some oblique references made about her over a three-day period in the London press, history would know nothing about her at all. She had apparently arrived unannounced on Monday, April 12, at the home that Bob Donnelly had rented next door to the O'Connors. She had asked if William was there,[24] and, upon being told that he wasn't, she evidently was invited inside to visit by Bob and Annie. Kate stayed long enough that the Donnellys felt obliged to extend an invitation for her to stay the evening (perhaps she lacked the funds to rent a hotel room for the night?) but, as there was only one bed in the house, she ended up bunking in with Annie and Bob (with Bob sleeping on the outside of the bed, Annie in the middle, and Kate next to the wall).[25] It was, even by today's standards, an odd situation and, when word got out about it later, it caused many Victorian tongues to wag.[26]

But prior to the sleeping arrangements being put into effect, Kate had taken it upon herself to venture next door to visit with the O'Connor children. Why she would visit with strangers (either the Donnellys or the O'Connors) is uncertain, but the fact remains that she did, and, once again, she was invited in by the occupants of the house. Shortly after Kate's arrival came Ellen Carty, the twenty-three-year-old first cousin of the O'Connor children, and Mary Ann Young. Next to arrive was Ellen's father, forty-nine-year-old Cornelius Carty, along with her brother, nineteen-year-old Patrick Carty.[27] The Cartys had made it a point to visit with Bridget and the O'Connor children every night to keep them company and to ensure that they were safe.[28] The Cartys arrived a little after 6:30 p.m. and didn't stay long.

Next to arrive was William Pratt (the newspapers would report that it was James Pratt who dropped in, but, as James Pratt was only seven years old, it is more likely that the Pratt who was visiting was William Pratt, the forty-two-year-old root beer manufacturer from town).[29] Bob Donnelly then walked over from his house to check in on the O'Connors, and, not long afterwards, W.J. Atkinson, the son of William Donnelly's old friend William Atkinson, arrived. The group talked, and some played cards and dominoes in the kitchen. Bob Donnelly was in at 8:30 p.m. and out shortly after 9:00 p.m. Bridget O'Connor did some baking, and by 9:30 p.m. all the guests had departed the house and the O'Connor children went to bed.[30]

Shortly before eleven o'clock that evening, the front doors of both the O'Connor and Donnelly houses were jammed so as to prevent exit.[31] A fire then broke out in the vicinity of the kitchen of the O'Connor home. As the flames spread and the smoke rose, the dogs within the house began to bark,[32] which woke up twelve-year-old Patrick O'Connor. He called out to his brother Thomas, "The house is on fire!"[33] and yelled for his sister Bridget to wake up.[34] Thomas rose from his bed in a panic, wrestled a window out of its casing and leapt from his bedroom on the second floor onto the ground.[35] Looking out her bedroom window, both Bridget and Patrick saw two men hurrying away from their house in the direction of the foundry down the street.[36] Concerned these two people had started the fire and that Thomas might run into them, Bridget called out, "There's two fellows going down the road! Keep back!"[37] Patrick continued watching as the two men climbed the gate to the foundry and disappeared. Smoke was now filling the house, obstructing the children's vision and making breathing both difficult and dangerous. Holding his breath, Patrick now charged down the stairs to the ground floor, opened a window and escaped from the house.[38] Bridget, however, was still trapped inside up on the second floor. The smoke was now so thick that Bridget couldn't see; she misjudged the stairway and ended up falling down the stairs. She tried to locate the front door but couldn't find it.[39] The smoke was now cutting off her air supply and she felt herself growing faint.

Thomas and Patrick ran to Bob Donnelly's house and pounded on the front door. "Fire! Fire!" they yelled.[40] Bob Donnelly sprang from his bed and ran to his front door. To his bewilderment, it was jammed; something was preventing it from being opened. Just why Donnelly's door had been jammed is intriguing and allows for some speculation. The door may have been jammed to prevent him from getting outside to rescue the O'Connor children, which, afterward, would have revealed to the O'Connor parents that the Donnellys were powerless to protect them. This, in itself, may have provided a powerful incentive for the O'Connors to break with the prosecution and pull Johnny from any further testimony against the prisoners. It is also possible that the arsonists were planning on setting fire to Bob Donnelly's house as well, but just after torching the O'Connors' place, they may have been scared off before doing the deed when the O'Connors' dogs started barking and waking people up. Whatever the reason for jamming Bob Donnelly's door may have been, it didn't much matter — Bob Donnelly broke through the obstruction and then ran to the O'Connors' house. He later stated, "As soon as I got out of my house I saw the kitchen of O'Connors' house on fire in the north and I then ran to the front door."[41]

With her brothers crying that Bridget was still trapped inside, Bob attempted to break down the front door to the O'Connor home. When that failed, he ran out to the front yard and yanked a pole free from a nearby fence.[42] He could see the fire had now burned through the roof of the kitchen at the north end of the house and spread to the gable end.[43] He charged at the door with the pole, breaking it open. He then ran into the fire-filled house and rescued Bridget.[44] Once the girl was safely outside, Bob ran back into the house to save what items he could for the family.[45] He removed some furniture,[46] but the smoke drove him back. At this point two neighbours, Frank Morky and Daniel Howe, arrived on the scene. According to Howe:

> Robert Donnelly was at the front door running into the house when I got there. I helped to take out a little stove and cupboard with Frank Morky. Bridget O'Connor was taking out a sewing machine at the door when I got there. I threw out two or three mats. I couldn't save anything else on account of the smoke. It was suffocating.[47]

Bob Donnelly tried one last dash inside the burning building. There was furniture upstairs that he wanted to save for the O'Connors. He fought his way through the smoke and flame until he made it to the top of the stairs, but by the time he had reached the upper landing the west end of the second floor had burned through. There was nowhere for him to go. The smoke and fire forced him to head back downstairs and outside.[48] He then attempted to scale the outside of the building to see if he could get in through a window on the second storey. Howe recollected, "I did see Robert Donnelly trying to climb up the wall on the outside. He got nearly to the top . . . It appeared to me that the great bulk of the fire was inside the kitchen."[49]

However, the fire had now reached the upstairs window, preventing Donnelly from entering the house and causing him to climb back down to the ground. More people had started to gather in front of the burning house by this point, and one of them, David McRoberts, approached Donnelly.

"How did the house get on fire?" he asked.

"It was set on fire," answered Donnelly matter-of-factly. "The boy saw two men running away from the fire."[50]

McRoberts would later claim that he said, "Robert, that is too thin. If they were setting the place on fire, it would be the stable where William's horse is."[51]

This certainly would have been true if the arsonists were attempting to send a message to William Donnelly. However, William was not their target this evening — the O'Connor parents were. Burning William's stable would not have sent them any message at all; burning down their house — with their children still in it — most certainly would.

By morning, the extent of the damage from the fire was plainly visible. Bob Donnelly had saved Bridget's life and at least some of the O'Connor family's possessions, but everything else had been incinerated. A local newspaper described the scene: "The ashes of the ruins contain a large sprinkling of iron-ware, castings, broken scales, sewing machines, saws, etc., the accumulation of a lifetime of one who was certainly devoted to the collection of portable property."[52]

Immediately, the views of the anti-Donnelly forces were made known to the press in an attempt to spin the tragedy to their advantage:

> Various rumours are afloat regarding the burning
> of O'Connor's house last night. Parties who were
> first there state that the furniture, if they had any,
> had been removed, and nothing of any consequence
> was in the house to get burned. Others freely
> state it as their opinion that it was set on fire by
> Bob Donnelly, who lives in another house owned
> by O'Connors, and situated on an adjoining lot,
> for the purpose of gaining public sympathy and
> trying if possible to circulate the report that some
> of the friends of the parties charged with the
> murder of the Donnellys had set it on fire to spite
> O'Connors.[53]

While Bob Donnelly would be legitimately accused of many things during his lifetime, a desire for public sympathy would never be one of them. Moreover, any sympathy that might have come forth from the O'Connors losing their home would have rightly gone to the O'Connors — not the Donnellys. Risking his life for a bit of sympathy would have seemed a needlessly risky gamble for Bob Donnelly to take. Plus, any plan carried out by any member of the Donnelly family that had the potential to impact the forth-coming trial would have had to have originated or, at the very least, been cleared by the "brains" of the family, William Donnelly, who was away from the house that night. It's doubtful William would have given his okay to a plan that would have involved starting a blaze that very easily could have spread to the stable where he kept his prize stallion. As one of the local newspapers stated:

Within twenty feet of the south end of the house
was a stable containing William Donnelly's stallion,
valued at $500, and immediately to the north was
Robert Donnelly's house. So that in addition to the
punishment inflicted on the O'Connor family, the
probability of burning the stable and the adjoining
dwelling was very great.[54]

The Committee knew blaming Bob Donnelly for setting the fire
was going to be a hard sell, because he could have been killed in
attempting to rescue Bridget O'Connor and in saving what items he
could from her house. Consequently, the Committee supporters then
put forth the possibility that the Donnellys had set the fire, so that
the O'Connors could collect the insurance money and they could
all move to London.[55] If that had been the O'Connors' plan, the
parents, clearly, had not been apprised of it. When news reached
the O'Connors in London they were devastated:

> The burning of their dwellings in Lucan was
> communicated to Michael O'Connor and his wife
> and children here this morning, and, of course,
> they were filled with grief. Mrs. O'Connor loudly
> lamented all the trouble that has come upon
> them through no fault of their own, and insisted
> on their going home at once, and taking Johnny
> with them. This the County Attorney would not
> allow. A vehicle was provided, however, and
> Michael, his wife and daughter [Mary Ellen] left
> for Lucan at one o'clock, under promise to return
> tonight. A detective accompanied them. Johnny is
> kept apart from his parents here in the special care
> of Constable Pope, who guards him night and day.[56]

Michael and Mary O'Connor returned to Lucan and, once again, the local press was there when they were brought face to face with the magnitude of their loss:

> Shortly after three o'clock this afternoon, Mr. and
> Mrs. O'Connor arrived from London, in company
> with Detective Phair, and on visiting the ruins the
> grief of the latter was very great. She looks upon it
> as a great trial, that, in addition to being thrown into
> an unenviable connection with the late tragedy, her
> house is burned down, and a portion of her family
> nearly consumed with it. She is fully convinced that
> it was done as a sort of bonfire over the refusal of a
> change of venue in the Biddulph murder case, and in
> consequence her alarm has been intensified.[57]

The Lucan coroner, Dr. Thomas Hossack, called for an inquest to determine the cause of the fire and quickly empanelled a jury later that evening. At ten o'clock the next morning the jury was brought together at the Lucan jail and, from there, proceeded to the ruins of the O'Connor home.[58] As Crown attorney Hutchinson would be occupying a seat on the bench at the inquest, the Vigilance Committee quickly called a meeting. It was decided their attorney, John Blake, should attend the inquest as well, to ensure there was nothing that could come back on either the prisoners or the Committee itself.[59]

Shortly after the inquest had commenced, it was obvious the jury was not sympathetic to the O'Connors. Michael O'Connor was called upon to testify and afterwards was cross-examined by Blake. O'Connor stated that he had been receiving threatening letters for several weeks leading up to the fire. Blake asked him what about the content of the letters caused him to believe he was being threatened. "I was threatened that I would be burned and was therefore expecting it. I got a letter saying that I would be used the same as the Donnellys if I did not leave the place. That was what I considered threatening me."[60]

"Was there any signature to the threatening letters?" a member of the jury asked.

"Well, by heavens, to ask a man such a question," replied an exasperated O'Connor, "as if anyone would be damned fool enough to put his name to a threatening letter!"[61]

A consultation then followed among the members of the jury, after which they announced they did not wish to hear any further testimony. The panel retired and returned four hours later to render their verdict on the matter:

> That Michael O'Connor's house was burnt on the
> night of the 13th instant [this month], and that the fire
> originated in the interior of the kitchen but we are not
> able to determine whether accidentally or willfully,
> but the jury do not believe that the fire was started
> from the outside of the building.[62]

Both Crown attorney Hutchinson and Coroner Hossack were taken aback by the jury's decision. "A more prejudiced jury I have never met with," Hutchinson said.[63] Michael O'Connor was also mystified by the jury's decision. He would later find evidence that was strongly suggestive that one of the Ryder family had been involved in the burning and charged him with arson. However, the case would be laid over and, as was getting to be typical in Biddulph, nothing ever came of it.[64]

The fire had caused Crown attorney Charles Hutchinson to grow even more concerned about the welfare of Johnny O'Connor. The entire O'Connor family was now relocated to London and a twenty-four-hour police guard was assigned to watch over them. Hutchinson posted a $2,000 bond out of his own pocket to secure the family's safety[65] with the belief that the attorney general's office would eventually reimburse him. A second constable was hired to live with the O'Connors; his job was to supervise Johnny at all times. Everywhere Johnny went — whether to church or school or throughout the city — the constable was beside him. The constable even slept in the same apartment with the O'Connors.[66] Hutchinson wrote to Oliver Mowat's office: "If we let Johnny out of our hands the chances are in favour of our never seeing him again."[67]

But Mary O'Connor saw an opportunity arise out of the tragedy. She knew the family held the whip hand[68] — the prosecution needed her son's testimony. She further knew there was government money that could be accessed. She now demanded that the Crown compensate her and her family for their losses; she wanted everything that was lost in the fire replaced, including clothing, furniture and the house itself. Hutchinson was growing frustrated.[69] When the prosecution was slow in complying, the parents exerted their influence on their son to communicate their position. "We are not getting our money," said Johnny, "and Hutchinson is going back on us. I hope the prisoners will get off — and they will get off too."[70]

Hutchinson had no alternative but to comply with the O'Connors' demands. He not only continued to pay for a constable's round the clock supervision of Johnny, but paid the O'Connors money to build a summer kitchen, a piggery, and some small outbuildings and repairs on the house he rented for them in London. Then came the claims for the board and lodging of Johnny, compensation for the loss of their Lucan home (and for losses of the contents therein), in addition to compensation for their having to leave Lucan, where they had income, and come to London, where they had none. And finally, they wanted to be compensated for "being deprived of the services of Johnny, who was old enough and able enough to assist in the support of the Family."[71] Their demands were bleeding much-needed funds out of the prosecution's coffers. But in fairness to the O'Connor family, they hadn't asked to be dragged into this matter. And their losses were real: they'd had their lives threatened, their home burned to the ground and had been uprooted. Even Charles Hutchinson had admitted that they were definitely entitled to some compensation. Nevertheless, the O'Connors' demands now started to outpace the prosecution's budget, and, with very little money coming in from the attorney general's office as it was, Hutchinson was losing valuable funds that could have gone to strengthen the prosecution's case.

Back in London, the malaise the Biddulph prisoners had been suffering had given way to agitation. When a prisoner who had been brought into the London jail spoke well of the Donnellys, James Ryder took note. He waited until the next morning when the cells were open and then attacked the man, knocking him to the floor and kicking him in the stomach and ribs. The new prisoner was immediately removed from his surroundings.[72] That the Biddulph prisoners should have the doors to their cells open at all was a point of contention for Charles Hutchinson. Given that the prosecution had but two eyewitnesses, a large part of their strategy had been to keep the prisoners isolated in their jail cells in the hope that one of them would confess. The Crown attorney wanted the prison experience of James Carroll, John Kennedy Jr., John Purtell, Martin McLaughlin and Thomas and James Ryder to be one of deprivation — no freedoms would be allowed, and they should have no contact with anyone save their attorneys.[73]

In truth, it was far more a gamble than a strategy, but Hutchinson and his prosecution team needed desperately for it to work. Consequently, when word reached the prosecution that Sheriff William Glass had bypassed the Crown attorney and contacted Oliver Mowat's office directly with a request to allow the prisoners to be freed from their cells to exercise outside, Hutchinson was irate. Glass protested that, because "they are all outdoors men and not used to inactivity,"[74] keeping the prisoners locked up in their cells was inappropriate. Even Hutchinson's fellow prosecutor Aemilius Irving was incensed.[75]

And things got worse. The prosecution later learned that the Middlesex jailer, Joseph Lamb, had been giving the prisoners unprecedented privileges while they were within his jail. Far from keeping them isolated from their family and friends, Lamb had set up the debtor's wing of the prison to allow the wives of some of the prisoners to stay overnight with their husbands.[76] Further, Lamb was still allowing the prisoners to be provided with tobacco and, rather than prison food, special meals were still being delivered to them from a hotel within the city. Lamb's explanation for going against the Crown's instructions was a simple one: he believed that the prisoners were innocent and therefore deserving of the privileges he had granted them.[77] The prosecution's strategy was being scuttled from within.

I n May 1880, William Lewis's trial for the stabbing death of Mike Donnelly took place before Justice Matthew Cameron in Simcoe, at the Norfolk County Spring Assizes. In the days leading up to the trial, Patrick Donnelly had left Biddulph to assist the prosecution, gathering what evidence he could and delivering subpoenas to those who had witnessed the killing in Waterford.[78] Despite the men whom Patrick Donnelly and the prosecution had brought forth to testify, and despite the fact that Lewis had brought a knife with him to the bar that night, it was ultimately ruled that Mike Donnelly's death had not been premeditated, but rather had resulted accidentally as a consequence of a fight between the two men. Lewis was convicted on the lesser charge of manslaughter and sentenced to five years in Kingston Penitentiary.[79] The local Simcoe newspaper was outraged at the lesser sentence; it pointed out that the witnesses had testified Lewis had vowed to "fix" Donnelly prior to the killing, which, from their vantage point, spoke to the crime having been committed with malice aforethought.[80] It would not be the last unsatisfactory legal ruling the Donnelly family would experience.

Like Kate Johnson, frustratingly little is known about William H. Lewis, save for the following facts: he was twenty-two years of age when he went to prison and was five feet nine. He was unmarried, and said to have grey eyes, light hair and a fair complexion. He could read and write and he made chairs as a profession when not working on the railway line. He was a Protestant (Methodist) who was born in the United States. Despite having been drinking in the tavern on the night of Mike Donnelly's murder, Lewis would claim on his prison report that he was not a drinker. Like Bob Donnelly, William Lewis would be released early from Kingston Penitentiary as a result of good behaviour, serving only four years and four months of his five-year sentence. During his incarceration the record shows that he was hospitalized for a few days with the flu (grippe), but apart from this, nothing else is known about him.[81] After his release from prison, Lewis shows up in census records in Frontenac (near Kingston) in 1881, and then West Flamborough (near Hamilton) in 1891. Thereafter, he seems to have vanished.

W ord about the O'Connor family receiving money from the Crown had reached the ears of their enemies. While attending an auction in London's Market Square, Michael O'Connor was viewing a buggy when someone from within the crowd piped up pointedly, "Mick, buy the buggy — the county will pay for it."[82] When O'Connor looked up he found himself staring at Patrick "Grouchy" Ryder. O'Connor wrote (or had written for him) a letter to the local paper detailing Ryder's insult, before adding an equally pointed one of his own:

> Were it not for my civility in allowing my son
> Johnny O'Connor to oblige the late Donnellys by

going to their place on the night of the tragedy, and had Mr. Grouchy's friends remained at home that night, said their prayers and gone to bed as I did, I would not be in a position to be thus insulted.[83]

In preparing their case for a change of venue, Charles Hutchinson sought to obtain affidavits from people of prominence in and around London. His plan was to then present these affidavits to the justices in Toronto. Many of the people who had backed his strategy to change the location of the trial were legal heavyweights in the township, and their opinion on the matter would be given serious credence by the magistrates in the city. However, to his surprise he found that the people who had agreed with his desire for a change of venue were now not willing to put their support in writing. Magistrates were among those who had initially agreed with Hutchinson's request in private, but they were now unwilling to take their concurrence public.[84] "No one whose affidavit would be of any use, would make one," Hutchinson lamented.[85] He was able to convince London Police Chief Williams to provide him with an affidavit, but its contents were so bland as to be useless, particularly when Williams only mentioned Biddulph — not London — as being inherently hostile to the prosecution's case.[86] By the time the prosecutors were ready to appear before the magistrates at Toronto's Osgoode Hall, Hutchinson had only two affidavits to present — and one of them was his own.[87]

By contrast, the defence team had no shortage of people willing to step forth to endorse London as being completely free from the taint of bias. William Meredith, the lead counsel for the defence (the leader of the provincial Conservative party), had no trouble securing a former Member of the Legislative Assembly for North Middlesex, John MacDougall, as well as Josiah Blackburn, the editor of the *London Free Press*, to write affidavits in support of keeping the trial in London. Blackburn even went a step further, using his newspaper to condemn the proposed change of venue as "an insult to the people of London and Middlesex."[88] Fellow defence lawyer Hugh MacMahon brought in support from his colleague in the Liberal Party Donald MacKenzie. Such men went on the record to state that, after years of public service in Middlesex, the members of their community of Biddulph were impartial, honest and held justice in the highest regard. More support followed — the reeve of Westminster township; a former London alderman; London's Liquor Licence commissioner; the reeve of Adelaide township; a former county warden and the current county warden — all threw their support behind the defence counsel for keeping the venue unchanged.[89]

By this point, the prosecution had given up any hope of getting Toronto as a venue for the trial;[90] it was clear that Oliver Mowat considered the proposed venue to be too close to home for his political comfort. With Toronto out, the prosecution thought perhaps Wellington or Guelph might be a possibility.[91] Looking to better their chances, the prosecutors filed writs to move two of the indictments handed down by the Middlesex Assize Court to the Superior Courts in Toronto — one, for the murder of Thomas Donnelly, was sent to the Court of Common Pleas; the other, for the murder of James Donnelly, was delivered to the Court of Queen's Bench.[92] The thought was that with two courts, each with two teams of High Court Justices considering two different cases, they would effectively double their chances of obtaining a change of venue.

After conferring among themselves, the defence team decided that the six prisoners should be brought to Toronto to attend the hearings and to present affidavits in support of why the venue should not be changed.[93] Defence counsellor John Blake had advised the prisoners that the defence team would tell the High Court justices that, since they lived in Biddulph and not London, London should be considered neutral territory in the matter. There was no denying that all the prisoners' families lived in Biddulph and, therefore, theoretically at least, they held no sway in a city that lay eighteen miles away to the south. Their game plan now clearly mapped out, the prisoners and their lawyers boarded a train bound for Toronto. A large crowd of their friends and supporters saw them off at the station and cheered them on.[94]

Toronto, like most cities in Canada, had once been the dominion of the indigenous peoples — bands such as the Wyandot, the Iroquois and the Ojibwa had lived on its land for several thousand years, almost as soon as the Laurentide Ice Sheet had receded from the region. The city's connection to its indigenous peoples can be seen in its name, which is derived from the Mohawk word "tkaronto," which, loosely translated, means "where there are trees standing in the water." The term originally referred to The Narrows, an area near present-day Orillia, where the Wyandot and other bands had set fish weirs. Soon the area was visited by the French (French topography from the late 1600s through to the mid-1700s indicate that what is modern-day Lake Simcoe was once known as "Lac de Taronto"). By the late 1700s, however, the British influence was in full stride and the name was changed to "Toronto."[95]

The first governor of the province of Ontario, John Graves Simcoe, saw the region as being a perfect place for a naval base and garrison. Its location was optimal to check any potential American aggression. Simcoe was English and, therefore, everything he did as governor was done with a nod to his mother country. He had named the first harbourfront town in the area "York" after the Duke of York, the son of King George III. There he secured his garrison. Through Simcoe's efforts, York became the capital of Upper Canada for a time, and during this time, parliament buildings and roads were created. Simcoe's York garrison region soon attracted settlement, and settlement brought business and prosperity to the area.

In short order, the rural regions along the garrison's fringe expanded, making the entire area a thriving marketplace. In 1812, the York settlement had but 700 people; by 1834, British immigration saw that number grow to over 9,000 inhabitants, and the former town of York was incorporated as the City of Toronto, with its own civic government and mayor. By the 1840s, the main streets had sewers and gas lighting. Toronto's port attracted steamboat traffic, which, in turn, brought more people to the area to settle. By the 1850s the railroad connected the city not only to Lower Canada, but also to the American cities of Chicago and Detroit. Toronto had blossomed in industry and commerce to such an extent that by the time of Confederation in 1867, it was named the capital city of the province of Ontario. Toronto's population would actually increase by five times between 1831 and 1891. It boasted agricultural manufacturing firms, clothing factories, publishing houses, metal foundries, department stores, banks, a hospital, horse-drawn streetcars, a police force, law courts, public schools, a university, distilleries, tanneries and money and prosperity enough to draw the jealous ire of the smaller cities and towns within the province.

By the late 1800s, Toronto was referred to by those in the rural areas of Ontario as "Hogtown," and not, as is popularly believed, because of the quantity of livestock that was processed in Toronto, largely by the city's largest pork processor and packer, the William Davies Company.[96] Instead, as a Toronto *Globe* editorial headline explained:

> In the smaller cities of the Province when a man
> wants to say nasty things about Toronto he calls it
> Hogtown. . . . The remark originally had no relation
> at all to our friend the hog, but was merely intended
> to convey an impression that the citizens of Toronto
> were porcine in their tendencies and had their
> forefeet in anything worth having.[97]

Rather than taking it as an insult, however, the people of Toronto came to embrace the moniker, accepting it as proof of their superiority to their more rural neighbours: "We are no longer desirous of putting aside the garland woven for us by our jealous neighbours . . ." trumpeted the Toronto *Globe*. "We accept it, and shall wear it blushingly on modest brows. For this is Hogtown, and growing more hoggy all the time."[98] And this was the attitude of the Torontonians who turned out in droves to see the Biddulph prisoners upon their arrival in Hogtown. To the fair citizens of Toronto these accused men represented living examples of how uncivilized the world outside of Toronto was, and so they were naturally curious to see what these cold-blooded murderers from the farmlands looked like. A Biddulph contingent also arrived in the city to show the urbanites that the accused were not without support. They came bearing gifts and food, including a basket of tropical fruit, and cheered the prisoners as they were led to and from their prison cells in York County.[99] The prisoners felt comfortable speaking to the Toronto press, and commented on how much they loved the scenery that had flashed by their train windows as they approached the city, and of their ease of life in the London jail. A fruitcake that had been baked especially for them in Biddulph even warranted a mention in the newspapers.[100]

One person in Toronto who made sure to keep away from the rural sideshow was the provincial premier, Oliver Mowat. As the Liberal leader in a largely Conservative province, he didn't want to be seen anywhere near the prisoners nor the prosecution lawyers. Nevertheless, his political adversaries drew him into the affair whether he wanted to be or not. Josiah Blackburn continued to editorialize in support of the defence team through the pages of his *London Free Press*, publishing articles suggesting that the prosecution was being directed by Mowat himself, for no other reason than to persecute Roman Catholic prisoners: "It is astonishing that Attorney-General Mowat should have insisted not only on asking for a change of venue, but, when it was refused, to drag the unhappy prisoners down to Toronto."[101]

When it came time for the justices in the Superior Court to hear the Crown's reasons for a change of venue, Aemilius Irving cited precedent by declaring that such had occurred several times during periods of political tension in Ireland. This might have played well back in the Irish settlement of Biddulph, but it fell flat before the British law courts in Toronto. The Conservative leader William Meredith then stepped forth on behalf of the defence and stated, "The Irish cases cited in which changes of venue had been granted had all arisen out of great political excitement. These cases therefore should not be made a precedent for an ordinary case of murder."[102] Neither the prosecution counsel's meagre number of affidavits, nor its attempt to cite precedent overseas impressed the Superior Court justices who declared, "In cases such as this, religion or politics would not affect the decision to be given."[103] As to Hutchinson's affidavit stating that it was impossible to obtain an impartial jury in Biddulph, Justice Cameron couldn't see how the jurors in Biddulph could possibly be prejudicial to the case. Moreover, Chief Justice Hagarty stated that he did not understand why the trial would be more likely to be impartial in Wellington or Huron than in Middlesex. Besides, he noted, in Toronto there were three daily papers, and for some time past those papers had printed lengthy articles about the "Biddulph Tragedy." Consequently, he believed that strong affidavits could likewise be procured that a fair trial could not be had in Toronto. He believed it would be establishing "an unwise precedent were this application to be acceded to."[104] And so the justices denied the prosecutors' appeal and sent the murder trial back to Middlesex. The prisoners, however, were not permitted to leave Hogtown until their York County jailer had feted them with a banquet at the Osgoode Hall restaurant. With their bellies and confidence now swollen, the defence lawyers and the prisoners returned to London on the train, where a crowd of three hundred stood waiting to welcome them home.[105]

Having lost their battle in Toronto, Hutchinson and the prosecutors conferred to assess the damage and to discuss what to do next. The venue was not going to change, which meant the potential jury for the trial would have to be scrutinized with a laser-like focus in the hopes of getting at least some impartial members into it. Hutchinson also retabled his "B" plan of trying to isolate the prisoners from having any contact with the outside world. He still believed jail time could wear down a prisoner's resistance to the point of causing him to confess his crimes — if the rules of the jailhouse were actually enforced. And the prosecutors evidently had some evidence for this belief. A reporter for the *London Advertiser*, for example, had been particularly struck by the appearance of James Carroll while the prisoner had boarded the train for Toronto to take part in the hearings. When he had first been arrested, Carroll looked to be a formidable adversary. But now, the newspaperman thought he appeared "anything but well."[106]

For the isolation strategy to work two things were required — the prison rules had to be followed so that the prisoners would be kept in a deprived state, and enough time had to elapse while the prisoners were in this state to wear them down.[107] Time was the big factor; like waves rolling against a rock, if enough time could lapse, the object the agent acted upon would eventually wear down or give way completely. Again, the Crown attorney ordered that jail regulations be enforced[108] — there would be no fancy meals from local hotels, no tobacco and no conjugal visits. Even outdoor activities would be off-limits.[109] Once again, however, the prosecutors received no compliance from the jailer, Joseph Lamb.[110] Hutchinson reported Lamb's insubordination to attorney general deputy John Scott, who, in turn, notified John Woodburn Langmuir, the inspector of prisons, asylums and public charities for the Province of Ontario. Langmuir immediately travelled to London to investigate the matter. The inspector's investigation didn't take long and resulted in Lamb's dismissal.[111]

Straight away the defence lawyer Hugh MacMahon started a campaign to have Lamb reinstated. This was to be expected — Lamb had treated the prisoners well, which had effectively thwarted the prosecution's attempts at isolation and deprivation in an effort to get them to break down and confess their crimes. What wasn't expected was that MacMahon would be joined in his efforts to bring back the jailer by none other than the prosecution attorney James Magee. Both Magee and MacMahon were members of the Liberal party, and Mowat's office had feared that firing a Roman Catholic prison guard who was treating other Roman Catholic prisoners well could be used against him politically. Consequently, it would have been disastrous to Mowat's political career to have a defence attorney under the direction of his political adversary, William R. Meredith, lead the charge for reinstating a public servant who was a favourite among a large segment of the Irish Roman Catholics in Biddulph. It was better to have one of his own men, Magee, take up Lamb's cause or, at least, be by MacMahon's side in doing so, than to be seen as standing on the sidelines in the matter. To his defence partners, MacMahon's action in the matter was seen as a simple matter of looking out for his clients' interests. To his colleagues for the prosecution, Magee's action in the matter was inexcusable. He had broken ranks with his fellow prosecutors out of loyalty to his political party, which had deliberately compromised their strategy in the case. Still, as Magee had been appointed to the case by Oliver Mowat, the Crown attorney couldn't fire him. While Magee would remain part of the prosecution team, Hutchinson certainly wasn't going to involve him in any strategy sessions going forward. Magee could no longer be trusted.[112]

Surprisingly, given the political considerations that were presently at play within the case, Mowat's office did not attempt to overrule Inspector Langmuir's decision to fire the jailer, and, despite the efforts of both MacMahon and Magee, Joseph Lamb was still out of a job. But Lamb was not dispossessed long. His friends within the Vigilance Committee, including James Maher and Patrick "Grouchy" Ryder, helped him move his family and belongings to Lucan, where he opened a store on Main Street.[113]

While all the legal wrangling had been going on, William Donnelly had been working non-stop to find more evidence and witnesses that would aid the prosecution's case against the killers of his family. As an aside, and as documented evidence of this, Donnelly researcher William Davison Butt compiled a list of William Donnelly's contributions to the prosecution (repeated below) that I found hard to believe until I checked his sources and found that he was absolutely correct. His contributions to the prosecution were staggering:

- He discovered the identity of the leader of the Vigilance Committee.[114]
- He ferreted out where the Committee members had met on the night of the murders.[115]
- He learned what alibis certain members of the Committee were planning.[116]
- Using his contacts in and knowledge of Biddulph, he discovered that Michael Powe had been refused membership in the Vigilance Committee owing to his friendship with the Donnellys — and he convinced Powe to testify to this in court.[117]
- He learned that John Kennedy Jr. had given his revolver to a man named Tom Fulton after the murders.[118]

- He brought to the prosecution evidence that meetings of the Vigilance Committee were still taking place.[119]
- He formulated a list of times that Committee members, such as Martin McLaughlin,[120] Patrick Ryder[121] and James McGrath[122] had targeted or were otherwise hostile to various members of the Donnelly family.

And Butt's list doesn't end there: William further discovered the names of people who had information that would help the prosecution's case and gave this information to the prosecutors in the hope that they would be able to find a means to make it worthwhile for these people to come forward and testify. For example:

- He discovered that his parents' neighbour, John Whalen, had witnessed the murders from his house across the road and had seen the mob leaving the Donnelly house.[123]
- He found out that John Whalen's brother, William, had also witnessed the mob leaving the Donnellys' house after setting it on fire.[124]
- He learned that his immediate neighbour at Whalen's Corners, John Walker, had seen the men who had surrounded William's home on the night that John Donnelly was shot.[125]
- He sought out and conversed with farmer John Doherty, learning that Doherty had seen a group of Committee members marching along his private sideroad on the night of the murders.[126]
- He delivered subpoenas for the prosecution and met with law enforcement.[127]

- He made models of the Donnelly homes in which the murders occurred for use as exhibits during the trial.[128]
- He gathered up more materials for courtroom exhibits from the ruins of his parents' home, including what remained of his father's guns and bone fragments.[129]

The prosecutors, particularly Hutchinson, marvelled at his tenacity. On multiple occasions, Hutchinson wrote to various people about William, saying things such as "He is there moving about from place to place, watching intently the movements of the enemy & although not by any means discreet he is intelligent & of course deeply interested";[130] "The township is guarded everywhere; no stranger can enter without being spotted. If we find out anything new, it will come through William Donnelly, who is constantly on the watch";[131] "He is sharp, & may find out something. I fancy he thinks of nothing but the murder."[132] Hutchinson was correct on that last notion, but William Donnelly had no choice. William had to occupy his mind because he was unable to occupy his hands. Unlike Patrick, who, when not in Biddulph, was back in Thorold, manufacturing wagons and sleighs and blacksmithing, and unlike Bob, who was now commuting to Glencoe where he had started his own cartage business, and unlike Jennie, who at this stage of her life had three children who not only occupied but demanded her time, William had nothing to distract him from the murders. And so, he busied his mind with attempting to dig up evidence, discern patterns and logical connections, and turning over whatever he came up with to the prosecutors.

However, while William Donnelly was tenacious and productive, he was also driving himself into debt. Gathering evidence against the killers had become his full-time job ever since his brother John lay dying on his bedroom floor. Unfortunately, it was a job that didn't pay. On June 25, 1880, Nora Donnelly gave birth to a daughter, whom William named Johannah, after his late mother. But with expenses now mounting up, he was torn between trying to find a regular job to provide for his family and doing what he could to bring the killers of his family to justice.

Shortly before Johannah's birth he had written to Charles Hutchinson to see if the prosecution could perhaps compensate him for his travel expenses while he was attempting to collect evidence.[133] Hutchinson was sympathetic; he had observed first-hand how hard William had been working on behalf of the Crown and how much his efforts had strengthened their case.[134] Finally, he was at least able to have William reimbursed for his out-of-pocket expenses.[135] The prosecutors, frankly, would have been lost without William Donnelly's efforts. Their attempts to bring in detectives to turn up evidence had thus far led to several wild goose chases that had resulted in nothing.

And while William Donnelly would continue to work without compensation for the prosecution, the O'Connor family remained safely in their house in London — and demanded even more of what little money Hutchinson was able to access. The Crown had already paid for the O'Connors' house, security, food and expenses, but Mary O'Connor wanted more. As had become her way, whenever she requested more funding, she threatened to remove Johnny from the case as leverage.[136] Her strategy was successful, as she always came away from her negotiations with new money in the family coffer.[137] And when she recognized that any and all money she had been receiving from Hutchinson had come from the attorney general's office, Mary O'Connor decided to bypass the middleman and boarded a train to Toronto to make her demands directly to the provincial premier. Mowat was of course unavailable to meet with her, and so his deputy, John Scott, was left to listen to her litany of complaints. He, too, capitulated to her demands,[138] and Mary O'Connor returned to London a happy woman.

Scott felt the pressure from the O'Connors, but, like Hutchinson, feared the repercussion from the family if he refused their money requests. He wrote to Hutchinson that, "I fear unless [payment] is done Mrs. Connors [sic] will attempt to take her boy away and it is quite possible his recovery would cost a good deal more than what is now proposed."[139]

But Mary O'Connor's threats weren't the only problems that assailed Hutchinson and his team. Their strategy in regard to the prisoners had previously been undermined by the actions of their colleague James Magee in the matter of the jailer Joseph Lamb. Hutchinson and Irving had long seen Magee as being dead weight in terms of what he brought to the prosecution, and knew that he was present merely as a mole for Oliver Mowat. However, they now became suspicious of their fellow prosecution teammate Edmund Meredith's loyalties as well. Ever since the preliminary hearing had ended, Hutchinson had noticed that the high-priced solicitor had all but disappeared from the proceedings. Hutchinson wrote to co-counsel Aemilius Irving, "He [Meredith] has pocketed a $250 retainer on behalf of the Donnelly family, for which he has done next to nothing."[140]

That peccadillo, however, paled in significance to what was then brought to the attention of William Donnelly. Meredith had been spotted riding in a sleigh seated next to the defence attorney, John Blake. The pair were later observed attending a church service at St. Patrick's on Sunday, June 27, 1880. This was particularly odd, given that Meredith was a Protestant. To make matters even more suspicious, Blake and Meredith dined later that same Sunday afternoon in the company of Father John Connolly — the man who had lately gone public with his support for the prisoners. William Donnelly immediately wrote to Hutchinson for an answer: "Mr. E. Meredith and lawyer Blake were at the Catholic Church here on Sunday, they dined with Father Connolly. What does this look like? Is Mr. Meredith giving us away?"[141] Hutchinson was shocked, and advised Donnelly to be guarded in what he henceforth shared with the solicitor: "It looks bad in Meredith to dine with Father Connolly. He ought not to have done so, especially in company with Blake. I do not however think he can give you much away, for since the close of the magisterial investigation he has not been admitted into our confidence much, and in future we will be still more careful letting him know what we are about. I would not advise you to let him see that you distrust him; at the same time, keep your own counsel. Do not give him any information as to anything you think may turn out advantageous."[142]

The prosecution was now understandably paranoid about potential leaks coming from within their team that would alert the opposition in advance to any strategies they might be planning. They needed their own inside man — one who could mingle freely within the Biddulph crowd and who would not be seen by the locals as being pro-prosecution. William Donnelly didn't qualify for obvious reasons. However, Hutchinson believed that the former Lucan constable Samuel Everett did. He certainly would not be seen as pro-Donnelly in the matter; after all, he had been the one whom Bob Donnelly was said to have taken a shot at back in 1877 that resulted in Donnelly's two-year stretch at Kingston Penitentiary. More recently, Everett had told the London press, "I am glad the Donnellys are dead."[143] After consulting with Coroner Hossack, however, Hutchinson shared the medical man's views that Everett would be loyal to whoever paid him.[144] The prosecutors ran the idea past William Donnelly. "He's a rotten stick to depend on," Donnelly had said about the ex–town constable.[145] Then, seeing how desperate Hutchinson was to obtain any additional evidence, he finally capitulated with the comment: "Still, rotten sticks make good manure sometimes."[146] Hutchinson brought Everett on board but put him on a tight leash, only giving him until September 8 to unearth evidence that the prosecution could use.[147]

William Donnelly's initial suspicions about Samuel Everett ultimately proved correct; on the Crown's dime, Everett had travelled to Berlin, Ontario (now Kitchener),[148] where he sent to the prosecution a letter, made out to the attention of Aemilius Irving, that purported to be from a witness he was chasing. The fugitive witness ("Mike") felt obliged to comment on Everett's excellent tracking skills, commenting on how close Everett was to him, and, thus, to the truth about the murders.[149] One problem arose, however, when Irving suspected that the handwriting was that of Everett himself.[150] Everett had now joined the ranks of the not-to-be-trusted, right alongside Magee and Meredith. His services were terminated.

Despite the efforts of William Donnelly, nothing was going the prosecution's way. The defence was winning the battle of the press because they had more people on their side who were still alive to talk. It was estimated that over twenty people had taken part in the murders versus only three Donnelly survivors. Each of those twenty people had families and friends, which meant if the prosecutors were successful, a whole community could be negatively impacted, along with the businesses that depended upon their patronage and the church that depended upon their tithing for its sustenance. By sheer strength of numbers, the anti-Donnelly forces had much more to lose, and so they brought every resource they had to bear on defending the prisoners. If even one prisoner was found guilty, a domino effect would be set into motion that would (or at least could) negatively impact the township. Consequently, all people of influence — the politicians, the store owners, the parish priest — were looking out for their own self-interests and of necessity threw their support behind the six prisoners. The Donnellys could muster no such support; if they lost the trial, not one ripple would appear to disturb the placid waters of daily life in Biddulph. To this end, an effort was made to paint the Donnellys as worse than those who murdered them. They were a family of rural terrorists; mad dogs that had to be put down for the safety of the community. Even successful Protestant merchants threw their support behind the prisoners: "Two years ago, the Donnellys were the terror of the township," said one.[151] "Without a doubt," said another, "the Donnellys were the terrors of the district, and their removal from the scene of their many depredations and acts of lawlessness is looked upon as a public gain."[152]

Given that Lucan was a small town, the hypocrisy of the above statements was astounding, as all the local people had a good idea that the above quotes were given to the press by one or both of the Stanley brothers. And they also knew that the Stanleys had acquired their vast wealth and political power through "depredations and acts of lawlessness" of their own. Bernard Stanley, for example, apart from being a Lucan hotelkeeper, distiller, hardware store owner, miller and the wealthiest man in town, had a history of violence and incendiarism. He had burned out and robbed members of the Black community in Wilberforce in 1848; he had led the attack on the Catholics, demolishing Andrew O'Keefe's tavern on Christmas Eve after the election in 1857; and, more recently, his name had been whispered as being behind the burning of Artemus Bice's barns on January 31, 1880.[153] William Donnelly, of course, knew the Stanleys were behind the above statements made to the newspapers, but also knowing libel law, when he responded to Bernard Stanley's allegations in the press, he did so without naming him directly: "Dear sir, your correspondent who wrote this contradiction lives in Lucan, and I must say that for the last thirty-five years he has been well used to the cries of fire and robbery . . ."[154]

This was a trait of the Donnelly family that surfaces again and again: the paying one back "in his own coin," a variant of the Golden Rule the Donnelly siblings had imbibed at their mother's knee since they were children. If someone showed kindness to them, they would return the gesture with kindness, but if someone displayed slander or violence to them, it would be returned to them in kind. Stanley had used the press to accuse the Donnelly family of being terrors of the district, and so William Donnelly used the press to alert Stanley to the fact he was throwing his stones from within a glass house. This tit-for-tat attitude of the Donnellys would explain much about the problems that followed them throughout their lives, and perhaps much about certain of their deaths.[155]

The surviving Donnellys trusted no one. When a Biddulph resident and Donnelly family friend, Tom Morkin, offered to purchase their late parents' property, the Donnelly brothers questioned his motive. After talking it over among themselves, Morkin's offer was firmly declined.[156] William Donnelly informed the press that "the homestead will be kept in our hands as long as we live. None of the Vigilants will ever get it."[157] Moreover, the Donnelly survivors announced that they were in the process of having a monument created to place atop their family's grave in the cemetery at St. Patrick's church. The gravestone would stand over eleven feet high and be constructed so as to have five sides — one for each member of their family who had been murdered.[158] Atop the gravestone was going to be a small statue of a young man in handcuffs, signifying the cowardly way the Committee members had manacled Tom Donnelly to render him defenceless prior to beating him to death. It would be as much a *j'accuse* monument as it was a memorial to the deceased.

While this stand-alone attitude defined them, it didn't help their cause. By contrast, the anti-Donnelly forces sought the protection and power of the group, always turning out in numbers to support their incarcerated brethren. Father John Connolly came (thus bringing religious sanction) to watch Vigilance Committee members sowing oats on a twenty-five-acre farm that James Carroll had recently rented.[159] Later that summer the Committee members returned to cut the thistles from John Kennedy Jr.'s fields.[160] By fall, forty Committee members showed up to harvest the crops from each of the six prisoners' farms and to do the threshing.[161] Such public displays of support sent a message to the people of Biddulph, and the message was received.

People now feared the Committee and its power. A local farmer mentioned that he "would sacrifice a large sum of money rather than sit on the jury. If a verdict were rendered against the prisoners, I know my barns would have to go."[162] He had cause to believe it; a juror (James Creighton) who had been sympathetic to the O'Connors when their house had burned down very nearly suffered a similar fate when someone attempted to set fire to his barn shortly afterwards.[163] A Lucan judge, James McCosh, who had earlier found Tom Donnelly not guilty of the Ned Ryan robbery, had indicated "I hope I don't have to come to court, it would be very inconvenient."[164] A man named Robert Ross had confessed in private to hearing John Kennedy Jr. say that he would shoot William Donnelly, but he declined to take his information public, stating, "I do not wish to have anything to say in this matter, as I am always travelling late at night."[165]

The playing board had tilted; the Vigilance Committee had cowed into silence those who could testify against the prisoners. Public opinion now favoured the accused, as had the Toronto justices, as had the London jailer. The Conservative Party had taken up their Irish Catholic cause, while the Liberal Party was awkwardly trying to distance itself from their prosecutors. The Vigilance Committee and its supporters now had full control over both the town of Lucan and the Township of Biddulph and, thus, the forthcoming trial. And what's more, everybody knew it.

THE FIRST TRIAL

Middlesex County Courthouse, circa 1895. Both of the Donnelly
murder trials were adjudicated within this courthouse.
(Ivey Family London Room, London Public Library)

James Carroll was exasperated. He had been expecting the town
barber to come to the jail earlier that evening when there would
have been plenty of ambient light available for him to do his job —
and for Carroll to inspect the stylist's handiwork. But now the sun
was setting, and, between the faint glow from outside and the flickering illumination from the odd candle within the jail, it was almost
too dark. Just as he had insisted on changing into a white shirt in
order to look "respectable" before going to Lucan on the day of
his arrest, James Carroll felt it was important that his hair look its
best for his appearance in court the next morning. Appearances

were important to the former farm implements salesman; indeed, he deemed even minor stylistic nuances to be significant, such as when he had his goatee trimmed to an Imperial prior to his appearance in the Assize court back in April.[1]

When the barber eventually arrived, it was decided that the environment was indeed too dark to shave the prisoner, and to apply the hair dye that Carroll had ordered. It was decided that it would be best for the barber to return early the next morning to work his tonsorial magic.[2] As the barber took his leave, Purtell called out, "Don't forget the dye!"[3] According to a member of the press who was present, "A responsive smile showed that the much-required article would be on hand."[4] This was acceptable to Carroll, who knew that when he walked into the Middlesex County Courthouse, a three-storey castle-like structure that sat adjacent to the prison overlooking the Thames River, the building would be full to capacity with the nation's press. A limited number of tickets had been printed out in advance and, if you didn't get one, you weren't getting into the courtroom.[5] In the months and weeks leading up to the trial the atmosphere surrounding the proceedings had taken on the air of a major sporting event, and, like most sporting events, the fan support was divided between two teams — those who favoured the prisoners and those who favoured the Donnellys.[6] Nobody was neutral in the matter.

When morning dawned, the six prisoners were taken from their cells and led into the courtroom to be arraigned. To a man, they each pleaded not guilty. The grand jury returned true bills (meaning that the prosecution had provided sufficient evidence of guilt to warrant proceeding with a trial) against all six prisoners and the magistrate set the start of the trial for October 4. The prosecution had decided to try the freshly shaved James Carroll first among the prisoners; if they were able to secure a conviction against him, then they would proceed with trying his five accomplices.[7] He would be on trial for the murder of Johannah Donnelly. Given that the testimony of Johnny O'Connor and William Donnelly placed Carroll at both murder sites during the early morning hours of February 4, Hutchinson and the prosecution team believed that this evidence against the defendant was particularly strong.

It wasn't.

In truth, the testimony of the prosecution's star witnesses could easily be quashed by alibis and, taken at face value, simply spoke to the fact that James Carroll had been present at the killings — not that he had murdered anybody. At best, the prosecution's evidence supported a charge that Carroll was an accessory to murder, and nothing more.[8] But he wasn't being charged with being an accessory; he now stood accused of murdering one specific person — and there was zero evidence to support that contention.

A quick examination of James Carroll's background reveals that being an overseer, rather than a direct participant, suited Carroll's profile. He had, after all, been a foreman for railway crews, a leader and an organizer, but seldom if ever did he roll up his sleeves and do any of the dirty work himself. Granted, upon his return to Biddulph, he had made out that he was a hard man but, as indicated earlier, there is no record of James Carroll ever emerging victorious in a physical encounter. Carroll typically expressed courage only from within the safety of a group, or when he had the drop on an adversary, such as when he had pulled a gun on John Donnelly.

That Charles Hutchinson and his legal team were of the opinion Johnny O'Connor's testimony, however truthful, was sufficient to indict James Carroll for the murder of Johannah Donnelly is inexplicable. By his own admission, O'Connor had been hiding under a bed in a darkened room and unable to see into the kitchen area on the night of the murders — and the kitchen was where Johannah had been murdered. By Johnny O'Connor's estimation, some twenty people had stormed into the Donnellys' house with clubs and other weapons and started hammering away at the family; it would be hard to know who'd killed whom that night even if he had been present in the murder room. Moreover, if the list of killers with which the former Lucan constable Samuel Everett had provided the prosecution was to be believed, it was Michael Carroll who had killed Johannah Donnelly, not James Carroll.[9] It was far more likely that Constable Carroll had served as the Committee's set-up man; he went into the house ahead of the mob to ensure the coast was clear for the murders that followed. And there was also the issue of whether or not it was the fire that had killed Johannah Donnelly, as, again according to O'Connor, the old woman had still been breathing when he had fled from the flames. And finally, William Donnelly had testified it had been James Ryder and Martin McLaughlin who had called John Donnelly to the door, and their guns that had caused his death. James Carroll had simply been spotted standing outside after the fact. Unfortunately for the prosecution, however, Carroll was considered their best shot at securing a conviction. Equally as unfortunate for the prosecution was the fact that none of the testimony they were about to bring forth would support their case that Carroll was the killer of Johannah Donnelly.

Nevertheless, the trial proceeded.

A fter some preliminary presentations in which maps of the territory and model reproductions of the homes of the murder victims were presented for the purpose of orienting the jury, the real meat of the trial was served up. The prosecution began its presentation by laying out a wealth of circumstantial evidence. The goal was to establish the existence of a sinister committee, the sole purpose of which was to work toward eradicating the Donnellys. With that as its base, they would add layers — members of the Committee, actions of these Committee members against the Donnelly family (to establish motive), culminating with the murders and the eyewitness reports identifying the people who were present on that night, specifically James Carroll. It was a rather large mountain the prosecution had chosen to climb, admittedly, particularly when what they were asking for was the death penalty for Carroll, which would require a unanimous consensus from the jury. The prosecution's star witnesses, William Donnelly and Johnny O'Connor, were then brought forth and once again provided their eyewitness evidence of James Carroll's presence at the two crime scenes. Despite aggressive cross-examination by defence attorney Hugh MacMahon, the pair were implacable.[10] The two cousins, Robert and Thomas Keefe, repeated their testimony from the preliminary hearing, that on the night of the murders they had both observed Patrick Ryder Jr. riding past their property carrying either a gun or a sword.[11] Martin Hogan Jr. was brought forth to share what he knew about the Vigilance Committee, testifying that he initially believed it to be part of Father Connolly's anti-crime society. However, upon attending one of the Committee's meetings he discovered that it was a sworn society and, when he refused to swear an oath on the Bible, he had been shown the door. He added that the Committee meetings were held at the Cedar Swamp Schoolhouse and that they were secret and restricted.[12] James Keefe Sr., Thomas Marshall, Edward Sutherby and Thomas Hines[13] spoke to the size of the group of Committee members that had shown up at the Donnelly property during the Thompson cow theft incident. Sutherby further testified that the mob had threatened him personally, while Hines spoke of hearing James Carroll threaten James Donnelly Sr., saying that he would "break his bones." Sutherby also brought forth another interesting piece of information. During the time the Committee had been searching for Thompson's missing cow, James Carroll had said in his presence that "I'll have them [the Donnellys] out of Biddulph if it costs me my life!"[14] Clearly this did not sound like the mission statement of a man who was supposed to be looking for a lost heifer. To underscore this point, Magistrate John Peters was called forth to provide a list of the number of times James Carroll had come to him to have warrants sworn out exclusively for the Donnellys.[15]

William Blackwell and William Walker confessed to seeing a large number of tracks surrounding their neighbour William Donnelly's property.[16] A great deal of testimony was presented to support O'Connor's claim that one of the killers had taken a spade to the head of Tom Donnelly:

- Detective Enoch Murphy testified he had seen such a spade in the ruins of the Donnelly house near the body of Tom Donnelly and also the remains of an axe.[17]
- Constable Alfred Brown reported he had observed this spade near Tom Donnelly's corpse.[18]
- *London Advertiser* reporter Charles Albert Matthews testified he had actually pulled this spade out from beneath the charred head of Tom Donnelly on February 4.[19]
- Robert Keefe Sr. stated he also had seen the blade of the spade (the handle having burned away in the fire) and that after it had been pulled away it was then placed next to Tom Donnelly's corpse.[20]

So far, Johnny O'Connor's testimony was both corroborated and convincing. Constable Gilbert Moore then told his story of the terrible condition of the bodies of the Donnelly family members that he observed on the property, and of the blood he had noticed in front of the Donnellys' front door.[21] This offered corroboration of O'Connor's testimony that he had heard the sounds of Tom Donnelly being beaten outside after he had witnessed him running through the front room of the house. Constable William Hodge was brought to the stand and stated that, after listening to Johnny O'Connor's account of Tom Donnelly being handcuffed, he had arrested James Carroll. And despite Carroll claiming he had his handcuffs on his person that day, when Hodge searched him they were nowhere to be found.[22] Constable Charles Pope swore that when he pointed out the Donnelly ruins to Carroll on their way to Lucan, Carroll refused to look at the property and exhibited no response.[23] The prosecution called other witnesses to support William Donnelly's testimony that the fire from his parents' house that night had made it brighter than usual for miles around, thus allowing a higher degree of certainty to his claim of being able to clearly see and identify the men who were standing outside his house after the murder of his brother.[24]

When it was time for the defence to present its case, the attorneys brought forth a simple strategy — that all six of the prisoners had alibis on the night of the murders:

- James Carroll, along with his brother William, was staying at the home of William and Mary Thompson on the night of the murders. Both of the Thompsons swore that that the Carrolls stayed inside all night and never left their house.[25]
- John Purtell was at the home of his employers, James and Matthew McGrath. According to their testimony Purtell stayed with them all evening.[26]
- Thomas Ryder swore that he was playing cards at his house that night with Valentine Mackey and James Toohey. The latter two men were then brought forth to swear that this was so.[27]
- James Ryder Jr. stated that that he had stayed in that evening at his father's house in the company of his five brothers: William, Michael, Patrick Jr., John and Morris.[28]
- Committee member Michael Blake was put on the stand to say that he had spent the night at Ryder's house as well.[29]

- Martin McLaughlin testified, saying that not only was he not a member of the Vigilance Committee, but also that he too stayed in all night[30] — his daughter, Temperance, was brought forth to testify that she had witnessed him sleeping during the time the murders were said to have occurred.[31]
- John Kennedy Jr.'s presence was also accounted for on the evening of the murders: he claimed that he had gone to Denis Carty's, where he played cards with constable William Hodgins and James Bryan.[32] When the game wrapped up around 9:15 p.m. they all headed home. However, Bryan added that he returned to John Kennedy Jr.'s house at 2 a.m. that morning, in order to borrow some medicine for a sick family member.[33]

The defence ran into its first stumbling block when they called Committee member James Maher to the stand. Maher testified under oath that he had been away in Stratford on the night of February 3. However, the prosecution brought Andrew Keefe to the witness box, who swore that Maher had approached him before the trial and asked if he would alibi him by stating that he had been with him in Stratford when the murders occurred. Allowing Maher's alibi testimony was a bad (and unnecessary) move for the defence to have made, but they still had other cards to play. That there was, in fact, a Vigilance Committee, could not be denied at this point — but perhaps its existence could be justified. And the fact that the Donnellys had been targeted by this Committee could also be justified if the defence could present the jury with a litany of the family's legal transgressions. However, when the defence started to head down that track, Justice Armour cut them off abruptly: "No number of their crimes, real or alleged, could justify the Donnelly homicides," he said.[34]

That avenue having been effectively sealed off to them, the defence then moved to pick apart Johnny O'Connor's testimony. They called to the stand Lucan's own political powerhouse William Stanley, and the merchant John Fox, who shared with the jury that the version of the murders they had heard from O'Connor on the stand differed in several details from the version they had heard him tell in town the morning after the tragedy.[35] Then came a stream of political and entrepreneurial heavyweights to the stand to testify in support of James Carroll's character: men such as Bernard Stanley and his partner in the local grain mill, Thomas Dight;[36] William H. Ryan (the Biddulph magistrate and reeve of Biddulph);[37] David McRoberts (who had been a juror at the O'Connor fire inquest);[38] Lucan merchant Tom Hodgins;[39] and the Member of Parliament for North Middlesex, Timothy Coughlin.[40] Certainly a man who could so impress people of this calibre could not be a lowly murderer. Several of these witnesses, while praising Carroll, made sure to cast aspersions on William Donnelly's character, referring to him as a dishonest and untrustworthy person. The hope had been that if Donnelly could be painted as a liar, his testimony regarding seeing James Carroll and John Kennedy Jr. outside his bedroom window could be called into doubt. However, when the witnesses were interrogated during cross-examination, they could not produce a single example of William Donnelly's behaviour that would support their contentions.[41]

Eventually, the defence presented its closing arguments — to wit, each of the prisoners had an alibi and, in some cases, multiple witnesses to support their alibi. Against this, all the prosecution had to offer was the testimony of a scared boy who claimed he'd heard and seen things in the black of night, from under a bed in a room far away from where the murder of Johannah Donnelly had taken place. Would the jury seriously send a man to the gallows on *that* evidence? As for William Donnelly's testimony, the defence dismissed it outright; it was from a man who'd had a long-standing grudge against several of the Committee members and whose word could not be trusted. Defence counsel William Meredith put it bluntly: what the jury had heard were "incredible lies, from the black heart of William Donnelly!"[42] Sure, there was a Vigilance Committee to ferret out crime in the neighbourhood and, yes, the prisoners and many others were members of it — but where was the crime in that?[43] Moreover, Johnny O'Connor had claimed that James Carroll had looked directly at him while standing in the doorway of the bedroom immediately prior to the killings. If this was so, and if Carroll had committed the murder, why had the boy's life been spared? And perhaps more importantly, as a Toronto newspaper would point out, a guilty verdict would be tantamount, once all the dominoes had fallen, to an indictment of half the township — did the boy's blinkered testimony warrant this?[44]

For the Crown's closing arguments, Aemilius Irving pointed out that the Committee had been created only to attack the Donnellys. Indeed, what other "criminals" had they gone after? James Carroll had stated he would have them out of Biddulph if it cost him his life — and then the family had been murdered. The prisoners' alibis were almost laughable; as prosecutor James Magee had dryly commented during the trial, "Is it not remarkable how many occurrences happened at two o'clock that night?"[45]

Then came time for Judge Armour to give his charge to the jury. He clearly had been impressed with the prosecution's case. The very idea of a "Vigilance Committee" had rubbed him the wrong way: "Such committees were outside the law and mothers of all sorts of crimes," he counselled.[46]

He noted that the alibis provided for the prisoners were highly suspect:

> If you decide the Society made up their minds to
> exterminate the Donnellys, everything is plain, so
> far as these alibis and this evidence is concerned;

for do you suppose that men who would join hands
to perform such an outrage as this would hesitate to
swear alibis for every person engaged in it?[47]

The Vigilance Committee's intrusion onto the property of James
and Johannah Donnelly disturbed him: "If the cow case had been a
charge of riot and not of trespass, it would have been sustained."[48]

That the Committee should have its own private constable and
magistrate was troubling: "It was an extremely unfitting thing that
a person should be appointed constable who was nominated at
such a meeting, and that a magistrate nominated in the same way
should receive appointment."[49]

He, frankly, could see no reason for another group of people
uniting to kill the Donnelly family: "Where did they come from, if
they were not members of this Committee?"[50]

Johnny O'Connor's testimony had seemed to him legitimate and
not something he had been coached to say by William Donnelly:
"As for John O'Connor's evidence, do you believe that the boy
could invent his story? Is there anyone capable of writing such a
history as that, and teaching it to a boy afterwards?"[51]

And, finally, he let the jury know that the repercussions of their
verdict on the guilt or innocence of James Carroll had the potential
to impact all such legal trials in the future:

> The disgrace of such a deed rests not only upon
> this part of the country, but upon the country at
> large, and it is of the utmost importance that the
> perpetrators of it should be brought to justice,
> otherwise this crime might stand as an example of
> what persons might do and go unpunished.[52]

Having said his piece, Justice Armour instructed the jury to formu-
late their verdict.

Such a judicial show of support had been unexpected but certainly welcomed by the prosecution. They could be forgiven if during the jury's deliberation period they felt an impulse to crack open a bottle of champagne — the judge had just directed the jurors to render a verdict to convict James Carroll. After four and a half hours the jury returned with their verdict, which was reported in the press and echoed across the nation:

The jury in the Biddulph case failed to agree, notwithstanding the strong charge against the prisoner by Judge Armour. Seven were for acquittal, four for conviction and one undecided. They were at once discharged, and matters now stand as before the trial.[53]

THE SECOND TRIAL

Lawyers William Meredith (left), for the defence, and Aemlius Irving (right), for the prosecution, faced off against each other during the second trial before Judge Matthew Crooks Cameron (middle). (Library and Archives Canada)

A hung jury had never been anticipated — by anybody. The defence had believed that with their volume of alibis, the quality of their character witnesses, the non-specificity of the prosecution's eyewitness testimony, and the lack of overall evidence against their client that James Carroll would be acquitted. The prosecution, for its part, had not been particularly optimistic about its chances heading into the trial, but after Justice Armour's charge to the jury, their belief that Johnny O'Connor's testimony carried significant legal weight had been buoyed.[1] A hung jury meant there could be a second trial, and now the thought trickled through their minds that, with a little more legal fine-tuning, they might just get a conviction yet. The friends and supporters of the Vigilance Committee who were present in the courtroom, not understanding the jury's decision, believed that the verdict had cleared Carroll of the charges, and rushed forward to congratulate him on his victory. By the time Judge Armour was able to restore order in the court, the prosecution announced they would not proceed with another trial at this time, but of course reserved their right to do so at a time in the future to be determined. This meant James Carroll and the rest of the prisoners would have to be returned to their cells in the Middlesex County Gaol.

The defence counsel, along with members and sympathizers of the Vigilance Committee, believed that, after eight months in jail, the prisoners had been incarcerated long enough. Hugh MacMahon applied for bail on their behalf. The prosecution denied it. MacMahon then submitted writs of habeas corpus directly to the attorney general's office. Again, the motion was denied.[2] Allies of the prisoners' cause had newspaper articles published in the press stating how unfair it was that the Biddulph men were still locked up.[3] Politicians weighed in, including North Middlesex's representative in the Ontario Legislature, John Waters, who was quoted in the *Catholic Record* newspaper, appealing directly to Mowat to give the prisoners (who were Waters's constituents) bail.[4] A petition was worked up and signed by many prominent members of the community, and then sent to the attorney general's office, once again appealing for the prisoners' release on bail.[5] All eyes now turned to Oliver Mowat. The trial had settled nothing, and both sides in the case wanted answers from the attorney general regarding direction.[6]

Hutchinson's initial optimism at Justice Armour's support of the prosecution's case took a hit when he learned what certain members of the jury were now saying publicly. One had spoken out that he would not have voted to convict Carroll even if he had witnessed the killings himself.[7] Another expressed the sentiment that, while he believed the prisoners to have been guilty, the prosecution's evidence was not strong enough to warrant a conviction.[8]

Others stated that Justice Armour had been too aggressive in his critique of the defendant's case, and so voted to acquit Carroll as an act of protest.[9] The sheer number of names affixed to the bail petition was also a cause for concern, particularly if another trial were to go forward within the same community.[10] Hutchinson and his team discussed the viability of taking another kick at the can to obtain a change of venue,[11] but they knew that since their previous two attempts had failed, there was no reason for optimism in attempting a third.

The press now zeroed in on Premier Mowat: would he call for a special commission to expedite a second trial? After all, the prisoners had been in jail for eight months, and, at this point, hadn't been convicted of anything.[12] The premier, for the moment, was indecisive; if the trial went forward and the prisoners were acquitted, he would lose currency within the Irish Roman Catholic community for putting "innocent" men through a second trial — but if the prisoners were prosecuted and convicted, a huge block of Irish Catholics would not forget the damage the premier had done to their community when it came time to vote in the next election. He couldn't win. It would be best if the whole matter were dropped and dropped quickly. But Mowat's department had to maintain the appearance of standing for justice, particularly in a murder case in which an entire family had been wiped out within the province that he represented.

The prosecution was content to give the attorney general all the time he wanted to reach his decision on the matter, and the longer he took the better. They still needed time to look into the change of venue issue, and to search for more evidence and witnesses to support Johnny O'Connor's testimony. They also still clung to the belief that the more time the prisoners spent in jail, the greater the likelihood that one or more of them would flip on the others.

And then came the attorney general's bombshell. In a move without legal parallel in Canadian history, Oliver Mowat ordered a

Special Commission from Ontario's lieutenant-governor to authorize a second trial to take place in January of 1881 — a little over two months' time.[13] The prosecution was stunned. January was far too soon. Hutchinson didn't see how a jury could even be empanelled before February 6 — three months away — and the rush worried him.[14] More news came from Mowat's office; it had already selected who would be adjudicating the forthcoming trial, and this time it would be not one, but two justices: Matthew Crooks Cameron and Featherston Osler.[15] Osler had a solid reputation but, unbeknownst to the prosecution, he had already decided to let Justice Cameron conduct the trial. Cameron's appointment raised some eyebrows, particularly on the prosecution side of the aisle — Cameron was the former Conservative Party leader of the province. Indeed, he had been the one who had passed the leadership torch on to his successor in the party, William Meredith, who was the lead counsel for James Carroll's defence team. Surely, he would be sympathetic to the political ramifications that would arise from either a victory or a loss to the leader of his party. And when the prosecution learned that Justice Cameron had made the comment that "the evidence is not sufficient to convict,"[16] their worst fears were all but confirmed; the attorney general, in an effort to project an image of impartiality to the Roman Catholic voters, had delivered unto the prosecution their destroyer. The forthcoming trial was going to be a façade; the outcome had already been decided.

While the prosecutors were reeling from the news out of the attorney general's office, the O'Connor parents began acting up again. Michael and Mary O'Connor announced that they no longer wanted a constable living with them.[17] Instead, they proposed, the Crown should take the salary they were planning on paying the constable for his guard duties and pay it directly to Michael O'Connor — he would guard their son. Again, the

O'Connors used Johnny's cooperation with the prosecution as leverage and, again, the Crown gave in to their demands.[18] Michael O'Connor quit his job in a London factory and was now paid to stay at home and keep an eye on his son.[19] This arrangement lasted less than a week, however, as Michael O'Connor took Johnny to Biddulph, and then promptly got drunk and assaulted someone in a store.[20] It was decided that it would be in everyone's best interests to move the family into a larger home in London where, continuously if not obtrusively, Johnny O'Connor could be watched by constables under the charge of Police Chief Williams.[21]

But the O'Connors had more demands. Mary O'Connor had decided that she wanted some additional items for her household and for a little shop she had opened — and wanted the Crown to pay for it. The Crown did.[22] And then Mary O'Connor received an interesting letter.

It hadn't taken much digging on the part of the Vigilance Committee to find out the O'Connors needed money. It was decided that perhaps an understanding could be arrived at between the Committee and the family that would serve the interests of both parties. At some point in December, an anonymous letter showed up at the London home of the O'Connors. It contained an intriguing proposition. Mary wanted money, and the Committee wanted the murder charge dropped against James Carroll. It wouldn't require much effort or even a formal dropping of the charge — the charge would have to be dropped if Johnny were to go away for a while. If Mary would allow her son to leave the country or otherwise prevent him from testifying, the Committee offered to make it worth her while.[23] They would be willing to match the attorney general's reward offer of $4,000 — a considerable sum in 1880 (approximately $134,000 in current Canadian dollars)[24] if she could make this happen. Both sides would get what they wanted.

Recognizing that there was now a short window available between the two trials in which to ply her leverage (as it was highly unlikely the prosecution would require her son's testimony for a third trial), Mary decided it was time to pay another visit to the attorney general's office in Toronto, where, once again, she was put onto Oliver Mowat's deputy, John Scott. She told Scott of the letter she received and implied she was considering the deal — but would stay loyal to the Crown if she received the government's reward money. She further told Scott that all her family's money had been spoken for in debts, that they had no clothes or bedding to get them through the winter months. She told him the O'Connor family had been victimized and wiped out by the tragedy and its aftermath. Scott comforted her but explained that any and all available money had to come from Charles Hutchinson's office in London. She then asked for, and received, train fare back to London.[25]

As she departed from the attorney general's office, however, Mary O'Connor was spotted by a reporter from the Toronto *Globe* who made mention of it in an article on December 13, 1880.[26] Her visit to Mowat's office soon became a matter of public knowledge, which added more ammunition to the defence's case that Johnny O'Connor's testimony was being bought and paid for by the Crown. In truth, the Committee may not have offered an amount equal to the government's four thousand dollar reward, but that was the amount she told Crown attorney Hutchinson she had been offered when she returned to his office from her visit in the city.[27] She wanted to know what Hutchinson could do to make it worth her while to keep Johnny available for the trial.[28]

The surviving Donnelly siblings weren't consulted on any of this. From the O'Connor family's perspective, it was none of their business. Johnny O'Connor had already helped them out by testifying at the coroner's inquest, the preliminary hearing and the first trial — at great personal risk to himself and the O'Connor family. Bob Donnelly risking his life to save Bridget O'Connor from the fire at their home was a nice gesture, but from here on out it was strictly business between the O'Connors and the Crown; the Donnellys had nothing to do with it. Doing the right thing going forward meant looking out for number one.[29]

After some back and forth between Charles Hutchinson and John Scott, a cash settlement was promised to the O'Connors — but only once the forthcoming trial was over.[30] This was no sooner agreed to than Mary O'Connor came asking for money again. Hutchinson made it clear to her that any monies advanced to her between now and the end of the second trial would have to be deducted from the amount agreed to for the cash settlement.[31] Mary O'Connor consented, and took her latest installment home with her.

Heading into the second trial the Crown saw their primary hope in, of all places, the potential jury for the trial. In the first trial, they had the benefit of a sympathetic judge but a hostile jury. This time around they hoped to reverse that; they knew that Justice Cameron would be hostile to the prosecution's efforts, but if they could — somehow — get a sympathetic jury, there was hope they might just win the case. To get the right jury, however, they would have to engage in a bit of subterfuge; they would need to send spies out among the various groups in the towns and villages from which the jury pool would be drawn. These spies would be tasked with listening to conversations involving potential jury members, taking down notes of who said what and returning with this information to the prosecutors, who would then put this information to use when it came time to select the jury for the trial. A sample of their notes survive to this day:

> Parsons John, London Farmer: Said, "it is a bad
> affair, hope they will get what they deserve, hardly
> know what that will be — hardly think a jury will
> agree." Seems a good fair man.

Davis Berry Sr., Westminster, Farmer: Rather
inclined to convict. thinks they have some of the
right men — a good man.

Harkuep Walter, Westminster, Blacksmith: Rather
inclined to convict — said to a bystander, "how
would you like to have had a mother or sister in that
house that night, sweet as that girl was." Not a first-
class man.

Dibb William, Westminster Farmer: Said, "I think
they will never get a jury to agree, I don't place much
faith in the boy's evidence nor Bill Donnelly's —
Donnelly has posted the boy." Church of England.

Flowers John, Westminster, Farmer: Said "I don't
think they will ever hang them, but will have to be
guided by the evidence." A Presbyterian.

Moore Samuel, W. Nipouri Farmer: Said, "We have
our private opinion but it would look hard to hang
those men on that boys' evidence."

Patterson James, W. Nipouri, Farmer: Sorry to be
summoned, thought they would never get a jury to
agree.

Kepler Jacob, N. Dorchester, Farmer: Rather
inclined to acquit but will not shrink from duty.

Mofsos John, Nipouri, Farmer: Seems inclined to
favour the prisoners. He is well acquainted with
nearly all the parties, a party man himself — and

an Orangeman. Not considered safe — on the other hand Donnelly and Lewis recommend him.

Walker James, Mosa, Farmer: Said, "Don't see why they were not dealt with before." He did not like to have anything to do with them, as he thought they were a bad lot, and believes they are guilty from what he has read through the papers.

Murray Donald: Said, "If there was not more evidence than had been, he could not convict. There was no doubt they were guilty, but would have to have better evidence."

Kitchen John D., Caradoc Farmer: Said, "Don't like to have anything to do with the case."

Lamount, John, Caradoc Farmer: Said, "think they should be punished." Believed them to be guilty.

Paterson, Duncan, Lobo, Farmer: Said if he could get out of service he would, as he thought his property would be in danger.[32]

Hutchinson, at least, saw no breach of ethics in such a procedure: "Why should we not find out all we can about these jurors, and why should we not adopt the best mode for attaining our object, so long as we do nothing underhand?"[33]

On Monday, January 24, 1881, the great trial began and the dawning of the day brought with it the arrival of the great crowds. Hundreds of people had arrived by train, stage and private conveyance to London, where, according to one newspaper report, "the scene in and around the principal hotels was lively in the extreme."[34] Despite the cold winter weather, the crowds had started to gather around the Middlesex County Courthouse early that morning. Some of those present were there to be considered for possible inclusion on the jury. Others had been asked to appear as witnesses for either the Crown or the defence. Still more had arrived to report on the matter for the Canadian press. But most came simply to observe the spectacle.

The courthouse doors swung open a little before 11 a.m. and a sea of people rushed forth into the building. Once again tickets were issued to the event, and, once again, those without tickets were denied admittance.[35] The respective legal teams gathered around their tables and discussed strategy, while the Court's High Constable, Henry Groves,[36] set up the display table featuring models of the Donnelly family's farmhouse and William Donnelly's home at Whalen's Corners. Groves also hung up a large map of Biddulph Township and a plan of the village of Whalen to aid the lawyers in orienting the jury as to the locales of significance in the case.[37] Next, the judges, the Honourable Matthew Crooks Cameron and the Honourable Featherston Osler, arrived and took their seats. And then James Carroll was led into the courtroom. It marked the first time many of the press, the jurors and the curious got their first look at the accused:

> James Carroll was now brought into court, hand-
> cuffed, and placed in the dock. On his appearance in
> court there was an unusual stir, and all eyes were fixed
> on him in order to see how he looked. The prisoner
> seems, if anything, slightly improved in appearance
> since the last court, although looking to a certain
> extent care-worn, yet the prisoner held his head up
> well. And on being placed in the box, before taking

his seat, looked steadily around the courtroom, not assuming by any means a dogged or defiant attitude, but on the contrary, more of an air of anxiety, or of a person who felt keenly the position and circumstances of the ordeal before him. In condition Carroll appears a trifle more fleshy, and by no means looked as if he suffered at the hands of the jail authorities.[38]

On that first day, Carroll was merely required to be present during the jury selection procedure, which turned out to be a lengthy process. The jury selection component of the trial had originally been set to start at 11 a.m., but had ended up being put off until two o'clock that afternoon. By the time things got underway it was three o'clock, and the process continued without stop until almost 6 p.m. By 4 p.m., only six jurors had been agreed upon by the defence and the prosecution; by 5 p.m. that number had risen to eight, and by 5:30 p.m. the twelve-person panel had been fully finalized.[39] Throughout this lengthy process (both the defence and the prosecution had to agree on each member selected — and there were 100 potential jurors for them to choose from),[40] William Donnelly once again proved himself indispensable to the prosecution. He knew something about most of the jurors who were being assessed and offered his opinion as to which ones would be sympathetic to the prosecution's case. A copy of the final list of jurists who would eventually sit on the trial contains notations with respect to how inclined they might be toward the prosecution's side:

1. John Carruthers — "thinks men guilty, good man, recommended";
2. William Hooper — "recommended by Donnelly";
3. Horace Hyatt — "believed they should be punished, believed them to be a hard lot, and punishment was

what they want, and what they would get in his belief — good man, recommended";

4. John Lamont — "said he thought they should be punished, believed them to be guilty; a good man, recommended";

5. George. M. Francis — "thinks men guilty, good man, recommended";

6. James F. Elliott — "not interviewed, absent, Presbyterian, a good man by repute, an assessor and collector";

7. Dougal Graham — "thinks the men guilty, a good man, recommended";

8. James Watterworth — "said if he could get out of serving he would, as he thought his property might be in danger; not recommended";

9. James Dores — "not interviewed, being absent, has good reputation";

10. Hooper Ward — "thought favourable, but would not say much, a good man";

11. Asa Luce — "said if it was not for the stubbornness of the jurors, the trials might have been decided at the other court. He did not want to have anything to do with it. He thought it might make some disturbance yet; recommended";

12. Ben Kilbourne — "could not see any chance to convict on evidence now given, not recommended."[41]

The jury was actually a bit of a wild card because each of its members was Protestant.[42] On the one hand, this meant that Father Connolly and the Roman Catholic Vigilance Committee would have little influence over the proceedings, and, therefore, the trial would not be settled along religious lines. But politically, Protestants tended to vote Conservative, and the provincial leader of that party was the lead attorney for the defence. Still, given that eight of the twelve men on the jury were believed to be predisposed in favour of conviction, the prosecution now liked its chances. They had never found themselves in such an advantageous position before. Throughout all the legal windmills they had passed through previously with this case the jury had been against them. With the scales of jurisprudence seemingly tipped in their direction, the case was now theirs to lose.

The next order of business was the calling of the witnesses — the Crown called over ninety, the defence over forty. The witnesses were instructed that, upon their arrival at court the next morning, they were to not to enter the courtroom, but rather to stay within the witness (and other) rooms within the building, where they were to remain until called upon to give their testimony.[43] The prosecution's strategy this time around was to forgo William Donnelly's testimony completely. As the trial was solely to determine whether or not James Carroll was responsible for the murder of Johannah Donnelly, how John Donnelly came to meet his death was irrelevant to the proceedings at this time. Besides, during the previous trial, a good deal of the court's time had been taken up by the defence attacking (and the prosecution defending) William Donnelly's character, and, thus, his trustworthiness under oath. This was time that otherwise could have been spent on attacking Carroll's alibi and the Vigilance Committee and buttressing the testimony of Johnny O'Connor, which had so impressed Justice Armour during the first trial. With the jurors selected and the witnesses in place, the trial was now ready to proceed.

As the trial involved the same charges and the same defendant, most of the witnesses called forth were simply asked to repeat their testimony from the previous trial. Joseph Whalen, for example, recounted his experience with Johnny O'Connor on the night of the murders. James Feeheley mentioned being at the Donnelly house in the hours before the tragedy and how, prior to this, James

Carroll had taken him aside and told him that "the Donnellys would have to be stopped."[44] Feeheley then went on to relate that he asked Carroll if he had a warrant for him. Carroll had replied in the affirmative. When Feeheley asked what the warrant was for he was told by the constable that that was Carroll's business.[45] The prosecution attorney, Aemilius Irving, immediately picked up on the implication of this — was Carroll attempting to blackmail Feeheley by threatening to enforce his arrest warrant unless Feeheley cooperated with him? If so, what did that cooperation entail? Suddenly Feeheley became very forgetful about the matter, as revealed in the following exchange between the prosecutor and the witness:

> IRVING: "Was there anything said about quashing
> the warrant if you shunned the company of the
> Donnellys?"
> FEEHELEY: "I don't know that there was."
> IRVING: "But I want you to remember. Didn't you
> say so at a previous trial?"
> FEEHELEY: "I can't say."

At this point, defence counsel Hugh MacMahon rose from his table. "I object to the Crown Counsel putting words into the witness's mouth," he said. Judge Cameron sustained the objection. Irving then attempted a different tack.

> IRVING: "Why, then, did you stop associating with
> the Donnellys thereafter?"
> FEEHELEY: "The reason I didn't stop at Donnellys
> was because they were said to be bad company, and
> I was afraid to be seen coming out of their house. All
> the people appeared to be against them."
> IRVING: "What people?"

FEEHELEY: "I can't mention the names of any who said so, only it was common report."[46]

Irving had hoped to show the jury that Carroll and the Committee were using Carroll's position as a county constable to bend people in the community to their will. Since the Committee wanted the Donnellys out of Biddulph, they would do whatever possible to make this happen — including murder. While this was certainly food for thought for the jurors, the witness they most wanted to hear from was Johnny O'Connor, as he was the only one who had witnessed the horrific murders and was willing to talk about it. The defence lawyers were likewise keen to get him on the stand; they knew the prosecution's case hinged entirely on the boy's testimony and they needed to find contradictions and inconsistencies in it that they could exploit to their advantage.

When O'Connor was finally brought forth to give his testimony, the energy in the courtroom was palpable.[47] Even the press was moved to state that "the jurymen, who were an intelligent and respectable-looking lot of men, leaned forward when he approached . . . and listened eagerly to every word."[48] He did not disappoint. Once more Johnny O'Connor was made to relive the horror of what he had experienced almost one year previously. The prosecution knew that his testimony represented their last kick at the can to secure a conviction, and they wanted it all out on the table for the jury to experience. And it was; from James Carroll standing at the bedroom door with his face illuminated by flickering candlelight, to the frenzied mob's storming of the Donnelly home, to the sickening thuds of shillelaghs, spades and axes beating into human flesh and bone, to Tom and Bridget Donnelly running for their lives and into eternity, to the house burning down all around him — Johnny O'Connor told it all. The jury was riveted, hanging on his every word. The prosecution was certainly getting every dollar's worth of testimony they'd paid for out of Mary O'Connor's boy. When

O'Connor spoke of the men heading up the stairs to kill Bridget Donnelly, James Carroll suddenly looked ill, but he managed to keep himself together until the boy had concluded his recollection.

With Johnny O'Connor's testimony now entered into the public record, the court was then adjourned until the next day. That would be when William Meredith would be given his opportunity to cross-examine the boy. Throughout the night Meredith and the defence team pored over O'Connor's statements from earlier that day and contrasted these with what he had said during the first trial, the preliminary hearing and the coroner's inquest. They further analyzed testimony from those with whom the boy had spoken in the days immediately following the murders to compare what he had told them with what he had said on the witness stand. They were looking for contradictions. And by the time O'Connor took the stand for cross-examination at eleven the next morning, they believed they had found some.

When Johnny O'Connor had given his testimony the day before, and as he sat waiting to be cross-examined on this morning, he was never more than ten feet away from James Carroll — the very man whom O'Connor was accusing of these horrible crimes. Carroll, as usual, had taken the occasion to appear in his finest clothes — a black suit, his "respectable" white shirt (only this time with gold studs in it) and a grey scarf pinned around his neck.[49] He had stared hard at the boy throughout the latter's testimony the day before. O'Connor, however, had not been intimidated, either by Carroll's appearance or by his reputation. At fourteen and a half years of age,[50] Johnny O'Connor was now a year older than he had been at the time of the murders, and, by this, his fifth appearance on the stand,[51] he was used to (if not fully comfortable with) testifying in a courtroom. Some had said that ever since the first trial he had been coached by William Donnelly on what to say and how to comport himself in the legal arena.[52] Perhaps it was true, for O'Connor now certainly boasted a Donnelly-like sense of style. He was outfitted in a new grey suit, a black tie and a white shirt. Gold studs glistened from his shirt-front and a gold chain stretched over his vest[53] and into his pocket where it connected to a gold watch. He calmly twirled a fur hat on his hand while he waited for the defence attorney to approach the witness box to cross-examine him.[54]

William Meredith, the Queen's Counsel, master politician and future Chief Justice of Ontario, slowly eased himself from his seat at the defence table. He was a regal figure, with snow-white hair and a full but carefully manicured beard, who carried himself with the bearing of someone who had been groomed for politics. He walked in confident, measured strides to the front of the stands where the jury sat. He stopped within three feet of where Johnny O'Connor was seated. The boy placed his arm on the rail of the witness box and leaned in toward the attorney.[55] And then the duel began.

> MEREDITH: "What is your name?"
> O'CONNOR: "John."
> MEREDITH: "You were christened 'Jeremiah,' were you not?"
> O'CONNOR: "Yes, sir."
> MEREDITH: "How do they call you John?"
> O'CONNOR: "How do they call anyone John?"[56]

The spectators laughed loudly at the boy's rejoinder. Meredith, however, took it in stride. He had raised an interesting point right out of the gate. Johnny O'Connor's christened name was, indeed, "Jeremiah." Meredith's reason for bringing the matter up was that he wanted to plant doubt as to O'Connor's credibility in everything, from his name to his testimony. However, the name issue was put to bed when the boy's godmother, Temperance McLaughlin, was called forth by the prosecution to testify that, while it was true that the teenager had been christened "Jeremiah," he had also been christened "John," and so either name equally applied.[57]

Meredith next focused in on the gold watch O'Connor was wearing. Where would he have gotten the money for that? Perhaps he had received it as a bribe from a Donnelly in order to back the prosecution's claim that James Carroll had committed these atrocious murders? The boy, however, replied that he had simply been loaned the watch by the local hotelier, John Lewis, a friend of the O'Connor family, solely for his appearance in court that week.[58] Meredith then proceeded to ask the boy several questions in quick succession: How old was he? Did he go out to the Donnelly ruins with Bob Donnelly the day after the funeral? Did Bob Donnelly ask him about the murders on that day? What woke him up on the night the murders occurred? What kind of candle holder was James Carroll allegedly holding when the boy saw him in the doorway?

O'Connor answered all the defence lawyer's questions almost as quickly as they had been posed. In answering the last question above, he replied that Carroll had been holding a brass candle holder with a candle in it. He added that the old man had told Carroll to hold the candle by the doorway so that he could have some light in the room while he put on his clothes. Meredith's eyes widened at this bit of news.

> MEREDITH: "You did not tell this to Mr. Irving."
> O'CONNOR: "He did not ask me."
> MEREDITH: "You did not say anything about the old man asking Carroll to hold the light for him at the last trial."
> O'CONNOR: "Yes, I did."
> MEREDITH: "I'm sure you did not."
> O'CONNOR: "I think I did."

Meredith changed the subject. He asked O'Connor how he knew it was Bridget Donnelly whom the boy said he had followed up the stairs in the front room.

> O'CONNOR: "I saw her back."
> MEREDITH: "Had she on a dress?"
> O'CONNOR: "Yes."
> MEREDITH: "Had she on an apron?"
> O'CONNOR: "No."

Here, Meredith thought he might be able to trip the witness up.

> MEREDITH: "How could you tell she had on no apron when you saw only her back?"
> O'CONNOR: "What would she have an apron on for?"

Again, the spectators laughed. However, the boy had scored a point with his response. Bridget Donnelly would have had no time or inclination to put on an apron when the murderers burst into the house and began clubbing the family to death. Again, Meredith showed no reaction. He asked the boy if he saw anybody actually being murdered.

> O'CONNOR: "As I ran by I saw a lot of men hammering with clubs."
> MEREDITH: "This is a new story about clubs."
> O'CONNOR: "I spoke about clubs last time."
> MEREDITH: "You did not."
> O'CONNOR: "I saw three clubs; then I got back and in under the bed again."[59]

The newspaper reporters from Toronto were impressed with the boy's composure under fire. The Toronto *Globe* wrote that "[h]is answers were, as a rule, given very promptly and with a fear-lessness that did him credit,"[60] while the *Toronto Mail* indicated that "he [O'Connor] is exceedingly bright and conducts himself in a manly way that goes far to strengthen the belief in what he says."[61]

For his part, Meredith kept pressing. He now followed up with a question regarding what specific acts of violence against the family the boy had actually seen in the dark of early morning on February 4.

O'CONNOR: "When I ran with Bridge in order to get upstairs I saw them hammering."

MEREDITH: "What were they hammering?"

O'CONNOR: "They were hammering the Donnellys! And I got around the head of the basket and looked out. I saw two or three . . ."

MEREDITH: "You said yesterday three — which is it, two or three?"

O'CONNOR: "Three, I think."

MEREDITH: "Why, then, do you say there was three?"

O'CONNOR: "It's all the same."

MEREDITH: "It is not all the same."[62]

As O'Connor spoke of the murders, and specifically that of Bridget Donnelly, James Carroll suddenly became ashen. He beck-oned for a constable to come to the dock and said something to him. The constable then walked to the prosecution table and spoke with Hutchinson. The Crown attorney nodded, and the constable then returned to Carroll, handcuffed him, and led him from the courtroom.[63] In the meantime, Meredith had moved in closer to the boy in the witness box. He asked him how he knew that it was in fact Tom Donnelly who had run past the bedroom door. Or, for that matter, how he knew the voice he had heard in the kitchen belonged to Tom Donnelly at all.

> O'CONNOR: "I could tell Tom Donnelly's voice. I
> could also tell Tom Donnelly by his stocking feet."
> MEREDITH: "How could you be sure that it was Tom
> Donnelly by his feet?"
> O'CONNOR: "What would the other men want to be
> out in their stocking feet for?"

This brought forth another round of laughter from the spectators in the courtroom.[64]

After what seemed an inordinate amount of time had passed without the accused being present in court, a messenger was sent downstairs to the jail to find out what was wrong with James Carroll. Reporters from Toronto followed the court clerk down to the prison cells to see for themselves. There they discovered Carroll walking in the corridor. He evidently was in some distress and complaining loudly about sharp pains in his abdomen: "He was deathly pale and exceedingly nervous and weak. He said that he had only once before experienced a similar sensation and that was years ago, when he awoke from a dream in which he thought he was dying."[65]

Upstairs in the courtroom, Meredith's tenacity was starting to pay off; he was finally able to catch the boy in a contradiction.

> MEREDITH: "Did you see a spade?"
> O'CONNOR: "I saw no spade."

The seasoned attorney moved in for the kill.

> MEREDITH: "At the last trial you swore you saw
> a spade. Here is your evidence: (Reading) 'I saw

someone carrying a spade, then someone hit him three or four times with the spade.' Now which is true?"

O'CONNOR: "I can't remember."

Meredith attacked again.

> MEREDITH: "Before the Magistrates, you said you peeped out and saw Carroll, Purtell and Ryder standing around Tom."

O'Connor corrected him. "I didn't say I saw Carroll." Meredith ignored the boy's statement and moved on to another contradiction.

> MEREDITH: "You said before the Magistrates, that you saw one stick, and here you say you saw three sticks. You said in March, you were looking out from behind the basket at the foot of the bed; now you say you were looking out at the head of the bed. What do you say to that?"
> O'CONNOR: "I don't know."

The boy was in trouble now.

> MEREDITH: "You said last March, you saw Ryder and Purtell twice."
> O'CONNOR: "I don't think I said that."
> MEREDITH: "Then that's down wrong, also?"
> O'CONNOR: "I don't know."
> MEREDITH: "You said at the inquest, that then a whole crowd rushed in and commenced hammering Tom Donnelly with sticks and spades. Is that the way it happened?"

O'CONNOR: "I can't say."

MEREDITH: "You said before the Magistrates you saw two men with their faces blackened; now you only saw one. What do you say to that?"

O'CONNOR: "I don't know."

At this point, Aemilius Irving came to the boy's defence.

"I'll go over the evidence with the boy," Irving told Judge Cameron, before adding, "which the learned counsel did at some length, referring to the great number of times the witness has been examined, having been brought up five times for examination, including the present court."[66] While William Meredith had not damaged the core of Johnny O'Connor's testimony in any significant way, he had revealed to the jury there were certain things that had occurred on the evening of the murders of which the boy was now not as certain as he had been before. It would thus not require a great leap to suggest that a man's life should not be taken based upon testimony that was in any way uncertain. It was a necessary step toward injecting reasonable doubt into the minds of the jurors. But then Meredith wasn't one who had risen to the top of his profession by accident; he was among the most skilful lawyers in the Dominion. He had succeeded in turning a rock-solid report from a cocky kid into a good, but perhaps not altogether reliable, recollection from an uncertain witness. The prosecution knew that Meredith's performance had tilted the playing field to the advantage of the defence, and they hoped that the money that had been paid to Mary O'Connor over the past year for Johnny's testimony had not just gone up in flames before their eyes. They now moved to bring forth witnesses to mitigate the damage. It was at this point, however, that Justice Matthew Cameron inserted himself directly into the proceedings — and the prosecution realized fully what they were up against.

They moved to call forth other members of the Whalen family to testify. They had done this in the previous trial in order to lend support to the boy's testimony and, thus, credibility, but this time around the defence objected that such testimony was hearsay. Justice Cameron sided with the defence. The prosecution next sought to bring to the stand the London policeman who had interviewed Johnny O'Connor on the morning of the murders, as his notes and recollections from the interview with the boy would likewise corroborate O'Connor's testimony. Again, the defence objected to such testimony as being hearsay. And again, Justice Cameron sustained the objection. The prosecution then attempted to call the witness James Hobbins, who had met Johnny O'Connor during the latter's ride from the Whalens' house to Lucan on the morning of the murders and who was told by the boy what he had witnessed. Hobbins's testimony would have agreed in its particulars with what O'Connor had testified to on the witness stand — but Hobbins's testimony was forbidden by Justice Cameron.

To the prosecution's shock, however, when the defence called forth witnesses such as William Stanley and John Fox, who wished to report their version of what O'Connor had said in their presence on the morning of the murders, Justice Cameron allowed their testimony to proceed. Aemilius Irving stood up to protest the inconsistency being displayed. "I do not think it fair that my learned friends should allow such evidence to be put in for a part of their case, and then objects when it suits their purpose."[67] But Justice Cameron dismissed Irving's complaint outright by declaring, "If you have permitted them to outgeneral you in this matter, it is clearly nobody's fault but your own."[68] Cameron then berated the prosecution: "If I were listening to the case on the first hearing, I would strongly protest against the manner in which the Crown presents the case."[69]

While the prosecution had suspected that Cameron would be favourable to Meredith and the defence, they hadn't anticipated his deference to Meredith's side of the legal ledger to be so blatant. The prosecution now had to adapt to the shifting legal ground beneath their feet. They would have to transition from being a force of attack to one of defence in order to patch up the testimony of their star witness from the torpedoes that had been launched into it by the defence team.

The prosecution had to introduce something that would buttress O'Connor's testimony in the eyes of the jury. Hutchinson and Irving believed the defence was going to argue there was a valance on the bed that O'Connor had been hiding under while the murders took place. And, as the valance had hung down to the floor, it would have obscured the boy's view of anything. Consequently, Irving and the prosecution wanted to launch a pre-emptive strike on this belief by having Nora Donnelly and Mary O'Connor take the stand. Both women would testify the valance had been removed long before the murders took place and, thus, O'Connor's view into the front room would have been unobstructed.

Nora Donnelly testified that on the day of Mike Donnelly's wake, his body had been laid out upon Mr. and Mrs. Donnelly's four-poster bed, and that the valances were on the bed at that time, but that Mary O'Connor had removed them on the day of the funeral.[70] This opened the door for Mary O'Connor to be called to the stand to confirm this. However, the defence had led the prosecution into a trap; they had no interest in whether or not the valance had been on the bed on the night of the murders. They simply wanted Mary O'Connor under oath so they could grill her about her recent visit to the attorney general's office in Toronto. They intended to wrest from her the confession that she had gone to Toronto solely to obtain the money the government had offered on its reward poster for information leading to the conviction of the Donnelly killers. If they could get her to admit this, then they felt they could prove to the jury that Johnny O'Connor's testimony in the case had never been based on seeing James Carroll at the murder scene at all. They would argue the prosecution needed a witness for its case, and the O'Connors were willing to provide one — if the price was right. Johnny O'Connor, then, was nothing more than a testimony-for-hire by Oliver Mowat's office and James Carroll had been made a scapegoat so that one family might prosper. Hugh MacMahon couldn't wait to get her on the stand.

Aemilius Irving began by asking Mary O'Connor about the valances. She replied that on the night of Mike Donnelly's wake the valances were indeed on the bed, but that she had removed the valances the next day for the funeral — just as Nora Donnelly had indicated. Satisfied that both women had provided sufficient evidence that Johnny O'Connor's vision from under the bed had not been obstructed, Irving announced he had no further questions for the witness. It was now Hugh MacMahon's opportunity to spring his trap.

He started off with some softball questions: How long had she been living in Lucan? Did she attend Michael Donnelly's wake? Did her daughter Bridget live with the Donnellys for a period of time? Did she and her husband host John Donnelly's wake? Mary O'Connor answered MacMahon's questions amiably. And then the lawyer abruptly changed direction.

> MacMAHON: "You were in Toronto a short time ago?"
> MARY O'CONNOR: "I was sir, an' what of it?"
> MacMAHON: "Did you go to see the Attorney-General?"
> MARY O'CONNOR: "To see who?"
> MacMAHON: "The Attorney-General. Did you see the Attorney-General?"
> MARY O'CONNOR: "No, sir, I did not see the Attorney-General."
> MacMAHON: "Who did you see?"

MARY O'CONNOR: "Who did I see?"

MACMAHON: "No nonsense, answer my question."

MARY O'CONNOR: "I can't tell who I saw and who I didn't see."

MACMAHON: "Now be careful."

MARY O'CONNOR: "What will I be careful for?"

MACMAHON: "Now, Mrs. O'Connor, I'll make you answer my question."

MARY O'CONNOR: "I'll not do anything to lose my soul for you or anyone."

Laughter now came from the press and the spectators.

MACMAHON: "Now, tell me where you went in Toronto."

MARY O'CONNOR: "I went to the office."

MACMAHON: "What office?"

MARY O'CONNOR: "Attorney-General's office."

MACMAHON: "What did you want there?"

MARY O'CONNOR: "I wanted to see what kind of place it was."

At this the spectators once again roared out with laughter. Justice Cameron banged his gavel and yelled out repeatedly for order to be restored to the court. Once order had been restored, MacMahon continued.

MACMAHON: "Your curiosity was excited as to the style and shape of the building. Did you go alone?"

MARY O'CONNOR: "I went alone."

MACMAHON: "What was your business in Toronto?"

MARY O'CONNOR: "To see my own friends."

MACMAHON: "Come, now, you must tell the jury
what you went to Toronto for."
MARY O'CONNOR: "I have nothing to tell the jury nor
anyone else."
MACMAHON: "So, you only went to see what kind of
an office the Attorney-General had?"
MARY O'CONNOR: "Maybe I did and maybe I didn't,
and I don't want to be questioned any longer."

Justice Cameron now intervened. Looking at Mary O'Connor, he declared condescendingly, "People in your position don't usually travel a great distance, and at considerable expense, merely to see an office in a city."

Mary O'Connor caught his meaning — perfectly. "Poor people, I suppose, can't go and see things as well as rich folks?" While her reply brought laughter from some quarters, others nodded at her distillation of the judge's comment. MacMahon proceeded with his cross-examination.

MACMAHON: "Then all you went to Toronto for was
to see the building. Did you see anyone there?"
MARY O'CONNOR: "Did I see anyone there?"
MACMAHON: "Yes! Did you see anyone there?"
MARY O'CONNOR: "I saw Mr. Scott."
MACMAHON: "Oh, you saw Mr. Scott, did you? Who
is he, pray?"
MARY O'CONNOR: "How would I know who he was?"
MACMAHON: "What did you want to see Mr. Scott for?"
MARY O'CONNOR: "What did I want to see Mr. Scott
for you say?"
MACMAHON: "Yes, what did you want to see Mr.
Scott for?"

MARY O'CONNOR: "I heard talk of him."

MACMAHON: "Who told you to go to Mr. Scott?"

MARY O'CONNOR: "How do I know?"

MACMAHON: "You want the jury to believe you don't know who told you to go to the office in Toronto?"

MARY O'CONNOR: "I don't want to be speaking to the jury or anyone else. What for do you be forcing a woman to answer agin' her will?"

MACMAHON: "You'll have to answer my question, Mrs. O'Connor; if you don't you'll be made to."

MARY O'CONNOR: "You may keep me here for a month, then!"

JUDGE CAMERON: "I'll commit you, Mrs. O'Connor, unless you answer the question."

MARY O'CONNOR: "You can send me to prison if ye like."

JUDGE CAMERON: "I will unless you answer the question."

MARY O'CONNOR: "Well, then, send me; it's nice work trying to get a woman to spake agin' her will."

MacMahon resumed his questioning.

MACMAHON: "What did you want to see Mr. Scott for?"

MARY O'CONNOR: "What for?"

MACMAHON: "Yes, what for?"

MARY O'CONNOR: "Because I wanted to get my way home on the [train] cars."

MACMAHON: "Nothing else?"

MARY O'CONNOR: "Nothing else."

MACMAHON: "You went all the way to Toronto, then, to get the price of your railway fare back. How long were you in Mr. Scott's office?"

MARY O'CONNOR: "How do I know how long I was?"

MacMAHON: "Were you one hour?"

MARY O'CONNOR: "How do I know?"

MacMAHON: "Were you half an hour?"

MARY O'CONNOR: "How can I tell?"

MacMAHON: "Were you a quarter of an hour?"

MARY O'CONNOR: "Maybe I was and maybe I wasn't."

MacMAHON: "Did you talk about the reward?"

MARY O'CONNOR: "I don't remember."

MacMAHON: "Who brought you a letter about a reward?"

MARY O'CONNOR: "I don't know who brought the letter; I never saw it."

MacMAHON: "Will you swear you never saw the letter?"

MARY O'CONNOR: "I can swear I don't know who wrote the letter."

MacMAHON: "What did you do with the letter?"

MARY O'CONNOR: "I didn't do anything to it, I suppose the children burnt it."

MacMAHON: "How long ago?"

MARY O'CONNOR: "A long time ago."

MacMAHON: "Did you tell Mr. Scott about the letter?"

MARY O'CONNOR: "I dunno whether I did or not."

MacMAHON: "Is that what you want the jury to understand, that you don't know whether you said anything or not about the letter?"

MARY O'CONNOR: "I don't think I said anything about the letter to him; I didn't say anything to Mr. Scott about the reward."

This went on for some time until Mary O'Connor finally admitted a portion of the content of the letter: "I heard the letter read. It said if I would let the boy go with these parties everything would be all right and settled."

> MACMAHON: "What do you mean by settled?"
> MARY O'CONNOR: "How do I know?"
> MACMAHON: "Where was the boy to go to?"
> MARY O'CONNOR: "How could I tell where he was to go to?"
> MACMAHON: "Who are the parties?"
> MARY O'CONNOR: "How can I tell who they are?"

Finally, Charles Hutchinson rose from his seat. "Lords, this is all a mystery to us about this letter, and I don't know what my learned friend is driving at."

"You'll find out soon enough," MacMahon snapped.

Mary O'Connor spoke up: "The letter said if he would go with the parties it would be all right. I could tell anything about what's in the letter."

> MACMAHON: "Did you tell Mr. Scott what was in the letter?"
> MARY O'CONNOR: "I think I told him. We got a letter that whoever took the boy away would get the reward."
> MACMAHON: "What did Mr. Scott say about the reward?"
> MARY O'CONNOR: "How can I tell what he said?"
> MACMAHON: "Did Scott say as to who would get the reward?"
> MARY O'CONNOR: "The man didn't say nothing."
> MACMAHON: "Didn't you tell Mr. Scott that your boy was entitled to the reward that the Government had offered?"

MARY O'CONNOR: "I can't answer that, Mr. MacMahon."

MACMAHON: "Well, you must answer it."

MARY O'CONNOR: "Well, I don't think I did."

MACMAHON: "What portion of the reward did you want?"

MARY O'CONNOR: "How do I know what I wanted?"

MACMAHON: "[W]hen you couldn't get the reward you were satisfied with getting your railway fare? How much did you ask him for?"

MARY O'CONNOR: "$5.60, to pay for my fare home."

MACMAHON: "Had you money enough with you to pay your fare back?"

MARY O'CONNOR: "I needn't be short; I had friends."

MACMAHON: "Answer me; had you sufficient?"

MARY O'CONNOR: "I hadn't sufficient."

MACMAHON: "Then I suppose you went in for blackmailing?"[71]

The defence's strategy had worked; it was now obvious to the jury that Mary O'Connor had been to Toronto for the sole purpose of trying to get money. That her testimony hurt the prosecution's case was not in doubt; whether or not they could recover from the damage remained to be seen.

The best the prosecution could hope for at this point was to discredit the alibis advanced by the defence. First, they targeted James Carroll's alibi. William and Mary Thompson had consistently claimed under oath, since their first appearance in court on February 26, 1880, that Carroll and his younger brother William had slept over at their house on the night of the murders. According to the Thompsons, they had slept that night with their bedroom door open — that was how both of them knew that neither of the Carrolls had left their house that evening; they would have heard or seen them walk past their open door. Moreover, the Thompsons claimed to have gone to bed late that evening — Mary Thompson claimed she had been ill that night. She went to bed shortly after her husband did, but got up at 11 p.m. For his part, William Thompson swore he went to bed before 10 p.m. but couldn't sleep right away. He remained awake, hearing the clock strike ten and eleven. He saw his wife get up and heard the clock strike twelve. He didn't sleep between ten and midnight at all. Carroll, therefore, could not have left without being heard, and, again, as their door was open, they would have seen him had he left the house.[72] The prosecution was allowed to call Police Chief Williams to the stand, and he stated that on February 7, he, together with Patrick Donnelly and reporter John Lambert Payne, had visited the Thompson home and interviewed the couple and he took notes of their replies. These notes stood in stark contrast to what the Thompsons had claimed under oath:

> I asked Mr. Thompson a few questions and I took down his answers. I have written down: "I went to bed about half past eight and got up about half past seven; [the] Carrolls went to bed upstairs before we did; they did not go out to my knowledge; could swear they did not; I did not hear them." I recollect asking them [the Thompsons] what time Carroll came there. He [William Thompson] said, "About eight o'clock." I asked if he went to bed almost immediately afterwards; he said, "Yes." That is all I took down at that time. I then called Mrs. Thompson in and he, [William] Thompson, went upstairs, . . . I had a talk with her, she said, "Carrolls went to bed before we did and did not get up till after we did. . . ."
>   I asked her if the door of her bedroom was shut: she said, "The door to my bedroom was shut but

I could hear if they went out." (I put that question
pointedly to her); I asked her if she slept soundly
that night, she said, "I slept very sound, always do
nights."[73]

To the jury's eyes, Chief Williams's testimony made it obvious
that the Thompsons were inconsistent on two key points: Mary
Thompson had stated that she was ill and up throughout the night
but had told the chief that she'd slept soundly through the night;
they had testified that their bedroom door had remained open all
night, but had told the chief that it had been closed all night. These
contradictions revealed that the Thompsons' ability to be aware
of who came and left their house on the night of the murders was,
perhaps, not as certain as they had claimed previously under oath.
While James Carroll's alibi was now revealed to be somewhat problematic, there were still other alibis that needed to be contested
by the prosecution. To this end, the Donnelly brothers had been
particularly helpful — if not always successful. William Donnelly
had ferreted out evidence that a farmer, John Doherty, had seen
several of the Vigilance Committee members heading down a
sideroad on the night of the murders.[74] He also found witnesses
who claimed that they knew how John Kennedy Jr. had disposed of
a gun that had been used in the killings. These witnesses had fled to
the Grey County Lumber camps,[75] but Donnelly had them brought
back.[76] Unfortunately for the prosecution, these witnesses were too
scared to come to court. Bob Donnelly had tracked a witness all
through the night in order to bring him back to testify.[77] Patrick
Donnelly had ridden over fifty miles in a sleigh to Grand Bend on
Lake Huron in order to locate a man named Robert Cutt and bring
him back to London.[78] Unlike the other witnesses the Donnellys
had been pursuing, Cutt was willing to appear on the witness
stand to refute Thomas Ryder's "card game" alibi. On the night
of the murders, Cutt said, he had stopped in at Thomas Ryder's

farmhouse to speak with Ryder, where he waited until 10:30 p.m. for the homeowner to show up — but he never did.[79]

While such testimony helped dismantle some of the prisoners' alibis, or at least cast doubt upon them, some of the prosecution's other attempts at this were prevented from getting off the ground by Justice Cameron. When the prosecution had learned that eighty-six-year-old farmer Patrick Nangle had witnessed his neighbour, James Toohey, returning to his farm on the morning of the murders wearing a woman's dress and sporting a black eye,[80] they recognized his was explosive testimony. It would call into serious doubt Toohey's claim of having "played cards" the night before at Thomas Ryder's house and lend considerable support to O'Connor's testimony that one of the men he saw that night was wearing a woman's dress. However, Justice Cameron ruled that the testimony was hearsay and, therefore, inadmissible. He was fine, however, with the defence bringing forth their witnesses to present hearsay evidence regarding the crimes that had allegedly been committed by the Donnellys. In the previous trial, Justice Armour had dismissed such statements outright as being irrelevant (the reader will recall his comment to the defence that "no number of their crimes, real or alleged, could justify the Donnelly homicides"). Not so with Justice Cameron, who permitted Committee member Martin Darcy to testify that, in his opinion, nearly all the crimes in the Biddulph area had been committed by the Donnellys,[81] thus lending support to the perceived need for a Vigilance Committee.

The evening before the verdict was to be rendered, the temperature in London had dropped to −24 degrees Fahrenheit. By 8:30 a.m., it had warmed to only −20 degrees Fahrenheit.[82] That didn't prevent the crowds from turning out. At 9:25 a.m., the doors to the Middlesex County Courthouse opened, and a steady stream of people entered to witness the finale of the trial. Henry Fysh, who had replaced Lamb as the guardian of the Middlesex County

Gaol,[83] accompanied by two large constables, led James Carroll back into court.

Both Justices Cameron and Osler arrived, and High Constable Groves proclaimed the court open. Judge Cameron rose and now delivered his charge to the jurors. He felt obliged to mention the prisoner could not be convicted if there was any doubt as to his guilt:

> Gentlemen of the Jury:
> In reviewing the evidence, if doubts arise in your
> minds, the law throws around the accused a shield
> of protection, in that the prisoner is at your hands
> entitled to the benefit of such doubt.[84]

He then stated the prosecution had raised some valid points:

> The Crown argues, and with a good deal of force,
> too, that if the boy went in for wholesale perjury, he
> would not only have identified Carroll but he would
> have said Carroll struck a blow or blows. Why
> should the boy invent the story of the handcuffs?
> Why should the boy say he saw the girl run across
> the kitchen and rush upstairs, that the men went
> upstairs, and that he did not see the girl with
> them? These are all arguments adduced for your
> consideration.[85]

But the defence, in his opinion, had scored some solid points of its own:

> Then you are asked whether you can rely on the
> statements of Fox for the purpose of discrediting
> young Johnny O'Connor by reason of statements

the latter made which were inconsistent with the
evidence here . . . What the boy said outside
the witness box is not evidence, but as a person
is supposed, when uninfluenced by improper
considerations, or by motives of interest, to speak
the truth. So, if Johnny O'Connor told deliberately
shortly after that horrible occurrence what had
occurred, and proclaimed then that he did not
know any of the parties, and afterwards came into
the witness-box and said he did know a particular
person, it might be very difficult to rely upon the
truth of his sworn statements.[86]

Justice Cameron went on to speak of the inconsistency of the prisoners' alibis, and the fact that the boy had not seen James Carroll murder anybody, but had primarily identified him by the sound of his voice:

It has been given in evidence that in answer to
questions put to him, he [Johnny O'Connor] stated
that he recognized one, and that one he said was
Carroll. He did not attach any Christian name to
that Carroll. It is said that there are a number of
Carrolls in that township, and that name might
have applied to any of them as well as the prisoner;
that it had no individual reference; and that it did
not point out the prisoner more than any other
Carroll. That is what the Whalens represent. They
state that the boy said that he recognized the
prisoner by his voice, not because he had seen him,
not because he knew him in any way, but by reason
of his voice . . .[87]

He further pointed out that the Thompsons were members of the same Committee as Carroll, and of the latter's ruthless persecution of the family through the courts. Finally, he announced: "You will now retire and deliberate on your verdict, and when you have arrived at the same, you will return to the Court again."[88]

At 11 a.m., the jury retired to arrive at their verdict. At one point during their deliberation, the jury foreman was approached by no less than six jurors who wanted to know if a guilty verdict automatically meant the death penalty for Carroll. They believed him to be guilty, but they were fearful that if Carroll hung, it would potentially result in the deaths of many others in the subsequent trials that would follow.[89] That was a lot of deaths that their guilty verdict would have set into motion. If, however, Carroll could be found guilty and only be sent to prison, then justice could be served without any more deaths coming to Middlesex County. The jury foreman told them that jail was not an option and that only capital punishment was on the table.[90]

The jury returned to the courtroom at 3:08 p.m., and after taking their seats, were asked amid the most breathless silence: "Gentlemen of the jury, have you agreed on your verdict?"

The foreman answered, "We have."

"How do you find the prisoner — guilty or not guilty?"

The jury foreman cleared his throat and announced:

"Not guilty!"[91]

JUSTICE DENIED

Pat Donnelly, long considered to be the most passive of the Donnelly brothers, would become the family's most aggressive advocate during the Feeheley matter. (By permission of Ray Fazakas, author of *The Donnelly Album* and *In Search of the Donnellys*)

J ennie Currie fainted and fell to the floor as soon as the verdict was announced.[1] Her brothers, Patrick and William, immediately moved to tend to her, while an enthusiastic round of applause swept through the courtroom from the prisoner's supporters.[2] The three Donnelly siblings had been awaiting the verdict while seated in the attorney's office within the Middlesex County courthouse. The brothers unsuccessfully tried to fight back tears as they attempted to console their sister. Back in the courtroom, a crowd of well-wishers rushed forth from the stands to shake James Carroll's hand.[3] The High Constable of the Court called repeatedly for order to be restored and it was — eventually.[4] The ordeal of the murders, the coroner's inquest, the preliminary hearing and the two trials had taken its toll upon the surviving members of the Donnelly family, but perhaps none more than Jennie, who had been earlier described by the press as "a fine-looking, intelligent woman"[5] but also with a "wan, pale appearance . . . not improved by the mourning which she wears."[6] The brothers were numb; they looked around for Bob Donnelly, but he was nowhere to be found.

Once order had been restored in the court, Aemilius Irving, speaking on behalf of the prosecution, rose from his seat and addressed the bench. He announced that with the acquittal of James Carroll, the prosecution did not intend to proceed with the indictments they held against the remaining five prisoners. The prisoners were then granted bail at $500 each, plus two sureties of $250 each, with the understanding they would have to appear should they ever be summoned again on the matter. The offering of bail made the acquittal official, which started another round of enthusiastic applause from Carroll's supporters. Once again, High Constable Groves called for order in the court.[7] Justice Cameron now called James Carroll to stand before him in the prisoner's dock, while he offered his final thoughts on the verdict:

> James Carroll, I am now in a position to inform you
> that after a lengthy and prolonged trial, that a jury
> of your own countrymen have concluded to return
> a verdict of "not guilty" in your favour, and you
> are now acquitted from the charge of the murder
> of Judith Donnelly — but not from the charge
> for which you may yet be placed on trial, for the
> murder of James Donnelly, Thomas Donnelly and
> Bridget Donnelly. The jury in your case have taken
> a most favourable view, and I hope a correct view
> has been taken by them. And I sincerely hope you

have not been guilty of the atrocious crime laid to your charge. There is one point, however, I must dwell on. You, James Carroll, are a member of the constabulary of your county, and you have in the discharge of your duties as constable exhibited the utmost asperity. In an especial manner it has been plainly shown that you were particularly anxious to prosecute the Donnellys, and if you have suffered a year's imprisonment you have yourself to blame for it. This, together with the continual dread and uncertainty hanging over you, for your life, may be regarded by you in some measure as a punishment for your dereliction of duty in the discharge of your duties as a constable. I trust you will leave the dock a better and a wiser man.[8]

Justice Cameron's statement about dread and uncertainty ever-after hanging over Carroll's head would certainly be true. Carroll's name henceforth was like a scarlet letter forever linking him to the Biddulph murders. (Indeed, 140 years later an online newspaper for the town of Golden, British Columbia, where Carroll later moved, would feature the headline "Carroll Was Respected in Golden Despite Being a Mass Murderer."[9]) For the moment, however, particularly among the Committee members and the supporters of the prisoners, James Carroll was a hero; he had survived the English court system and had come out unscathed, while in the process throwing a blanket of protection over a multitude of his Roman Catholic brethren in the township who had been part of the eradi-cation of the Donnellys. His acquittal may indeed have saved the lives of over forty people.[10]

The relief and joy of the anti-Donnelly forces were evidenced by the loud cheering, the shaking of hands and back-slapping that now occurred. Carroll and the other prisoners were pulled by their supporters toward the front door of the courthouse that led outside to freedom — and the chance to really celebrate the victory. News of the raucousness spread quickly; a newspaper in Guelph (some seventy-five miles away to the northeast) reported:

> The scenes of joy enacted last night in the several
> resorts frequented by the Biddulph people during the
> trial were very enlivening. Drinking, singing, dancing
> and boisterous conversation were heard continually
> over the results.[11]

After celebrating in the London taverns, the prisoners (save for John Purtell, who remained behind in London[12]) boarded the evening train to Clandeboye, and from there were ushered into sleighs and taken to Lucan, where the celebrations continued. They were greeted upon their arrival by seven sleigh-loads full of supporters and a standing crowd that was estimated to have exceeded two hundred people. A dance band was hired for a special victory celebration at the Central Hotel, where over five hundred people turned out.[13]

During this pandemonium the Donnellys had stayed behind in the courthouse, trying to make sense of what had just happened. Once Charles Hutchinson and the prosecution packed up their materials, they returned to Hutchinson's office and there attempted to console William, Patrick and Jennie. Years later, William Donnelly would recollect:

> I cannot lose sight of the words used by Mr. [Aemilius]
> Irving, Q.C., who was Crown Prosecutor at the trials.
> After Carroll and the rest of the prisoners were turned
> loose on the world again, my sister, Mrs. Currie, was
> sitting crying in Crown Attorney Hutchinson's office,
> when Mr. Irving said to her, "Do not cry, my dear

woman; there is a just God, who sees all and who will try the case without lawyers or jury, and He will give you ample satisfaction in the way of retribution before ten years passes."[14]

While Jennie and her two brothers took some measure of solace in the thought of divine intervention asserting itself at a point yet to be determined within the next decade, Bob Donnelly hadn't been present to get the message. There is no evidence from the press that he was in the courtroom when the verdict was read, nor that he wanted any part of being consoled by a pair of British barristers[15] who, in his eyes, had just bungled whatever justice the courts might have delivered for his late family members. Indeed, in the past year of arguing over procedure, evidence hunting, change-of-venue proposals and trying to coax testimony from reluctant witnesses, he believed that something rather important had been overlooked: the murder of five of his family members. Bob Donnelly had not forgotten this at any point in the past twelve months. He had gone along with his older brother's wishes to have the matter settled in the courts — and *this* had been the result. He had watched as the prisoners who had beaten his family members to death exited the courthouse and into a party atmosphere of euphoria among their supporters. And he watched as they paraded themselves along London's King Street toward the taverns. Every hotel tavern was packed with supporters of the prisoners — the City Arms, the Western, the City Hotel, among others. Even the jury members got caught up in the elation; they banded together to have their photograph taken at a local portrait studio. They wanted an enduring memento of their role and contribution to such a historic event.

The press from the larger cities, meanwhile, had been left as dumbfounded as the Donnellys. They immediately rushed to file their dispatches to their respective city newspapers. None were complimentary of the jury's verdict:

Toronto Mail: The acquittal of Carroll, with
the virtual abandonment by the Crown of the
prosecution against his fellow-prisoners, ends for
the present the most famous and most brutal case in
our criminal annals. That five persons should have
been barbarously put to death was bad enough in
all conscience; but this failure of justice is even more
deplorable. It simply means that with all our boasted
civilization, human life is not safe, and the law may
be defied with impunity in certain sections of Canada.
No more humiliating confession is possible. . . . That
a whole family may be butchered under circumstance
of the greatest atrocity, and that the arm of the law
cannot reach the murderers, are facts which will
forever disgrace the good name of this Province.[16]

Toronto *Globe*: The failure of justice in this case
has so far been most complete. In a thickly settled
neighbourhood three members of one family are
cruelly murdered in cold blood and their house is
burned over their dead bodies, within a very short
time afterwards, on the same night, a fourth is
shot dead a few miles off, in a still more thickly
settled spot; and yet it has been found impossible to
bring either of these crimes home to anyone to the
satisfaction of a jury. There is something terribly
wrong in such a state of affairs. . . . The crime
committed by the men who killed the Donnellys was
immeasurably greater and darker than anything ever
urged against the latter, and the failure to convict
anyone of committing so foul a deed will remain a
blot on our administration of justice. The acquittal
of Carroll by the jury will not entirely absolve him

in public opinion from complicity in the crime. Stronger evidence, both direct and circumstantial, has rarely been brought against any man who in the face of it escaped the gallows.[17]

Hamilton Times: How far local prejudices, or fear of future results, influenced the jury may never be ascertained. We cannot but think, after all has been said and done, that it would have been more satisfactory had the judges at first changed the venue of the trial, and thus removed jurymen from even a suspicion of being unduly influenced in any manner whatever. In view of what has transpired in Middlesex within the last twelve months, and with all due deference to their Lordships, we believe that such a course would have given the greatest satisfaction to the people at large.[18]

The Toronto *Globe* report cited above claimed in its copy that only four of the Donnellys had been murdered, when, of course, there had been five. It was an unfortunate oversight, as by focusing on the immediate members of the Donnelly family that were killed, they had ignored the death of perhaps the most innocent of all the victims — Bridget Donnelly — who had caused no one grief of any kind throughout her short tenure in Canada, and most certainly was undeserving of the fate she had received at the hands of the killers. Be that as it may, Biddulph's Catholic community was celebrating. To them, the arrest and trial of their fellow parishioners was never about the murder of a local family; it was a direct attack on their very faith. They celebrated their victory by attending a special High Mass that was held in the prisoners' honour later that same evening.[19]

Clearly there had been a serious disconnect between the press from the cities and a large portion of the local community. To the city press, the Donnelly brothers were almost one of their own:

> The published pictures of [William Donnelly] do not
> convey a good impression of him. His face is thin and
> pale, and his hair clusters in curls over his head,
> and intelligence beams from his keen eyes. A thin
> sandy moustache and a small goatee gives his face
> much the appearance of the faces seen in old cavalier
> pictures. His brother Pat is also a fine-looking man.
> They dress neatly, speak English properly, are men
> of deep penetration and sense, and are in strong
> contrast with other residents of the Roman Line, who
> are in the main unprepossessing and unlettered, and
> of the "Cracker" species. The advantage which the
> Donnellys possess over the others is that they had
> the benefits of a more liberal education and had seen
> more of the world than their fellows, and were
> therefore better informed generally. It is hard to
> believe, judging from the manners of the two surviving
> male members of the family, that they were the
> ruffians the evidence makes them out to be.[20]

By contrast, the city newsmen's assessment of the Biddulph townspeople resembled something out of a horror movie:

> When the Court opened all the Biddulphers were
> on hand — men who had their noses bitten out by
> the roots, men who had left some of their ears in the
> mouths of their antagonists, men who bore the scars
> and scratches of many a faction fight, clustered in

the corridors and damned the constables because they were not admitted.[21]

This disparity of opinion regarding the outcome of the trial and of the character of its participants explains much about the confusion that would attach itself to the Donnelly story for well over a century, with those from outside the district opining on the travesty of justice that had occurred in the matter, and those from within Lucan and the surrounding areas preferring not to discuss it at all. The press would soon have another story to file, however, when Bob Donnelly walked into the bar of the Western Hotel on the night of the acquittals.

The crowd within London's Western Hotel was boisterous. It was filled with supporters of the Vigilance Committee, members of the jury, and perhaps certain of those who had previously been charged with the murderers of the Donnelly family but who hadn't taken the train back to Clandeboye: men such as James Maher Sr., James Maher Jr., Grouchy Ryder, Patrick Ryder Jr., John Darcy, Michael Heenan, among others. They were now well into their cups and toasting one another on the legal success of James Carroll and his team of defence lawyers. To those rejoicing within this hotel tavern, the legal decision was a vindication of the Vigilance Committee, and the night was theirs. Their jubilation was loud and raucous. Bob Donnelly had been stewing about the verdict for several hours, and had finally decided that if he couldn't receive satisfaction from the courts, he would obtain it on his own. Tracking the sound of the merrymaking to its source, he slammed open the door to the Western Hotel and walked in. Donnelly was by himself, yet all activity in the tavern suddenly stopped and the room became silent. This was the man who had beaten Constable Rhody Kennedy down with a pistol on Lucan's main street, and who had served two years in

Kingston Penitentiary for shooting at Constable Samuel Everett. His presence in this particular bar on this particular evening was unsettling. People who had gathered by the countertop of the bar now cleared way and gave him space. He walked to the front of the tavern and turned to look out upon the faces within the room. Many had been his neighbours when he was growing up on the Roman Line. But there was nothing neighbourly in the way he was staring at them right now. The youngest surviving son of James and Johannah Donnelly finally spoke: "I want all you *murderers* to come and have something."[22]

The men in the crowd suddenly found something else to occupy their attention — the floor, their drinks, the artwork on the walls. None dared to make eye contact. Observing the level of discomfort he had brought to the room gave Bob Donnelly some measure of satisfaction. To his mind, this was *not* a time for celebration. When it became obvious that there were no heroes to be found within the Western Hotel on this evening, Donnelly gave the barroom a final scan, and then turned, pushed open the door and walked out into the night. It has not been reported if the merriment resumed upon his departure that evening. Evidently Donnelly would repeat his offer at the City Hotel, where certain prisoners and their supporters had gone to celebrate Carroll's victory. When a London man stepped forth to calm Donnelly and to diffuse the situation, it was reported that he ended up being scared "pretty badly" before Bob Donnelly left the premises.[23]

The national drama having now played itself out, those involved in the proceedings of the past year attempted to get on with their lives. The prosecutors and defence attorneys picked up cases of a considerably lower profile; the magistrates made rulings on other cases brought before them; the farmers returned to their fields. As for the Donnellys, Jennie returned to her home in the Glencoe area where she and her husband James focused their attention on raising their three children. Patrick Donnelly and his wife also relocated to Glencoe for the time being, while William and Bob and their spouses opted to remain in Lucan.[24]

James Carroll now found himself a free man; he also found himself out of a job. Both he and Samuel Hodgins (who had loaned Carroll a pair of his handcuffs prior to the Donnelly murders) were unceremoniously dismissed from their constabulary duties. At an adjourned Sessions of the Peace held on February 5, 1881, Judge Elliot passed the following order:

> In consequence of the facts which were elicited during the late trial of James Carroll for murder, he and Samuel Hodgins of Granton are both dismissed from the constabulary of County of Middlesex. Both these men by their conduct have shown their disinclination to aid in the discovery of crime and their consequent unfitness for the position of Constable.
>
> By order at the adjourned Sessions,
> — William Elliot, Chairman[25]

The Vigilance Committee, meanwhile, began to actively take steps to raise money to cover the legal costs that the prisoners had incurred during the trials. They held a public meeting at the Cedar Swamp Schoolhouse to announce they were starting a fund-raising campaign.[26] Committee members were sent out to canvass the townships of Lucan, Granton, Usborne, Exeter, McGillivray, London and Blanshard, in addition to all the concession roads within Biddulph to search out financial contributions. Grouchy Ryder was assigned to collect whatever funds he could from the businesspeople in London, and made a point of dropping in at the office of Crown attorney Charles Hutchinson to see if he would care to contribute to the prisoners' cause. According to Hutchinson: "I told him I would not like to say what I thought about it, and so he gave it up at last, apparently much surprised that I would not 'help the poor boys who had suffered so much and had been put to so much expense.'"[27] Hutchinson had also been surprised one afternoon prior to this when James Carroll had shown up unannounced at his office. When Hutchinson asked him his business there, Carroll submitted a bill for his constabulary service for his arrest of Johannah Donnelly in St. Thomas in January 1880. Hutchinson lamented in a letter to Aemilius Irving that the ex-constable would probably be paid.[28]

William and Bob Donnelly started work on constructing a new house on their parents' property,[29] and completed the project in the spring of 1881. During his trips to Lucan to obtain materials for the construction, Bob Donnelly had always kept his eyes peeled for any of the men who had been accused of his family's murder — and for James Carroll specifically. The murders, and particularly the thought of his younger brother having been put in handcuffs by Carroll, who then looked on passively as the young man was beaten to death, had fuelled a fire of rage within Bob Donnelly so deep that no passage of time would ever see it extinguished. And then, in mid-March, he spotted Carroll walking along a sidewalk in Lucan. Donnelly stopped what he was doing and directly made his way to where Carroll was standing. Having no desire to talk to the ex-constable, he instead punched him square in the face, sending the man who had formerly boasted that he "could lick all the Donnellys" sprawling to the ground.[30] Carroll had no interest in attempting to fight Bob Donnelly, however, and instead rushed to have Donnelly charged with assault. The case was heard in magistrate's court on March 14, 1881, where it was promptly dismissed.[31] But Bob Donnelly wasn't through with Carroll just yet. Later that same month he again spotted Carroll in Lucan and made it a point to drive his shoulder hard into Carroll's chest, which again knocked the ex-constable from the sidewalk and into the street. Donnelly then stopped and glared at the Vigilance Committee member, hoping that this time Carroll would retaliate.[32] Carroll, again, ignored the challenge.

Sometime after this occurred, a reporter from the *London Advertiser* spoke to Carroll about the incident. True to form, the ex-constable bragged that he "put up with it all, and only laughed at him."[33] He also related additional details of the incident. According to Carroll, in the moments prior to the assault he had been walking along the sidewalk toward the Queen's Hotel when he spotted Bob Donnelly standing in the doorway:

> Bob Donnelly was standing at the door, and when
> I passed by he said to the crowd, "You can tell by
> that man's shoulders that he is a murderer." I took
> no notice of what he said, but passed on. About five
> minutes afterward the jostling occurred. His object
> was to raise a fight. I was standing on the sidewalk
> opposite [Bernard] Stanley's store, when Bob
> Donnelly came walking along and knocked against
> me. I paid no attention to him. About five minutes
> after he came along again [and] hustled still harder
> against me.[34]

While Carroll told the reporter that he had laughed it off, in reality he was concerned. And with good reason; Bob Donnelly was dangerous and he was, in the case of James Carroll at least, rather strongly motivated. Rather than laughing, Carroll instead took his concern directly to his ally, the magistrate William Stanley, and sought to have Bob Donnelly arrested. As Carroll would admit: "I thought it advisable to put a stop to such conduct and applied to Squire Stanley for a warrant. The Squire said he had no blank forms, but to come on Monday following and he would proceed.

During the interval my friends advised me to let the matter drop for this time."[35] Nothing more ever came of the incident.

I n April 1881 William Donnelly had almost died. He had been in the grip of the same condition that had claimed the life of his older brother Jim — inflammation of the lungs.[36] Unlike his late brother, however, William pulled through, although the condition would periodically return to him throughout the remainder of his life. He had always loved horses and was now focused on his business of breeding them, for which, by all accounts, he had something of a knack.[37] Nevertheless, he had not given up the idea of having the killers of his family punished in the courts. He had met a newcomer to Lucan, Francis West, whom Donnelly believed might be a man who could gather intel for him about the murders. After all, none of the local people knew West, and so they had no reason to be guarded around him. William Donnelly wrote to Charles Hutchinson to see if the Crown would be willing to pay West to snoop around on its behalf.[38] After all, while James Carroll might have been acquitted, the murder case could be reopened at any time if sufficient evidence could be brought forth to warrant it. Hutchinson was dubious that West would be able to turn up anything new, however, writing back that they had had little success with any of the detectives they had hired to ferret out meaningful evidence in the past.[39] Nevertheless, Hutchinson forwarded William's letter on to John Scott at the attorney general's office to see if the province might want to advance funds for the proposed surveillance.[40] His request was promptly denied.[41]

The one former prisoner William Donnelly had most wanted to have shadowed was John Purtell. The general consensus regarding Purtell was that he was weak, and that he might be tempted to roll over on certain of the other prisoners in return for the reward money the government had offered. Indeed, Purtell had recently been overheard saying as much during a drinking binge in one of the London hotels.[42] What gave William Donnelly optimism in this pursuit was the fact that Purtell had earlier quarrelled with James Carroll when the pair had been incarcerated in the Middlesex County Gaol. When this had been brought to the attention of the prosecution, Charles Hutchinson had approached Purtell about confessing what he knew in exchange for a lesser sentence, but the prisoner had declined the offer. For while Purtell had no use for James Carroll, he did not want to jeopardize the lives of the other prisoners.[43] However, now that Purtell had been released, and given what he had been saying recently in the London taverns, William Donnelly thought that he might be worth approaching again. He was surprised by the lack of enthusiasm coming from Oliver Mowat's office, writing to Hutchinson, "It seems strange that the Attorney-General will not adopt some means of finding out all about the murder as I am confident he could if he chose."[44] Despite the setback, William Donnelly would not let the matter rest; he resolved to find new evidence upon which to base a new trial.[45] He intended to keep his ear to the tracks in the hope that something might break his way. And then, surprisingly, something did.

While Francis West may not have been hired by the Crown to spy on John Purtell, he nevertheless had remained in Lucan — and happened to observe something that proved to be of significant interest to both William Donnelly and Charles Hutchinson. He had witnessed a very public dispute between William Feeheley and James Carroll on the main street of Lucan. While Feeheley had never been a suspect in the murders, there were some — including Patrick Donnelly — who believed that he knew far more about the killings than he had been letting on.[46] As West watched, the dispute between Carroll and Feeheley escalated to the point where Feeheley finally challenged the ex-constable to a fight. Carroll, as was his wont, refused. This caused William Feeheley to scream out that Carroll was a murderer and that he could prove it.[47]

This bit of news certainly piqued William Donnelly's interest when it was subsequently brought to his attention. Donnelly told Francis West to inform Charles Hutchinson of the incident. He also decided that someone now needed to work on William Feeheley in order to find out exactly what he knew about the murders. He had hoped that West might do this, but as he couldn't interest the Crown in hiring him, he knew that, once again, it would be up to the Donnelly brothers to gather whatever evidence there was — and then bring it to Hutchinson's attention. William himself was not a suitable candidate for the job, for if William Feeheley was, in fact, a member of the Vigilance Committee, he wouldn't say a word to William Donnelly about what he knew. As a London newspaper would report:

> In addition to hating William Donnelly, the Vigilants of Biddulph fear him. They cannot hide it. He has always been known to them as a shrewd, cunning man, who could govern his temper and keep his tongue quiet when he liked. They call him "the lawyer." His determination, too, was as marked as his cunning, and his fearless movements among them when danger seemed greatest, has given them an instinctive dread of him.[48]

Such was William's reputation among the Committee members. Bob Donnelly was also out of the question for being a candidate to gain the Feeheleys' confidence — if he learned they were involved in the murder of his parents, he would undoubtedly take matters directly into his own hands. That left Patrick Donnelly, who, upon receiving the news, hastened back to Lucan from his home in Thorold and immediately sought out the Feeheley brothers. Having known the two brothers for years, Patrick borrowed a page out of his brother Bob's playbook and confronted both William and James Feeheley directly about what they knew of the murders:

> I says, "Bill, I always thought you knew something about it!" He asked me "for God's sake" to forgive him, as he was led into it by others. [James] said he went there that night to see who was in the house. He said he did not think they were going to murder them, if he did he would not have done it.[49]

Upon pressing William Feeheley further, Patrick Donnelly learned more about the night of the murders and of the Vigilance Committee:

> William Feeheley told me in presence of James [Hogan] that James Toohey, Pat Quigley and James Maher were the three men that carried Tom Donnelly into the house after he was killed. Also told me that Pat Breen made all the bylaws and Dan Keenan kept the books. That there was an oath in connection with the society, and that he knew all about it as he had taken the oath himself. He said it was Pat Quigley's spade Tom's head was split with after he was carried into the house. . . . He told me Toohey came to him last summer and offered him more money than would buy our farm if he, Feeheley, would swear there was no oath in the society.[50]

No sooner had William Feeheley said his piece about the murders than his brother, James Feeheley, started talking. The county constable Thomas Shoebottom reported that while giving James Feeheley a ride into town in his buggy one day that "I was speaking to James Feeheley about the Donnelly murder. He said that Carroll should have been smart enough not to have any part in it as he was sure to be blamed for it. But he said Carroll was there [at the murders] as sure as you and I is riding in this buggy."[51]

John H. McConnell, a clerk of the municipality of the village of Lucan, recollected that

> [h]e [James Feeheley] told me then he was sent
> by the Vigilance Committee that night to see who
> was in Donnelly's house, and when he went out
> to the road after leaving the house, he met James
> Carroll and James Maher and some others whose
> names I don't remember, and he told them who
> was in the house. I asked him if he told them
> Johnny O'Connor was there — he said he didn't;
> he thought it was John Donnelly who was in bed
> with the father. He said the Vigilants sent him on
> to Whalen's Corners, to see who went in or out of
> Will Donnelly's house.[52]

Robert Keefe Sr. then came forward and stated that James Feeheley had told him some of the names of the thirty-one men he had witnessed moving in on the Donnelly house on the night of the murders.[53]

The Feeheleys' statements were certainly intriguing, and speculation as to whether or not they would be willing to repeat them under oath would fill the columns of the local newspapers over the months that followed. On the surface, their tale was certainly a plausible one and was supported by much of the circumstantial evidence. That James Feeheley had visited the Donnellys at their home shortly before the murders was undeniable, as both Johnny O'Connor and James Feeheley had testified to this during the trials. And it certainly was not a stretch to believe that Feeheley had been instructed to go to the Donnelly household beforehand by James Carroll, who held an arrest warrant over his head.

However, the Feeheley history also shows that the brothers were master pragmatists. Perhaps as a result of their troubled family background, they had grown to cultivate a talent for securing the protection and largesse of others. They had certainly demonstrated they were willing to play whatever role was required of them in order to facilitate getting what they wanted. They had, for example, been willing to be brought into the Donnelly family home over the years to be fed and cared for by Johannah Donnelly whenever their own home was no longer a welcoming place to be. They then signed on to Father Connolly's anti-crime society (they had both signed the copybook at the church) when the majority of their neighbours did (despite the fact that the Donnellys did not). And, once the Donnellys lost power in the community, William Feeheley was said to have joined the Vigilance Committee, whose sole purpose was to destroy the only family that had ever been kind enough to take in him and his brother.[54] If James Feeheley had, indeed, agreed to spy on the Donnellys on the evening of the murders, it followed that he would have done so because he feared James Carroll would have had him arrested and sent to jail if he didn't oblige the request. Again, the expediency of the moment ruled the day.

That the Feeheleys had no loyalty to anyone but themselves is evidenced by the fact their attitude toward the Donnelly family would change depending on with whom they were speaking. Consider the following: Francis West had pretended to not know anything about the Donnellys other than rumours. To the Feeheley brothers, then, he was not pro-Donnelly. Consequently, when West mentioned to William Feeheley that he had heard "the Donnellys are a hard lot," William Feeheley had replied, "Yes but there is not many of them left — God damn them!" Similarly, when West was alone with James Feeheley one night, the latter had told him, "One of the Donnellys nearly beat me dead once — but I have had good satisfaction since. . . . I helped put one son of a bitch out of the way, and know who finished four more."[55] The "one son of a bitch" that James Feeheley was referring to had to be Tom Donnelly (for reasons to follow). However, when he spoke with Patrick Donnelly, James Feeheley sang a different tune:

- "There was only one thing I ever done I was sorry for. That was selling Tom, the best friend I ever had [to the Vigilance Committee]."[56]
- "I know nothing about the murder. There is not any person in the world that I would sooner see or liked than your brother Tom."[57]
- "I did not think they would murder them. If I did I would not have done it."[58]
- "Pat, for God's sake forgive me, as I was led into it by others."[59]

In short, the Feeheleys told people what they wanted to hear in order to get what they wanted. Consequently, once word reached the Donnellys that the Feeheley brothers had accused Carroll of being a murderer, the Feeheleys sought to calm the waters between them and the Donnelly survivors by offering the Donnellys the hope of a new trial with the understanding that the Feeheleys were "led into it by others" and that they had no idea the mob was going to murder the Donnelly family members. That way, they might escape any retribution from the Donnellys and perhaps avoid being prosecuted for their role of being accessories to the murders.

Problems arose, however, when the people with whom the Feeheleys had shared their story asked the brothers to repeat their claims in court. Suddenly the Feeheleys came up with multiple excuses as to why they couldn't testify just yet:

- It wasn't safe to testify while their father was alive.[60]
- They would testify, but didn't want to be kept in Middlesex County over the fall.[61]
- They couldn't testify while their parents were still in the country.[62]
- They would testify, but only once they were safely out of the country.[63]
- They would tell all they knew about the murders right now if they could be offered protection.[64]

But when protection from a constable was offered, they declined the offer and boarded a train bound for Michigan.[65]

Charles Hutchinson had received reports, not only from the Donnellys but from others in the community, about what the Feeheleys were now saying about James Carroll and the Committee members who had taken part in the murders. Hutchinson believed that, with the Feeheleys' assistance, he could now make a much stronger case against James Carroll and other members of the Vigilance Committee for their role in the killing of the Donnellys. The fact that the Feeheleys had fled to Michigan was not a deterrent. Together with Patrick Donnelly and the detective H.R. Schram, Hutchinson boarded a train to Saginaw, Michigan. There the three men sat down with the Feeheley brothers for a parlay. Hutchinson offered them full immunity from prosecution if they would return with him and testify against the men they had seen kill the Donnellys. However, the Feeheleys now had changed their tune; they denied all knowledge of the crime and refused to return to Biddulph.[66]

Patrick Donnelly had grown tired of the brothers' doublespeak. In his last encounter with the Feeheley brothers he had dismissed them with the statement "If the Feeheleys were murdered and I to know about it, I would get up and tell. . . . If you will not have those men arrested and you know all about it, I look upon you as being as big a murderer as any one of the party."[67]

Patrick's parting words evidently brought no more than a shrug from the Feeheley brothers.

The real motivation for the Feeheleys, however, had little to do with conscience and everything to do with money. After all, if what they were saying was true, then they had been fine with Carroll and his group (and the horrendous crime of which both parties were guilty) for the past year. They were fine with the murder of a family who had provided for them over the years; they were fine to watch those murders occur from a front-row seat directly across the road at John Whalen's place. They were fine with it to the point they were willing to go through a coroner's inquest, a preliminary hearing and no fewer than two trials and still keep their mouths shut about what they knew. However, as soon as they believed there was money at risk, they suddenly developed a strong sense of moral propriety.

The backstory to their new-found sense of conscience occurred shortly after their father, Michael Feeheley, passed away. He had died less than a week after the second trial ended.[68] When Michael Feeheley died, the Donnelly brothers, among others, were among the Feeheley family's many creditors. Michael Feeheley's debts were so great, in fact, that there was no way for his widow or their sons to get out from under them.[69] Consequently, the family farm had to be put up for auction. It would be acquired by Vigilance Committee member Michael Carroll. As a gesture of goodwill toward the bereaved family he offered Michael Feeheley's widow Bridget the sum of $500. However, when James Carroll (no relation) found out about this, he advised his uncle, James Maher (who also was owed money from the Feeheley estate), to move to block the goodwill payment that Michael Carroll had pledged to the widow Feeheley. It was upon learning that the $500 that had been offered to the family was now off the table that the Feeheley brothers once again switched allegiances — this time from the Vigilance Committee to their mother. That's when they had started making threats that they would expose James Carroll and other members of the Committee unless they received the money that had been promised them.

As tensions continued to rise between the Feeheleys and the Committee members, who should step forth to calm the waters but Father John Connolly. The priest gave Bridget Feeheley $350 out of his own pocket to defuse the situation. At this point, the Committee overruled James Carroll's objections, and paid the widow $500.[70] The widow then repaid the priest the $350 he had given her, and the Feeheleys left the country.

Charles Hutchinson was excited about the developments, but he also knew that he had to proceed cautiously. As Oliver Mowat was away, Hutchinson spoke with the acting attorney general, Adam Crooks, about his desire to retry James Carroll for the murder of the Donnellys, but this time using the testimony of the Feeheley brothers to win a conviction: "James Feeheley's evidence in the event of another trial would carry sufficient weight to turn the score in favour of a conviction. From what I have heard I don't think Carroll's nerve would stand another trial."[71]

To his surprise, the acting attorney general supported the proposition:

> Dear Sir,
> I now beg to confirm the instructions given you by me yesterday to proceed upon the information obtained by you from the several parties whose statements were considered by me in conjunction with Mr. Magee. This will involve the immediate arrest of the several parties who according to James and William Feeheley took part in these murders.

You will please proceed to the State of Michigan
with such assistance as you may think necessary
for the purpose of arresting the two Feeheleys and
bringing them to London. Please consult with Mr.
Magee as Counsel at each stage of the proceeding
and take advantage of his personal assistance as
Counsel whenever you think it desirable. Be good
enough to send me copies of the several statements
for placing on file here.

I am
Yours truly,
Adam Crooks,
Attorney General, pro tempore[72]

Things had suddenly taken a dramatic turn. Both the Crown
and the surviving Donnellys felt a sense of optimism and confidence
for the first time since the trials began. But there was also danger
lurking beneath the excitement: there was evidence that would
come out when the Feeheleys went to trial that Father Connolly
had paid the Widow Feeheley what appeared to be hush money —
and this represented a significant problem to Oliver Mowat's office.
The priest's having done so now brought the Catholic Church
directly into the matter. Hutchinson, together with Crooks, quickly
arranged a meeting with the bishop of the London diocese to discuss
the problem and how the case could be reopened without bringing
any taint to the church.[73] Evidently a solution was worked out and
Hutchinson felt comfortable proceeding with his case.

The only problem that now remained was how to get the
Feeheleys back to Canada to testify. Since the brothers had refused
Hutchinson's offer of immunity in exchange for their testimony,[74]
the Crown attorney now understood the brothers would have

to be forced to return to Canada if there was to be any chance of them giving up their evidence. To this end, Hutchinson had Patrick Donnelly charge both the Feeheley brothers with abetting the murder of Tom Donnelly. Patrick Donnelly and the Crown attorney then travelled to Saginaw, Michigan, to file extradition papers. Hutchinson arranged for Johnny O'Connor and his mother to come to Detroit for the hearing as well, in addition to Constable Thomas Shoebottom and John McConnell.[75] The extradition commissioner was suitably impressed with the testimony these people provided and ruled that the Feeheleys were to be extradited to stand trial in London.[76]

But the Feeheleys dug in; they secured the services of Hugh MacMahon, one of the defence lawyers who had represented James Carroll and the prisoners during their two trials. Despite MacMahon's efforts, however, at the Fall Assizes, the magistrate found true bills against the Feeheleys. MacMahon then pushed to have his clients tried at the same Assizes right away to deny the prosecution the opportunity to fully prepare its case. Hutchinson wanted to put the trial over to the Spring Assizes, believing that he might actually be able to secure a change of venue[77] this time around, and that the Feeheleys might become more cooperative after a few months in jail. The magistrate ruled in Hutchinson's favour; the trial would take place at the Spring Assizes of 1882.

Hutchinson's enthusiasm for the case, and for his strategy of keeping the Feeheleys in jail in the hopes they would soften, were buoyed after he had sent Donnelly friends Robert Keefe Sr. and James Keefe Sr. into the cells to try to convince the Feeheleys to assist with the prosecution. If they cooperated, they could free themselves and bring the guilty parties to justice. The Keefes reported back that James Feeheley had told them he was waiting to see if they would be bailed. If not, then the brothers would definitely tell all they knew about the murders.[78] But Hutchinson had forgotten that the entire Donnelly matter was nothing but a headache to his superior, Oliver Mowat, who, upon returning to Toronto and learning of Hutchinson's desire to retry the Donnelly case, saw the Feeheley matter as an unnecessary expense to his office and a political nightmare that he had no intention of rehashing. And so, while Hutchinson planned his prosecution strategy, Oliver Mowat went behind his Crown attorney's back and ordered the prisoners to be released on bail with the understanding they would show up at the Spring Assizes for their trial. Their bail would eventually be covered by members of the Vigilance Committee,[79] and there was no chance that the Feeheleys would ever return for the trial. The premier had effectively ended the matter. Hutchinson was understandably furious about what Mowat had done and wrote to his former co-counsel Aemilius Irving:

> This bail matter has given me more annoyance than
> I can give you an idea of. I would like to know
> whether Mr. Mowat consulted you before consenting.
> I can hardly think that he did, and yet it would seem
> such a want of courtesy, apart from every other
> consideration, to consent without speaking to us, that
> if it is so, I can only suppose that he was so tired of
> the Donnelly case as to seize the first opportunity of
> getting rid of it forever.[80]

And thus was closed the book on the Donnelly murder trials.

THE DONNELLYS' LAST STAND

William Donnelly, the legendary brains and wit of the Donnelly family.
(By permission of Ray Fazakas, author of *The Donnelly Album*
and *In Search of the Donnellys*)

Francis Morrison West had $700 in his pocket when he had first set foot in Lucan.[1] But that was twelve months ago. He hadn't a penny left. With the information he had helped to collect on the Feeheley brothers, and their recent extradition back to London to stand trial, it had looked for a time like he might be line to receive the $4,000 government reward for information that would lead to the conviction of one or more of the Donnelly murderers. But Oliver Mowat's decision to grant bail to the Feeheleys had effectively put an end to both the trial and any chance of his collecting on the reward.

He had arrived from the United States, where he had lived in various places, such as Preston and River Falls, Wisconsin; Crookston, Minnesota; Grand Forks, North Dakota; and St. Louis, Missouri.[2] He had no fixed occupation, having tried his hand at various enterprises, including helping out as a farm hand, working in a slaughterhouse, bookkeeping and owning a meat store. He was also a piano player of some note.[3] After the collapse of his meat business in Preston, West had headed to Minnesota to visit a friend, Thomas Long. It was there he first learned of the Donnelly murders that had occurred the better part of a thousand miles away on the Roman Line and, at twenty-one years of age and with money in his pocket, he thought he would like to take a trip to Canada to learn more about the matter. He headed southeast, entering Canada through the Michigan border and eventually making his way to Lucan.[4] He would meet some of the surviving Donnellys, by his recollection, either in December 1880 or January 1881,[5] while living out of the Queen's Hotel in Lucan and advertising his services as a piano teacher. He had a few clients ("enough to pay my board," he said[6]), but in the meantime he began to loiter, playing billiards and drinking heavily.[7] His February conversation with William Donnelly had opened his eyes to a potential new line of work: that of private detective. This, and the government's $4,000 reward for information obtained that would lead to the conviction of the guilty party that had murdered the Donnellys, held considerable appeal.[8]

Around the time that the attorney general's office had nixed the plan of hiring him as an investigator, however, West had run out of money. Soon thereafter, he took to stealing. In April, he had stolen two rifles from the Lucan Armory[9] and had attempted to sell them to an old friend of Tom Donnelly's, John Kent.[10] Then West moved on to pilfering livestock — first stealing two hens,[11] then a cow.[12] In late fall, he accepted a less risky job helping John Kent with the threshing at the old Donnelly property. Kent had rented the fifty-acre farm from the Donnelly brothers and help was always needed at threshing time. The job had paid thirty-five dollars,[13] but that wasn't enough. Soon West had pawned his watch, a coat and a pair of boots.[14] By this time he had developed a reputation in certain circles for a willingness to engage in criminal activity and was soon approached and offered a sum of money to burn down a barn belonging to a man named Thomas Hall, who owned the town sawmill.[15]

The barn fell under the torch on Saturday, October 1, 1881. Eight days later, on the evening of Sunday, October 9, 1881, another fire was attempted in Lucan, but this time the arsonists were set upon by guards during the commission of the act. The target of the attempted arson was the Stanley, Dight & Co. grist mill in Lucan. One man, later identified as Simon Howe, escaped from the guards by running away into the woods; the other man was apprehended. The man who was captured was Francis Morrison West. However, in a bizarre turn of events, by the morning five people had been arrested for the crime, and West, who had been captured at the scene, was no longer a suspect. A local newspaper reported the story:

> LUCAN, Oct. 9. — Parties were captured in the
> act of firing Stanley, Dight & Co's mills at eleven
> o'clock to-night. They succeeded in boring four
> holes through one side of the building and pouring
> coal oil in the hole, and were in the act of applying a
> match when they were pounced upon by a constable
> and posse who were lying in wait for them. One of
> the parties escaped to the woods, but Bill Donnelly,
> Bob Donnelly, Cornelius Carty, his son Patrick, and
> John Kent have been arrested, and are now safe in
> the lock-up.[16]

William Donnelly had been at his home when he was arrested, while Bob had been pinched while returning from a visit with his sister Jennie, who was going to accompany him back to Glencoe the next morning.[17] The reporters rushed to William for a comment, and received the reply that "the whole affair's a vile conspiracy to get us into jail and difficulty. But it's nothing new."[18]

Suddenly, the Donnelly brothers were back in the news. By Monday morning the Lucan streets were filled with people talking about the latest Donnelly story; the hotels were filled, men talked among themselves about the incident, women warned their children of the evil of arson, and the young people tried to sneak a peek at the prisoners detained within the Lucan jail.[19] Reporters examined the scene of the would-be crime and filed their dispatches. One of the first townspeople to step forward and speak to the press was Bernard Stanley, co-owner of the mill, who stated that the prosecution's case was a strong one and that the evidence against the prisoners was solid.[20]

Spotted among the people who had swarmed into Lucan that morning were many members of the Vigilance Committee — Grouchy Ryder and his brother Thomas, Patrick Breen, James Toohey and James Carroll — all had come into town to rejoice in the news.[21] The Donnellys were in deep trouble now, and the Committee members wanted a front-row seat to watch their downfall. Bernard Stanley brought Vigilance Committee member Thomas Ryder in to see the Donnelly brothers as they sat within the animal pound/fire department/Lucan jail. They arrived under the pretense of commiserating with the Donnellys, but it was just to get a look and gloat. William Donnelly wrote a letter to the local newspaper about the visit, in which he sarcastically referred to the town jail as "the Lucan Boarding House" and to Lucan as "this village of Saints": "In about an hour and a half after our arrest Tom Ryder (whom Johnny O'Connor saw at the murder of our family) came into the lock-up with Barney

Stanley, and told us he was sorry for our trouble. It seems strange to me that he was not at home playing cards."[22]

Back outside, Grouchy Ryder decided to impress his friends from the Committee who had gathered around him in front of the Central Hotel by accosting William's wife, Nora Donnelly, as she walked by on her way to visit her husband.

"How are you, Mrs. Donnelly?" he inquired.

"Pretty well, thanks," she replied. And then, noting the satisfaction on Ryder's face, she mentioned, "You seem to be happy."

"Yes, I'm well. How's Mr. Donnelly?"

"He's all right."

"Yes. He's where he ought to have been long ago."[23]

The preliminary hearing commenced within the small courtroom above the Lucan jail at 3:45 p.m. that same Monday. The magistrates presiding were William Stanley, Patrick McIlhargey and James McCosh, while Edmund Meredith represented the defence, and W.P.R. Street of Street & Becher (London) handled the prosecution. Charles Hutchinson, as the Crown attorney, sat at the prosecution table to oversee the case on behalf of the province.

Right away, John Kent's charges were dropped owing to a lack of evidence.[24] Magistrate William Stanley then announced that the charges against the remaining parties had been amended, but when members of the press asked to see a copy of the amended charges, he refused to reveal it.[25] Later in the day the press obtained a copy and right away eyed the amended charges with suspicion:

> Persons who at the first rumour held skeptical views
> as to the likelihood of the Donnelly boys being
> implicated in any attempt at incendiarism, where
> particularly one that presents so many features of

bungling and clumsiness, became confirmed in their
opinions on perusing the plain statements of the
case as detailed in the morning *Advertiser*. No end
of comment was made concerning the fact of the
leading spirit in the prosecution apparently changing
the basis of attack from a direct charge of attempt at
arson to that of conspiracy.[26]

With the Donnellys now being charged with conspiracy to commit arson, the magistrates ruled that the hearing would be resumed on Thursday, October 13, 1881, at 10 o'clock in the morning. Francis West was then released and allowed to go on his own recognizance. Meredith requested that the prisoners also be bailed, but his request was denied. He then asked if his clients could be held in a different jail, owing to the filthy conditions of the Lucan lock-up. Again, his request was denied, but with the proviso that the prisoners could be watched in the upper level of the building during the day and only be returned to their cells below to sleep at night.[27]

By now, bits of the prosecution's evidence had leaked out. Evidently a pair of overalls, boots and a coat had been found in William Donnelly's barn that were believed to have belonged to Simon Howe, the man who had fled into the woods. Francis West, it was said, had been approached by William Donnelly while the former was working for John Kent on the old Donnelly property. William had allegedly instructed West to meet him at William's home later that evening and there William laid out his plan to burn down the mill and of West's role in the enterprise. His motive? "The Stanleys had sworn hard against him at the Carroll trial."[28]

This bit of news immediately raised the suspicion of Crown Attorney Charles Hutchinson, who recollected that in his experience of working alongside the Donnelly brothers (and particularly William Donnelly) during the course of the two murder trials, that "their idea throughout has been to bring the murderers to justice through and by the law, and I have frequently heard them repudiate the idea of having recourse to unlawful means for obtaining vengeance on the murderers of their family."[29] That the brothers would now stoop to criminal activity in order to attack a man who had not been present at the murders, nor a member of the Vigilance Committee — indeed, who had been nothing more than a witness called by the defence counsel during the trials — struck the Crown Attorney as unlikely in the extreme.[30]

According to West, his motive for allowing himself to be drawn into the plan was solely to gather evidence against the Donnelly brothers and, once William Donnelly had hatched his plan to put the torch to the town's flour mill, West believed he had the means to bring them down. He promptly sought out William Stanley and alerted him as to the Donnellys' intentions.

Almost immediately the local press raised an eyebrow at the particulars of the case, and reported its thoughts in the pages of their newspapers:

> The more the matter is talked over, the more absurd it
> appears to be that the Donnellys had any connection
> with the affair. That a person of Bill Donnelly's well-
> known shrewdness would associate with him four or
> five other persons in a job which could better have
> been done by one is considered highly improbable. . . .
> The fact that this Detective West should be the only
> person captured, after him stating distinctly who else
> would be concerned in the affair, at once throws a
> shade of distrust over the whole story. If, as was stated
> by him and his friends, he had given all the necessary
> information, there should have been no difficulty in at
> least securing the persons engaged in the incendiarism.
> But none of the prosecutors attempt to assert that

anybody was recognized, except the man "West." To an unprejudiced mind, the whole thing looks a "little thin" to say the least of it. In this city and Lucan there are not a few who openly express the conviction that the whole affair is a very clumsily contrived plot to get rid of the Donnellys, at least till after the Feeheleys are disposed of.[31]

It must be pointed out that despite the Feeheleys having been granted the right to bail by the attorney general's office, it had not been paid yet, as most of the Vigilance Committee members did not have access to the kind of cash necessary to cover their bond.[32] Consequently, the Feeheley brothers were still within the Middlesex County gaol, and, from the perspective of the Vigilance Committee, Father Connolly, and certain members of the Lucan business community, they remained a potential threat. After all, as long as they were still in the county they might be convinced to testify about what they knew regarding the murder of the Donnelly family. Taken as a whole, nothing about the arson allegation seemed legitimate. Even Magistrate William Stanley's actions were called into question:

It was stated also that a dispatch from Lucan this morning was to the effect that Squire Stanley wished it to be distinctly understood that he was not sitting as a magistrate upon the case, but was only there yesterday as a spectator. This, however, is not in accordance with facts, as may be seen from our report of the proceedings. Squire Stanley was the most active man on the Bench. If he is an interested party in connection with the ownership of the mill, objection may be taken to his presiding at the examination by any of the prisoners.[33]

That one of the Stanley brothers should be involved in a frame-up of the Donnellys was hardly surprising. After all, it was a Stanley who had suggested (in another bit of railroading) that a man be placed in a cell next to Bob Donnelly to covertly obtain evidence to be used against him in court (evidence that would later turn out to be fabricated but that, nevertheless, saw Donnelly put away in Kingston Penitentiary for two years); it was a Stanley whom the defence lawyers for the Vigilance Committee had called to the stand to refute the testimony given by Johnny O'Connor and to vouch for the character of James Carroll; it was likely at the Stanleys' urging that Patrick Flanagan had sought out the services of the private detective Hugh McKinnon to come to Lucan and do everything in his power to have the Donnellys sent to jail. And, of course, it was believed to have been a Stanley who had attempted to spin the murder of the Donnellys as "a public gain," as "where did anybody ever get the best of the Donnellys in law?"

In the meantime, the prosecution had acquired an additional attorney, Henry Corry Rowley Becher, a man who had history with the Donnelly family. He had served as the presiding magistrate in James Donnelly Sr.'s trial for having taken a shot at Patrick Farrell in December of 1855. Becher had been hired to prosecute the case by a consortium of Lucan businessmen who have never been specifically named.

Since those who had purchased his services were high-ranking Lucan businessmen, he was able to bring on board no fewer than twelve witnesses from the town of Lucan and neighbouring areas who had indicated their readiness to testify for the prosecution (Bernard Stanley and James Carroll among them).[34] And, to ensure that the Donnellys would not be getting out of jail any time soon, he also secured a statement from a local insurance company that it would cancel every fire policy in Lucan if the Donnellys received bail.[35] Clearly Francis West, the piano teacher and former meat merchant, now had friends in high places. Indeed, when he had been unable to pay a recent hotel bill in London, it was paid by none other than the magistrate in the preliminary hearing, William Stanley.[36] How could a man who was dead broke come to have his debts paid by the town's leading businessman, magistrate and reeve? The man who connected them, it would appear, was Thomas Hall — the man whose barn West was believed to have burned down.

West was certainly aware that, among his new friends within Lucan's political and merchant classes, the Donnellys were anathema.[37] But this was a sentiment that had been held for some time before West arrived on the scene, perhaps reaching its zenith (or nadir by some perspectives) during the stagecoach war that had taken place between the Donnelly brothers and Patrick Flanagan in the mid-1870s. More recently, since the Donnelly murders, William Stanley had spoken out against the Donnelly family in the local press. And the animosity was mutual; in September 1880, William Donnelly had also spoken to the press, and made a veiled reference to Bernard Stanley, claiming that he was a "high flyer" in Lucan who had amassed his material success as a result of being "well acquainted with fire and treachery."[38] Clearly there was bad blood between the two parties, and the implication was obvious: the Stanley brothers would look favourably upon anyone who could rid the township of the Donnelly brothers. More importantly to West, however, the Stanleys had power and money, the latter being something the music teacher sorely needed. The Donnellys, by contrast, had lost their trials against those who had murdered their family, and had expended almost all their money in the process of attempting to bring the killers to justice. Consequently, they were not candidates to put any dollars into West's empty pockets and, thus, were of little use to him.

Pat Donnelly's role in the recent Feeheley extradition had brought a lot of the dormant anti-Donnelly sentiments back to the surface. Both the Vigilance Committee members in Biddulph and the business class in Lucan recognized that if the Feeheleys could be made to confess what they knew about the murders an avalanche of problems was certain to descend upon them. There would have followed another high-profile trial, and perhaps the hanging of some nineteen to twenty men. Father Connolly would also have to come forth from the shadows to answer for certain things, such as why he gave money from the church to Bridget Feeheley after her boys had threatened to expose the Donnellys' killers. Those who had put their reputations on the line to serve as character witnesses for James Carroll, men like William Stanley, would also be publicly embarrassed by the Feeheleys' testimony, and their judgement would then be called into serious question. And once again, the town of Lucan and the township of Biddulph would be the foci of a flood of negative publicity by the North American press. The town would thereafter be stained by the blood of the murdered family. Certainly, this had to be the attitude of the Vigilance Committee members and the leading merchants of Lucan who had the most to lose, such as the Stanley brothers. Something had to be done about the Donnelly brothers so that any attempt at reviving the murder case would be dropped — but who would bell the cat? Thomas Hall believed he had found just the man for the job.

Granted, it was a relationship that made no sense, unless the burning of Hall's barn had been surreptitiously arranged for insurance purposes. It is, after all, hard to envision a scenario whereby a person who has had his property destroyed by someone suddenly embraces the person who had destroyed it. According to William Porte's diary, Thomas Hall's barn went up in flames on Saturday, October 1, 1881, but in the eight days that elapsed between that fire and the attempted arson of the Stanley, Dight & Company mill (which Porte's diary incorrectly indicates took place on the evening of October 8, one day earlier than it actually did),[39] West had not only informed Hall about his role in the burning of his barn,[40] but had then been invited to stay overnight at Hall's house.[41] Later, during the trial that followed, Hall would bring West medicine[42] and, later, together with William Stanley, pay West's bail.[43] Hall was clearly in the loop with William Stanley regarding the intended arson at the mill owned by the latter, as Stanley would claim on the witness stand that he had asked Hall to be among the group waiting with him in the mill to pounce upon the would-be arsonists.[44] West apparently became even closer with William Stanley, who would state under oath that the down-on-his-luck music teacher had visited him at his house "several times" in the week before the arson attempt and also after the preliminary hearing.[45] This was confirmed by West under oath while being cross-examined by defence attorney Edmund Meredith, who additionally got Francis West to admit he had stayed for several nights at the home of a Vigilance Committee member:

> MEREDITH: "Where have you been since the examination in Lucan?"
> WEST: "I was — I was in — well, different places."
> MEREDITH: "Were you in Bill Ned's [William E. Stanley's] house?"
> WEST: "Yes, for several nights."
> MEREDITH: "Were you in Barney Stanley's store?"
> WEST: "For five or six days — and some nights at Toohey's."
> MEREDITH: "Is that the Vigilance man?"
> WEST: "Yes, he is."
> MEREDITH: "How long were you there?"
> WEST: "I slept two nights in his barn."[46]

That Hall was friendly with Stanley, and that both men backed West, as evidenced by both men paying his bail and inviting him to sleepovers, speaks to purpose. William Stanley was not one known to hobnob with the downtrodden. A deal of some sort was clearly in place, an understanding had been arrived at: West was to bring charges against the Donnellys — the Stanleys would handle the rest. Perhaps West had been apprehended and threatened with arrest by Hall for the burning of his barn unless he was willing to implicate the Donnellys in a future crime, in much the same way James Carroll had used a warrant to cow James Feeheley into spying for the Vigilance Committee. It may have been that Hall approached West with a deal brokered by Stanley (who had the power and position to do so) to bring charges against the Donnellys in return for immunity from his crimes. We can only speculate. Money may well have changed hands, as West certainly had need of it and Stanley had plenty of it. Indeed, the Donnellys' defence counsel, Edmund Meredith, was convinced of this fact when he later crossed legal swords with the prosecution's John Idington:

> IDINGTON (representing the prosecution): "Then, what was West's motive?"
> MEREDITH: "Money."
> IDINGTON: "Who would supply it?"
> MEREDITH: "I have no doubt his friend Mr. Stanley would do so."[47]

Whatever had brought Francis West to this pass, by the time the preliminary hearing resumed on October 13, it was time for him to uphold his end of the bargain. Once again, he appeared before the magistrates Stanley, McCosh and McIlhargey. By this point, however, the charges against the Cartys had been dropped, John Kent's likewise, Simon Howe was nowhere to be found, and Francis West was now a Crown witness and, thus, faced no charges at all. That left only William and Robert Donnelly to be charged with the crime, which, perhaps, had been the objective from the beginning. During the preliminary hearing West related the intricate details of the plan that, he claimed, had been cooked up by William Donnelly: on the night the arson was to occur, West and Howe would approach the mill through a field so as to leave no tracks. They would bore holes into the mill siding, pour coal oil into the holes and light a match. Once the fire started, Howe would run back to William Donnelly's, where he would be alibied by the Cartys and Kent. West would head for the Queen's Hotel and enter a room he had already rented through a rear window, so he would not be seen. He could later claim he had been there the entire night. William, in the meantime, would surreptitiously feed his baby daughter brandy (unbeknownst to her mother), which would make the baby drunk. Nora Donnelly would mistake the baby's inebriation for sickness, and Bob Donnelly would then be sent out from the house to get an "old woman" (presumably a nurse) to return with him to check on the baby. That would be his reason for leaving the house. However, once he was outside, he would notice the fire at the mill, run to it and work alongside whoever else was there in an effort to suppress it, thus removing the Donnellys from suspicion. That, evidently, was the great plan masterminded by William Donnelly. However, the piano teacher had a plan of his own: "I thought to work this case up, bring the men to justice, gain a reputation, and so secure work as a detective in the future."[48]

West's testimony was considered impressive and substantial enough by William Stanley and the other two magistrates that they ruled that the Donnelly brothers should be tried in the Middlesex County Court in London on November 8. The prisoners were then ordered to be transferred to the Middlesex County Gaol on the evening train out of Clandeboye. Once again, West was able to enter into his own recognizance in the amount of $400 and was ordered to appear in London on November 8 to give his evidence at the trial. But there was another matter that required West's attention first.

The Crown had caught scent of something in the air that could prove damaging to its star witness. It had somehow come to light that

Francis West had stolen two rifles from the Lucan Armory at some point during the previous summer and had attempted to sell these items to the farmer John Kent. It was probably suggested to West by his legal counsel that, if he still had these weapons in his possession, he should surrender them to the armoury as soon as possible. That would go some way in reducing the likelihood that the integrity of their star witness might be called into question during the trial, and, hopefully, prevent his being prosecuted for theft by the government. But then another idea suggested itself. What if, upon returning the rifles, West should mention the theft was, like the attempted arson, a plan of one of the Donnelly brothers? Perhaps West could obtain immunity from the Crown in return for his testimony against the Donnelly in question. And, since William and Bob were already in jail, maybe Patrick Donnelly could be named as the accomplice in the weapons theft? After all, Patrick had been the most aggressive of the Donnelly brothers during the Feeheley extradition — and no one wanted *that* matter brought before the courts again. In a best-case scenario, all three Donnelly brothers might be sent to jail. And so, immediately after delivering his testimony on Thursday, October 13, Francis West marched over to the Lucan Armory with the two stolen rifles and put the plan into effect. As the press reported:

> It appears that last summer the rifles were missed
> by Captain Thom, and all efforts to discover their
> whereabouts proved futile. It is alleged that on
> Thursday last, West appeared at the armory with the
> rifles. He informed the caretaker that the arms had
> been taken by himself and Patrick Donnelly, and that
> they had brought them to the farm of John Kent and
> hid them there.[49]

Now that he had returned the stolen property, it was decided that it might be best for West to leave the country for a little while —

at least until it was known if any charges would be forthcoming. West somehow found the funds necessary to travel to Port Huron, Michigan, and there he awaited word as to when and if he should return.[50]

After the preliminary hearing had concluded, William and Bob Donnelly were handcuffed and marched from the jailhouse to the Queen's Hotel in Lucan, where they were to await the arrival of the horse-drawn paddy wagon that would take them to the Clandeboye train station some three miles outside of town. There, they would board the train that would deliver them to London, and, ultimately, to the Middlesex Gaol to await their trial. They were escorted to the hotel by detective H.R. Schram and constables William Hodgins and Thomas Shoebottom. The men sat down in a quiet corner of the barroom and were soon joined by the Donnelly brothers' longtime friend Robert Keefe, who had come to town to wish them luck during their forthcoming trial and to keep them company until the conveyance arrived to take them to the train station. The time for departure was rapidly drawing to a close when into the bar walked thirty-nine-year-old "Red Bill" Stanley. Stanley was a relative of William and Bernard Stanley[51] and worked at the mill that had almost fallen under the torch. With him on this night were the Vigilance Committee members James Maher, Grouchy Ryder and his brother "Sideroad" Jim Ryder. William Donnelly watched the men as they strutted up to the bar and ordered their drinks. He concluded they were looking for trouble.[52] Looking around the bar, Stanley spotted the Donnelly brothers. In an effort to impress his companions and also to mock the siblings' predicament, he flashed an insincere smile toward his adversaries.

"Bob! William! Come and have a drink with us!" he beckoned. To the considerable surprise and discomfort of Stanley and his cohorts, both brothers immediately stood up from where they had been seated and walked up to the men at the counter of the bar. The Donnellys ordered their drinks and Stanley was speechless. He hadn't expected the Donnellys to take him up on his bravado. The silence was awkward. Grouchy Ryder and James Maher suddenly became uneasy. Feigning civility, Maher said, "Good luck to ye, boys." Ryder nodded and grunted.

The bartender now placed the two drinks before the brothers. William turned to the men and returned Stanley's sarcasm.

"Thank you. To your good health."

Bob nodded and the brothers downed their drinks. The insincerity of the toast was not lost on the Committee members, who proceeded to bite their tongues, particularly with a detective and two constables not more than twenty feet away. Picking up on the tension, Robert Keefe now rose and walked up to the bar.

"Good luck to you, Robert Keefe," Grouchy Ryder said sardonically.

Keefe now extended his hand toward the elder of the two Ryders, almost daring him to shake it.

"No, I wouldn't shake hands with no man such as you," snorted Ryder.

Keefe had a low threshold for verbal abuse, and dropped all pretense of civility. "I'm an honest man, and that's more'n you can say." Ryder's eyes widened at the insult. But Keefe wasn't finished quite yet. "You're a rogue, and you murdered the Donnellys — and Brimmacombe on the Roman Line in '57!"

It was now Jim Maher's turn to enter the fray. He jumped to his feet and attempted to berate Keefe. As William would later recall, "The answers and questions came fast and loud, and for a few minutes there was every appearance of a row."

At this point the wagon pulled up in front of the Queen's Hotel, which caused the constables to interrupt the proceedings and escort the Donnelly brothers outside and into the omnibus. Inside the conveyance were the attorneys Charles Hutchinson, Henry Becher and Edmund Meredith, who would also be taking the train to London that evening. However, no sooner had everyone climbed aboard when a loud smashing of glass was heard. The constables and Detective Schram immediately rushed back into the hotel, followed by the attorneys and the Donnelly brothers. According to William Donnelly: "On entering we saw Rob Keefe holding old Ryder's head through the window, and noticed an odd tuft of grey hair floating in the air. It looked to me at first as if Keefe was playing circus and trying to get the wild beast into his cage."

"Oh, merciful Heavens, I'm going to be scalped!" screamed Grouchy Ryder. Ryder's words evidently caused the constables to start laughing, which incensed the old man, along with his fellow Committee members.

"The Constables are laughing instead of holding the prisoners!" Grouchy Ryder hollered at his companions. At this point, several people moved forward to break up the fracas, including the Donnelly brothers, Constable Shoebottom, Charles Hutchinson and Alexander McFalls, the proprietor of the hotel. Evidently William Donnelly applied a little too much force in pulling Sideroad Jim Ryder out of the scrum, which incensed Ryder. He drew back his fist and went for Donnelly who inhaled deeply, stood up straight and locked eyes with the man.

"Keep your blood-stained hands off me!" Donnelly said through gritted teeth.

The words stopped Ryder dead in his tracks.

Donnelly's eyes were now like daggers as he spoke: "Your time for striking is four hours and a half away yet." (Both statements were scathing. The hotel encounter took place at approximately eight o'clock; the Donnelly murders that "Sideroad" Jim Ryder participated in took place at approximately 12:30 a.m., thus, the "four and a half hours away" reference. Jim Ryder had never been placed on trial for the murders, and so for William Donnelly, the son of the couple whom Ryder and his crew had murdered, to now publicly point out that Ryder's hands were bloodstained from the act, caught the Committee member off guard.) Ryder suddenly went limp as the impact of William's words hit him harder than any punch ever could have. The constables now moved between the pair. When all of the combatants had been pulled apart and order finally restored, the constables, attorneys and the Donnellys returned to the wagon that would take them to Clandeboye to meet the train. When asked later about the altercation at the hotel, William smiled and referred to it as "a bit of the usual diversion."

Later that evening the *London Advertiser* would report on the Donnellys' arrival into the city:

> A large crowd were assembled at the station in London when the L. H. B. R. train, bearing the prisoners came in. Both William and Robert are in the best of spirits, and take their present inconveniences in a manner as agreeable as possible. They have no doubt about the favourable termination of the case. "Every man in Middlesex," said William with a smile, at the examination in Lucan, "is helping to pay for the business, even to Jim Maher himself," as that individual walked past behind him.[53]

The next morning the London press couldn't wait to hear William Donnelly's side of the story regarding the attempted arson of William Stanley's mill. They hurriedly made their way over to the Middlesex County Gaol, where William and Bob were being held. William was in fine form as the reporters asked their questions.

"How are you both doing?" asked a reporter.

"I never was better, sick or well," William replied.[54]

"How do you like the London jail?"

"This is a little different quarters from the cells in Lucan. Of all the pig sties you ever saw, that den is the foulest. The air would almost smother you. In one corner is a slop-bucket, and one is supposed to sleep within a few feet of this all night — when you can sleep. However, two of the constables were kept in with us, and we had the satisfaction of knowing they were as bad off as ourselves."

"Were any of your friends allowed in to see you?"

"Sure," William replied. And then, turning to Bob, William asked, "didn't we have young Ryder come to us half an hour after we were in the cells and say, 'Boys, I'm sorry for you?'"

"Yes, he's got very kind all of a sudden," Bob replied sarcastically.

"I suppose West didn't come near you?" asked the reporter.

"Very clear of it," William replied. "He knows too much for that."

"Is he any ways smart?" asked another newspaper man.

"Yes, he is in a certain way. He is ready with his tongue, but he got badly mixed up in giving his evidence yesterday. He can rattle the piano, I can tell, at a lively rate."

"How did it come that a music teacher should be engaged in working on the farm?"

"Well, I'll tell you. Hands were very scarce with so many people going off to Manitoba that the farmers were willing to take any kind of men. However, I had my suspicions about this fellow, and when I heard he was working for Jack Kent I went out to Lucan and told Jack that West wasn't there for any good."

"What reason had you to suspect him?"

"Oh, I can't say; but I never liked his oily and insinuating manner — did you ever see him?"

"Not that I'm aware of."

"Well, he has the queerest-looking head you ever saw. He would do to travel in a circus. Once seen, he can never be mistaken."

"Did he ever live in this city?"

"He was here for a week some time ago, but is said went away without paying his board bill at the City Hotel. I guess he gets his living by his wits."

"Was he working for money in this affair?"

"I couldn't say. He said at the examination he was working for a reputation. But maybe he'll get one he doesn't like before he's through with it."

"Then you don't think this case will amount to much?"

William now brought his wit and sarcasm to the fore: "Oh! I can't tell what they may swear against me. The plot to go out in the moonlight is such a clever one that of course I don't like to deny having something to do with it. Then, you see, I planned to have augur holes bored, although there were hundreds of cracks I could have poured the oil into. This showed *caution*. Then, see my *daring*, instead of going on the dark side and being sheltered by a woodpile ten feet high, I must go out where every person going by could see me. Oh! But the plot was a clever one!"

Just as William Donnelly had finished his anecdote, a messenger of the court arrived at the cell to inform the brothers that they were required in court. Detective Schram and members of the jail staff accompanied the Donnellys upstairs and into the courtroom, where they stood before Judge William Elliot. Charles Hutchinson read aloud the particulars of the case, giving the age of William at thirty-five and Robert at twenty-eight. Judge Elliot then inquired of the prisoners if they wished to be tried in the matter by a judge and jury, or by judge alone. Both men opted for a summary trial by the judge. Charles Hutchinson then turned to the prisoners to receive their pleas on behalf of the Crown.

"Are you guilty or not guilty, William Donnelly, of the charge alleged against you?"

"Not guilty."

"What say you, Robert Donnelly?"

"Not guilty."

Hutchinson then turned to the defence counsel. "Are you ready for your trial?"

Edmund Meredith rose from his table. "Not quite. I would like the trial postponed for a couple of weeks to secure some facts for the defence."

Judge Elliot then set down the date for the trial — November 8 at 10 a.m.

Meredith requested bail for the prisoners. Hutchinson opposed the motion. W.P.R. Street then rose from his table to lend his support to Hutchinson's objection.

"It would be extremely improper to let these parties out, considering the strong feeling there is between the Stanleys and them."

Meredith immediately challenged the prosecution's contention. "It would be unjust to detain them in jail on such a flimsy scheme as this one developed by West. Any person who knew the Donnellys would not for one moment believe that they would have anything to do with such a loud-mouthed tattler as West."

Judge Elliot declared that he would reserve his decision on the question of bail until 11 a.m. the next morning.[55] When the designated hour arrived the next day, Judge Elliot ruled that he deemed it proper to accept bail for the Donnellys. The brothers were required to pay two sureties of $250 each, and then were released — much to the chagrin of the prosecuting attorney Henry Becher and at least one insurance company back in Lucan. On their way out of the courthouse, a reporter asked William Donnelly if, after all that happened, the two brothers were actually going to return to Lucan. "Of course, we're going back to Lucan. They can't keep us away," Donnelly replied. "We will go out this evening, if nothing happens."[56]

Bob decided he would forgo Lucan and head home to Glencoe to see his wife.[57] William, however, took the train to Clandeboye station, where he intended to catch one of the few remaining stagecoaches to Lucan to be reunited with his wife and daughter. While aboard the train, word had evidently gotten out about its infamous passenger, as William would recollect:

> While on the train, the passengers, who were
> nearly all strangers, were made aware of the fact
> Bill Donnelly was on board and from the way they
> looked at me, I came to the conclusion that if the
> Vigilants confessed to the Biddulph butchery, it
> would not have caused any greater surprise.[58]

When he finally returned home, the reunion was brief — Nora had work for him to do: "I was handed a bucksaw and told to cut some wood while I was resting myself."[59]

Crown attorney Charles Hutchinson had lost himself in thought. After a full year of working to get justice for William and his siblings, he had gotten to know and befriend the surviving Donnelly family members. To now be prosecuting them seemed strange. Hutchinson had developed a particularly deep respect for William Donnelly during this time, which evidently had been reciprocated. William had written to him on two separate occasions, indicating "I can never repay you"[60] and that "it would be my meanest turn to do anything contrary to your wishes, being as you were a father to the remaining members of the family for the last year."[61] It's true that these words had been written seven and eight months previously, and that the passage of time can change a lot of things, but the sentiment the words expressed had been sincere and from the heart. For William Donnelly to then do something that would put him at loggerheads with the family's surrogate father made no sense. Masterminding an arson attack on the Stanley, Dight & Company mill seemed so out of character for the man that Hutchinson knew and had worked so closely with during the murder trials. It just wasn't a crime that the attorney could see William Donnelly's brain wasting energy on. Bob Donnelly was impulsive, to be certain, but if William Donnelly was going to be involved in any enterprise, be it criminal or otherwise, he would have been the brains of the operation. And after listening to the testimony given by Francis West, and weighing it in light of his personal knowledge of William's acumen, the Crown counsellor had concluded that William's brain would never have come up with anything so convoluted and, well, sloppy. And then there was the direct involvement of the long-time Donnelly antagonist William Stanley. This was certainly suspicious. In fact, the more that Hutchinson thought about it, the more he became convinced the entire case against the Donnelly brothers was nothing but a sham:

> I think this is a put-up job, but of course keep this
> opinion to myself. It is quite possible that Robert
> Donnelly, who is a foolish, reckless fellow and made
> well-nigh desperate by the course things have taken,
> may have been inveigled into doing something as
> wrong as charged against him, but there is no fear of
> William — who is as shrewd a man as I know —
> being drawn into so miserably concocted a plot as
> this. The feeling exhibited against the accused is
> intense and they have been dealt with very cruelly
> in my opinion, having been consigned for three
> days and nights to cells in the Lucan lockup which
> are altogether unfit for the occupation of human
> beings. This was done under the influence and by the
> direction of William Stanley, who is principal owner
> of the mill, which the accused are charged with
> having attempted to set on fire.[62]

In a clear case of grappling with his conscience, and of his conscience winning the battle, Hutchinson penned a letter to the attorney general indicating that he was stepping down from prosecuting the case.[63] The attorney general's office then assigned the Crown attorney from Perth County, John Idington, to take over Hutchinson's duties on behalf of the Province.[64]

During Francis West's sojourn in Michigan, Constable Thomas Shoebottom decided to ride over to John Kent's farm to interview the farmer about the rifle theft — and about Pat Donnelly's possible involvement in the caper. Kent informed the constable that, indeed, West had come to him with the rifles, and had even inquired if he would purchase them from him, but that he had declined the offer. Kent further stated that West had been alone that day; that Pat Donnelly was nowhere to be seen and that his name had never once been mentioned. Shoebottom concluded that West's statements about Pat Donnelly's involvement in the matter was a complete fabrication. He returned to town and obtained a warrant for West's arrest, charging him with robbery.[65] Upon learning that an arrest warrant had been issued for the prosecution's star witness, attorney Henry Becher prepared an immunity request for the AWOL music teacher and sent it along to the attorney general's office.[66] Mowat's office agreed to grant West immunity, and word was sent on to Port Huron that the coast was now clear for West's return to Canada.[67] The promise of immunity didn't immediately nullify the arrest warrant, however, and, upon West's return to Lucan, Constable Shoebottom arrested him on the charge of "feloniously stealing the above-mentioned weapons, the property of Her Majesty the Queen."[68] West was brought before Magistrate McIlhargey and entered into his own recognizance to the amount of $400, and ordered to appear before Squire Hannah on Thursday, November 17, 1881, to answer the charge.[69] His lawyers weren't worried.

The Donnelly brothers' trial began at 11 a.m. on Tuesday, November 8, 1881, before Judge William Elliot in the Interim Sessions Chamber of the Middlesex County Courthouse. Henry Becher, together with Charles Hutchinson's replacement, Queen's Counsel John Idington, appeared for the prosecution, while Edmund Meredith and A.J.B. MacDonald represented the defence. Prior to the start of the trial, Meredith had requested that all witnesses who hadn't yet been summoned to give evidence leave the courtroom. Judge Allison granted the request, which upset several of the anti-Donnelly forces that were present, such as Bernard Stanley. Despite the latter's protests, Judge Elliot saw to it that Stanley was removed from the courtroom.[70]

The prosecution called William Stanley as their first witness. The Lucan reeve, magistrate and businessman proceeded to tell his story of how West had informed him of the plot to burn the grist mill earlier that week, and how he had posted guards every night at the mill in the days leading up to the attempted arson. He further related how he had been lying in wait for the perpetrators on the night of the crime, along with Thomas Hall, Thomas Cubbins, William Hodgins and Edward Hodgins. Having given his evidence, Stanley was then available to be cross-examined by the defence attorney Edmund Meredith, who, like Crown attorney Charles Hutchinson before him, had a strong suspicion that Stanley was both the mastermind and the money behind what was nothing more than an attempt to frame the Donnellys.

> MEREDITH: "Has there not been a great deal of trouble in Lucan?"
> STANLEY: "Yes."
> MEREDITH: "Have you not been a sympathizer with the prisoners charged with the murder of the Donnellys?"

STANLEY attempted to deflect the question: "Not very much so."

MEREDITH: "Did you not congratulate the prisoners when they got off?"

STANLEY: "Yes, I was there, but made no speech from a wagon."

MEREDITH: "Have you not been strongly opposed to the Donnellys?"

STANLEY: "Not very; I have not been on very unfriendly terms with them, nor friendly terms either."

MEREDITH: "Do you remember a conversation with Constable Shoebottom after the alleged [arson] attempt?"

STANLEY: "Don't remember."

MEREDITH: "Didn't you say: 'If this thing was carried out all right it would end the Feeheley case?'"

There, within the compass of a sentence, was the entire reason for the prosecution of the Donnelly brothers. Stanley, of course, denied having said any such thing, but now the pieces of the puzzle had started to be pressed firmly into place. More pieces were provided when Constable Shoebottom was brought to the stand. He testified that Francis West had been furnished "with funds for this case" but didn't know the name of the person who had bankrolled him. The prosecution was now in trouble and needed support. James Carroll had tried to sneak into the courtroom to witness the proceedings; however, his presence was spotted by Meredith, who had the court attendants promptly remove the ex-constable from the room.

Francis West was finally called to the stand. His attorney had him repeat his narrative of the events leading up to the attempted arson of Stanley's mill and how he had kept William Stanley apprised of the incendiary plan. After delivering his testimony, West was Edmund Meredith's witness to cross-examine. The defence attorney asked West if it was true that he had told William Stanley repeatedly throughout the week that the arson was going to take place specifically on the evening of Sunday, October 9. West replied this was so. That being the case, Meredith inquired, then why did Stanley testify he had posted guards at the mill throughout the *entire* week, rather than just on the Sunday night the arson was set to take place? West had no answer. But Meredith certainly had more questions.

MEREDITH: "If you wanted to catch the Donnellys, why did you not insist on William or Robert going with you to the fire?"

WEST: "I knew they wouldn't go. They never did."

MEREDITH: "Yes, but Pat Donnelly went and stole rifles with you?"

WEST: "He did. In the fire business the Donnellys were laying the plans."

MEREDITH: "What about the baby story?"

WEST: "Bill was trying to get the baby drunk."

MEREDITH: "Wouldn't his wife smell its breath?"

WEST: "I did not think about that. It was Bill Donnelly's scheme."

MEREDITH: "Who was the 'old woman' that was to be sent for?"

WEST: "I did not hear her name."

MEREDITH: "Well, what was the old woman sent for?"

WEST: "To console Mrs. Donnelly, I suppose, in the dying hours of the child!"

MEREDITH: "But the child was only to be *drunk* and not *dying* at all?"

Meredith then proceeded to get West to admit to his history of larceny.

MEREDITH: "What was the first theft you were connected with?"

WEST: "Taking two rifles from the Lucan Armory."

MEREDITH: "When was that?"

WEST: "On the first day of April."

MEREDITH: "Why didn't you tell about the theft then?"

WEST: "I did not consider I had the case properly worked up against the Donnellys. . . . William and Patrick Donnelly got up the plan to steal the guns, and then these guns were to be shot through a window of William Donnelly's house. William Donnelly had been sick, and this was to be published in the papers. Then the story was to be got up that the Vigilance Committee were still persecuting the Donnellys and had shot through the windows. It was arranged that no one was to be in that room. I received the following letter: 'Lucan, April 2nd. Come down tonight. Don't fail — Patrick Donnelly.' Patrick Donnelly and I took the guns and left them at William Donnelly's house; the shooting did not take place."

MEREDITH: "But yet you saw the theft committed and the stolen property put in the hands of William Donnelly?"

WEST: "I did not have them sure."

MEREDITH: "What was the next thieving business you were in?"

WEST: "Stealing hens from McLean. Two hens."

MEREDITH: "What was the next theft? You stole a cow, I understand?"

WEST: "Yes, I helped John Kent to steal the cow, but afterwards told the owner where to get the cow."

MEREDITH: "Did you not talk to Frank Kent about robbing the Lucan bank?"

WEST: "No, never."

MEREDITH: "Well, what about burning a barn in London township?"

WEST: "Frank Kent and I talked over the matter, but I was to get six dollars from John Kent for the job."

Meredith was further able to corral West into committing perjury. In the preliminary hearing on October 13, West had testified that William Donnelly did not know the content of West's written statements regarding the information he had collected on the Feeheley case:

October 13 Testimony:

MEREDITH: "Are the statements true you signed about the Feeheleys?"

BECHER (to West): "Don't answer that question."

MEREDITH: "Oh, this is getting too near home?"

BECHER: "You must produce the statements or define what they were."

MEREDITH (to West): "Did you make statements in writing about the Feeheley case?"

WEST: "I believe I did."

MEREDITH: "Did you have an interview with several parties about the Vigilants and Feeheleys?"

WEST: "I never made any verbal statements."

MEREDITH: "Not to the Donnellys?"

West: "We are not on the Feeheley case now."

MEREDITH: "Ah! Ah! But we are, and will be on a good many cases before we get through with you."

WEST: "I'll swear I never told the Donnellys I could prove anything about the Feeheleys."

MEREDITH: "Did you ever tell the Donnellys what was contained in these written statements?"

WEST: "No. I had no business to. I was minding my own business."[71]

And yet in his sworn testimony during the trial, West had stated that he had written the statements about the Feeheleys in the presence of the Donnellys — and under William's instructions:

November 8 Testimony:

WEST: "I signed the papers at the Queen's Hotel, and wrote them relating to the Feeheley case. There was no one in the room but myself. I copied the statement from a book I kept; William Donnelly told me at his house what to write, I took notes down on pieces of paper, and afterwards destroyed them. I don't think William ever saw that book; these statements are all a pack of lies, dictated by William Donnelly."
MEREDITH: "Did you send statements to the Crown Attorney about the Feeheley case?"
WEST: "Yes, but there is not a word of truth in them, not a single word."
MEREDITH: "It's signed by you. Did you try to mislead these persons?"
WEST: "No. I did it for William Donnelly."
MEREDITH: "So you perjured yourself."[72]

The first day of the trial had ended badly for the prosecution. The headlines in the evening paper told the story:

A WITHERING CROSS-EXAMINATION
OF WITNESS WEST.
HE PRONOUNCES HIS OWN
WRITTEN STATEMENT TO BE LIES.[73]

The next day the defence didn't even feel the need to present its case. Edmund Meredith simply asked that the prisoners be discharged. And in considering the evidence, Judge Elliot was inclined to agree. In his final charge he stated that the prosecution's case had rested wholly upon the evidence of Francis West, whom the judge deemed to be "an accomplice of questionable character,"[74] and a man who, from the very start, had looked to "fix guilt of some kind or other upon the Donnellys." West, by his own admission, had "readily agreed in several conspiracies to burn buildings" since arriving in Lucan. The judge then touched on the written statements that West had sent to Crown attorney Hutchinson on the Feeheley case, and that West now declared these statements to be lies from beginning to end. West had claimed that William Donnelly had dictated to him what to write and he had written out these notes in Donnelly's presence. But then these original notes were claimed to have been destroyed, and could not be produced at trial. "Throughout this whole story," declared Judge Elliot, "whenever anything important seemed to come near the Donnellys, something essential appeared to drop out." An agent from the press who was present for the judge's charge reported the magistrate's concluding remarks:

> Mention was made of the murder of the Donnelly
> family, which His Honor characterized as one of the
> most brutal inhuman butcheries ever recorded in the
> annals of Canada, and it was quite natural that the
> remnant of the family should never cease their efforts
> to bring to justice the murderers of their parents.
> People knew this and doubtless many in that section
> of the country would gladly see the Donnelly boys
> put out on the road, as they feared the developments
> that might someday be made. Points in the evidence
> were next considered. . . . The prisoners were men
> of intelligence, William being reputedly shrewd, and

it seems strange that they should so instantaneously bestow their confidence in West. . . . There was nothing in all the evidence that was essentially corroborative, and West's story itself could not be believed. In order to convict the prisoners, there must be evidence against them of a fair and reasonable character. He therefore found them not guilty. The prisoners were forthwith discharged, and received the congratulations of their friends.[75]

Francis West's testimony had done more harm to him than to the Donnellys. He had come to Lucan a music teacher; he would leave the town a felon. Upon the cessation of the trial, West was arrested and charged with three counts of larceny (for the theft of the hens, the cow and the rifles from the Lucan Armory) and one count of perjury.[76] He was placed in the Middlesex County Gaol on the same day that the Donnelly brothers were acquitted. William Stanley and Thomas Hall came forth to pay his bail and Francis West promptly fled Canada, never to return.

It marked the first trial the Donnellys had won in a while. Their acquittal on the conspiracy to commit arson charge saw them defeat some powerful enemies who had schemed so successfully against them in the past — the Vigilance Committee and the Stanleys. But it was a pyrrhic victory. Those who had murdered their parents still had not been brought to justice. And that was the only legal victory that held any meaning for them.

F ate, however, has a strange way of working out its own form of justice, as William Donnelly would point out some three years later. It was 1884, and a London reporter spotted William and Bob Donnelly when the pair were standing together on the London train platform. The newspaperman approached and asked

William if he still had any hope of convicting the murderers of his family. "You bet I have," he answered. And then he paused to consider the question in greater detail. As he looked out over the tracks that led north toward Biddulph, the land where his parents had lived and where their killers lived still, a thought came to his mind. It was a thought that seemed to bring him some measure of satisfaction, and that would have brought chills to those surviving Vigilance Committee members who read it in the paper the very next morning:

Isn't it strange what a number of deaths have taken place among the people in Biddulph? Just after the first trial, six of the McGrath people were driving across the McGillivray crossing of the London, Huron and Bruce Railway. An express train ran into the wagon. Four were killed and two escaped. The killed were Jim McGrath and his wife, his brother, Matt McGrath, and his cousin. Those people were called as witnesses, and swore an alibi for John Purtell, one of the prisoners, a man in the employ of McGrath. Dr. McGrath, son of the old man, was sick at the time of the trial. He would have been called as a witness to swear to Purtell's alibi but for that. He died since. Then there was old Mick Feeheley. His boys were extradited from Detroit, you remember, charged with being concerned in the murder. One of them, Jim, was the last man at my father's house the night of the murder. He was sent there to see who was in the house. The old man gave his evidence at the trial and as he stepped down from the box he said, "One man damned his soul today and had to do it." Then he went and got drunk and died in two or three days. While he was

sick the Vigilants wouldn't let anybody near him.
They were afraid he'd give them away. . . . He
knew that what he had sworn to wasn't true, and
it broke his heart. He had to do it for the sake of
his boys. Then a brother of Jim Carroll, who was
here at one of the trials, though he was not at the
murder, was killed while felling a tree in Michigan.
They just buried him; held no wake, nor nothing.
The quieter they keep, the less chance there is for
disputes that might let the public into the secret of
the murder. Then Martin [Darcy]; he was one of the
leading Vigilants, though he was not charged with
being present at the murder. He was in Lucan one
day about two years ago; went home and was dead
in three days. He just took sick and died. Nobody
could account for it. His father, Dennis [Darcy], died
the day after. He was a decent man and had nothing
to do with the Vigilants, but everybody allowed that
he knew his son was guilty, and when Martin died,
it broke his heart. Then Jim Kelly died. He was a
man about forty, and supposed up to that time to
be healthy. Well, he died after two or three days'
sickness. You remember old [Patrick] Whalen? His
house was near the Donnelly homestead, and yet
he heard nothing of the murder, and saw nothing
except the brightness of the fire that night, but
neither curiosity nor humanity led him to go over
and see what was the trouble. We were over at
the old farm, building a new house. The old man
[Whalen] came over to get a plank or something.
He took a pain in his back, went to bed, and died
in six weeks. The Vigilants never left his bedside,
afraid that he would say something that would give

them away. Mick Carroll got a paralytic stroke that took away his speech, and he died in a short time afterwards. He was a Vigilant and a brother-in-law of old Ryder, that had his barns burned. The other Ryder, one of the accused murderers, was his uncle. There was Mrs. Jim Ryder, too — there were two Jim Ryders — this was "Sideroad" Jim's wife. Jim was a Vigilant and a brother of Tom Ryder, one of the prisoners. Mrs. Jim took a pain in her side, a hard lump formed there and swelled to a great size. She died in a few days. John [Darcy], one of those arrested, took sick with a pain in his back and died in three or four days. A relative of his suffers with paralysis and cannot move about. Old Mrs. Pat Ryder (their barns were burned you know) got wrong in her mind and died. They kept close watch on her till death, for fear she would say something against them. Jim Quigley was a brother of Pat and John Quigley, leading Vigilants. Jim had nothing to do with the murder, but I believe he knew all about it. He took sick in the harvest field and died a short time afterward. And then, let me see . . . there was Mike McLaughlin, brother of John and Neil McLaughlin, leading Vigilants. He knew about the murder. He is dead now — caught a cold, and it finished him. Do you remember a fellow [Francis] West, who came from the other side, and was a party to putting up a job on us to have us convicted for trying to burn Stanley's mill in Lucan? He was one of the victims in the Milwaukee Hotel fire last winter. There was a man named [Samuel] Everett, a constable in Lucan, who swore my brother Bob here into the penitentiary for two years on a charge of trying to shoot him. He acknowledged afterwards that it was a put-up job, and that some big men in Lucan had made him do it. He dropped dead in the streets of Chicago not long ago. And I came pretty near forgetting Pat Sullivan. He was a brother of Ned Sullivan, a leading Vigilant. He had nothing to do with the murder, but he knew about it. He took paralysis and died in a few days. A first cousin of Jim Carroll's is out of his mind. It was in the papers some time ago that he wanted to see the county Crown Attorney, and they allowed that knowing of the crime, it preyed on his mind, and he wanted to tell what he knew. But they kept him from saying anything and he went crazy. A son of Jim Ryder went to Michigan and got his leg broken. There are other things of the same kind among the Vigilants and their friends, but I can't call them all to mind just now.

And isn't it strange that with all these deaths and accidents among them, there hasn't been a death, and hardly any sickness, on our side?"[77]

EPILOGUE

Bob Donnelly (left) and his nephew James Donnelly stand in front of the home that Bob and his brothers built on their parents' original lot in 1881. At the time this photo was taken, in 1905, Bob had just purchased the fifty-acre property from his remaining siblings, in addition to purchasing the adjoining fifty acres that his parents had once owned (but lost) in the late 1850s, thus reuniting the Donnelly property after a separation of some 50 years. (By permission of Ray Fazakas, author of *The Donnelly Album* and *In Search of the Donnellys*)

Twenty-four years now pass by, and we find a man running along a darkened country road at three o'clock in the morning. The man is Bob Donnelly — and he is exhausted and terrified. He continues running until his fifty-five-year-old legs can carry him no farther. He walks now, occasionally stealing a quick glance over his shoulder for a non-existent adversary who might still be pursuing him out there, somewhere, in the darkness.[1] When he finally stops, he is three miles outside of Lucan.[2] The mercury can dip to 52 degrees

Fahrenheit in Middlesex County during the month of September, and so the clothing he is wearing ("a pair of trousers, an undershirt, a pair of house slippers without socks and a light-coloured fedora hat")[3] is insufficient to block out the chill of the early morning. Through the darkness he spots a straw stack on a farmer's field. He advances toward it, climbs in and waits for his enemies to appear.[4]

It has never been revealed what motivated Bob Donnelly to run away from his house during the early morning hours of September 28, 1908. Perhaps the paranoia had returned. If so, it is understandable. Bob Donnelly had lived a good deal of his adult life amid schemes by others to do him harm, and he had witnessed more than his fair share of death during this time.

According to Bob's nephew, James Michael Donnelly, his uncle's absence from home had lasted exactly twenty-four hours.[5] Bob Donnelly was returned to the London Asylum for the Insane the following week, where a Dr. Forster presented him to a conference of four physicians and concluded that the patient was suffering from "Melancholia Vera,"[6] a condition characterized by deep depression. Throughout the next eleven months, Bob Donnelly would be signed out and returned home for extended stays twice more without incident. However, on April 26, 1909, while out with a walking party on the grounds of the asylum, he would escape again.[7] Upon discovering his absence, attendants from the asylum immediately took to the surrounding streets in an effort to locate him, not knowing that Donnelly had headed straight for the Proof Line Road and was already walking the nineteen and a quarter miles back to his home in Lucan. Not wanting to jeopardize any future releases, his nephew contacted the asylum and told the medical superintendent where his uncle was. In short order, attendants from the institution showed up and returned Bob Donnelly to London.[8] It would prove to be his last act of defiance. Bob Donnelly would be temporarily discharged from the London Asylum for the Insane in July, and permanently discharged on October 30, 1909.[9]

He returned to his home in Lucan, and there he would live out his remaining years in relative peace, alongside his wife and nephew (whom the couple had more or less adopted since the death of his father Mike Donnelly in December 1879).

William and Nora Donnelly moved to Glencoe not long after the arson trial had ended, and there, for a time, William was employed as a constable. The couple would eventually move on to Appin, where they would assume proprietorship of a modest-sized hotel. William and Nora would bring two more children into the world to join their daughter Johannah (John, named in honour of William's late brother, and Nora, named after her mother). Patrick would remain content living near Niagara, where he would remarry in 1884, and he and his new wife Mary would raise five children of their own (Mary, Margaret, John, Edith and Matthew). Jennie Currie had lived in and around Glencoe most of her life and would remain there. Together with her husband, James, she watched as their children grew in number to twelve (Robert, Johannah, James, John, Rosemary, Jane, Margaret, Anna, Catherine, Michael, Clara and Patrick). Bob and Annie Donnelly would live for a time in Glencoe as well. They would have no children of their own, but they did ensure that Mike and Ellen Donnelly's two children wanted for nothing.

Bob Donnelly, to the surprise of many, became the most financially successful of the Donnelly brothers, making considerable money from a haulage business he started while living in Glencoe. No matter where he lived, however, it seemed that the lives of others depended upon his vigilance. In almost a mirror image of his heroics in saving his neighbour Bridget O'Connor on the night that her family's house burned down in Lucan, Bob Donnelly's bravery would be called upon yet again. While he was living in Glencoe, three children of a neighbour had been left alone in their house when one of them accidentally knocked a lit coal-oil lamp onto the floor. Soon the flames spread and engulfed the home. Hearing the children's screams, Bob Donnelly ran from his house in time to see one of the neighbour children escape from a window. With two children still trapped inside the home, he broke through the front door of the house and fought his way through the smoke and flames until he found the two children and carried them outside to safety.[10] He may not have been in Biddulph to save his parents on the night their home burned to the ground, but since that fateful night three children would live into adulthood as a result of Bob's ability to take quick and fearless action.

While life was good in Glencoe, Bob Donnelly was determined to maintain a presence in the land of his birth — if only to show the surviving Vigilance Committee members that the Donnelly family would not be run off their land. In time, he purchased his parents' fifty-acre farm on the Roman Line from his siblings, along with any and all quit claims on the property, completing the transaction in 1900.[11] His next purchase came in 1901, when he bought the old Western Hotel in Lucan. This was the same hotel where his brothers had gotten into a brawl with the town strongman, Joseph Berryhill, back in 1875. The brawling evidently didn't stop with the arrival of the new proprietor, however. One night at the hotel, one of the patrons, Edward Brown, got a little out of line and Bob Donnelly smacked him. Brown immediately filed charges and the pair appeared in court. Enid McIlhargey picks up the story:

> The evening of the trial Robert stepped briskly into
> court a few minutes late and excused himself quite
> politely to the judge for delaying the proceedings. The
> judge said, "That is quite all right, Mr. Donnelly."
> And he continued, "Mr. Donnelly, you are here
> charged with striking Edward Brown. How do you
> plead, guilty or not guilty?"

"Not guilty, your Honour," answered Robert. "I just hit him a slap. If I had really hit him there would have been a wake and funeral. What is the fine, please?" Upon being told what amount the fine was, he took a large roll of bills from his pocket and handed the judge the amount. Then, politely bidding them all good evening, he walked out.[12]

John McIlhargey worked for Bob and Annie Donnelly during this time period and recalled a humorous incident that occurred between Bob and a local liquor store owner:

At one time Bob Donnelly kept a hotel in Lucan and a Mr. Pelltier, a Frenchman, kept a liquor store. At a hotel, liquor or beer could be sold only by the glass, and at a liquor store only by the bottle. They were not very friendly and were always watching each other like hawks. Tom Creighton kept a little hotel at Elginfield and was not very well off. One time, Creighton was out of beer and had no money to buy more. He went to Bob, who gladly gave him a keg. He was always ready to help any person in need, and perhaps he saw a chance to have a joke on Pelltier. Someone, perhaps it was Pelltier, squealed on Creighton for getting beer by the keg at the hotel. Creighton went to Bob who told him not to worry; they would fix it up okay. When the court day came the judge asked Creighton, "Did you on such a day buy a keg of beer from Mr. Donnelly?"

He answered, "No, your Honour."

The judge asked, "Are you sure?"

"Yes, your Honour. I got it from Mr. Pelltier. I remember quite clearly because I had just a dollar and I still owe him twenty-five cents."

Of course, he had been coached by Bob Donnelly to answer so. Bob took Tom home for dinner and after dinner drove to the liquor store. Tom went in and said "here is the twenty-five cents I still owe you Mr. Pelltier," but Pelltier was too angry to speak.[13]

Bob and Annie, along with their nephew James, would manage the hotel for several years, selling it only when another real estate opportunity came their way that was too meaningful to pass up. The reader will recall that the Donnelly family had originally farmed one hundred acres on Lot 18 on the Roman Line, but they had lost the southern fifty acres to Michael Maher in 1855. Bob, together with his nephew James Michael Donnelly would purchase the southern fifty acres in 1905.[14] This purchase resulted in finally reuniting the two halves of the property to the full one hundred acres it had been when Bob's father, James Donnelly Sr., had first cleared it a half-century earlier. The acquisition marked one of the proudest days of Bob's life — "The deed jumped up and kissed me," he said with a laugh.[15]

Of all the Donnellys' many antagonists, James Carroll deserves special mention. While a jury of his peers had cleared him of the murder charge, he would never be free from the stigma that attached itself to him for his alleged role in the killings. He would remain in Biddulph for only two years after the second trial, by which point it was clear that he had no future there. His fellow Vigilance Committee members had either died or slowly turned their backs on him. His Biddulph pugilistic record would drop to 0 and 3[16] when he lost a return engagement against his old foe Thomas Keefe. In fairness to Carroll, however, he was outnumbered in this match as Keefe had gotten involved after Carroll had become locked up with James "Buckshot" Ryder. The James Ryder in question was related to Grouchy Ryder but had fallen out with his relatives because he had remained on friendly terms with the Donnellys. Carroll had evidently acquired the habit of trespassing upon Ryder's property in order to take a short cut to wherever it was that he was going and, after watching this occur one too many times, and after repeatedly telling Carroll to stop, Buckshot had had enough. According to a newspaper account:

> He [James Carroll] was going quietly along when
> Ryder rushed toward him with a stick, shouting at
> him to stop, which he did. The two then clinched,
> and while he was on the ground Tom Keefe ran
> up and kicked him on the side of the head, inflicting
> a bruise, the effects of which still remain.[17]

James Ryder took Carroll to court over the incident, and the former constable ended up paying fines for trespassing, assault and then court costs, which, all told, came out to $20.75.[18] Two interesting points would come out of this particular fight: the first was the suggestion that a bulldog that Keefe had brought with him to the altercation may have recognized James Carroll as having been present on the night of the Donnelly murders. According to Keefe, the bulldog ("Jack") was "no common dog. He once belonged to old Mr. Donnelly; was present on that awful night; probably saw the whole tragedy, and some of the actors. One thing appears certain: Carroll and he are not friends."[19] The second rather telling point to come out of the altercation is that despite the fight being observed by Carroll's relatives (and fellow Vigilance Committee members) the Mahers, not one of them opted to come to his aid.[20]

James Carroll had run out of reasons to stick around. He had hoped his work with the Stanley brothers might parlay into his ultimately acquiring his late father's farm in Stephen Township. But the trustees, his uncles Bartholomew Carroll and John Delahay, fought him in court over the matter and James Carroll lost. And on Saturday, May 26, 1883, William Porte wrote in his diary: "James M. Carroll of Tragedy Renown, left here on Friday the 25 under the shadow of the Rocky Mountains in the great lone land. Won't he be lonely. Well, so be it."[21]

James Carroll left Biddulph for the west coast of Canada. A little over a year later the *Winnipeg Times* newspaper would report that

> James Carroll, who figured so prominently in the
> Biddulph racket two or three years ago, is working
> on the railway out west. It is said that he scarcely
> eats anything, works only enough to provide himself
> with the necessaries of life, and holds but little
> intercourse with those around him. He seems to be
> a victim of melancholy, and it is feared his reason is
> giving way.[22]

Carroll would ultimately settle in the East Kootenay district of British Columbia, after putting in stops in Golden and Beaver. He died in 1915 in New Westminster, British Columbia, at the age of sixty-four.

B ob Donnelly never forgave the Vigilance Committee. Words that have echoed through the corridors of time speak of how, whenever a member of the Committee died, Bob Donnelly would make sure to attend the funeral, and would invariably walk up to the casket — in front of the bereaved friends and family — and spit on it, saying "There goes another of the bastards to hell!"[23] Postcards, particularly around the holidays, would arrive at the homes of Vigilance Committee members that read:

Dear Mr. ____,

When you go to church on Sunday and bless
yourself with your bloody hand, think of the poor
Donnellys who you sent to their death without any
chance of repentance.[24]

A story recounted in 1952 by James Collisson, whose father
Michael lived in Biddulph and had been a friend of the Donnelly
family, bears repeating. James had stepped inside the City Hotel in
London in the hope of locating his brother — and that's where he
encountered Bob Donnelly:

When I went into the hotel the proprietor was
talking to Donnelly, and seated all around the room
was a large number of young fellows from Biddulph
whose fathers had been arrested for the murders. I
went and asked my cousin if my brother was in and
he said no. And he then turned to Bob Donnelly
and said, "Do you know this boy? He comes from
Biddulph." I think I can still see and feel the look
of hatred which came into his eyes when he looked
at me. My cousin said, "Now hold on, this boy is
all right, he is the son of Mike Collisson." Donnelly
shouted at the top of his voice and held out his hand
to me, "Shake, my boy, we don't have to go out in
every rainstorm to wash the blood off our hands." I
knew all the people sitting around and had gone to
school with some of them, and you can imagine how
I felt and how quick I got out.[25]

Despite an enduring hatred for those who had murdered their
family, the surviving Donnellys still retained that sense of compassion

for the less fortunate that their mother had inculcated in them at a very young age — and that had so often brought trouble into the family home. A Lucan resident, Leonard D. Stanley, who worked at the mill in Lucan that William and Bob had once been accused of plotting to burn down, recalled seeing Bob Donnelly come out of his hotel one morning and spying a young, handicapped girl trying her best to walk along the Lucan railway tracks:

> One morning I was working in the grain elevator at Lucan I saw something that has impressed me ever since. It was early, and there wasn't very much of a stir on the station platform, the elevator being just down the track a few yards from the station and quite close to the hotel then run there by Bob Donnelly. As I looked out of the end of the elevator I saw the hotel door open and Bob Donnelly come out onto the platform. He looked up and down and I could see that his gaze had fallen upon something at the other end of the platform, for he stood there with tears in his eyes and slowly put his hand in his pocket and I could see he pulled out a bill. I then looked through a crack in the end of the elevator and beheld the object of his pity. There, coming along the track was a poor, terribly crippled girl, almost in rags, a pitiable sight. And as she came along, though she wasn't asking for any help, Bob Donnelly stepped out and pushed the bill into her hand and said: "Here, lady, take this. And if you ever come this way again, come into this house here, and stay as long as you like and it won't cost you a cent." Now there wasn't another living soul about the place, only me, and Donnelly couldn't see me for I was looking out

through a wide crack in the boards, so he didn't do it
for show — but that's the kind of fellows they were.[26]

This was a Donnelly trait that was too ingrained to ever be extricated. It would even be extended to include those who would do them harm, or whom they had harmed. For example, on July 2, 1884, Bob Donnelly moved to break up a fight between two patrons of the Simpson House Tavern in Glencoe. In so doing he inadvertently bumped into a man named Charles Burchell, knocking him off balance. When Donnelly eventually left the establishment that night Burchell was waiting in the shadows for him. As Donnelly walked past, Burchell leapt upon him, whereupon Donnelly tore himself free and blasted his adversary with one solid punch, which caused Burchell to fall to the street unconscious. William Donnelly, who was then serving in his capacity as town constable, arrested his brother for the assault, but when witnesses came forth to say that Bob had not initiated the fight, he was released.[27] However, when Bob Donnelly discovered how seriously he had hurt Burchell,[28] he brought the man into his home and nursed him back to health. He further covered Burchell's medical and hotel bills, and paid the man compensation for any wages he might have lost during the period of his convalescence.[29]

William Donnelly likewise shared this trait of having compassion for the disadvantaged and was said to have provided money to some of the widows in Appin to help them make ends meet after their husbands had died.[30] Other stories have come down to us that, prior to the murders, the family was known to take strangers into their home who were passing through Biddulph. They would feed and shelter both the rider and his horse, and then bring the horse, which had been groomed and fed, to the front door for their guest the next morning so that he could continue on his journey.[31] The Donnellys were said to always offer riders who passed by their farmhouse the use of their water trough and were the first to help any neighbour who had fallen sick.[32] If one of the Donnellys considered you a friend, all of them did. A man who was friends with Bob Donnelly told his son about the day he first met Bob's brother Pat.

> Bob Donnelly was making Dad acquainted with
> his brother, Pat, from Hamilton, St. Catharines,
> or somewhere down there, and when Dad met the
> Donnelly, [Pat] stuck out his hand and said, "Aw,
> you're my friend before ever I saw you! And if you
> ever get in trouble, off comes my coat the very first
> thing." And that's exactly as Dad told it to us.[33]

But the kindness the family extended was only one half of their disposition. The other half dwelt in shadow; the Donnelly brothers — even after the murders — seldom thought twice about using violence when they believed doing so was justified:

> *Glencoe Transcript*, November 1883:
> At a late hour on Saturday night Robert Donnelly, of
> the village, assaulted Constable Hugh McKay, and
> was on Monday arrested and taken to London by
> Constable G. Moore. Donnelly's explanation of the
> affair is that for some time past he has been missing
> geese from his flock, and determined to keep a watch
> for the party or parties who were making inroads
> upon them. Accordingly, on Saturday night, while on
> sentry, he saw some person leaving his premises and
> accosted him. The intruder turned out to be McKay.
> Donnelly says he was determined to take the law in
> his own hands, and gave McKay a good thrashing.
> McKay has since been arrested for larceny; the arrest
> being made by Constable William Donnelly.[34]

Thorold Post, June 1888:
Patrick Donnelly, charged with stabbing Joseph
Roberts in the Osborne house on Monday night.
Roberts, a waterworks employee, swore that after
some words regarding a chum in the bar of the
Osborne house, the prisoner followed him into the
hall, knocked him down and stabbed him in the
breast with a large pocket-knife, which was produced.
Roberts showed an ugly wound, and signs of having
lost considerable blood. The prisoner, he said,
threatened to cut his heart out. . . . after Roberts was
struck, the blood spurted from his breast. They threw
Donnelly out and sent for a doctor; during the first
scuffle on the floor each accused the other of biting.
Donnelly's face was bleeding when they separated
them; a witness kicked the knife out of Donnelly's
hand and put him out of doors. Case adjourned until
Wednesday, when a doctor was ordered to attend to
Donnelly's face. The magistrate closed the case, and in
the afternoon sentenced Donnelly to three months in
jail at Welland.[35]

Bothwell Times, July 1888:
Randolph Parker was on the sidewalk in front
of the St. Nicholas House, wanting someone to
come and settle a little difference, and was making
more noise than William Donnelly, the proprietor,
thought proper. So taking the law into his own
hands, [Donnelly] struck Parker, so it is said, with
a slingshot, knocking him off the sidewalk, then
kicking and beating him with his cane [shillelagh]
about the head and body. Upon others interfering,

Donnelly flourished a revolver and declared he would shoot any person who would come near him.[36]

It was stories such as these, reported as they were in the press of the day, that would provide grist for the Donnellys' many enemies, while also cementing their reputations and legacy into the future as being tough people whom one didn't want to cross.

William Donnelly would be the first of the surviving brothers to pass away. His death record from 1897 states that he had been suffering for two years prior to his passing from "liver and stomach complaints."[37] However, he had also suffered for some time from periodic bouts of inflammation of the lungs,[38] which would later return to him as pleurisy[39] and influenza.[40] When Bob Donnelly had been interviewed in May of 1908 by Dr. James Sutton, he had been asked specifically about the cause of death for each family member who had perished by that point in time. When asked about his brother William, Bob had replied that his death was "due to some form of lung trouble."[41]

It would appear that "lung trouble" ran throughout the family; Jim Donnelly had died of pneumonia, and Pat would succumb to pneumonia as well in 1914.[42] According to one author, Jennie Currie would ultimately die of tuberculosis in 1917,[43] following the death of her daughter, Rosemary, from tuberculosis in 1914.[44]

And as for Bob Donnelly, he continued to live in his little white frame house on South Main Street in Lucan for the remainder of his days, which, in the event, lasted only two years after his release from the London Asylum for the Insane. He died quite suddenly in 1911 from a paralytic stroke and was buried in the family plot at St. Patrick's Church, next to his family members. However, upon her death in 1919, Bob's wife Annie stipulated in her will that she wanted Bob's remains to be exhumed from St. Patrick's Cemetery and reinterred next to hers in St. Peter's Cemetery in London.[45] Her wishes were fulfilled and Bob was separated from his family for the second time; the first in life, the second in death.

With Bob's death, Patrick and Jennie became the only surviving children of James and Johannah Donnelly. Both attended Bob's funeral in Biddulph, and Patrick would make an interesting comment in a letter he wrote to the press upon his return to the Niagara Peninsula: "Permit me to extend my sincere thanks to the citizens of Lucan and surrounding country for the respect and sympathy shown at the death and burial of my deceased brother. I assure you I dearly love the land of my birth — with all its faults I love it still."[46] After the murder of his family members, William Donnelly, knowing how superstitious his Irish neighbours were in Biddulph, had never missed an opportunity to suggest to the newspapers that the Divine Hand of God would ultimately smite down those who had slaughtered his family.[47] While he may have seen "no use crying over burnt bodies," William Donnelly nevertheless saw considerable value in passing prophesy over them.

But Patrick's comments about loving the land of his birth would prove to be the most prophetic of any spoken by a Donnelly family member. The family's love for their Biddulph land was what had caused their late mother and father to stay and die upon it rather than flee to safety. It was their love for this land that had caused the surviving brothers to rebuild the family home upon it. And it had been Bob Donnelly's love for this land that had caused him to return to Lucan and to purchase his parents' original one-hundred-acre lot. In some respects, even death could not remove the Donnellys from their land. Indeed, their legend would grow out of it.

While their enemies had tried to drive the Donnellys from the town of Lucan and the township of Biddulph so that even the memory of the family would be eradicated, now, over 140 years later, it is the Donnelly name that has grown to become synonymous with these areas. Indeed, the present cultural museum in Lucan is named the "Lucan Area Heritage & Donnelly Museum." A "Black Donnellys Brewery" has sprung up, tours upon the site of James and Johannah's former plot of land went on for decades and two websites are presently dedicated to their story. The family's refusal to be cowed by their neighbours, their church or the Lucan power brokers has caused the family to be discussed and ultimately to become the focus of an enduring fascination that would never have occurred had not the Vigilance Committee laid them in their graves. In one of life's ironies, it is the names of those who had sought to destroy them that have now faded from the history books, only to resurface when some scribe rehashes the saga of the doomed family. In many respects, the Donnelly story has endured simply because it is an all-too-human story, filled with all of our species' vices and some of its virtues.

In 1881, a nameless reporter from the *London Advertiser* inquired in his newspaper column if, after all that had already been written about the Donnellys by that time, "could it be possible for this to go on for five or ten years?"[48] We must smile at the scribe's shortsightedness. Not only would the Donnellys' story endure for ten years, but it would continue to do so for well over a century. Indeed, as the author tosses his present offering on the topic into the ring, he finds that it falls alongside dozens of books, several documentaries, one film, six plays, four songs, at least two PhD theses, and countless magazine, newspaper and online articles that have been created about the Donnelly family in the 140 years since the reporter first posed his question.

In 1889, a tombstone was erected over the graves of the murdered family members by the Donnellys who survived. It stood over eleven feet high. St. Patrick's Church ordered it removed in the mid-1960s, owing to the number of people who had trespassed upon the church property to see it. It would be replaced by a more modest headstone. But perhaps the problem lay in the fact that the original marker wasn't large enough; for even then the Donnellys had become bigger than Biddulph. They had become as much a part of the fabric of Canada as the ships that brought the immigrants across the seas, or the land that needed to be cleared so that farms could exist and flourish, or the backroom political deals that lined politicians' pockets and brought the railway that interconnected the territories of the new Dominion. After all, the Donnellys had been a part of all these things. Both the family and the country had shared the same desire for autonomy and opportunity, both had struggled to crawl out from beneath the thumb of British rule and both made outsiders and the dispossessed feel welcome in their home. And both had their dark side.

"How time passes; it's a kind of a way time has," William Donnelly once dryly observed.[49] And time's way of passing would carry on for 138 years after William wrote those words until the author found himself standing before William and his family's headstone in St. Patrick's cemetery.

Having now researched the Donnelly story as thoroughly as I could, and presenting the facts as culled from the various newspapers, court transcripts, letters and diaries from the time, I get a strange feeling standing in front of this important monument.

The feeling is amplified as I look around the cemetery and note some of the other names on the various headstones — Kennedy, Quigley, Ryder, Toohey, McLaughlin, Heenan . . . almost every member of the Vigilance Committee is buried here too. No wonder Annie Donnelly wanted Bob's remains disinterred and moved to another cemetery.

I begin to question whether or not presenting the tale yet again is the right thing to do. After all, it is hard for the Donnellys (or their enemies for that matter) to rest in peace when yet another scribe disturbs their grave. What would they think of the fuss that has been made after them? No word of answer comes forth from the headstones. Perhaps it was just my naïveté coming to the surface. After all, what little is left of the Donnellys and their enemies' bones were long ago reclaimed by the very earth that once nourished them. Ashes to ashes, dust to dust.

I leave the cemetery and return to my truck. I pull the shift into drive and head north a little way on the Roman Line one last time. I hook a right onto Breen Drive, which I know to be the road along which the killers walked on their way to murder the family in the early morning hours of February 4, 1880. The realization sends a slight shiver up my spine. Crime has continued in Biddulph since then, of course, just as it has all over the vast world that lies outside of Middlesex County. But, as in the Donnellys' time, premeditated mass killings are still something of a rarity in this neck of the woods.

I turn left on 59, and then right onto the Whalen Line. Another left and I'm heading northeast along Perth Road 139. I'll be back at the arena in St. Marys in time for the puck to drop for Ben's next game. I hope that his team wins and that he scores another goal. I smile at the prospect. The thought takes some of the gloom out of the day I've had. I know that when the tournament is over and we're driving home to Bracebridge later this evening he'll ask me where I went today — and why. The answer is too long for the car ride home. Maybe he'll read the books someday.

Some strange things can come out of a hockey tournament in St. Marys.

DRAMATIS PERSONAE

THE DONNELLY FAMILY (IN ORDER OF BIRTH)

JAMES SR.: The paterfamilias of the Donnelly clan, James Sr. was born in 1816 and moved from Ireland to Canada in the early 1840s. He believed that Canada was a land of opportunity that gave Irish people the chance to own their own land and he was very protective of the land he would acquire. He would spend seven years in Kingston Penitentiary for killing a neighbour, Patrick Farrell, during a fight at a logging bee. He was murdered on February 4, 1880, in his home on the Roman Line.

JOHANNAH: The matriarch of the Donnellys, Johannah was born in 1820 in Ireland and immigrated to Canada with (or one year after) her husband. She was the primary caregiver in the Donnelly home. A tough but compassionate woman, she taught her children to stand up for each other and for the family. She was murdered on February 4, 1880, in her home on the Roman Line.

JAMES (JIM): The first-born son of James and Johannah, Jim was the only one of the Donnelly children to be born in Ireland (1841). He was perhaps the most violent of the Donnelly brothers. He died of pneumonia in 1877.

WILLIAM: Born in 1844 in London, Ontario, William was the second-born child of the Donnellys and the wittiest. He was also the smartest, often serving as the legal counsel for both his family and friends. He married Nora Kennedy and they had three children: Johannah, John and Nora. He died from a respiratory condition (most likely pneumonia) in 1897.

JOHN: The third child of James and Johannah, John was born in 1847 in Biddulph. He was considered a happy-go-lucky person, but would defend his brothers at the drop of a hat. He was briefly married to Francis Durham and was shot to death at his brother William's home by members of the Vigilance Committee on February 4, 1880.

PATRICK: The fourth child of James and Johannah, Patrick was born in 1849 in Biddulph. He moved out of the family home before notoriety attached itself to the family name and became a blacksmith and carriage maker in the Niagara Falls region of Ontario. He was briefly married to Mary Ryan, who died, and later to Mary Donnelly, and together they had five children: Mary, Margaret, John, Edith and Matthew. He and his brother William were the most active of the surviving family members in assisting the prosecution of his family's killers. He died of pneumonia in 1914.

MICHAEL (MIKE): The fifth child of James and Johannah, Michael was born in 1850 in Biddulph and had no legal problems until the stagecoach wars (he was partners with his brother William in the Donnelly stagecoach line). He married Ellen Hines, and together they had two children, Catherine (Kate) and James. Never one to shy away from a fight, he was killed after being knifed during an altercation in a barroom in Waterford in 1879.

ROBERT (BOB): The sixth child of James and Johannah, Robert was born in Biddulph in 1853. Bob was perhaps the most courageous of the Donnelly siblings, unafraid of a fight no matter the odds, but, like his mother, deeply compassionate for the less fortunate. He and his wife Annie Currie had no children of their own, but took care of his brother Mike's children after his death. He suffered from mental illness near the end of his life and died in 1911.

THOMAS (TOM): The seventh child of James and Johannah and the youngest son, Thomas was born in Biddulph in 1854. He's generally considered to be the strongest of the Donnelly brothers, and one who seldom thought before he acted. He was murdered after being handcuffed in the Donnelly home on the Roman Line. He is believed to have a child outside of marriage with Flora McKinnon, whom she named Tom Donnelly Jr.

JENNIE: The eighth and final child of James and Johannah — and the only daughter — Jennie was born in 1858 and, unlike her brothers, never faced a legal charge throughout her lifetime. With her husband, James Currie, she had twelve children: Robert, Johannah, James, John, Rosemary, Jane, Margaret, Anna, Catherine, Michael, Clara and Patrick. She died in 1916 of tuberculosis.

SECONDARY CHARACTERS

ANTI-CRIME SOCIETY, THE: The Anti-Crime Society was created in 1875 by Father John Connolly. Its purpose was to take a stand against crime in the community and to show support for Father Connolly. The priest had requested that the members of his congregation within St. Patrick's Roman Catholic Church agree to have their homes searched for stolen property when asked and to support their priest (him) in this undertaking. Those who were in favour were asked to sign a document that he had drawn up and placed in the church. It was signed by 78 parishioners.

ATKINSON, WILLIAM: Born in 1840, William Atkinson was one of William Donnelly's friends and admirers. He would be a part of his "Adventurers" who attempted to rescue William's girlfriend Margaret Thompson from being held against her will by her parents. Atkinson would later be tortured by Private Detective Hugh McKinnon in an attempt to have him give up information about the Donnellys.

BAWDEN, JOHN: Constable Bawden was part of a group, led by Private Detective Hugh McKinnon, that was responsible for the torture of Donnelly friend William Atkinson. He was also involved in the Ryder wedding brawl when he attempted to place John Donnelly under arrest. He once arrested Mike Donnelly without cause and held him prisoner illegally in a Lucan hotel room for over a week.

BRIMMACOMBE, RICHARD: Brimmacombe (1821–1857) was an English settler in Biddulph who was murdered on the Seventh Concession road in 1857, allegedly by Patrick "Grouchy" Ryder and William Casey.

CARROLL, JAMES: James Carroll (1851–1915) would prove to be the Donnelly family's chief antagonist. He was a founding member of the Vigilance Committee that was created to run the Donnellys out of town and have them arrested and, finally, orchestrated their deaths. Carroll would be made a constable specifically to persecute the Donnelly family. He, together with his younger brother, William, would be arrested for the murders of the Donnellys, but ultimately only James would stand trial for the crime.

CARROLL, JAMES: James Carroll (1857–1936), was the son of Michael Carroll and nephew of Mary Thompson, and lived on a farm just across from the Donnellys. He was no relation to the James Carroll of later infamy in the story.

CARSWELL, JOSEPH: Joseph Carswell was awarded a property that had been taken away from Jim Donnelly. Trouble plagued his farm afterwards, which he blamed solely on the Donnelly brothers.

CASEY, WILLIAM: Casey (1830–1901), together with Patrick Ryder, was believed to have killed the English farmer Richard Brimmacombe in 1857. He would later become a member of the Vigilance Committee and justice of the peace.

CONNOLLY, FATHER JOHN: The parish priest at St. Patrick's Church, Father Connolly (1829–1909), was an educated man who sincerely wanted peace within his parish; he was led astray by reports from within his congregation that were anti-Donnelly. His statements from the pulpit against the family had unintended consequences for the Donnellys that would prove fatal.

CURRIE, ANNIE: Annie was born in 1859 and would marry Robert Donnelly in 1873. The couple would unofficially adopt the son and daughter of Mike Donnelly after his death in Waterford, Ontario. She died in 1919.

CURRIE, JAMES: James was the brother of Annie Currie. Born in 1849, James married Jennie Donnelly in 1874. The couple would have twelve children. He died in 1931.

DONNELLY, BRIDGET: Bridget Donnelly was born in Ireland in 1844 and came to visit (and perhaps settle) in Canada from Ireland. She was the niece of James Donnelly Sr. and would later be brought to court to testify after Patrick "Grouchy" Ryder's barn burned down as a witness for her uncle. She was later murdered by a mob that raided that Donnelly home on the Roman Line on February 4, 1880.

DONNELLY, HANORAH (NORA): Nora was born in 1852 and married William Donnelly in 1875. She was the sister of John Kennedy Jr. and Rhody Kennedy, who would later become fierce adversaries of the Donnelly family. She died in 1937.

DONNELLY, MARY: Mary was born in 1856 and was Patrick Donnelly's second wife (her maiden name was Donnelly). They married in 1884 and had five children. Mary died in 1915.

DURHAM, FRANCIS: Francis Durham was born in 1852 and was briefly married to John Donnelly in 1871. She died in 1930.

EVERETT, SAMUEL: Constable Everett (1841–1882) was a corrupt constable who worked for the town of Lucan. When certain business interests within the town wanted the Donnellys in jail, Everett claimed that Bob Donnelly had attempted to shoot him. Donnelly was then convicted of the crime and would spend two years within Kingston Penitentiary. Everett would later change his testimony on the matter when he was removed from his job as town constable.

FARRELL, PATRICK: Patrick Farrell (1816–1857) was a man who had quarrelled with James Donnelly Sr., when the two men lived in Ireland. After immigrating to Canada, a land deal between the two went south, and Donnelly fired a shot at him. When they met a year later at a logging bee, both men drank heavily and their bad blood boiled over yet again. During a fight, James Donnelly Sr. struck Farrell with a handspike, killing him. Donnelly would serve seven years in Kingston Penitentiary as a result.

FEEHELEY FAMILY: The Feeheleys had been friendly with the Donnellys but turned against them when the Vigilance Committee came into existence. Michael (1818–1881) and Bridget Feeheley had an abusive relationship, and their children James (1857–1932) and William (1860–1926) were often taken in by the Donnelly family during such times. James would later spy for the Vigilance Committee on the night of the murders to let them know who came in and out of the Donnellys' home. William would watch Tom Donnelly's murder from a vantage point across the road.

FLANAGAN, PATRICK: Flanagan was the Donnellys' chief competition during the stagecoach wars. He came from a successful family in Clandeboye, and later, at the behest of certain business interests in Lucan, Flanagan hired or was the contact person to bring private detective Hugh McKinnon to Lucan to dig up dirt on the Donnelly family.

HINES, ELLEN: Ellen was born in 1858 and would marry Michael Donnelly in 1874. The couple produced two children prior to Michael's death in 1879. Their son would be informally adopted and raised by Bob and Annie Donnelly. She died in 1929.

HODGINS, WILLIAM: Constable Hodgins (born 1842) worked with James Carroll and the Vigilance Committee to try to remove the Donnellys from Biddulph. He once fought with John Donnelly in a back-alley brawl that lasted thirty minutes.

HUTCHINSON, CHARLES: Hutchinson (1826–1892) was the Crown attorney for Middlesex County whose job was to prosecute wrongdoings on behalf of the province. He prosecuted cases against the Donnellys throughout their lifetime but worked on their behalf during the murder trials that followed the murders.

IRVING, AEMILIUS: Irving (1823–1913) was a talented lawyer and member of Parliament in the 1870s. He worked with Charles Hutchinson to prosecute James Carroll for the murder of Johannah Donnelly.

KEEFE FAMILY: The Keefe family would be lifelong friends of the Donnellys. The patriarch was James Keefe Sr. (1821–1890). His sons, Daniel Keefe, James Keefe Jr., Patrick and Thomas (1857–1902) were particularly close with the Donnelly brothers, as was their cousin Robert Keefe. The Keefe sons were particularly tough and fought frequently.

MACMAHON, HUGH: MacMahon (1836–1911) was part of the defence team that defended James Carroll during the latter's murder charge in two trials.

MAHER FAMILY: James Maher Sr. (1823–1906) was an uncle of James Carroll and allowed James and his brother William to live at his home on the Roman Line. Both Maher and his son, James Jr. (born 1862), would be members of the Vigilance Committee and were said to have taken part in the murder of the Donnelly family.

MCKINNON, HUGH: McKinnon (1843–1903) was a brutal ex-policeman-cum-private investigator from Hamilton, Ontario, who had been hired by the Donnellys' rival in the stagecoach business, Patrick Flanagan, to rid the community of the Donnellys. Apart from nearly killing a friend of the Donnellys and re-charging certain of the Donnelly brothers with crimes of which they had already been acquitted, his investigations resulted in nothing.

MEREDITH, EDMUND: Edmund (1845–1921) was the brother of William Ralph Meredith, whom the Donnelly survivors employed to represent their interests in the trials against the murderers of their parents. His loyalty to his clients would later be called into question.

MEREDITH, WILLIAM RALPH: William (1840–1923) was the leader of the provincial Conservative Party — the opposition party to Oliver Mowat's Liberal government. He was also part of the defence team for James Carroll and the prisoners accused of murdering the Donnellys. Despite being Protestant, he tried to position himself politically as a strong advocate for the rights of Irish Catholics within the province and to paint the Donnelly murder trials as a persecution against the Catholic community within Lucan and Biddulph.

MOWAT, OLIVER: The premier of Ontario and the attorney general of the Province, Mowat (1820–1903) was a career politician who wanted justice pursued in the trial of James Carroll for the murder of Johannah Donnelly, but upon learning that there were upwards of twenty people who could be accused of the crime, all of whom were Roman Catholic, he began to fear he would alienate Irish Roman Catholic voters if he was seen to support the prosecution of the killers. His interference in the trial against the Feeheley brothers for the murder of Tom Donnelly resulted in their fleeing the country.

O'CONNOR FAMILY: Michael (1818–1883) and Mary O'Connor (born 1841) were friends with the Donnelly parents. Their son, Johnny O'Connor (born 1866), barely escaped with his life from the scene of the murder of the Donnelly family on the Roman Line on February 4, 1880. He would go on to testify against those he saw commit the murders, which marked him and his family out as targets by the Vigilance Committee members. Robert Donnelly would save the lives of two of the O'Connor children when their home was set on fire prior to the trial.

PORTE, WILLIAM: Porte (1823–1899) was the postmaster of Lucan and also served on its town council. He kept a diary of the goings-on within both the town of Lucan and throughout Biddulph township. He believed the Donnellys had been unfairly blamed for much of the crime that occurred within the region. He would remain friendly with the family throughout the ordeal and afterwards.

PURTELL, JOHN: John Purtell (born 1857) was a hired hand of the McGrath family and was identified by Johnny O'Connor as being present at the Donnelly home during the murders.

RYAN, MARY: The first wife of Patrick Donnelly, she was born in 1853 and married Patrick in 1871. Mary died during childbirth in 1873. Their baby would die as well.

RYDER FAMILY: Patrick "Grouchy" Ryder (1822–1906) had known the Donnellys for years but after his barn burned down in January 1880, he believed that the Donnellys had been the culprits. He and his family members — sons Patrick Jr. and James Jr. — and brothers James, Thomas and Daniel were said to have taken part in the murder of the Donnellys.

STANLEY BROTHERS: Bernard (1825–1911) and William Stanley (1834–1911) were the most powerful men in Lucan, Ontario. Ruthless and politically savvy, they were not above using terror tactics in acquiring businesses and properties. They would side with James Carroll during the murder trials and were involved with bringing charges against William and Bob Donnelly for an alleged arson attempt in 1881.

THOMPSON, WILLIAM JR.: William Thompson Jr. (1845–1929) lived on the lot adjacent to the Donnelly homestead. His sister Margaret had once been in love with William Donnelly, but William Thompson

Sr. forbade their union. William Donnelly and his friends raided their homes looking for Margaret but the father had hidden her at a relative's home. William Thompson Jr. would join the Vigilance Committee and was a hardened adversary of the Donnelly family.

TOOHEY, JAMES: James Toohey (1844–1931) was the man who hid William Thomson Jr.'s sister, Margaret, from William Donnelly's group. He was also said to have been present at the murder of the Donnelly family on the night of February 4, 1880.

VIGILANCE COMMITTEE, THE: A second society, originally called the Peace Society, but later referred to as the Vigilance Committee, was formed in August 1879 to bring some muscle to the plan of ousting the Donnelly family from the community. James Carroll, John Kennedy Jr., Martin McLaughlin and other people who held anti-Donnelly sentiments created the group (numbering somewhere between fifty and one hundred in total), which was said to have planned and orchestrated the murder of the Donnelly family.

WEST, FRANCIS MORRISON: West (no record exists as to his birth, but he died in the United States in 1882) was a music teacher and small-time thief who tried to become a private detective. Working on behalf of a Lucan faction led by the Stanley brothers, he concocted charges against William and Bob Donnelly for attempting to set fire to a grist mill owned by the Stanleys.

WHALEN FAMILY: The Whalens lived across the road from the Donnelly family. Patrick (1816–1882) and Ann Whalen (born 1810) lived north of the Donnellys, while their son John (born 1846) lived directly across the road. It was to Patrick and Ann's house that Johnny O'Connor ran immediately after the murders. John Whalen, like William Feeheley, witnessed the murder of Tom Donnelly from across the road.

CHRONOLOGY: 1840—1916

Jennie Donnelly would be the last of the children of James and Johannah
Donnelly to pass away. (By permission of Ray Fazakas, author of
The Donnelly Album and *In Search of the Donnellys*)

1840 — Johannah Magee and James Donnelly marry in Ireland.

1841 — Their son, James Jr., is born in Ireland.

1842 — James, Johannah and James Jr. sail to Upper Canada (it is
believed that James may have arrived first in order to get estab-
lished and then sent for Johannah and James Jr. in 1843).

1844 — William Donnelly is born in London, Ontario.

1845 — James Donnelly builds a home on a one-hundred-acre lot
owned by John Grace (Lot 18, Concession 6, in Biddulph).

1847 — John Donnelly is born in Biddulph, Ontario.

1849 — Patrick Donnelly is born in Biddulph, Ontario.

1850 — Michael Donnelly is born in Biddulph, Ontario.

1853 — Robert Donnelly is born in Biddulph, Ontario.

1854 — Thomas Donnelly is born in Biddulph, Ontario.

1855 — John Grace , seeking to take advantage of increased real estate values, sells half of Lot 18, Concession 6 (the southern fifty acres), to farmer Michael Maher for £200.

— Shortly after attempting to sell a lot that he has leased to recent immigrant Patrick Farrell, James Donnelly Sr. is charged with shooting at Farrell (a man James Donnelly Sr. is believed to have quarrelled with when both men lived in Tipperary, Ireland).

1856 — John Grace sells the northern fifty acres of Lot 18, Concession 6, to James Donnelly Sr. for £50. This is 75 percent less than what Maher had paid for the southern fifty acres of the lot, which fosters ill will between Maher and Donnelly.

1857 — A fight breaks out at a logging bee between James Donnelly Sr. and Patrick Farrell. Both men pick up handspikes and Donnelly kills Farrell with one blow. The Ontario government posts a $400 reward for Donnelly's capture.

1858 — Jennie Donnelly is born in Biddulph, Ontario.

— James Donnelly Sr. decides to submit to the authorities and turns himself in. At his trial, he is convicted of murdering Patrick Farrell and is sentenced to be hanged. Johannah Donnelly begins to circulate petitions to have spare her husband's life. Her actions are rewarded; James Donnelly's sentence is commuted to seven years in Kingston Penitentiary.

— Johannah Donnelly and her children work hard to make the farm successful enough to support them. James Donnelly's brother arrives to lend some help, but soon leaves. Johannah is forced to take out several mortgages on the farm to make ends meet but is able to pay all the mortgages back. The Donnellys sell a small section on the northern side of the property to the township to be used as a yard for the local school. It is thereafter referred to locally as "the Donnelly Schoolhouse."

1865 — Having served his seven-year sentence, James Donnelly Sr. is released from Kingston Penitentiary and returns home to Biddulph.

1869 — William Donnelly is charged with stealing a revolver by
speakeasy owner John Graham. Donnelly defends himself
impressively in court and is acquitted.

— William Donnelly, along with his older brother Jim and others,
are acquitted at trial for the robbery of the Granton post office.

1870s —Jim Donnelly takes over a small farm, but soon moves off to
Michigan. His brothers Michael, Robert and Thomas farm
the property during his absence. William helps his parents
on their Biddulph farm. Patrick leaves Biddulph to work in
the carriage business in London, where he marries a woman
named Mary Ryan. John Donnelly elopes but returns to run a
tavern in Lucan. The marriage is short-lived.

1871 — William Donnelly secures his first job outside the family farm
as a stagecoach driver for the McPhee and Keefe stage line.

1873 — William Donnelly purchases the stage line from McPhee and
partners with the Calder stagecoach line. He hires his brothers
Michael, Robert and Thomas Donnelly as drivers. Their
competition is a stage line owned by a man named Hawkshaw.

— William Donnelly is dating Margaret Thompson, a girl who
lives with her older brother William in a farmhouse next to
the Donnellys' property. Soon they decide to marry. Margaret's
father, William Thompson Sr., forbids the union and takes her
away from Biddulph.

1874 — Margaret Thompson writes to William Donnelly to come and
rescue her from her parents. William Donnelly, along with some
of his brothers and friends, stages a raid on William Thompson
Sr.'s house in an effort to rescue Margaret. In the process they
raid the home of widow Ellen Fogarty and Margaret's brother,
William Thompson Jr. They are unable to locate Margaret and
are charged with trespassing but later acquitted.

— A man named Patrick Flanagan takes over the Hawkshaw
stage line and the rivalry between the Donnelly stage and the
Flanagan stage line becomes known as the "stagecoach wars."

— Jim Donnelly is ordered to vacate his property in Biddulph on
Lot 26, Concession 11. The land is sold to a farmer named

Joseph Carswell. However, not long after he takes possession, fires break out on his property.

1875 — Much to the chagrin of her brothers Rhody and John, Nora Kennedy marries William Donnelly.

— Jim Donnelly, while in the employ of his brothers' stagecoach line, assaults a fruit peddler. He is originally charged with assault and theft but after his brother William's legal wrangling, the theft charge is dropped.

— The stagecoach wars continue; a stagecoach owned by Flanagan is destroyed. A driver for Flanagan is killed when a wheel falls off his stage during an ill-advised race against Michael Donnelly's stage on the main road into London. A Flanagan driver, Robert McLeod, cuts off the Donnelly stage driven by Tom Donnelly, causing it to topple over and injure some of the passengers. William Donnelly charges McLeod and is awarded damages. However, the two injured passengers from the Donnelly stage, Louisa and Martha Lindsay, win their suit against the Donnelly Stagecoach Line and William is ordered to pay damages. He opts for a short-term jail sentence instead of paying.

— Local strongman Joseph Berryhill challenges the Donnelly brothers' friend James Keefe to a fight. Keefe and the Donnellys attack Berryhill in a bar. Keefe temporarily disappears and Thomas Donnelly is charged and convicted of assault.

— During the same night as the Berryhill fight, a man named James Curry claims that Keefe, James Donnelly Jr. and Thomas Donnelly assaulted and robbed him. However, the local constable recognizes that Curry was too drunk to know what happened to him and decides not to pursue the charge against Tom Donnelly and Keefe.

— The stables of stagecoach owners Flanagan and Crawley are set on fire. Later, Flanagan himself is beaten while returning from his stable. Rhody Kennedy falls out with the Donnelly brothers and testifies they were the ones who threatened to burn Flanagan's stables. William Donnelly defends his brother against the charge with the result that Tom Donnelly is acquitted. He further charges Rhody Kennedy with perjury.

1876 — Flanagan stagecoach driver Peter McKellar has an altercation with Michael and Robert Donnelly on the Main Street in Lucan. Michael Donnelly is charged (and later convicted) of threatening McKellar's life. However, William Donnelly charges McKellar with threatening him with a revolver. Rhody Kennedy, now a constable, decides to single-handedly arrest Robert Donnelly, and ends up being pistol-whipped in the street.

— A private detective from Hamilton, Ontario, Hugh McKinnon, is hired by Donnelly rival Flanagan (and other business owners in Lucan) to ferret out information that will lead to the arrest of the Donnellys. He tortures a friend of the family, William Atkinson, to attempt to get him to confess the Donnellys' crimes, but Atkinson says nothing. Later he has local constable John Bawden illegally imprison Michael Donnelly in a hotel room in Lucan, but Donnelly escapes.

— Constables John Bawden, John Coursey and John Reid attempt to arrest two Donnelly brothers while they're at the wedding of Thomas Ryder in Lucan. A brawl breaks out and a constable is shot. The Donnellys flee the scene and the local militia is sent out after them. John and James Donnelly are arrested. William later turns himself in to the London authorities.

— Due largely to William's legal manoeuvring, most of the charges brought against the Donnelly brothers are dropped. However, William, James and John are sent to prison in Toronto. William is released within weeks of being incarcerated due to an illness. The other two brothers remain behind to serve their full sentence.

1877 — The Donnellys' stables and stages are burned, as well as the home of Michael Donnelly.

— Jim Donnelly dies at home of pneumonia.

— The Donnelly stage line shuts down operations owing to the market being taken over by the London, Huron and Bruce Railway.

— James Carroll, a man in his mid-twenties and a relative of the Mahers, comes to Biddulph. He immediately attempts to cause trouble for the Donnellys. When challenged to a fight by John Donnelly, Carroll pulls a revolver on him and also threatens to shoot Johannah Donnelly.

— Robert Donnelly is sent to Kingston Penitentiary after being charged with shooting at Town Constable Samuel Everett. The constable later claims that he wasn't sure it was Robert Donnelly who shot at him.

1879 — Constable Everett assaults fellow constable William Hodgins, after words are exchanged about fear of arresting one of the Donnellys.

— A new priest arrives at St. Patrick's Catholic Church in Biddulph, Father John Connolly. He immediately is inundated by anti-Donnelly stories by several parishioners who wish to drive the family out of the township. He is offended by a letter sent to him from William Donnelly.

— Father Connolly creates an anti-crime society, the function of which is to put down crime in the Biddulph area. He wants all his parishioners to sign a pledge indicating their willingness to have their properties searched for stolen goods. The Donnellys refuse to sign the pledge, believing that it is just a ruse for their enemies to set them up for crimes they didn't commit.

— Having grown disillusioned with Father Connolly's anti-crime society, another group forms, made up of more violent members. The group becomes the "Vigilance Committee" and their sole goal, seemingly, is to have the Donnellys arrested and/or driven from the township. James Carroll, John Kennedy Jr. and many of the Donnellys' enemies are members of this new group.

— William Thompson Jr. loses one of his cows and tells the Vigilance Committee he believes it was stolen. The Committee members believe the Donnellys to be the culprits and stage a raid on the Donnelly farm. Not finding the animal there, they threaten James Donnelly Sr. with physical harm and then head toward William Donnelly's home to look for it. William is tipped off by his mother that the Vigilance Committee is coming for him and so waits for them outside of his front door with a pistol in his hand. When the mob arrives, they lose their nerve to proceed.

— With the Vigilance Committee's backing, James Carroll is made a constable. He pledges he will drive the Donnellys out of Biddulph and immediately sets about looking through old court cases for loopholes that would allow him to arrest or re-arrest members of the Donnelly family. He arrests Tom Donnelly on an old charge that he had been acquitted of and Tom is promptly acquitted again. Carroll keeps re-charging him on the same offense. During one attempt to arrest Tom Donnelly, the latter is given a horse by his brother John and outrides his pursuers. Tom turns himself in and Carroll charges John Donnelly with aiding Thomas's escape. He is acquitted. The Donnellys now charge the Vigilance Committee members with trespassing on their property when they were in search of Thompson's cow.

— Through the efforts of the Vigilance Society, James Carroll and Father Connolly, a campaign to encourage people not to associate with the Donnellys is put into play. In a small community, this is the equivalent of solitary confinement.

— Michael Donnelly is stabbed to death in a bar fight in Waterford, Ontario. The man who killed him, William Lewis, had vowed to "fix" him prior to the encounter. Lewis is arrested.

1880 — Robert Donnelly is released from Kingston Penitentiary and, after a brief stop in Biddulph to visit his parents, returns to his home and wife in Glencoe.

— The barn of Donnelly neighbour Patrick "Grouchy" Ryder burns down. The Vigilance Committee meets with Ryder and instructs Carroll to prepare charges of arson against the Donnelly brothers. However, the brothers were all at a wedding on the night in question and so are alibied. The

Vigilance Committee then decides to have James and Johannah Donnelly charged with the crime. Despite the lack of evidence, the elderly couple is arrested and brought to trial. The trial is repeatedly postponed as Constable Carroll attempts to find evidence against them.

February 3, 1880 — The Vigilance Committee meets in the Cedar Swamp Schoolhouse. Their inner circle has decided that the Donnellys will be murdered later that night. They recruit one-time Donnelly friend James Feeheley to go to the Donnelly home that evening and then report to the Committee as to who is inside the house.

February 4, 1880 — At approximately 1 a.m., a mob made up of between twenty and forty Vigilance Committee members advances on the Donnelly farmhouse. Constable James Carroll sneaks in through the kitchen door and immediately handcuffs Tom Donnelly, the strongest of the Donnelly brothers. Once Tom is thus handicapped, the mob breaks into the home and clubs James, Johannah, Tom and Bridget Donnelly to death. A boy, Johnny O'Connor, hides under the bed and witnesses the massacre. The mob then sets fire to the Donnellys' home and heads out toward William Donnelly's home. O'Connor escapes from the burning home and runs to the home of Ann and Patrick Whalen. He tells the Whalens what he has witnessed, but the Whalens don't head over to the Donnelly home until it is too late, and the Donnellys' home burns to the ground. Around 2 a.m., the mob arrives at William Donnelly's home and begin calling his name and pounding on his door. The noise awakens John Donnelly, who had been staying overnight at William's. When John answers the door he is shot at close range with both a shotgun and a large-calibre hunting rifle. He dies within minutes. By morning neighbours and curiosity seekers gather round the ruins of the Donnelly home. Many pilfer mementoes, ranging from pocket watches to skulls. In the afternoon Coroner Thomas Hossack empanels a jury that visits the ruins of the Donnelly home and observes the bodies. The police arrive afterwards and put the charred bones into a single small wooden box.

February 5, 1880 — James Carroll and twelve other members of the Vigilance Committee are arrested for the murders of the Donnelly family.

February 6, 1880 — The funeral is held for James Sr., Johannah, Thomas, Bridget and John Donnelly. Father John Connolly delivers the funeral address, which is a mixture of sorrow for the victims and contempt for the magistrates who didn't put the Donnellys behind bars. During the service, Patrick Donnelly challenges the priest to defend his actions.

February 11, 1880 — The coroner's inquest is resumed. Witnesses (such as can be found) tell what they know of the Donnelly murders. William Donnelly and Johnny O'Connor offer the strongest testimony. The coroner's inquest continues on February 18 and concludes on March 2. The jurors conclude that the Donnellys were murdered by "persons unknown."

February 21, 1880 — A preliminary hearing takes place, running from February 21 to March 13. Six prisoners are committed to stand trial at the Spring Assizes. The remaining prisoners are released on bail.

April to May, 1880 — The prosecutors believe that the jurors in Biddulph and London are prejudiced in favour of the prisoners. They attempt to obtain a change of venue but the magistrate denies their request. They bring their appeal to the city of Toronto and, again, are denied. The trial will take place in London.

October 4–9, 1880 — The first trial commences on October 4 under Justice Armour. The prosecution's strategy is to first try James Carroll, as he was spotted at both murder scenes. Again, the witnesses testify, but it is clear the Vigilance Committee has intimidated the majority of the township into supporting the prisoner. Justice Armour issues a pro-Donnelly charge to the jury, but only four members of the jury vote to convict, seven vote to acquit and one is undecided. The case must be re-tried.

November to December, 1880 — The attorney general (and premier of the Province of Ontario), Oliver Mowat, fearing a potential backlash from the Catholic community he depends on to retain power, orders a special commission to have the next trial in just over two months' time (not long enough for the Crown to mount an effective prosecution). He appoints two justices to adjudicate the trial — Matthew Crooks Cameron and Featherston Osler (the latter of which has already indicated the evidence in the matter is insufficient to convict).

January 24 to February 2, 1881 — The second trial gets under way. The judge doesn't allow the prosecution to call many of their witnesses and indicates that there is reasonable doubt as to Carroll's guilt. Carroll is acquitted of the murder of Johannah Donnelly. The Crown decides not to prosecute the remaining prisoners.

February 1881 — James Feeheley confesses to Patrick Donnelly about what happened on the night of the Donnelly family murders, and gives names. However, what the Feeheleys really want is money to get out of town.

April 1881 — In an effort to avoid testifying, Michael and James Feeheley leave Canada for Michigan.

September 1881 — The Feeheleys are extradited to Canada and charged with the murder of Thomas Donnelly. Oliver Mowat goes behind the prosecution's back and allows the Feeheleys to be freed on bail (which is paid by the Vigilance Committee and Father Connolly). The Feeheleys flee to Michigan and never return.

October 1881 — William and Robert Donnelly are framed on an arson charge, set up by Bernard Stanley, the wealthiest man in Lucan, along with several other Lucan businessmen who support the Vigilance Committee. The Donnellys are acquitted.

1897 — William Donnelly dies.

1908 — Robert Donnelly is committed to the London Asylum for the Insane.

1911 — Robert Donnelly dies.

1914 — Patrick Donnelly dies.

1916 — Jennie Donnelly, the last surviving immediate member of the Donnelly family, dies.

NOTES ON TEXT

CHAPTER SEVENTEEN: THE MASSACRE

1   Unless otherwise indicated, the activity and dialogue pertaining to
the murders of the Donnelly family on the Roman Line are taken
from the testimony of Johnny O'Connor, during both the coroner's
inquest in Lucan on February 11, 1880, and the preliminary inquest
of the criminal charges against the prisoners that took place
on February 21, 1880. Evidence at The Coroner's Inquest and
Preliminary Examination, Aemilius Irving Papers, F 1027-3, File
82-8, Transcript of the Donnelly Murder Case, 1880 (MS 6500)
Public Archives of Ontario, Toronto. Similarly, unless otherwise
indicated, the activity and dialogue pertaining to the murder of
John Donnelly are drawn from the testimony of William Donnelly,
Nora Donnelly and Martin Hogan during both the coroner's
inquest and preliminary examination.

2   "I saw John Donnelly going north on horseback, at about five
o'clock." Testimony of John Whalen, Aemilius Irving Papers,

F 1027-3, File 82-8, Transcript of the Donnelly Murder Case, 1880 (MS 6500) Public Archives of Ontario, Toronto.

3   J. Robert Salts in conversation with the author on Saturday, November 8, 2014. See also: "That same year [1870] a builder named Robert Thompson got the boys to help him get four big field-stone and he built a standard 18 by 26 foot squared-log cabin. . . . . In 1871, Thompson returned and constructed a large frame kitchen on the back. There was a small bedroom on the south wall and the back door also faced south." *You Are Never Alone: Our Life on the Donnelly Homestead*, J. Robert Salts, Publisher, London, ON, 1996, p. 37.

4   "I asked him [James Feeheley] if he told them [James Carroll and James Maher] Johnny O'Connor was there — he said he didn't; he thought it was John Donnelly who was in bed with the father." Testimony of John H. McConnell. J.J. Talman Regional Collection, University of Western Ontario Archives, Donnelly Family Papers, B4877, File 54, Various Authors, Information on Murders, 1881, ca. 1881.

5   "He [James Feeheley] told the witness then about being sent by the Vigilant Committee to the Donnellys' house to see who was there, as they intended to take the family out that night and hang them unless they told who burnt Ryder's barn. He said he went to the house, and when he came out to the road he saw James Carroll, and James Maher. They sent him then to Whalen's Corners to watch Will's house, and see who went in or out." *Huron Signal-Star*, July 15, 1881. See also testimony of John H. McConnell: "He [James Feeheley] told me then he was sent by the Vigilance Committee that night to see who was in Donnelly's house, and when he went out to his road after leaving the house, he met James Carroll and James Maher and some others whose names I don't remember and he told them who was in the house." J.J. Talman Regional Collection, University of Western Ontario Archives, Donnelly Family Papers, B4877, File 54, Various Authors, Information on Murders, 1881, ca. 1881.

6   *Toronto Mail*, March 5, 1880.

7   As an example: "Mrs. Donnelly fell upon her knees at the foot of the ringleader and implored, with mingled tears and blood pouring down her fading cheeks, for one minute to pray for the salvation of her soul. With a savage laugh and a bloodcurdling curse, the fiend replied, 'Pray, you bitch? You have prayed too long already,' and with a heavy instrument the poor woman was felled senseless at his feet . . ." *Toronto Telegram*, February 8, 1880. This anecdote has been picked up and put forth as factual by various authors of the Donnelly story over the years. However, it is unsourced (it is not attributed to anyone who was present during the murders) and is not corroborated by anything that Johnny O'Connor heard being said during the time that the murders took place and, thus, is highly suspect.

8   According to an annotation made next to a name on a list of suspects compiled by Lucan constable Samuel Everett during the time that the murders were being investigated, Michael Carroll was the one who delivered the coup de grace to Johannah Donnelly. J.J. Talman Regional Collection, University of Western Ontario Archives, Donnelly Family Papers, B4877, File 39, Samuel Everett, List of Suspects by Everett, ca. 1880.

9   Donnelly Family Papers, B4877, File 39, Samuel Everett, List of Suspects by Everett, ca. 1880. According to Everett's list, "James Maher killed the old man."

10 James Toohey was observed later that same morning sporting a black eye and, given that he had been among the group that had chased Tom Donnelly from the house, it is likely that he received the shiner as a result of a punch from Tom. "Luke Nangle told Charles Nangle & John Grace, that on the morning after the murder they saw [James] Toohey dressed in woman's clothes and taking them off in the stable. Toohey had a black eye (this can be proved by James McLaughlin, Daniel Keefe and Patrick Keefe and Patrick Donnelly). He can prove that there were several meetings of part of the Vigilance Committee at Toohey's house, between the night of the Ryder fire and the murders, when the windows

were screened with bed quilts." J.J. Talman Regional Collection, University of Western Ontario Archives, Donnelly Family Papers, B4878, File 15, Charles Hutchinson to Aemilius Irving, Charles Hutchinson Letter Book, ca. January 15, 1881. See also: "When the crown presented evidence that vigilante James Toohey was seen sporting a black eye the morning after the murders, Cameron stopped them short by ruling the information inadmissible." *London Advertiser*, January 29, 1881.

11 There is an enduring belief that Tom Donnelly, while running from the front door, was intercepted by Thomas Ryder, who thrust a pitchfork into his abdomen, bringing the youngest Donnelly brother to his knees whereupon the mob caught up to Tom and finished him off with their clubs. The belief seems to be based on the belief that Ryder later was given the nickname "Pitchfork" Tom Ryder as a result of his role in the murder. However, the author has had trouble finding a source for Thomas Donnelly being stabbed by a pitchfork. While there is no doubt as to Ryder's nickname being "Pitchfork," there is a consid-erable lack of evidence that he used such an implement upon Tom Donnelly. Further, in an era when the death penalty was in play for those found guilty of committing murder, it strikes the author as rather an unnecessarily dangerous and foolish moniker to give someone who would be looking to keep his role in the Donnelly murders on the down-low. Moreover, most of the Ryder family had odd nicknames — "Grouchy," "Young Grouch," "Buckshot," "Sideroad," "Pitchfork" — and it seems more likely that a scenario was thereby created after the fact to fit an already existent nickname. In addition, Johnny O'Connor (the only witness who was willing to speak on the record of what happened within the Donnellys' house that night) makes no mention of Tom Donnelly being killed by a pitchfork (or even seeing one), but he does mention clubs and sticks.

12 "William Feeheley afterwards told witness he saw the whole thing, that he was inside Whalen's fence, and that Jack Whalen saw it too." *Huron Signal-Star*, July 15, 1881.

13 "William Feeheley told me in presence of James Hodgins that James Toohey, Pat Quigley and James Maher were the three men who carried Tom Donnelly into the house after he was killed." Statement by Thomas Shoebottom, County Constable, J.J. Talman Regional Collection, University of Western Ontario Archives, Donnelly Family Papers, B4877, File 63, Unknown, Statements About the Feeheleys, ca. April 31, 1881 — July 31, 1881. See also: "That night witness [Patrick Donnelly] and James slept together, and prisoner said the only thing he ever did for which he was sorry was that he had sold Tom Donnelly to the Vigilance men, saying that he went to the house on the evening of the murder to see who were there. He said it was James Toohey, Pat Quigley and James Maher who carried Tom Donnelly into the house . . ." *Huron Signal-Star*, July 15, 1881.

14 "This scene, Feeheley said to a friend, would never fade from his view while life should last, and often in the darkness of his chamber he saw the bleeding head of Tom rise slowly up, and his lips part, as they did on that fateful night of the murder." *London Free Press*, May 21, 1881.

15 "He [William Feeheley] said it was Pat Quigley's spade Tom's head was split with after he was carried into the house." Statement by Thomas Shoebottom, County Constable, J.J. Talman Regional Collection, University of Western Ontario Archives, Donnelly Family Papers, B4877, File 63, Unknown, Statements About the Feeheleys, ca. April 31, 1881 — July 31, 1881. See also: "He [William Feeheley] said . . . that it was Quigley who smashed Tom's head with a spade." *Huron Signal-Star*, July 15, 1881.

16 O'Connor's testimony about seeing a man at the murders in a woman's dress was corroborated by Luke Nangle: "Luke Nangle told Charles Nangle and John Grace, that on the morning after the murder they saw [James] Toohey dressed in woman's [sic] clothes and taking them off in the stable. Toohey had a black eye (this can be proved by James McLaughlin, Daniel Keefe and Patrick Keefe and Patrick Donnelly)." J.J. Talman Regional Collection, University of Western Ontario Archives, Donnelly Family Papers, B4878,

File 15, Charles Hutchinson to Aemilius Irving, Charles Hutchinson Letter Book, ca. January 15, 1881.

CHAPTER EIGHTEEN: AFTERSHOCK

1   Unless otherwise indicated, Johnny O'Connor and the Whalen family's actions and dialogue on the night of the murders are taken directly from their testimony given at the coroner's inquest and preliminary examination, Crown v. James Carroll, Aemilius Irving Papers, F 1027-3, File 82-8, transcript of the Donnelly Murder Case, 1880 (MS 6500) Public Archives of Ontario, Toronto.

2   Testimony of John Whalen. Coroner's Inquest, February 4, 1880.

3   Testimony of John Whalen. Coroner's Inquest, February 4, 1880.

4   Testimony of Johnny O'Connor, Archives of Ontario, Aemilius Irving Papers, Evidence at the Coroner's Inquest and Preliminary Examination, F 1027-3, File 82-8, Transcript of the Donnelly Murder Case, 1880 (MS 6500).

5   Public Archives of Ontario, Irving Fonds, F1027, 82 80, MS6500, Deposition of Patrick Whalen, March 31, 1880.

6   Testimony of Patrick Whalen. Preliminary Hearings, March 12, 1880.

7   Testimony of William Blackwell. Archives of Ontario, Coroner's Inquest, March 2, 1880.

8   "The reflection of the fire at old Donnelly's was sufficient to increase the light of the night around my place and [William] Donnelly's. The colour of the window with frosted panes, was pink colour, from the fire: quite a bit of light was thrown on my window from the reflection of the fire." Testimony of William Blackwell. Archives of Ontario, Coroner's Inquest, March 2, 1880.

9   Testimony of Nora Donnelly. Preliminary Hearings (London), March 31, 1800.

10 Testimony of William Donnelly. Preliminary Hearings (London), February 28, 1880.

11 Testimony of William Donnelly. Preliminary Hearings (London), February 28, 1880.

12 Testimony of William Donnelly. Preliminary Hearings (London), February 28, 1880.

13 Testimony of William Donnelly. Preliminary Hearings (London), February 28, 1880.

14 Testimony of William Blackwell. Preliminary Hearings (London), March 31, 1800.

15 Testimony of William Donnelly. Preliminary Hearings (London), February 28, 1880.

16 Testimony of William Donnelly. Preliminary Hearings (London), February 28, 1880 and March 1, 1880.

17 Testimony of William Donnelly. Preliminary Hearings (London), February 28, 1880 and March 1, 1880.

18 Testimony of William Donnelly. Preliminary Hearings (London), February 28, 1880.

19 Testimony of William Donnelly. Preliminary Hearings (London), February 28, 1880.

20 "I remember James Carroll coming to our house on the night of the murder: he used to come and sleep there often: any time that his brother was there he slept with him: he slept with his brother three or four times: he stopped for nearly two weeks at one time." Testimony of Mary Thompson. Preliminary Hearings, (London), February 31, 1880.

21 "I had business with Carroll and went to Granton to meet Carroll. . . . Mr. Carroll had a warrant against me, and I went to Granton to pay the costs." Testimony of Patrick Whalen. Preliminary Hearings (London), March 12, 1880.

22 "I was then on my way to Granton. I left my house about six." Testimony of Patrick Whalen. Preliminary Hearings (London), March 12, 1880.

23 "I met James Hobbins while going to Granton before I met Casey; I told him what had happened. . . . I told Casey, Hobbins and Curtain that I saw two of the bodies in the house." Testimony of Patrick Whalen. Preliminary Hearings (London), March 12, 1880.

24 Testimony of Patrick Whalen. Preliminary Hearings (London), March 12, 1880.

25 "I first heard of the burning of the Donnellys about seven or half past seven in the morning, from Mr. Whalen; he was on his way to Granton . . . he said that he saw no signs of them around the place, and that the place was burned down . . . Mr. Whalen did not tell me anything about seeing bodies." Testimony of William Casey. University of Western Ontario, Middlesex County, Clerk of the Peace, Criminal Records, Queen v. James Carroll, Murder of [Johannah] Donnelly, February 4, 1880; testimony of William Casey, October 6, 1880.

26 "I told Casey, Hobbins and Curtain that I saw two of the bodies in the house." Testimony of Patrick Whalen. Preliminary Hearings (London), March 12, 1880. Also, testimony from William Casey: "On my way to Granton I met a Mr. Curtain, who told me that Whalen had told him that a little boy had come to his place from the Donnelly fire." University of Western Ontario, Middlesex County, Clerk of the Peace, Criminal Records, Queen v. James Carroll, Murder of [Johannah] Donnelly, February 4, 1880; testimony of William Casey, October 6, 1880.

27 "Carroll overtook me on my way to Granton, he was on horseback. . . . I was on foot." Testimony of William Casey. Preliminary Hearings (London), March 9, 1880.

28 Testimony of William Thompson Jr. Preliminary Hearings (London) February 27, 1880.

29 Testimony of Mary Thompson. Preliminary Hearings (London), February 27, 1880.

30 Testimony of Mary Thompson. Preliminary Hearings (London), February 27, 1880.

31 Testimony of Mary Thompson. Preliminary Hearings (London), February 27, 1880.

32 Testimony of Johnny O'Connor. Preliminary Hearings (London) February 21, 1880.

33 Testimony of Johnny O'Connor. Preliminary Hearings (London) February 21, 1880.

34 "The reason I did not tell was that I was afraid they would arrest me for being there: that was my own idea." Testimony of Johnny O'Connor. Preliminary Hearings (London) February 21, 1880.

35 Testimony of Theresa Whalen as reported in the *London Advertiser*, January 26, 1881.

36 "I could distinguish what appeared to be two persons in the morning when the fire burned down." Testimony of Patrick Whalen. Preliminary Hearings (London), March 12, 1880.

37 "At about nine o'clock this morning when the fire was low, I could distinguish the remains of four human beings, but could not tell who they were." Testimony of John Whalen. Coroner's Inquest, February 4, 1880.

38 "I stayed in bed till eight o'clock, I think when I got breakfast I went over to Donnelly's again. When we got there, we saw the burnt bodies — I saw four. I could not distinguish them." Testimony of Johnny O'Connor. Preliminary Hearings (London), February 21, 1880.

39 Toronto *Globe*, March 11, 1880.

40 Testimony of William Casey. Preliminary Hearings (London), March 9, 1880.

41 The account of this encounter between William Casey and James Carroll is taken from Casey's testimony during the preliminary examination. While such a conversation might well have occurred, there much within it that is suspect. For one thing, it is an incredibly vague exchange between the prosecuting constable and one of the sitting magistrates on the Ryder arson case, which was to have concluded that afternoon. Given the trial that both men were heading to Granton to take part in depended solely upon James and Johannah Donnelly being alive to see it through, and that neither one would think that the fact that James and Johannah Donnelly's home had been burned to the ground with reportedly four bodies inside should be worth their while investigating beggars belief.

42 Testimony of Patrick Whalen. Preliminary Hearings (London), March 12, 1880.

43 "John Taylor of Granton says he knew by Carroll's and Kennedy's actions in Granton the morning after the murders that there was something wrong. They had a long conversation together before there was any word of the murders." J.J. Talman Regional Collection, University of Western Ontario Archives, Donnelly Family Papers, B4878, William Donnelly to Charles Hutchinson, December 14, 1880.

44 Testimony of William Casey quoting Patrick Whalen. Preliminary Hearings (London), March 9, 1880.

45 "I told him [Casey] I had settled my matter, and he did not come in early." Testimony of Patrick Whalen. Preliminary Hearings (London), March 12, 1880.

46 "He asked me what the boy told me when he came to my place, but I would not tell him." Testimony of Patrick Whalen. Preliminary Hearings (London), March 12, 1880.

47 "On my way to Granton I met a Mr. Curtain, who told me that Whalen had told him that a little boy had come to his place from the Donnelly fire." Testimony of William Casey Preliminary Hearings (London), March 9, 1880.

48 Testimony of William Casey. Preliminary Hearings (London), March 9, 1880.

49 "I saw Whalen in Granton and asked him about the boy, when he said in an insulting way, that he wasn't going to tell me what he knew." Testimony of William Casey. Preliminary Hearings (London), March 9, 1880.

50 Unless otherwise indicated, all dialogue between Johnny O'Connor and his mother Mary O'Connor is drawn from Mary O'Connor's testimony at the Preliminary Hearings (London), February 21, 1880.

51 All dialogue between Constable William Hodge and Michael O'Connor is drawn from William Hodge's testimony at the Preliminary Hearings (London), March 5, 1880.

52 Testimony of William Hodge. Preliminary Hearings (London), March 5, 1880.

53 Testimony of William Hodge. Preliminary Hearings (London), March 5, 1880.

54 "The reason that I stayed in Granton was that I considered that I ought to stay till two o'clock, and then dismiss the case and thus free myself from any further responsibility." Testimony of William Casey. Preliminary Hearings (London), March 9, 1880.

55 "Feeheley was still calling Dorey [Darcey] a murderer, and told him he could produce the boy they sent to Whalen's Corners the morning of the murders to see if William Donnelly was dead." Written statement of Francis West, University of Western Ontario, Middlesex County Clerk of the Peace, Criminal Records. Queen v. William & Robert Donnelly, Arson, October 15, 1881 (Note dated April 16, 1881).

56 Testimony of Police Chief William T. Williams. Preliminary Hearings (London), March 1, 1880.

57 Testimony of William Donnelly, Preliminary Hearings (London), February 28, 1880.

58 List of jurors for the coroner's inquest, as published in the *London Free Press*, February 12, 1880.

59 Testimony of Police Chief William T. Williams. Preliminary Hearings (London), March 1, 1880.

60 Testimony of Police Chief William T. Williams. Preliminary Hearings (London), March 1, 1880.

CHAPTER NINETEEN: DEALING WITH THE DEAD

1 "Christopher William Flock," https://ckphysiciantribute.ca/doctors/christopher-william-flock/ (accessed January 2, 2020).

2 "I saw the boy O'Connor about ten o'clock that night before the postmortem began — between nine and ten o'clock. That was the first time I saw him. I had no conversation with him then; I had no conversation with him until after the funeral, which took place on Friday." Testimony of William Donnelly. Preliminary Hearings (London), March 1, 1880.

3 *London Free Press*, February 12, 1880.

4   "On the evening of February 4, 1880, at the residence of Mr
Michael Connors [sic] in Lucan I made a postmortem examination of the body of the late John Donnelly of Biddulph. The body,
although not fast, was well nourished and in a state of rigor mortis.
There were no bruises or appearance of injuries to the head. Some
blood on the right eyebrow, but when washed off there was no
wound. Blood [was] also on the hands and face, but no wounds.
At the upper part of the right side of the chest, in front of and at
the base of the neck adjoining, there were numerous small holes or
openings somewhat blackened by contusion, about thirty in number,
such as might be made by a gunshot. They covered a space of about
three or four inches, covered by blood. In one of them was a small
sliver of wood not a half long and as thick as a match. None of these
wounds were large but a few were a little larger [in the area] of the
right side in the neighbourhood of the groin, about two inches from
the anterior superior spinous process of the ilium. Between that
and the os pubis ovo pouparts [sic] ligament there was one wound
somewhat contused. It was about a half inch across in one direction
from without inwards and a little less in the other direction. . . . Here
the ligament and skin was depressed and the edges of the wound
inverted. On the right side over the nates or the buttocks near the
middle of the body and low down was another wound irregularly
circular with inverted and ragged margin and protruding with no
discolouration or contusion. These were all the marks or wounds
observed externally. Upon laying open the chest and exposing it,
beneath the external wounds on its upper part and the base of the
neck I found a great quantity of extravasated blood in the parts
beneath the skin and deeper. The soft parts were liberally mangled
and torn. The clavicle (or collar bone) and first rib fractured. The
large vessels in this region lacerated. I probed among these parts
with my finger but could not find any foreign body. The broken
ends of the bones and the fragments broken from them and the
lacerated soft parts were all I could feel. The right side of the cavity
of the chest contained a large quantity of blood — at least 3 pints,

some of it coagulated, the greater portion fluid. I then removed the
right lung and found in its upper part numerous small holes corresponding with those on the outside of the chest. The substance of the
lung here contained a considerable quantity of extravasated blood.
These holes appeared in both the front and back parts of the lung,
as if whatever made them had passed through its substance. In its
substance I got two or three gun shots. I sponged out all the blood,
searching through it with my finger for more shot but got none.
After wiping the cavity dry I examined its posterior wall and discovered two or three ribs fractured towards the spinal column. Between
that and the middle of the ribs I felt in these fractured ends for more
shot but did not get any. It appeared as if they had scattered and,
passing in different directions, had buried themselves deeply in the
soft parts of the body, out of sight and reach. When passing a boujie
or probe from the wound at the lower part of the abdomen on the
right side it proceeded inward and backward into the pelvic cavity.
I then laid back a flap of the abdominal wall and in its layers found
extravasated blood but no great quantity. I moved back the intes-
tines exposing the pelvic cavity with its contents and there was no
blood in it and upon passing my fingers down I found the horizontal
barrier of the pubis near its junction with the ilium was fractured
through to the acetabulum, shattering the bone forming this cavity.
I introduced a boujie at the wound in the nates (or buttocks) and
passing through the pelvis which now comments with the hip joint.
It emerged in front corresponding with the wound there. I made a
general examination of the other organs of the chest and abdomen;
they appeared to be in a healthy condition. I am of the opinion
that John Donnelly came to his death by shooting. I considered
the immediate cause of death to be haemorrhage in consequence
of the laceration of the large blood vessels at the base of the neck
and upper part of the chest together with haemorrhage from the
lung. The other injuries inflicted on the parts below would probably have proved fatal but not so soon unless from nervous shock.
I examined the shirts which I had removed from it [the corpse] and
they presented holes corresponding with those on the body. There

was considerable blood on the shirts on the upper parts, not much below." University of Western Ontario, Post Mortem Report on John Donnelly by C.W. Flock, MD, found within Legal Papers: Post Mortem Reports On The Bodies Of The Late James, Julia, Thomas and Bridget Donnelly, Donnelly Papers, February 1880, Box 35.

5 Testimony of William Donnelly. Preliminary Hearings (London), February 28, 1880.

6 *London Advertiser*, February 7, 1880.

7 *London Free Press*, February 12, 1880.

8 "There was some information laid that night [Wednesday]. We went out the following day, Thursday, in the morning about ten or eleven; I gave Hodge and Pope a warrant with instructions to arrest Carroll and get him quietly to Lucan." Testimony of Police Chief William T. Williams. Preliminary Hearings (London), March 1, 1880.

9 Testimony of Constable Alfred Brown. Coroner's Inquest, February 11, 1880.

10 "At an early hour this morning the remains of the other four victims, that is, father, mother, brother Tom and the cousin Bridget, were collected and placed together in one coffin and conveyed here, and now lie alongside the corpse of John in O'Connors' home." *London Free Press*, February 12, 1880.

11 Testimony of Dr. C.W. Flock. Coroner's Inquest, February 11, 1880.

12 *London Free Press*, February 12, 1880. Interestingly, the interment records for St. Patrick's indicate that the burial did not take place until Saturday, February 7, 1880 (rather than Friday, February 6, 1880).

13 "Canada. A Whole Family Murdered By Masked Men. LUCAN, Ont., February 4th – About 12 o'clock last night, masked men entered the dwelling of the somewhat notorious Donnelly family and murdered the father, mother, son and one niece. A boy named Connor [sic], the only other inmate, took refuge under a bed and escaped. The band then set fire to the house, which, together with the murdered bodies, was totally consumed. Another son, residing about three miles from the homestead, was called to his door about the same hour, and shot dead. The township is wild with excitement." *Oakland Daily Evening Tribune*, Wednesday, February 4, 1880.

14 The *New York Times*, February 5, 1880.

15 Reaney, *The Donnelly Documents: An Ontario Vendetta*, p. 126, note 561.

16 *London Advertiser*, February 5, 1880.

17 "Although a report was in circulation this morning that the bodies would be interred in the Church of England Cemetery, but on enquiry I find that the rumour is without foundation. They will be interred in the Roman Catholic burying-ground, the church of their forefathers." *London Free Press*, February 12, 1880.

18 *Maclean's* magazine, November 1, 1931.

19 The author is speculating on the identity of the *London Advertiser* reporter but it most likely was Charles Albert Matthews, as he was covering the case for the *London Advertiser* and would later give testimony in the murder trial on Day Two: Tuesday, October 5, 1880. University of Western Ontario, Middlesex County Clerk of the Peace, Criminal Records, Queen v. James Carroll, Murder of [Johannah] Donnelly, February 4, 1880.

20 "He [Father Connolly] appeared to be in great anxiety and expressed fears of being arrested. He assigned as a reason for his fear the bitter hatred which the Donnelly boys, and especially William, had against him." Also (quoting Father Connolly): "I expect to be arrested, as I know that from this bitter hatred which William Donnelly bears me he will do all in his power to have me arrested." *London Advertiser*, February 6, 1880.

21 *London Advertiser*, February 6, 1880.

22 *London Advertiser*, February 6, 1880.

23 "It is not true that I have excommunicated or placed the Donnellys under the ban of the Church." Father Connolly quoted in the *London Advertiser*, February 6, 1880.

24 *The Biddulph Tragedy*, London, 1880. This booklet consisted of chronological excerpts from *London Advertiser* newspaper columns on the murders, published to take advantage of the growing interest in the murders from the general public. CIHM series 02301, pp. 42–43.

25 "Thursday, in the morning about ten or eleven, I gave Hodge and Pope a warrant with instructions to arrest Carroll and get him quietly to Lucan." Testimony of Police Chief William T. Williams. Preliminary Hearings (London), March 1, 1880.

26 "My orders were not to let him know that I had a warrant for him till I got him to Lucan. I told him we wanted him to help us work on this being as he was a constable." Testimony of Constable William Hodge. Preliminary Hearings (London), March 5, 1880.

27 Unless otherwise indicated, all dialogue and activity regarding the arrest of James Carroll are drawn from the testimony of constables William Hodge (on March 5, 1880) and Charles Pope (February 26, 1880) during the Preliminary Hearings (London).

28 The account of the arrests of the various members of the Vigilance Committee on February 5, 1880, are taken from a report by John Lambert Payne published in the *London Free Press*, February 12, 1880. Interestingly, William Donnelly had been surprised at John Darcy's arrest and moved to have him released: "I gave orders to the Chief to have Dorsey [sic] let out when I became satisfied that Mr. Dorsey [sic] had not been there." Testimony of William Donnelly from the Preliminary Hearings (London), February 28, 1880. Darcy would in fact be released seven days later, on February 12, 1880. According to William Donnelly, however, John Darcy's son was an associate of Vigilance Committee Member James Maher: "James Maher, one of the prisoners in this murder case, and Jack [John] Darcy, a son of the old man discharged the other day, stole the bells off a respectable Protestant man's cutter at the church gate, while Father Connolly was reading prayers at Mrs. Andrew Keefe's funeral." Toronto *Globe*, March 2, 1880.

29 James Maher's statement as repeated by the arresting officer Charles Pope during the latter's testimony at the Preliminary Hearings (London), February 26, 1880.

30 Toronto *Globe*, February 3, 1881. It is interesting (and rather telling) that both Kennedy parents appear to be solely on the side of their daughter (Nora) and the Donnellys in the matter. Not

only did John Kennedy Sr. point out to the detectives the direction in which his son had fled, but an article published in the *London Advertiser* (February 10, 1880) states that "Mrs. Kennedy is reported to have told a detective today that she felt satisfied that her son [John Kennedy Jr.] and the man [Martin] McLaughlin were the leaders of the gang who killed the Donnellys."

31 Statement of John Kennedy Jr. made on February 5, 1880, as reported by John Lambert Payne in the *London Free Press*, February 12, 1880.

32 Report of Martin McLaughlin's arrest taken from *The Biddulph Tragedy*, pp. 17–18.

33 Arrest of the Ryders on February 5, 1880, taken from the report by John Lambert Payne published in the *London Free Press*, February 12, 1880.

34 *London Free Press*, February 12, 1880.

35 *London Advertiser*, February 6, 1880.

36 The description of the prisoners arriving in London is drawn from the report published in *The Biddulph Tragedy*, p. 19.

37 *London Advertiser*, February 6, 1880.

38 The description of the prisoners is drawn from the report published in *The Biddulph Tragedy*, pp. 19–20.

39 *The Biddulph Tragedy*, p. 20.

40 All information on how the Irish waked their dead has been derived from several sources: "Irish Wakes and Superstitions," https://connollycove.com/insight-irish-wake-superstitions-associated/; "The History of a Traditional Irish Wake," https://andersonfuneralservices.com/blogs/blog-entries/1/Articles/35/The-History-of-a-Traditional-Irish-Wake.html; "The Irish Wake," https://celticlifeintl.com/the-irish-wake/ (accessed on October 4, 2019).

41 *London Free Press*, February 12, 1880.

42 *London Advertiser*, February 9, 1880.

43 *Toronto Mail*, February 5, 1880.

44 *London Free Press*, February 12, 1880.

45 *London Advertiser*, February 7, 1880.

46 *London Advertiser*, February 5, 1880.

47 *Montreal Star*, February 6, 1880.

48 For over one hundred years it has been alleged that the Donnellys' pet dog had been killed on the night of the murders. While it is true that this was reported as being the case in the *Toronto Mail* on February 5, 1880 ("The body of the little dog was found near what is called the remains of the unfortunate young woman Bridget Donnelly"), it's important to bear in mind that not every item that appeared in the newspapers about the Donnelly murders was true. Such may well have been the case with regard to the alleged death of the Donnelly family's pet dog. Two years after the murders, Thomas Keefe, a longtime friend of the family, wrote a letter to the editor of the *London Advertiser* newspaper, in which he stated that he was the proud owner of a bulldog that 'once belonged to old Mr. Donnelly; was present on that awful night, probably saw the whole tragedy and some of the actors . . .'" (*London Advertiser*, May 15, 1882). Keefe had apparently been gifted the dog by one of the family members (so Jennie Currie, unfortunately, did not end up with it). It's possible that the Donnelly family owned more than one dog; however, both Bridget Donnelly and Bridget O'Connor during their testimony at the Ryder arson trial only make reference to one dog, not "dogs," plural (they say, "the dog," University of Western Ontario, Middlesex County, Clerk of the Peace, Criminal Records, Queen vs. James and [Johannah] Donnelly, Arson, January 15, 1880). If this is true, that Thomas Keefe later claimed that he owned a dog that had been in the Donnelly home on the night of the fire, the researcher is left with a puzzle. If the Donnellys owned only one dog, it could not have died in the fire and then gone on to live with Thomas Keefe. Authors such as William Butt have indicated that the Donnellys' dog was a terrier, but he provides no source for this (Butt, *The Donnellys: History, Legend, Literature*, p. 448). In testimony from Johnny O'Connor during the second trial, the boy, when asked if he saw anything else as he left the house, is reported as saying that he saw something like the head of a dog (Miller, *The Donnellys Must Die*, p. 176). However, none

of the constables (nor Chief Williams, nor reporter John Lambert Payne) who were on the site of the crime and who saw the charred bodies in the ruins of the Donnelly home reported seeing a severed dog's head. And while O'Connor is quoted from the second trial as saying that he saw something that looked like the head of a dog, it must be remembered that he never claimed to have seen the body of James Donnelly Sr., which was found the next day next to the stove in the kitchen; the boy might merely have caught a glimpse of the bloodied hair and hammered head of James Sr. by the stove and thought that, through the smoke and fire, it looked in appearance like the head of a dog (and, again, his testimony wasn't that it *was* the head of a dog, but only that it looked something like the head of a dog). We know that Mike Donnelly owned a bulldog, and it's possible that Henry Phair delivered Mike's dog to the family, or perhaps a puppy of that dog (or from the same litter) shortly after Mike's death. That Keefe would claim to own James Donnelly's dog in a public forum, such as a letter written to the editor of the local newspaper, would seem a needless claim to make if it weren't true. Consequently, like William Davison Butt, this author believes the story of the dog's death to be apocryphal (a "Bambi story" as Butt refers to it), in order to add more public sympathy to the tale, and that the dog was a bulldog that later ended up in the care of Keefe.

49 Jennie Currie's letter, written in a response to a telegram sent by her brother Patrick Donnelly, was published in the *London Free Press*, February 12, 1880.

50 "I was not at home the night of the murder: I was at St. Thomas; I first heard of the murder on Wednesday; I came home about two o'clock on Friday morning; I went to Mr. Connor's in Lucan." Testimony of Robert Donnelly. Preliminary Hearings (London) February 27, 1880. There is confusion as to where Bob Donnelly was coming in from. In the preliminary hearings (cited above), he claimed that he had been in St. Thomas (which was where his sister Jennie arrived from). However, the following newspaper report had him arriving from Glencoe: "LUCAN, Ont., Feb. 6 — Robert

Donnelly, the youngest son of the ill-fated family, arrived here from Glencoe about two o'clock this morning. His was driven to the house of Michael Connors [sic], where the body of his murdered brother, John, was laid out." *Toronto Mail*, February 13, 1880.

51 Toronto Mail, February 13, 1880.

52 Toronto *Globe*, February 19, 1880.

53 *London Free Press*, February 12, 1880.

54 *London Advertiser*, February 6, 1880.

55 *London Advertiser*, February 6, 1880.

56 *London Advertiser*, February 6, 1880.

57 *The Biddulph Tragedy*, p. 21.

58 *The Biddulph Tragedy*, p. 22.

59 Unless otherwise indicated, all the information on the procession and funeral is drawn from the booklet *The Biddulph Tragedy* (p. 36), as well as the *London Advertiser*, February 6 and February 7, 1880.

60 *London Advertiser*, February 6, 1880. The reason for the prevalent belief among some in attendance that Father Connolly might well condemn the Donnellys from the pulpit during the funeral was the fact that Father Connolly had, on prior occasions, apparently done so. According to County Constable Henry Phair, when he had arrested Patrick Ryder Jr., the young man had informed him that the priest had cursed the Donnellys from the altar. Testimony of Henry Phair, Preliminary Examination, Aemilius Irving Papers, F 1027-3, File 82-8, transcript of the Donnelly Murder Case, 1880 (MS 6500) Public Archives of Ontario, Toronto.

61 Unless otherwise indicated, all excerpts that follow from Father Connolly's sermon and his interaction with Patrick Donnelly are taken from the newspaper report on the funeral that was published in the *London Advertiser* on February 6, 1880.

62 "A violent burst of weeping followed, and the priest bowed his head on the railing, while his body rocked to and fro with emotion. The majority of those assembled, male and female, wept bitterly, and it was full five minutes before quiet was restored and the speaker sufficiently recovered to proceed." *Toronto Mail*, February 13, 1880.

63 *Toronto Mail*, February 13, 1880.

64 *Toronto Mail*, February 13, 1880.

65 Toronto *Globe*, March 2, 1880.

66 Toronto *Globe*, March 2, 1880.

67 Toronto *Globe*, March 2, 1880.

68 The dialogue between Father Connolly and the reporter is taken from the *Toronto Mail*, February 13, 1880.

69 Toronto *Globe*, March 2, 1880.

70 Toronto *Globe*, March 2, 1880.

71 *Toronto Mail*, February 13, 1880.

CHAPTER TWENTY: THE CIRCUS COMES TO TOWN

1   "Between February 5 and March 4, 1880, William Porte filed 90,937 words of telegraph copy." Miller, *The Donnellys Must Die*, p. 180.

2   Quoted in *London Free Press*, February 12, 1880.

3   Quoted in *London Free Press*, February 12, 1880.

4   Quoted in *London Free Press*, February 12, 1880.

5   *London Free Press*, February 12, 1880.

6   *London Advertiser*, reprinted from *Petrolia Topic*, February 13, 1880.

7   Quoted in *London Free Press*, February 12, 1880.

8   *Stratford Weekly Herald*, February 11, 1880.

9   "The funeral has occupied the public mind, and now the scenes in the church and the words of Father Connolly are in everybody's mouth." *Daily Journal*, Evansville, Indiana, February 7, 1880.

10 *Oakland Daily Evening Tribune*, Wednesday, February 4, 1880.

11 The *Glencoe Transcript* reported on June 3, 1880, that "Patrick Donnelly was at Lucan last week and paid up all his father's debts."

12 "It has been generally stated and believed that to his [Pat Donnelly's] absence from the paternal roof at an early age may be attributed, in a great measure, all the evil-doings with which the rest of the family stand accused, for the simple reason that he was fair and honest

in his intercourse with the community amongst which his lot was cast; that he ever and always, during periodical visits to his early home, stood aloof from taking any part with the brothers' quarrels or their supposed grievances; that, on the contrary, he denounced in the strongest terms the line of conduct pursued by them, and upon several occasions tried to prevail upon them to sell their possessions and make for themselves a home in some other land, to the end that they might be away from the influence and cause that gave rise to so much ill-feeling amongst them and their neighbours." *London Advertiser*, February 9, 1880.

13 *Toronto Mail*, February 7, 1880.

14 "So much had this line of conduct gained the respect of the community which surrounded his father's home, that a large number of farmers made offers today that if he [Patrick Donnelly] would agree to go and live upon the homestead himself they would erect a residence thereon, suitable for his accommodation, without any cost or charge whatever to him, but that they would not do so for any other member of the survivors." *London Advertiser*, February 9, 1880.

15 "Patrick Ryder . . . nicknamed "Grouchy" . . . godparent of Patrick Donnelly," Reaney, James, *The Donnelly Documents*, p. 14, note 336.

16 *London Advertiser*, February 7, 1880; Toronto *Globe*, February 9, 1880; see also, General Register of the Gaol at London, February 7, 1880.

17 "Purtell, the party under arrest in London . . . formerly resided in this town. Three years ago, a party of Germans were attacked on Sunday in the huckleberry swamp, in the Township of Ellice, and brutally beaten, one of them being stabbed so seriously that his life was despaired of. Several of the gang were arrested, among them Purtell and Maher, and when tried before the Police Magistrate they were convicted and sentenced to six months each in the Central Prison, where they both served their full time. Purtell's record while in this section was remarkable for ruffianism and cowardly conduct in several rows in which he was mixed up."

London Advertiser, February 14, 1880, reporting the story from a newspaper in Stratford, Ontario.

18 "The ruins of the house of James Donnelly, Sr., were still smoking when our reporter arrived there. Not a stick, with the exception of the two logs which formed the steps to the front door, but was entirely consumed." *The Biddulph Tragedy*, p. 10.

19 "I went to my father's place on Saturday [February 7]; one of the [O'Connor] boys was with me; Johnny [O'Connor], it was nobody else." Testimony of Bob Donnelly. Preliminary Hearings (London), February 27, 1880.

20 Testimony of Bob Donnelly. Preliminary Hearings (London), February 27, 1880.

21 "Joseph Whalen came over when we were there." Testimony of Bob Donnelly. Preliminary Hearings (London), February 27, 1880.

22 *London Advertiser*, February 9, 1880.

23 *London Advertiser*, February 9, 1880.

24 *London Advertiser*, February 9, 1880. See also University of Western Ontario Archives, J.J. Talman Regional Collection, M443, Unknown, Admittance of Carroll et al. to Middlesex County Gaol, February 6, 1880–February 8, 1880.

25 Toronto *Globe*, February 10, 1880.

26 *London Free Press*, February 16, 1880.

27 *London Advertiser*, February 6, 1880.

28 "I have got a good many threatening letters lately to leave the place. Made me more afraid of being burnt out than usual. . . . I got a letter saying that I would be used the same as the Donnellys if I did not leave the place. . . . Got three one day." Testimony of Michael O'Connor. Middlesex Coroner's Inquests, 1880, inquest into burning at O'Connor residence, April 15, 1880. See also London *Advertiser*, April 16, 1880.

29 *Hamilton Spectator*, February 20, 1880.

30 *Hamilton Spectator*, March 30, 1880.

31 *Hamilton Spectator*, March 2, 1880.

32 "My wife is at her father's and I do not sleep any two nights in the same house." J.J. Talman Regional Collection, University of

Western Ontario Archives, Donnelly Family Papers, B4878, File 2, William Donnelly, Letter to Charles Hutchinson from William Donnelly, June 9, 1880.

33 Toronto *Globe*, February 20, 1880.

34 Toronto *Globe*, February 20, 1880. "'Don't put my name in the paper,' he said, 'because if you do I'll get another torch before two months.'" Certain statements within the article are highly suggestive that the man who made these comments was Joseph Carswell. Carswell, for example, had lost his barn to arson, for which he blamed the Donnellys. The article mentions that "he had suffered, he added, at their hands to the extent of $2,300, his barns and other outbuildings having been consumed by fire; and evidently he has not yet recovered from his loss." The article also mentions that the interviewee is a Protestant and Carswell was Presbyterian.

35 *London Advertiser*, February 6, 1880.

36 *London Free Press*, February 15, 1880.

37 *London Free Press*, February 12, 1880.

38 Toronto *Globe*, March 1, 1880. See also: "The following letter, written by Rev. Father Connolly, and addressed to the editor of a Quebec journal, may properly be inserted here: . . . 'it must be said that with the exception of the Donnellys, whose reputations were bad, I never met a more honest or more upright people in every line of life than my present broken-hearted parishioners. There is no man whatever in this place who believes the persons now accused would be guilty of the crime laid to their charge.'" (Father John Connolly quoted on page 26 of the pamphlet put out by the *London Free Press* entitled *The Great Biddulph Tragedy: A Complete and Graphic Narrative of the Massacre of the Donnelly Family By Their Neighbours in Disguise*, published 1880. London, Ontario.) And: "The murders were the work of the Vigilance Committee, unless we are much astray, and the Vigilance Committee is the offspring of the Parish Priest, Father Connolly, who has openly, in a published letter, declared his belief in the innocence of the accused, and has taken every opportunity of denouncing the Donnellys, and of inflaming public opinion against

them." Letterbooks from the Office of the Clerk of the Peace, Middlesex County, Hutchinson to Mowat, March 6, 1880.

39   Toronto *Globe*, February 20, 1880.

40   *London Free Press*, February 12, 1880.

41   Letterbooks from the Office of the Clerk of the Peace, Middlesex County, Hutchinson to Scott, February 14, 1880.

42   "James Feeheley told me . . . Pat Ryder said to him one day, 'We did murder them but can they prove it?'" J.J. Talman Regional Collection, University of Western Ontario Archives, Donnelly Family Papers, B4878, File 4, Patrick Donnelly, Letter to C. Hutchinson from Patrick Donnelly, April 25, 1881.

43   Letterbooks from the Office of the Clerk of the Peace, Middlesex County, Hutchinson to Scott, February 24, 1880.

44   Letterbooks from the Office of the Clerk of the Peace, Middlesex County, Hutchinson to Mowat, March 9, 1880.

45   *London Free Press*, February 12, 1880.

46   Letterbooks from the Office of the Clerk of the Peace, Middlesex County, Hutchinson to Mowat, March 6, 1880, and to Scott, March 29, 1880.

47   *London Advertiser*, February 11, 1880.

48   *London Advertiser*, February 12, 1880.

49   The Donnelly survivors were so upset with the news that they had intended to place a small statue of Tom in handcuffs atop the tombstone they were having created in memory of their fallen family members, so that all who saw it in the future would know of the cowardly tactic the mob had used against the one member of their family that had a chance of fighting back (*Glencoe Transcript*, Thursday, June 3, 1880). See also Reaney, James, *The Donnelly Documents*, p. xcii and McKeown, Peter, *A Donnelly Treatise: After the Massacre* (self-published, 2004), Kindle edition, pp. 372–382.

50   "Carroll, who was reading from the [London] ADVERTISER the evidence again him at the inquest, remarked in the course of conversation, 'The boy goes pretty strong for me.'" *London Advertiser*, February 12, 1880.

51 "Some of those who were friends or favored the accused, freely stated their opinion that the boy had been 'stuffed' . . ." *London Advertiser*, February 12, 1880.

52 *London Free Press*, February 23, 1880.

53 "I found a stick there accidentally on the 12th or 13th. The stick produced is the one; I found it in a field about ten rods from the house, north of the house in the direction of the schoolhouse — that would be in the direction of my brother William's place. I was driving some cattle from the old homestead to James Keefe's; one of them got back on me, she went in the gate. I took a short cut through the field about half ways between the schoolhouse and the gate. I was walking about two feet from it; I saw it on the ground and I picked it up and looked at it and I saw what I supposed to be blood on it. I laid it standing at my father's wood pile. I afterwards took the stick to Lucan and gave it to my brother William to hand it to the chief. That is all I know about the stick. I found the stick four or five rods from the road; it was not near enough the road to have been thrown in." Bob Donnelly Testimony. Preliminary Hearings (London), February 27, 1880.

54 *Toronto Mail*, February 7, 1880.

55 *Morning News*, January 1, 1884. J.J. Talman Regional Collection, University of Western Ontario Archives, Donnelly Family Papers, B4878, File 26.

56 *London Free Press*, September 8, 1880.

57 London Free Press, June 24, 1880.

58 London *Free Press*, September 9, 1880.

59 Toronto *Globe*, September 10, 1880.

60 *London Free Press*, September 8, 1880. .

61 Toronto *Globe*, September 10, 1880.

62 "On one side of the house destroyed is situated a dwelling used jointly since the tragedy by William and Robert Donnelly and their families." *Toronto Mail*, April 15, 1880.

63 *London Free Press*, February 18, 1880.

64 *Toronto Mail*, February 19, 1880.

65 Toronto *Globe*, February 19, 1880.

66 *London Free Press*, February 18, 1880.

67 *London Advertiser*, February 21, 1880.

68 Hutchinson, Charles, Letters and Papers, Clerk of the Peace Correspondence, Irving to Hutchinson, March 6, 1880.

69 Edmund Meredith was the same lawyer whom James Sr. had written to on February 3, 1880, requesting his legal assistance on the Ryder arson case. Meredith would later become the mayor of London (1882–1883). One of eight brothers ("The Eight Merediths of London"), who were all very successful and well connected in the fields of law, politics and finance, Edmund was described as "an excellent jury lawyer." (W. Arnot Craick, "The Eight Merediths Of London," *Maclean's*, June 1, 1913).

70 *London Advertiser*, February 12, 1880.

71 *London Advertiser*, February 18, 1880.

72 *London Advertiser*, April 21, 1880.

73 *Toronto Mail*, February 11, 1880.

74 *London Advertiser*, March 2, 1880.

75 Toronto *Globe*, March 3, 1880; *Toronto Mail*, March 3 and 4, 1880; *London Free Press*, March 6, *London Advertiser*, March 3, 1880.

76 *London Daily Advertiser*, March 3, 1880.

77 *London Daily Advertiser*, March 3, 1880.

78 *London Daily Advertiser*, March 3, 1880.

79 *London Daily Advertiser*, March 3, 1880.

80 *Stratford Times*, March 10, 1880.

81 *Toronto Mail*, February 5, 1880.

82 *London Free Press*, February 22, 1880.

83 *London Advertiser*, February 23, 1880.

84 *London Free Press*, February 27, 1880.

85 *Toronto Mail*, March 13, 1880.

86 "The preliminary hearings close. Mr. Hutchinson on behalf of the Crown having closed the case for the Prosecution & Mr. MacMahon for defence on behalf of the prisoners. Magistrates decided to commit the accused parties to the common gaol for trial on the charge of murder of James Donnelly and others as charged in the information hereunto annexed." *London Advertiser*, March 15, 1880.

87 Letterbooks from the Office of the Clerk of the Peace, Middlesex County, Hutchinson to McKinnon, February 6, 1880.

88 Letterbooks from the Office of the Clerk of the Peace, Middlesex County, March 16, 1880. Irving to Hutchinson. "Gross falsifications," said lead prosecuting attorney Aemilius Irving regarding Clay's "discoveries."

89 *London Free Press*, April 16, 1880.

90 "Sir Oliver Mowat," https://bac-lac.gc.ca/eng/discover/politics-government/canadian-confederation/Pages/sir-oliver-mowat.aspx (accessed January 1, 2021).

91 "Canadian Statistics in 1867," https://www65.statcan.gc.ca/acyb07/acyb07_0002-eng.htm (accessed January 1, 2021).

92 University of Western Ontario Archives, J.J. Talman Regional Collection, Mowat to Magee, February 16, 1880.

93 University of Western Ontario Archives, J.J. Talman Regional Collection, Scott to Hutchinson, February 16, 1880.

94 Letterbooks from the Office of the Clerk of the Peace, Middlesex County, Hutchinson to Magee, February 19, 1880.

95 Province of Ontario Sessional Papers, 1875–76, No. 59.

96 *Toronto Mail*, March 6, 1880; see also *London Free Press*, March 12, 1880.

97 Biggar, C.R.W., *Sir Oliver Mowat — A Biographical Sketch*, Toronto: Warwick Bros and Rutter Ltd., 1905, pp. 719–20. Biggar indicates that Meredith's efforts were largely political in the matter.

98 "Mr. Irving was here yesterday, & held a consultation with Mr. Magee & myself, relative to these cases. The conclusions we arrived at are as follows: [. . .] That a reward of at least $5000 should be offered for such information as will lead to the conviction of all or any of the guilty parties." Charles Hutchinson Letter Book, 1878–80, p. 718, J.J. Talman Regional Collection, University of Western Ontario Archives, Donnelly Family Papers, B4878, File 12, Hutchinson to Mowat, March 18, 1880.

99 "Our intention was, in the draft we sent you, to avoid casting any reflections upon the evidence already obtained." Charles Hutchinson Letterbook, 1880–81, p. 26, J.J. Talman Regional

Collection, University of Western Ontario Archives, Donnelly Family Papers, B4878, File 12, Hutchinson to Mowat, March 29, 1880. See also draft of the reward poster submitted by Hutchinson to Mowat: "The Government of Ontario hereby offers a reward of $5000 to such person or persons as will hereafter give such information as will lead to the conviction of any of the persons who were guilty of the said murders or all of them." J.J. Talman Regional Collection, University of Western Ontario Archives, Donnelly Family Papers, B4878, File 12, Charles Hutchinson Letter Book, March 18, 1880.

100 *London Advertiser*, March 19, 1880.

101 *London Free Press*, March 23, 1880.

102 *London Free Press*, March 23, 1880. See also: "I have under advice of Mr. Irving had placards of the proclamation posted in the city & even sent others to Biddulph & elsewhere to be distributed was widely as possible. I observe the alteration in the wording. Our intention was, in the draft we sent you, to avoid casting any reflections upon the evidence already obtained. I fear there will be an opportunity of doing so, as the proclamation is now worded, & that the restrictions as to the distribution of the reward will have a discouraging effect. I have heard strong expressions of opinion to this effect, since the proclamation appeared." Letterbooks from the Office of the Clerk of the Peace, Middlesex County, Hutchinson to Scott, March 29, 1880.

CHAPTER TWENTY-ONE: FRIENDS IN LOW PLACES

1 Letterbooks from the Office of the Clerk of the Peace, Middlesex County, Hutchinson to Mowat, March 18, 1880.

    Mr. Irving was here yesterday, & held a consultation with Mr. Magee & myself, relative to these cases. The conclusions we arrived at are as follows:

1st That it is desirable to change the venue, as there
seems to be no chance of a fair trial in this county, &
that the trial should be held in Toronto.

2   "But the Premier and Attorney-General refused resolutely to
consider Toronto. His own need was public invisibility in the
Donnelly prosecutions. But nowhere else would publicity be greater
than in Toronto, nowhere else would people be more aware of
his presence than here at the seat of his government." Butt, *The
Donnellys: History, Legend, Literature*, p. 258.

3   Charles Hutchinson, Letters and Papers, Clerk of the Peace,
Cameron to Hutchinson, March 12, 1880. The author of the
letter is likely Malcolm Colin Cameron, a Goderich justice and
Liberal Member of Parliament for South Huron, as indicated in
Reaney, "Crown Attorney Hutchinson was anxious to change
the venue from Middlesex to some other place where the anti-
Donnelly prejudice was not so strong. . . . This decision was
supported by a letter from Justice Malcolm Colin Cameron who
knew Biddulph well." *The Donnelly Documents: An Ontario
Vendetta*, pp. cxxii–cxxiii.

4   "A rumour is abroad that James Keefe, who was depended on as a
witness for the Prosecution in the Donnelly case, has left the country.
The report goes that he purchased a ticket last Thursday or Friday
for Nebraska. It will be recollected that Keefe is the man that William
Donnelly is said to have first told his story to, and he was expected to
corroborate the evidence of Donnelly. It is hard to say what the effect
of this will be. The Crown intended to call him tomorrow before the
Magistrates." *London Advertiser*, March 8, 1880.

5   *Glencoe Transcript*, April 1, 1880.

6   "I have employed a constable to guard young O'Connor, fearing
mischief. His evidence is so essential, & it would be easy for the
friends of the prisoners to get him out of the way, unless carefully
watched." Letterbooks from the Office of the Clerk of the Peace,
Middlesex County, Hutchinson to Scott, March 29, 1880.

7   "We have been silent while column after column of matter maligning ourselves, our pastor, our friends, our nationality, and our community have remained uncontradicted. We have never even hinted that the crimes of the Donnelly family (cruel and terrible though they were) were a justification of their murder. Then why should it be demanded (at least indirectly) that we should be punished because, as it is alleged (though falsely), others, with the majority of whom we had no connection, may have done wrong?" James Carroll quoted in the *Irish Canadian*, September 15, 1880.

8   "Bill Donnelly received an anonymous letter today stating that if he made a tramp among the Orangemen and Protestants of Biddulph and McGillivray, he could collect all the money he wanted to meet his legal expenses. The writer said he would divulge his name hereafter." Toronto *Globe*, February 10, 1880.

9   "The feeling in Biddulph still appears to run very high, and popular opinion seems to be divided into two classes — Donnelly and anti-Donnelly. On Thursday last a farmer on the 8th concession, who has been friendly with the Donnellys, had a bee. The next neighbour had an excellent well of water, and some of those present went to his well to get some water. The second time they went the found the following notice posted on the pump: 'No water for Blackfeet here. Go to old Donnelly's homestead and you will get all you want.'" *London Advertiser*, June 24, 1880.

10 *London Advertiser*, June 24, 1880.

11 *London Advertiser*, June 29, 1880.

12 "Here the reader is maliciously informed that there are two contending factions in Biddulph, or at least that such factions existed there prior to the tragedy; that the most intense enmity existed between such factions, who have been continually quarreling with each other, and that their quarrels have culminated in the fearful Donnelly tragedy; and above all that the ex-prisoners are among those immediately implicated in the unfortunate quarrel which he says terminated so fearfully in the terrible slaughter of a number of the Donnelly family on the memorable fourth of February, 1880. Now, sir, all this is a malicious lie. . . . there never were two factions

or contending parties in Biddulph in the odious sense that such factions are known to exist anywhere. Therefore, there is not or never was any standing quarrels between any two classes of the community; and by consequence, the Donnelly tragedy was not (as your correspondent says) the result of any quarrel whatsoever." Letter to the editor, published in the *Irish Canadian*, April 21, 1881.

13 "In making use of the word 'faction' it was done merely to avoid tautology; it was not intended . . . to convey the idea that there were an importation in our midst of 'Terryalts,' 'Cummins and Daraghs,' 'Corcorans and Feehans,' 'Black Feet' and 'White Feet,' 'Orange' and 'Green,' &c. Not the slightest wish had I of conveying any such idea; but will 'Veritas' [the nom de plume of his literary adversary] attempt to deny that there was not two contending parties in our midst — one advocating respect for the law of the land, and the other violating it in various ways?" The *Irish Canadian*, April 28, 1881.

14 Orlo Miller devotes 38 pages to the topic in his book *The Donnellys Must Die*, pp. 19–57.

15 Moreover, if associating with Protestants was sufficient to warrant being labelled a member of the Blackfeet clan, then many members of the Vigilance Committee would have qualified for membership. James Carroll, for example, often associated and sought the counsel of the Stanley brothers, two affluent Protestant businessmen in Lucan, while the lead attorney for the prisoner's defence team was William Meredith, who was also a Protestant.

16 *London Advertiser*, April 5, 1880.

17 "It is also reported that the remainder of the Donnelly family are about removing from the village, but the locality of their future residence is not definitely indicated, probably it will be Toronto." *Toronto Mail*, April 15, 1880.

18 *London Advertiser*, April 7, 1880.

19 *London Advertiser*, April 7, 1880.

20 Toronto *Globe*, April 9, 1880; see also *London Free Press*, April 10, 1880.

21 Toronto *Globe*, April 13, 1880.

22 ". . . the danger of young O'Connor being in the meanwhile made away with . . . a strong effort will be made to get him out of the way & in such a manner as to render his evidence before the Coroner & magistrates as a mischief. We are opposed to a desperate & unscrupulous party, who will shrink from nothing. . . . I do not think it would be safe to let the boy go back to Lucan." Letterbooks from the Office of the Clerk of the Peace, Middlesex County, Hutchinson to Mowat, March 6, 1880.

23 Even the local press was baffled by her presence: "Quite a mystery seems to hang around this young lady. She came from no one knows where, and disappeared as mysteriously as she came. She is a perfect myth." *London Free Press*, April 16, 1880.

24 Testimony of Bob Donnelly: "The Monday [the day] before the fire was the first time I ever saw Miss Johnson. She came to my place enquiring if Will Donnelly lived there. . . ." *London Free Press*, April 16, 1880; see also University of Western Ontario, J.J. Talman Regional Collection, Donnelly Family Papers, Middlesex Coroner's Inquest, April 15, 1880.

25 "She [Johnson] left [the O'Connors'] before he [Bob Donnelly] did, and went to his house. She stopped there all night. Then slept in the same bed with his wife and him. She slept next to the wall and his wife slept in the middle. They had only one bed in the house, and they all had to 'bunk' together." *London Free Press*, April 16, 1880.

26 "This part of the evidence caused great merriment. Some reference was made to Bryan O'Lynn, who, it seems, used similar economy in bed and bedding" [Bryan O'Lynn is an Irish comedic folk song about a fellow who has a way of making do with things at hand. At the end of the song he claims to a mother and her daughter, "Whoo! I'll marry you both!"] — and "The inquest on the O'Connor fire was resumed at ten o'clock this morning. Long before the opening of the room used by the jury quite a crowd had collected, in spite of the rain, and were eagerly discussing the pros and cons. A rumour was in circulation that the now celebrated Johnson girl would be present, and her appearance was eagerly looked for, but she failed to put in an

appearance, greatly to the disgust of the Court House frequenters and the gossips generally." *London Free Press*, April 16, 1880.

27 The names of the people who visited at the O'Connors' house that night is taken from the testimony of Bridget O'Connor and Bob Donnelly, University of Western Ontario, J.J. Talman Regional Collection, Donnelly Family Papers, Middlesex Coroner's Inquest, April 15, 1880.

28 "Cartys came every night to keep me company. Mary Ann Carty stayed up all night with me one night." Testimony of Bridget O'Connor. Donnelly Family Papers, Middlesex Coroner's Inquest, April 15, 1880.

29 Donnelly Family Papers, Middlesex Coroner's Inquest, April 15, 1880. See also Reaney, *The Donnelly Documents: An Ontario Vendetta*, p. 186, note 604: "James Pratt is the son of William Pratt, but at seven years of age is surely too young for even a domino party at the O'Connor house. The inquest's juror and visitor to the O'Connor house is William Pratt [the London journalist was in error by calling him "James"]; root beer manufacturer, (b. 1838), English, Grand Trunk Railway watchman."

30 "The other parties named except Cosens stayed until about 9 o'clock. They were playing Cards and Dominoes in the Kitchen." Testimony of Bridget O'Connor. University of Western Ontario, J.J. Talman Regional Collection, Donnelly Family Papers, Middlesex Coroner's Inquest, April 15, 1880.

31 "Tom and I went to Robert Donnelly's and called him and said the house was on fire. Robert had some difficulty in opening his door." The fact that Patrick O'Connor also testified that "I went downstairs. I could not open the door . . ." and that the door could not be opened from the outside either, resulting in Bob Donnelly having to break it down with a pole, speaks to the doors having been blocked. Testimony of Patrick O'Connor. Donnelly Family Papers, Middlesex Coroner's Inquest, April 15, 1880.

32 "The dogs awakened me up the first by barking." Testimony of Patrick O'Connor. Donnelly Family Papers, Middlesex Coroner's Inquest, April 15, 1880.

33 Testimony of Patrick O'Connor. Donnelly Family Papers, Middlesex Coroner's Inquest, April 15, 1880.

34 Testimony of Patrick O'Connor. Donnelly Family Papers, Middlesex Coroner's Inquest, April 15, 1880.

35 "I jumped out as soon as the window was taken out." Testimony of Thomas O'Connor. Donnelly Family Papers, Middlesex Coroner's Inquest, April 15, 1880.

36 "I then looked through the window and saw two fellows walking down the road going towards the foundry and going over the gate at the foundry. . . . The reason I stood and watched the men going down street was because I knew the house was on fire and I thought they had set it on fire, and I wanted to know which way they were going. . . . The two men on the street were opposite [the house that Bob Donnelly had rented] — walking past not running. I did not know who they were." Testimony of Patrick O'Connor. Donnelly Family Papers, Middlesex Coroner's Inquest, April 15, 1880.

37 "Bridget and Pat said they saw two fellows going down the road and told me to keep back. I did not see them . . ." Testimony of Thomas O'Connor. *London Free Press*, April 15, 1880.

38 "I went downstairs. I could not open the door but then got out of the north window downstairs." Testimony of Patrick O'Connor. University of Western Ontario Archives, J.J. Talman Regional Collection, Donnelly Papers, Middlesex Coroner's Inquest, April 15, 1880.

39 "When I got up I went in their [her brothers'] room — had to go through it to go downstairs. I tried to find the stairs and fell down it. There being no railing around it. There is [sic] about eleven or twelve steps in the stair. I fell down about half way. The door at the bottom of the stairs was open. I could not see anything for smoke. I tried to find the front door and couldn't." Testimony of Bridget O'Connor. Middlesex Coroner's Inquest, April 15, 1880.

40 "On the night of Tuesday between 11 and 12 o'clock I was awakened by one of O'Connor's boys. Both Pat & Tom were then calling 'fire.'" Testimony of Bob Donnelly; see also testimony of Patrick O'Connor:

"Tom and I went to Robert Donnelly's and called him and said the house was on fire." Middlesex Coroner's Inquest, April 15, 1880.

41 Testimony of Bob Donnelly. Middlesex Coroner's Inquest, April 15, 1880.

42 "I then ran to the front door and when I went out on the street to get a stick to break the door." Testimony of Bob Donnelly. Middlesex Coroner's Inquest, April 15, 1880.

43 "I saw the fire on the roof of the Kitchen in the north end and on the gable end of the house." Testimony of Bob Donnelly. Middlesex Coroner's Inquest, April 15, 1880.

44 "Bob Donnelly broke in our front door with a pole and he then went into the house and let Bridget out." See also: "The O'Connor girl states that she certainly would have been smothered to death only for her timely rescue by Bob Donnelly by forcing in the door with the end of a heavy fence rail." Testimony of Patrick O'Connor. Middlesex Coroner's Inquest, April 15, 1880. *London Free Press*, April 14, 1880.

45 "Robert Donnelly was at the front door running into the house when I got there." Testimony of Daniel Howe. *London Free Press*, April 16, 1880.

46 "I then took out some furniture; chairs, etc." Testimony of Bob Donnelly. University of Western Ontario Archives, J.J. Talman Regional Collection, Donnelly Papers, Middlesex Coroner's Inquest, April 15, 1880.

47 Testimony of Daniel Howe. *London Free Press*, April 16, 1880.

48 "I went upstairs to the top step [but] could get no further; the west end was burnt through." Testimony of Bob Donnelly. University of Western Ontario Archives, J.J. Talman Regional Collection, Donnelly Papers, Middlesex Coroner's Inquest, April 15, 1880.

49 Testimony of Daniel Howe. *London Free Press*, April 16, 1880.

50 Testimony of David McRoberts, University of Western Ontario Archives, J.J. Talman Regional Collection, Donnelly Papers, Middlesex Coroner's Inquest, April 15, 1880.

51 Testimony of David McRoberts, Donnelly Papers, Middlesex Coroner's Inquest, April 15, 1880.

52 *Toronto Mail*, April 15, 1880.

53 *London Advertiser*, April 14, 1880.

54 *London Free Press*, April 15, 1880.

55 "As the Donnellys have failed to secure the change of venue in the murder case some think they are trying the plan of burning the old log house of their friend, in order that he may get his insurance money and move to London. . . . Public feeling is very much worked up and very little sympathy is manifested for O'Connor in his loss." *London Advertiser*, April 14, 1880.

56 *Toronto Mail*, April 15, 1880.

57 *London Free Press*, April 15, 1880.

58 *Toronto Mail*, April 15, 1880.

59 "A number of the friends of the prisoners in London jail held a consultation this afternoon, and sent word to Mr. MacMahon to attend the inquest and look after the interests of his clients." MacMahon then tapped John Blake to attend. *London Free Press*, April 15, 1880.

60 *London Advertiser*, April 16, 1880.

61 *London Free Press*, April 16, 1880.

62 *London Free Press*, April 16, 1880.

63 The full quote from Charles Hutchinson on the matter: "I thought & still think it was an act of incendiarism. I think the evidence shows clearly that the fire could not have originated inside. It broke out inside the building undoubtedly, but nothing could have been easier than to introduce the fire from the outside. The jury based their verdict on the fact that the fire was first observed inside the building, & paid to attention or next to none to the evidence by which it appeared clear to me, that when the young O'Connors went to be, (the old people were in London) there was no fire in the house at all, nor had been for some time before they retired. A more prejudiced jury I have never met with. The Coroner concurred in my opinion as to this, also as to the advisability of holding the inquest." Letterbooks from the Office of the Clerk of the Peace, Middlesex County, to Scott, July 23, 1880.

64 Miller, *The Donnellys Must Die*, p. 199.

65 "I became bail for the boy's appearance at the next assizes, on the sum of $2000 . . ." Letterbooks from the Office of the Clerk of the Peace, Middlesex County, Hutchinson to John Scott, July 10, 1880.

66 ". . . my putting [Johnny O'Connor] in charge of a constable to be with him day & night, sleeping in the same apartment & accompanying him to school, chapel & every where." Letterbooks from the Office of the Clerk of the Peace, Middlesex County, Hutchinson to John Scott, July 23, 1880.

67 Letterbooks from the Office of the Clerk of the Peace, Middlesex County, Hutchinson to John Scott, April 19, 1880.

68 "Without the boy we can do nothing." Letterbooks from the Office of the Clerk of the Peace, Middlesex County, Hutchinson to John Scott, July 10, 1880.

69 "She is a troublesome woman, and her husband is more trouble-some still. Nothing satisfies them, and no one can keep on good terms with them." Letterbooks from the Office of the Clerk of the Peace, Middlesex County, Hutchinson to John Scott, July 10, 1880.

70 Letterbooks from the Office of the Clerk of the Peace, Middlesex County, Hutchinson to Irving, April 21, 1880.

71 "I agreed to furnish the O'Connors with a suitable dwelling house & to pay the rent, also to put up a summer kitchen, piggery & other small outbuildings & to repair generally, towards which the landlord agreed to allow 1 month's rent, & the material used for said buildings to belong to me. I also agreed to pay $3 per week for board & lodging of Jones the constable. Mrs. O'Connor was satisfied so far as above, but claimed beyond this to be paid for the board & lodging of Johnny. She also claimed compensation for the breaking up of their Lucan home, for being obliged to leave Lucan, where here husband & herself were able to support themselves, & come to London where neither could find suitable employment, & for being deprived of the services of Johnny, who was old enough & able enough to assist in the support of the family — also for losses sustained by reason of the fire which destroyed their dwelling house & its contents only very partially insured on the ground that the fire was an act of an incendiary & the motive their

connection with the Donnelly matter." Letterbooks from the Office of the Clerk of the Peace, Middlesex County, Hutchinson to Scott, July 23, 1880..

72   The incident was reported in the *Toronto Mail*, April 20, 1880, and the *London Advertiser*, April 20, 1880.

73   Regional History Collection of the D.B. Weldon Library, University of Western Ontario, Spencer Armitage-Stanley, Papers re Queen v. James Carroll, et al., Scott to Hutchinson, April 7, 1880, and to Glass, May 3, 1880.

74   Armitage-Stanley, Papers re Queen v. James Carroll, et al., Glass to Scott, May 7, 1880.

75   Armitage-Stanley, Spencer, Papers re Queen v. James Carroll, et al., Irving to Hutchinson, May 17, 1880, in which Aemilius Irving refers to the Biddulph prisoners as Sheriff Glass's "family"; see also: "The sheriff's conduct is unsatisfactory." Armitage-Stanley, Papers re Queen v. James Carroll, et al., Irving to Hutchinson, May 6, 1880.

76   To wit, Mrs. John Kennedy, Ellen Maher and Ann McLaughlin all stayed overnight in the prison with their respective husbands. Letterbooks from the Office of the Clerk of the Peace, Middlesex County, Hutchinson to Irving, May 5, 1880; see also *London Free Press*, May 28, 1880.

77   *London Free Press*, July 13, 1880.

78   *Toronto Mail*, May 21, 1880.

79   Archives of Ontario, Toronto, Norfolk County Gaol Register, 1876–1925.

80   *Norfolk Reformer*, May 21, 1880.

81   William H. Lewis Prison Record, Kingston Pen. 1843–1890, Canada's Penitentiary Museum, Kingston, Ontario. Microfilm T-2044, Vol. 1047.

82   *London Daily Advertiser*, May 19, 1880.

83   *London Daily Advertiser*, May 19, 1880.

84   "Judge Davis, L. Lawrason, J. Peters J.P., James Fisher J.P. — all these absolutely refused. Mr. Lawrason took a night to consider, Peters several days; Judge Davis refused promptly, but gave a very

decided opinion as to the necessity for the change. I afterwards had several conversations with Judge Elliot on the same subject, who was equally convinced of the necessity — in fact rather more so, & while I did not directly ask him for an affidavit, it was became he had approved Judge Davis' refusal before I had the opportunity. I knew therefore there was no use in asking. These are the most important people I asked. I asked the chief [Williams] & others on the force to endeavour to get affidavits, but their reports coincided with my own experience . . ." Letterbooks from the Office of the Clerk of the Peace, Middlesex County, Hutchinson to Irving, May 15, 1880.

85 Letterbooks from the Office of the Clerk of the Peace, Middlesex County, Hutchinson to Irving, May 15, 1880.

86 Donnelly Family Papers, Regional History Collection, D.B. Weldon Library, University of Western Ontario, contains a handwritten copy of Chief Williams's deposition.

87 "Crown Attorney Hutchinson's affidavit and the vague generalities of Chief Williams were all that the Crown prosecutors could muster." Butt, *The Donnellys: History, Legend, Literature*, p. 255.

88 "Our esteemed local contemporary the *Free Press* is greatly exercised over the proposal of the authorities to obtain a change of venue in the Donnelly murder trial. . . . What we desire to call attention to is the statement of our esteemed contemporary that a change of venue will be an insult to the people of London and Middlesex, as implying that a fair verdict cannot be here obtained." *London Advertiser*, March 8, 1880.

89 Butt, *The Donnellys: History, Legend, Literature*, pp. 255–56.

90 "Would there be any use in speaking again to the Attorney General on the subject?" Letterbooks from the Office of the Clerk of the Peace, Middlesex County, Hutchinson to Irving, May 5, 1880.

91 For Wellington as a possible location please see: "Upon the prisoners appearing in court they will be arraigned and then a motion made to enter suggestion to have the trials in some county other [than] Middlesex (Wellington to wit)." D.B. Weldon Library, University of Western Ontario, Irving to Hutchinson, May 3, 1880.

For Guelph as a possible location please see: "It would be easier to tamper with the jury in Guelph than in Toronto, & this is one of the chief if not the chief danger we have to encounter against securing a fair trial." Letterbooks from the Office of the Clerk of the Peace, Middlesex County, Hutchinson to Irving, May 5, 1880.

92   "Today at Toronto I obtained Writs of Certiorari to remove the indictment for the murder of James Donnelly into the Queen's Bench, and to remove the indictment for the murder of Thomas Donnelly into the Common Pleas." D.B. Weldon Library, University of Western Ontario, Irving to Hutchinson, May 3, 1880.

93   Affidavits from Martin McLaughlin and Thomas Ryder can be found in the *London Advertiser*, May 25, 1880. The affidavit from Patrick Ryder can be found in the *London Advertiser*, May 26, 1880.

94   "Despite the early hour, 6 o'clock this morning, there was a large crowd of friends of the prisoners, and persons eager to gaze with morbid curiosity upon the men charged with the heinous murder of the Donnelly family, on their departure for Toronto. The prisoners were awakened at 5 o'clock this morning and served with breakfast. They were then handcuffed in pairs; James Ryder and Carroll; McLaughlin and Thomas Ryder; and John Kennedy and Purtell, and with a strong guard of constables under command of Sheriff and Deputy Sheriff Glass, marched to the G.W.R. station, where they arrived at about twenty minutes to six o'clock. Their arrival was the signal for a rush of the crowd and they were speedily surrounded by about three hundred persons, foremost among them the Biddulphers, of whom a large number were present to make farewell. Relatives of every prisoner were present, cheering them by kind words. The first greeting over, the rollicking Irish wit commenced to bubble over and for a few brief moments the prisoners seemed to forget the terrible position in which they were placed, and when the word 'all aboard' was given there was a general handshaking and numerous wet eyes. The party occupied a special car at the rear end of the train, and at the hour set for departure the train moved out of the station and a faint cheer was given by the prisoners' friends. The prisoners evidently anticipated

a stay of one or two days as each of them took a change of clothing packed in a large trunk. They were also well supplied with refreshments on the road. . . . Mr. H. MacMahon, Q.C., the prisoner's Counsel, was also upon the train. Mr. J.J. Black, who is also engaged with Mr. McMahon on behalf of the prisoners, was on the platform to see them off. Great credit is due the Sheriff for the regularity and order which was preserved and the good judgment displayed under the trying circumstances." *London Advertiser*, May 17, 1880.

95 History of Toronto is culled from "Toronto," https://thecanadianencyclopedia.ca/en/article/toronto (accessed June 7, 2019).

96 "Toronto Pork Packing Plant." http://lostrivers.ca/points/pork-packing.htm (accessed June 8, 2019).

97 Toronto *Globe*, June 23, 1898.

98 Toronto *Globe*, June 23, 1898.

99 *London Free Press*, May 26, 1880.

100 Toronto *Globe*, May 18, 1880; see also *London Free Press*, May 20, 1880.

101 *London Free Press*, May 28, 1880.

102 Toronto *Globe*, May 26, 1880.

103 Toronto *Globe*, May 27, 1880.

104 *London Advertiser*, May 27, 1880.

105 *London Free Press*, May 27, 1880; *Glencoe Transcript*, June 3, 1880.

106 "The confinement, after a life on the farm, has told upon the appearance of the prisoners. Carroll, especially, looked anything but well, and a prolonged term of confinement would undoubtedly have any other but a favourable effect upon his health." *London Advertiser*, May 17, 1880.

107 "I see the papers occasionally referring to the hardship of keeping the prisoners so long in gaol awaiting trial. Our best chance is in delay." Letterbooks from the Office of the Clerk of the Peace, Middlesex County, Hutchinson to Irving, June 24, 1880.

108 *London Free Press*, May 28, 1880.

109 *London Advertiser*, June 3, 1880.

110 "We might do something in the gaol to obtain evidence in the Donnelly case if we had anyone we could rely upon, but with him [Joseph Lamb] there as gaolor, it is useless to think of it." Letterbooks from the Office of the Clerk of the Peace, Middlesex County, Hutchinson to Magee, July 15, 1880. "The gaol suggestion is wholly impracticable by reason of the unsatisfactory attitude of the officer connected therewith." Regional History Collection of the D.B. Weldon Library, University of Western Ontario, Armitage-Stanley, Papers re Queen v. James Carroll, et al., Aemilius Irving to Hutchinson, June 30, 1880.

111 "You will probably have heard that Mr. Langmuir held an inquiry the other day into the conduct of the London gaolor Mr. Lamb, in connection with the Biddulph prisoners, & as the result, ordered the Sheriff to dismiss Lamb from his office, & to take away the keys of the gaol. This was accordingly done. The charges were brought on my information, & were fully made out." Letterbooks from the Office of the Clerk of the Peace, Middlesex County, Hutchinson to Scott, July 15, 1880.

112 "With reference to Lamb the gaoler, a strong effort will be made for his reinstatement. I need not tell you that this will not be in the public interest, if successful. . . . I understand MacMahon is setting himself in his behalf, & Mr. Magee is also interested for him MacMahon is the counsel for the Biddulph prisoners. There is no difficulty in accounting for the part he is taking. Why Magee is moving in thee matter I can't say; perhaps for some political reason. He & MacMahon are, as you no doubt know, influential men on the Govt side . . ." Letterbooks from the Office of the Clerk of the Peace, Middlesex County, Hutchinson to Langmuire, July 15, 1880. See also: "I do not think that [Deputy Attorney General John] Scott understands, by any means, that Magee's services are at an end." Regional History Collection of the D.B. Weldon Library, University of Western Ontario, Armitage-Stanley, Papers re Queen v. James Carroll, et al., Aemilius Irving to Hutchinson, April 18, 1880.

113 Toronto *Globe*, August 19, 1880.

114 "Pat Breen who is supposed to be leader of the Vigilants was at old Pat Whalen's nearly every second night last spring before the assizes. He is now visiting there again. This is something Breen [had] never done before." J.J. Talman Regional Collection, University of Western Ontario Archives, Donnelly Family Papers, B4878, File 2, William Donnelly to Hutchinson, September 18, 1880.

115 "Dear Sir, I never gave up the trail yet and am satisfied now as to where they all met previous to the murder. Old Pat Ryder has a farm 1/2 mile north of my father's on the east side of the road. There is a side road running by it which leads to Heenan's and Kennedy's. There's a house on this farm with stove in it. The Ryder family use this house when working on the farm. The morning after the murders there were about fifteen tracks covering this untraveled side road to this house." J.J. Talman Regional Collection, University of Western Ontario Archives, Donnelly Family Papers, B4878, File 2, William Donnelly to Hutchinson, June 7, 1880.

116 "Ryder will endeavour to prove that he was at Mick Carroll's threshing on that day. I heard of Carroll being threshing two days, but [he] does not know the date. If it is of any use to you I can find out the date and also whether Ryder was at Carroll's or not." J.J. Talman Regional Collection, University of Western Ontario Archives, Donnelly Family Papers, B4878, File 2, William Donnelly to Hutchinson, September 15, 1880.

117 "Michael Powe of this place went to join them one night but they would not take him because he was friendly with us. It will be very hard to get them to tell the like of this as there is no doubt Father Connolly is trying to seal all their mouths for the sake of Catholicity." J.J. Talman Regional Collection, University of Western Ontario Archives, Donnelly Family Papers, B4878, File 2, William Donnelly to Hutchinson, June 29, 1880.

118 "There are three independent witnesses working up near Wireton in Colpoys Bay, namely the two Hodgins that slept at Bryant's on the night of the murder, and John Fulton who saw Kennedy give his revolver to Tom Fulton." J.J. Talman Regional Collection, University

of Western Ontario Archives, Donnelly Family Papers, B4878, File 2-3, William Donnelly to Hutchinson, December 10, 1880.

119 "William says that the Vigilants hold frequent meetings, but at no stated place. They have deserted the swamp school house. He was heard that they have agreed to employ no strangers, they should chance to entertain a detective unawares." Letterbooks from the Office of the Clerk of the Peace, Middlesex County, Hutchinson to Irving, May 11, 1880.

120 Regional History Collection of the D.B. Weldon Library, University of Western Ontario, Armitage-Stanley, Papers re Queen v. James Carroll, et al., June 9, 1880. Note to the reader: in the instance of this footnote (as well as the two that follow), I was unable to locate the cited source material in the University of Western Ontario Archives. After the passage of 140 years, it is possible that they have either disappeared since Butt wrote his thesis or simply were not transferred onto microfilm. In this instance, I have gone with Butt's original footnote information.

121 Armitage-Stanley, Papers re Queen v. James Carroll, et al., Donnelly to Hutchinson, April 3, 1880.

122 Armitage-Stanley, Papers re Queen v. James Carroll, et al., August 14, 1880.

123 "William Donnelly was here yesterday. He told me that John Whalen, son of old Patrick, has important information, which he thought he would be willing to communicate, if assured of safety & of participation in the reward. He can identify some of the parties who were at the old Donnelly's & who participated in the murder. . . . Donnelly says that John Whalen is friendly, & is only kept back by fear. He would like to leave the country, as he is regarded with suspicion by the Vigilants. He says there are others in the same position & who are only deterred by fear from telling what they know." Letterbooks from the Office of the Clerk of the Peace, Middlesex County, Hutchinson to Irving, August 25, 1880.

124 "In your next [letter] let me know if you were speaking to Johnny O'Connor in reference to William Whalen." J.J. Talman Regional Collection, University of Western Ontario Archives, Donnelly

Family Papers, B4878, File 2, William Donnelly to Hutchinson, June 29, 1880. See also: "Jim Feeheley set the trap at my father's and left William Whalen and William Feeheley to watch the house that no one should leave or come to it unknown until they fixed the hour . . ." J.J. Talman Regional Collection, University of Western Ontario Archives, Donnelly Family Papers, B4878, File 2, William Donnelly to Hutchinson, April 8, 1881. Additional evidence that William Whalen witnessed the murders was provided in a written statement from Enid McIlhargey, dated June 27, 1960 (provided to the author by Enid's daughter, Ely Errey, in an email on January 15, 2021): "The Donnelly murder, which happened on the evening of the 3rd or the morning of the 4th of February 1880 was planned by those who took part in it but it's believed that only one other person knew all the members of the gang . . . . [William] Whalen, a native of Biddulph, suspected that something was planned for that evening but had never been included in any of the meetings. He walked to the Donnelly home on the evening of February 3rd and soon saw the gang coming. Knowing that it would not be safe for him to be seen around there, he hid under some trees just south of the house. He saw everything that happened but was seen by nobody. The house was burned, Mr. & Mrs. Donnelly, their son Tom and a niece Bridget Donnelly were all murdered. Bridget Donnelly had come out from Ireland just a short time before. Johnny O'Connor, a little friend from Lucan who was spending the night at the Donnellys, escaped and ran across the road to the home of [Patrick] Whalen. William (Bill) Whalen was often heard to say, 'I may not know all that happens in Biddulph in the daytime, but I could tell you a lot that happens in Biddulph at night.'"

125 "I have been speaking to Walker at Whalen yesterday and found that whatever Sutherby says is law with him as they are brotherinlaws [sic]. Walkers saw the party of the 4th of February but is afraid to depend on either me or Everett but will do as Sutherby says. A proof of him getting the reward is all he wants." J.J. Talman Regional Collection, University of Western Ontario

Archives, Donnelly Family Papers, B4878, File 2 and 3, William Donnelly to Hutchinson, September 17, 1880.

126 "All the tracks led by John Doherty's house, which is situated by this side road. I understand Doherty saw them going and heard some of their conversation but he is afraid to say anything. He is a decent man but is in poor circumstances and I am going to find out in an indirect way how the reward would affect him. I am confident he knows them all, at least the ones that passed his place." J.J. Talman Regional Collection, University of Western Ontario Archives, Donnelly Family Papers, B4878, File 2, William Donnelly, Letter to C. Hutchinson from William Donnelly, June 7, 1880.

127 Middlesex Sheriff's Daybook, 1880–85 volume, pp. 19 and 20. Weldon Library, University of Western Ontario, London.

128 "Mr. Robert Thompson who built my father's house is summoned by the Crown. He says he should have a model of the house as high as the lofts, similar to the ground plans I have showing the windows and doors as there will be great swearing about the kitchen door where my mother was found." J.J. Talman Regional Collection, University of Western Ontario Archives, Donnelly Family Papers, B4878, File 2 and 3, William Donnelly to Hutchinson, September 18, 1880.

129 ". . . for the purpose of going to Lucan on the 2nd of October to bring in all the firearms destroyed in the fire together with the tin dish and the bones, in case they would be wanted at the trial." J.J. Talman Regional Collection, University of Western Ontario Archives, Donnelly Family Papers, B4878, File 4, William Donnelly to Johnson, February 18, 1881.

130 Letterbooks from the Office of the Clerk of the Peace, Middlesex County, Hutchinson to Irving, July 2, 1880.

131 Letterbooks from the Office of the Clerk of the Peace, Middlesex County, Hutchinson to Irving, June 29, 1880.

132 Letterbooks from the Office of the Clerk of the Peace, Middlesex County, Hutchinson to Irving, May 7, 1880.

133 "I am quite satisfied that if the Crown gave me anything towards helping me to move around I would find out plenty of convicting

evidence before the trial comes off." J.J. Talman Regional Collection, University of Western Ontario Archives, Donnelly Family Papers, B4878, File 2, William Donnelly to Hutchinson, June 9, 1880.

134 "I wish something could be done for the poor fellow. He ought at all events to leave Lucan for his own safety, although perhaps it is as well he stays there in the interests of the prosecution. He is sharp, & may find out something." Letterbooks from the Office of the Clerk of the Peace, Middlesex County, Hutchinson to Irving, May 7, 1880. See also: "However lest his fame should not have reached you, I will explain that William Donnelly is that one of the Donnelly family who lived in Whalen's Corners & whose life was sought, when poor John Donnelly was killed. I sent for him on 2 or more occasions for the purpose of obtaining information, not desiring to communicate with him either by telegram or mail, not having confidence enough in either mode of communication with the place of Lucan, where Donnelly resided. The information I required was essential at the time." Letterbooks of the Office of the Clerk of the Peace, Hutchinson to Scott, July 23, 1880.

135 "I enclose for your time & expenses on 28th when you came to me at my request. Please sign & return receipt." Letterbooks from the Office of the Clerk of the Peace, Middlesex County, Hutchinson to William Donnelly, June 30, 1880.

136 Armitage-Stanley, Spencer, Papers re Queen v. James Carroll, et al., Hutchinson to Scott, July 23, 1880. Charles Hutchinson: "They [the O'Connors] have unsparingly used the potent argument that they would remove Johnny."

137 Armitage-Stanley, Papers re Queen v. James Carroll, et al., Hutchinson to Scott, July 10, 1880. Charles Hutchinson: "When she claims money, I have to give in. I battle with her as long as possible, but eventually she carries her point, and gets, at all events, part of what she wants."

138 Regional History Collection of the D.B. Weldon Library, University of Western Ontario, Armitage-Stanley, Spencer, Papers re Queen v. James Carroll, et al., Scott to Hutchinson, July 9, 1880.

139 Armitage-Stanley, Spencer, Papers re Queen v. James Carroll, et al., Scott to Hutchinson, July 9, 1880.

140 Letterbooks from the Office of the Clerk of the Peace, Middlesex County, Hutchinson to Irving, June 29, 1880.

141 Regional History Collection of the D.B. Weldon Library, University of Western Ontario, Armitage-Stanley, Spencer, Papers re Queen v. James Carroll, et al., William Donnelly to Hutchinson, June 29, 1880.

142 Charles Hutchinson, Letters and Papers, Clerk of the Peace Correspondence, Hutchinson to Donnelly, June 30, 1880.

143 *London Free Press*, February 12, 1880.

144 "In regard to Everett, I think which[ever] party employed him would have his confidence, the defence in your suit do not appear to be at all friendly with him, neither are the Donnellys. I think it would by all means be to his interest to serve you in the matter." Regional History Collection of the D.B. Weldon Library, University of Western Ontario, Armitage-Stanley, Papers re Queen v. James Carroll, et al., Hossack to Hutchinson, August 30, 1880.

145 Armitage-Stanley, Papers re Queen v. James Carroll, et al., Donnelly to Hutchinson, August 14, 1880.

146 Armitage-Stanley, Papers re Queen v. James Carroll, et al., Donnelly to Hutchinson, August 14, 1880.

147 Letterbooks from the Office of the Clerk of the Peace, Middlesex County, Hutchinson to Everett, August 29, 1880.

148 Regional History Collection of the D.B. Weldon Library, University of Western Ontario, Armitage-Stanley, Papers re Queen v. James Carroll, et al., account of S.L. Everett for services to the Crown, August 28 to September 29, 1880, dated October 11, 1880. See also October 12 account for services to the Crown for October 3 and 4, 1880. For certification of Everett's accounts by John Scott, see Hutchinson, Letters and Papers, Clerk of the Peace Correspondence, Scott to Hutchinson, November 8, 1880.

149 Regional History Collection of the D.B. Weldon Library, University of Western Ontario, Armitage-Stanley, Papers re Queen

v. James Carroll, et al., letter to "Mr. ervin" [sic], signed "Mike," October 6, 1880.

150 "The enclosed letter in pencil has just arrived. It was probably posted at Berlin the day Everett was here? <u>Is it in his handwriting</u>?" Armitage-Stanley, Papers re Queen v. James Carroll, et al., Irving to Hutchinson, October 12, 1880.

151 Toronto *Globe*, February 7, 1880. The speaker is believed to be William Stanley.

152 Toronto *Globe*, February 10, 1880.

153 Reaney, *The Donnelly Documents: An Ontario Vendetta*, p. 69, note 474.

154 *London Free Press*, September 9, 1880.

155 *To pay one back in their own coin*: There are so many instances of this attitude throughout the Donnelly story: James Donnelly Sr.'s willingness to use a handspike against a man who threatened to use one on him; James Donnelly Sr.'s willingness to use force against those who would use force against him in attempting to drive him off his property; John Donnelly telling James Carroll's relatives negative things about Carroll after hearing that Carroll had made negative statements about the Donnellys; William Donnelly sending letters to the Bishop of London complaining about Father Connolly (thus going over the head of Father Connolly to his superior) after Father Connolly had complained about him; William Donnelly leaving the priest a letter threatening legal action on the Tom Ryan affair after the Father had threatened Ryan; Tom Donnelly refusing to let Ryan's fields be threshed as a result of the latter's attempts to persecute him in court; Tom Donnelly not giving the priest his permission to have Ryan's field threshed as the priest had opposed him during his legal trials with Ryan. The stagecoach wars are full of such tit-for-tat behaviour — if a fire was set in a Donnelly stable, a fire was set in a Flanagan stable, and so it went. If you were good to the Donnellys, they would be good to you ("very decent neighbours and not in the least quarrelsome if left alone," *London Advertiser*, February 11, 1880). And

this tendency would continue after the murders. Witness William Donnelly's replies to A. Riddell, who criticized William's constabulary performance in the local newspaper — Donnelly responds in kind by criticizing Riddell's marital infidelities in the same paper. This is the Donnelly version of the golden rule of "do unto others." It may have been based on religious and ethical concerns, but since so few people in the community paid more than lip service to ethics, it was not an attitude that, when stringently enacted, endeared the Donnelly family to their neighbours and community.

156 "Mr. Tom Morkin, of Biddulph, the other day offered the surviving members of the Donnelly family to purchase the old Donnelly homestead from them. The boys would not sell it." *London Advertiser*, June 24, 1880.

157 Letter from William Donnelly, published in the *London Free Press*, June 24, 1880.

158 *Glencoe Transcript*, June 3, 1880.

159 *Toronto Mail*, May 7, 1880. James Carroll had rented a twenty-five-acre farm on the north end of the Roman Line (Biddulph Township Assessment Roll, 1881) about the time he became a constable. It may have been property leased to him by his uncle James Maher.

160 Toronto *Globe*, June 25, 1880.

161 Toronto *Globe*, August 24, 1880.

162 Letterbooks from the Office of the Clerk of the Peace, Middlesex County, Hutchinson to Irving, May 7, 1880. See also *London Advertiser*, May 18, 1880.

163 James Creighton, on April 18, 1880, almost lost his stable containing five horses. His stable had one corner partitioned off such that it could serve as bunkhouse for two stable hands, William Atkinson and Simon Howe. Atkinson woke up at 3 a.m. as a result of a cramp and discovered a lit candle burning in a haystack. *Glencoe Transcript*, April 23, 1880.

164 Clerk of the Peace, Middlesex County, McCosh to Hutchinson, September 24, 1880, Weldon Library, University of Western Ontario.

165 Clerk of the Peace, Middlesex County, Ross to Hutchinson, September 28, 1880.

CHAPTER TWENTY-TWO: THE FIRST TRIAL

1   "He [Carroll] had shaved off his chin whiskers, leaving an Imperial on his upper lip. His moustache had been given a fierce twist, and this assisted him in getting up a bold look upon his entrance into Court." *London Daily Advertiser*, April 13, 1880.

2   "Last evening a city barber went to Carroll's cell to give him a 'clean shave,' but as the shades of night were not far off, it was decided to leave the matter over till this morning at an early hour." *London Advertiser*, September 30, 1880.

3   "Just as the barber was leaving, Purtell, one of the persons in the cell, exclaimed in a deep whisper, 'Don't forget the dye!'" *London Advertiser*, September 30, 1880.

4   *London Advertiser*, September 30, 1880.

5   "Passes are now required to secure admittance to the Court House. The Sheriff was busy yesterday serving them out." *London Advertiser*, September 30, 1880.

6   "The feeling in Biddulph still appears to run very high, and popular opinion seems to be divided into two classes — Donnelly and anti-Donnelly." *London Advertiser*, June 24, 1880.

7   "The trial of James Carroll, for the murder of Judith [Johannah] Donnelly (the result of which would decide the guilt or innocence of those indicted with him), commenced before Mr. Justice Armour, at London, on the 4th October, 1880, and proceeded day by day until the 9th of the same month. Messrs. Irving, Q.C., and Jas. Magee, for the Prosecution, and Messrs. MacMahon, Q.C., Meredith, Q.C., Macnabb and Blake for the prisoners." *The Dominion Annual Register and Review, For the Fourteenth and Fifteenth Years of the Canadian Union*, 1880–1881, Edited by Henry J. Morgan (Keeper of Records, Canada), p. 388, Montreal: John Lovell & Son, 1882.

8   "From the evidence elicited at the trial, the majority will also agree that the evidence against the prisoner would scarcely have justified a verdict of guilty. The evidence of the boy Connors pointed directly to Carroll [as being], if not the murderer . . . at least being present." *Listowel Banner*, October 15, 1880.

9   "Dennis Henan, Mike Henan, John Henan, James Toohey Sr.,
James Harigan, John Thompson, John McGlochlin, John Ryder,
Mike Carroll (he killed the Old Woman), James McGraw, William
Casey (J.P)., James Ryder, Dan Ryder, John Quigley, Pat Quigley,
Edward Ryan, John Ryan, John Cain, Wm. Thompson, James
Maher (killed the Old Man), John Dorsey, Jon Bryen, John
[Lamplin?], Pat Ryder and his two sons, William Feehley, John
Ryan (little Johney), Mike Madigan, Mike Blake, James Kelly,
Pat Breen (pres. of the Committee), Pat Dewar, Ted Toohey."
J.J. Talman Regional Collection, University of Western Ontario
Archives, Donnelly Family Papers, B4877, File 39, Samuel Everett,
List of Suspects by Everett, ca. 1880.

10   Testimony of Johnny O'Connor and William Donnelly. University
of Western Ontario, J.J. Talman Regional Collection, Middlesex
Court Records, Queen v. James Carroll, Murder of [Johannah]
Donnelly, February 4, 1880.

11   "I saw one of the Ryders between half past nine and ten o'clock on
the night of the murder; it was Patrick Ryder Jr. I was standing at
our gate, he was on horseback going south towards his own house.
He was carrying something; I could not say what it was; it was rolled
up in white. I considered it was a gun." Testimony of Thomas Keefe.
Archives of Ontario, Aemilius Irving Papers, "Copy Of Evidence,"
taken February 21 at the preliminary examination of Witnesses
before John Peters, Esq., J.P., and James Fisher, Esq., J.P., in the presence of James Carroll, John Kennedy, Martin McLaughlin, Thomas
Ryder, John Purtell, and James Ryder, charged with the murder
of James Donnelly, Judith Donnelly, Thomas Donnelly, Bridget
Donnelly, and John Donnelly, on the 4th day of February, A.D.,
1880, at the Township of Biddulph, in the County of Middlesex."

12   Testimony of Martin Hogan Jr. University of Western Ontario, J.J.
Talman Regional Collection, Middlesex Court Records, Queen v.
James Carroll, Murder of [Johannah] Donnelly, February 4, 1880.

13   Testimony of James Keefe Sr., Thomas Marshall, Edward Sutherby
and Thomas Hines. Middlesex Court Records, Queen v. James
Carroll, Murder of [Johannah] Donnelly, February 4, 1880.

14   Testimony of Edward Sutherby. Middlesex Court Records, Queen v. James Carroll, Murder of [Johannah] Donnelly, February 4, 1880.

15   Testimony of John Peters. Middlesex Court Records, Queen v. James Carroll, Murder of [Johannah] Donnelly, February 4, 1880.

16   Testimony of William Blackwell and William Walker. Middlesex Court Records, Queen v. James Carroll, Murder of [Johannah] Donnelly, February 4, 1880.

17   Testimony of Enoch Murphy. Middlesex Court Records, Queen v. James Carroll, Murder of [Johannah] Donnelly, February 4, 1880.

18   Testimony of Alfred Brown. Middlesex Court Records, Queen v. James Carroll, Murder of [Johannah] Donnelly, February 4, 1880.

19   Testimony of Charles Albert Matthews. Middlesex Court Records, Queen v. James Carroll, Murder of [Johannah] Donnelly, February 4, 1880.

20   Testimony of Robert Keefe Sr. Middlesex Court Records, Queen v. James Carroll, Murder of [Johannah] Donnelly, February 4, 1880.

21   Testimony of Gilbert Moore. Middlesex Court Records, Queen v. James Carroll, Murder of [Johannah] Donnelly, February 4, 1880.

22   Testimony of William Hodge. Middlesex Court Records, Queen v. James Carroll, Murder of [Johannah] Donnelly, February 4, 1880.

23   Testimony of Charles Pope. Middlesex Court Records, Queen v. James Carroll, Murder of [Johannah] Donnelly, February 4, 1880.

24   Testimony of Frank Forbes, William Spettigue, James Cunningham, James Gunning and Thomas Cunningham. Middlesex Court Records, Queen v. James Carroll, Murder of [Johannah] Donnelly, February 4, 1880.

25   Testimony of William and Mary Thompson. Middlesex Court Records, Queen v. James Carroll, Murder of [Johannah] Donnelly, February 4, 1880.

26   James and Matthew McGrath. Middlesex Court Records, Queen v. James Carroll, Murder of [Johannah] Donnelly, February 4, 1880.

27   Testimony of Thomas Ryder, Valentine Mackey and James Toohey. Middlesex Court Records, Queen v. James Carroll, Murder of [Johannah] Donnelly, February 4, 1880.

28 Testimony of James Ryder Jr. Middlesex Court Records, Queen v. James Carroll, Murder of [Johannah] Donnelly, February 4, 1880.

29 Testimony of Michael Blake. Middlesex Court Records, Queen v. James Carroll, Murder of [Johannah] Donnelly, February 4, 1880.

30 Testimony of Martin McLaughlin. Middlesex Court Records, Queen v. James Carroll, Murder of [Johannah] Donnelly, February 4, 1880.

31 Testimony of Temperance McLaughlin. Middlesex Court Records, Queen v. James Carroll, Murder of [Johannah] Donnelly, February 4, 1880.

32 Testimony of John Kennedy Jr., Denis Carty, William Hodgins and James Bryan. Middlesex Court Records, Queen v. James Carroll, Murder of [Johannah] Donnelly, February 4, 1880.

33 Testimony of James Bryan. Middlesex Court Records, Queen v. James Carroll, Murder of [Johannah] Donnelly, February 4, 1880.

34 *Toronto Mail*, October 7, 1880.

35 Testimony of William Stanley and John Fox. Middlesex Court Records, Queen v. James Carroll, Murder of [Johannah] Donnelly, February 4, 1880.

36 Testimony of Bernard Stanley and Thomas Dight. Middlesex Court Records, Queen v. James Carroll, Murder of [Johannah] Donnelly, February 4, 1880.

37 Testimony of William H. Ryan. Middlesex Court Records, Queen v. James Carroll, Murder of [Johannah] Donnelly, February 4, 1880.

38 Testimony of David McRoberts. Middlesex Court Records, Queen v. James Carroll, Murder of [Johannah] Donnelly, February 4, 1880.

39 Testimony of Tom Hodgins. Middlesex Court Records, Queen v. James Carroll, Murder of [Johannah] Donnelly, February 4, 1880.

40 Testimony of Timothy Coughlin. Middlesex Court Records, Queen v. James Carroll, Murder of [Johannah] Donnelly, February 4, 1880.

41 "They . . . said that William Donnelly's reputation was bad, although none could say why from personal experience." Butt, William Davison, *The Donnellys: History, Legend, Literature*, p. 290. See also McKeow, Peter, *A Donnelly Treatise: After the Massacre*, Kindle edition, p. 2999.

42 Closing statement of William Meredith. *London Advertiser*, February 5, 1880.

43 "There was nothing unjustifiable in what was done at the Cedar Swamp Schoolhouse." Closing statement of William Meredith. *London Advertiser*, February 5, 1880.

44 Toronto *Globe*, October 11, 1880.

45 Statement of James Magee taken from University of Western Ontario, J.J. Talman Regional Collection, Middlesex Court Records, Queen v. James Carroll, Murder of [Johannah] Donnelly, February 4, 1880.

46 Justice John Armour quoted in the *Toronto Mail*, October 11, 1880.

47 Justice John Armour quoted in University of Western Ontario, J.J. Talman Regional Collection, Middlesex Court Records, Queen v. James Carroll, Murder of [Johannah] Donnelly, February 4, 1880.

48 Justice John Armour quoted in the *Toronto Mail*, October 11, 1880.

49 Justice John Armour quoted in the *Toronto Mail*, October 11, 1880.

50 Justice John Armour quoted in the *Toronto Mail*, October 11, 1880.

51 Justice John Armour quoted in University of Western Ontario, J.J. Talman Regional Collection, Middlesex Court Records, Queen v. James Carroll, Murder of [Johannah] Donnelly, February 4, 1880.

52 Justice John Armour quoted in the *Toronto Mail*, October 11, 1880.

53 *Huron Signal-Star*, October 15, 1880.

CHAPTER TWENTY-THREE: THE SECOND TRIAL

1 Charles Hutchinson in his report to Attorney General Oliver Mowat wrote, "I need not tell you that the case for the Prosecution depends entirely upon Johnny's evidence, which since Mr. Justice Armour's charge to the jury has increased in value ten-fold in the public estimation." Letterbooks from the Office of the Clerk of the Peace, Middlesex County, Hutchinson to Mowat, October 25, 1880.

2 Regional History Collection of the D.B. Weldon Library, University of Western Ontario, Armitage-Stanley, Papers re Queen v. James

Carroll, et al., Scott to Hutchinson, November 24, 1880, sending the writs.

3   "It is to be hoped that the case will be settled shortly, as it is manifestly unfair to keep so many men imprisoned and away from their families and farms on a charge that may never be proved against them." *Huron Signal-Star*, October 15, 1880.

4   *Catholic Record*, October 29, 1880.

5   Toronto *Globe*, October 22, 1880.

6   "Mr. Attorney-General Mowat bears the responsibility of action or inaction in the matter." *Toronto Mail*, October 14, 1880.

7   "Three days after the last trial James McMartin, pro[prietor] City Hotel, heard Rodgers, one of the jurymen, say if he saw the prisoners committing the deed he would not find them guilty. He will I think make affidavit to this if you require it in trying to move the trial." Regional History Collection of the D.B. Weldon Library, University of Western Ontario, Armitage-Stanley, Papers re Queen v. James Carroll, et al., William Donnelly to Hutchinson, November 9, 1880.

8   "I heard a leading wholesale merchant say openly at the club the other day, that although he thought the men were probably guilty, he would not find them so on the evidence so far brought against them." Letterbooks from the Office of the Clerk of the Peace, Middlesex County, Hutchinson to Irving, October 26, 1880.

9   *London Advertiser*, October 11, 1880.

10 "What think you of the petitions to admit them to bail? . . . rather significant of a pretty strong feeling in their favor." Letterbooks from the Office of the Clerk of the Peace, Middlesex County, Hutchinson to Irving, October 22, 1880.

11 "I think still the chance of convicting here much less than it would be almost anywhere else." Letterbooks from the Office of the Clerk of the Peace, Middlesex County, Hutchinson to Irving, October 18, 1880. See also: "I am sorry the trial has to be in this county, as I have no hope whatever of a conviction being got here under any circumstances. The verdict will amount to 'served them right' — whatever evidence we have, & we are no likely to have

more than we [had last] time." Letterbooks from the Office of the Clerk of the Peace, Middlesex County, Hutchinson to Irving, October 30, 1880.

12 "The Biddulph murder case will probably be tried by a special commission, Hon. Mr. Mowat being favorable to that course of procedure. It is hardly probable that the prisoners will be allowed out on bail. It is to be hoped that the case will be speedily settled, for the prisoners have been about eight months in gaol." *Huron Signal-Star*, October 29, 1880. See also *Huron Signal-Star*, October 15, 1880.

13 *London Free Press*, November 18, 1880.

14 "I presume you intend me to express an opinion as to whether jurors can be summoned in time for 17 or 24 January, the precept to sheriff being received on 3 January. It seems to me hardly possible for the jurors to be served in time for either of these days, unless the sheriff were authorized to employ extra hands. With his ordinary staff, it would take from 10 to 12 days to serve 100 jurors, & not many days less to serve a smaller number — say 10 days. The men could not be got ready to start until 13th; 10 days would bring it to the 23rd, & the jurors are entitled to 8 days notice, so that the jurors last served should to be required to attend before 31 January. . . . Why all this hurry at the last moment? For private reasons of our own (the Crown's I mean) I would like to have plenty of time to serve the jurors. . . . This cannot be done in a hurry. The men must be throughly reliable & intelligent & must have plenty of time. If we are to submit to the forlorn hope of a fair trial in this county, it certainly ought to be under the most favourable circumstances possible, & these I regret to think will give us little chance of a favourable result. I see no reason for changing the opinion that the trials cannot be brought in conveniently sooner than the 6th February, & I would much prefer a week later." Letterbooks from the Office of the Clerk of the Peace, Middlesex County, Hutchinson to Irving, November 8, 1880.

15 "Special commission of Oyer and Terminer to be held by MC [Matthew Crooks] Cameron for trial of the Biddulph Murders." Public Archives of Ontario, Featherston Osler Family Fonds,

F1032 MU2300, 1881, Justice Featherston Osler, Diary of Justice Featherston Osler, January 22, 1881-February 7, 1881.

16 Hutchinson, Letters and Papers, Clerk of the Peace, Everett to Hutchinson, November 18, 1880.

17 "I think it proper to let you know how things stand in connection with the O'Connors. After the trial Mr. & Mrs. O'Connor refused to allow the constable to remain in charge of Johnny any longer." Letterbooks from the Office of the Clerk of the Peace, Middlesex County, Hutchinson to Mowat, October 25, 1880.

18 "The O'Connors now have the boy in their hands; and in my opinion, I regret to say they have but little thought except as to the amount of money they can make out of the situation." Letterbooks from the Office of the Clerk of the Peace, Middlesex County, Hutchinson to Mowat, October 25, 1880.

19 Letterbooks from the Office of the Clerk of the Peace, Middlesex County, Irving to Hutchinson, October 18, 1880. See also Letterbooks from the Office of the Clerk of the Peace, Middlesex County, Hutchinson to Mowat, October 25, 1880.

20 Letterbooks from the Office of the Clerk of the Peace, Middlesex County, Hutchinson to Irving, October 14, 1880: "I fear O'Connor is not to be trusted with the care of Johnny, & that the boy is not safe. O'Connor took him with him to Lucan a day or two ago, & got drunk there or on the way back. When he got home in the evening, he was very drunk. He met old Mr. Marshall in Jones' store in Petersville, & when Marshall remonstrated with him in respect of his condition, he attacked him violently & was with difficulty restrained. Constable Jones tells me that it is the habit of the old woman to get drunk also."

21 Letterbooks from the Office of the Clerk of the Peace, Middlesex County, Hutchinson to Williams, November 8, 1880.

22 ". . . after enduring a great deal from her [Mary O'Connor] only the other I advanced her $100 to provide absolutely necessary, as she said, for her household & for the little shop she is now carrying on. The more you give her, the more she wants." Letterbooks from

the Office of the Clerk of the Peace, Middlesex County, Hutchinson to Scott, December 9, 1880.

23 The fact that she had received such a letter is evidenced in Mary O'Connor's quote: "We got a letter that whoever took the boy away would get the reward." *London Advertiser*, January 28, 1881. See also: "Mrs. O'Connor says she was actually offered $4,000 by friends of the prisoners, if she would give up the boy, & that the money was actually tendered to her. . . . This may or may not be all truth, but I believe there is truth in it." Letterbooks from the Office of the Clerk of the Peace, Middlesex County, Hutchinson to Scott, December 16, 1880.

24 According to the *Globe and Mail*, "1854–1914: The Dominion of Canada is under the gold standard. The value of the Canadian dollar was fixed in terms of gold and valued at par with the U.S. currency. Both U.S. and British gold coins are legal tender in Canada." Tavia Grant and Claire Neary, "A brief history of the Canadian dollar," https://theglobeandmail.com/report-on-business/economy/a-brief-history-of-the-canadian-dollar/article1366590/ (accessed February 14, 2019). So, $4,000 Canadian dollars in 1880 would be the equivalent of $4,000 U.S. dollars. $4,000 U.S. dollars in 1880 would be equal to $101,000 U.S. dollars in 2020. "Value of $4,000 from 1880 to 2019," https://in2013dollars.com/us/inflation/1880?amount=4000 (accessed February 14, 2019). When present-day conversion differentials between U.S. and Canadian dollars are accounted for, as of February 2020 $101,000 U.S. would convert to $134,000 Canadian. https://xe.com/currencyconverter/convert/?Amount=101%2C165.10&From=USD&To=CAD (accessed February 15, 2019).

25 University of Western Ontario, Armitage-Stanley, Papers re Queen v. James Carroll, et al., Correspondence, Scott to Hutchinson, December 9 and December 15, 1880, File 3.

26 Toronto *Globe*, December 13, 1880.

27 "She did not scruple to say that she could get $4000 from the friends of the prisoners, & therefore that she intended to receive

money from the Govt. . . . I have no doubt she could make a good bargain with the prisoners' friends, & see no reason to question the offer of $4000 having been made." Letterbooks from the Office of the Clerk of the Peace, Middlesex County, Hutchinson to Scott, December 9, 1880.

28   "It is quite in the cards that if incensed she will try to make terms with the prisoners' friends, and put Johnny out of the way." Letterbooks from the Office of the Clerk of the Peace, Middlesex County, Hutchinson to Scott, December 16, 1880.

29   "I have little doubt that efforts will be made on behalf of the prisoners to get the boy out of the way before the next trial, and that it will be in question, which the O'Connors will not be above considering, whether it will pay best to be true to the Crown, or to fall in with the views of the other side." Letterbooks from the Office of the Clerk of the Peace, Middlesex County. Hutchinson to Mowat, October 25, 1880. See also: "I feel very uneasy about the safety of the boy, as I have lost control of him. I have not the slightest confidence in his father. Its would not surprise me at any time to find that he had gone over to the enemy. I place a little more reliance upon Mrs. O'Connor, but not very much. I think they are both determined to make as much money as possible out of this matter, & that if they are led to believe they can make more by betraying us they will not scruple to do so. When [Constable] Jones had charge of the boy, I always knew what was going on. Now I have no means of keeping any watch over him, & yet the danger is greater than it ever was." Letterbooks from the Office of the Clerk of the Peace, Middlesex County, Hutchinson to Mowat, October 26, 1880.

30   "I am authorized by the Attorney General to say that you may intimate to the O'Connors that the government will, after the Donnelly cases are concluded, take any application they may be advised to make into careful consideration with a view of granting them some compensation in respect of the losses which it is believed they have suffered on account of their connection with these cases." University of Western Ontario, Armitage-Stanley, Papers re Queen

v. James Carroll, et al., Correspondence, Scott to Hutchinson, November 2, 1880, File 3. And: "I have warned her distinctly that the amount of my advances beforehand will then be taken into account . . ." Letterbooks of the Office of the Clerk of the Peace, Middlesex County, Hutchinson to Scott, December 17, 1880.

31 Charles Hutchinson: "You cannot eat your cake and have it." Letterbooks from the Office of the Clerk of the Peace, Middlesex County, Hutchinson to Scott, December 17, 1880.

32 J.J. Talman Regional Collection, University of Western Ontario Archives, Donnelly Family Papers, B4877, File 51, Unknown, List of Potential Jurors, ca. 1881.

33 Letterbooks from the Office of the Clerk of the Peace, Middlesex County, Hutchinson to Irving, November 17, 1880.

34 *London Advertiser*, January 25, 1881.

35 Evidently two sets of tickets had been printed up and distributed: "The blue ones are season tickets while the red ones are only for one day's admission." *London Daily Advertiser*, January 25, 1881.

36 *London Advertiser*, January 25, 1881. For Groves's first name, see *The Province of Ontario Gazetteer and Directory, Containing Precise Descriptions of the Cities, Towns and Villages in the Province with the Names of Professional and Business Men and Principal Inhabitants Together with a Full List of Members of the Executive Governments, Senators, Members of the Commons and Local Legislatures, and Officials of the Dominion, and a Large Amount of Other General, Varied and Useful Information, Carefully Compiled from the Most Recent and Authentic Data.* C.E. Anderson & Co., Proprietors, M. McEvoy, Editor and Compiler, Toronto: Robertson & Cook Publishers, Daily Telegraph Printing House (Directory Branch), p. 275, 1869.

37 *London Advertiser*, January 25, 1881.

38 *London Advertiser*, January 25, 1881.

39 *London Advertiser*, January 25, 1881.

40 "One hundred potential jurors had been summoned; the selection of twelve jurors occupied half of the first day. The prosecutors with their private reports on those one hundred men selected

the best jury possible." Butt, *The Donnellys: History, Legend, Literature*, p. 305.

41 Donnelly Family Papers, notes on the jurors. Weldon Library, University of Western Ontario.

42 "All the jurymen belong to one or the other of the leading Protestant denominations — Methodist, Presbyterian, Baptist, and one Church of England. They are nearly all Canadians. After the most careful and rigid enquiries, we fail to hear the first whisper against the standing of a single individual constituting the Biddulph panel." *London Advertiser*, January 26, 1881.

43 *London Advertiser*, January 25, 1881.

44 "I had a conversation with Carroll about the Vigilance Committee. And he said the bad doings would have to be stopped. If the Donnellys were in it, they would have to be stopped. Carroll also told me to shun the Donnellys." Testimony of James Feeheley. *London Advertiser*, January 26, 1881.

45 "I then asked Carroll if he had a warrant for me. He said he had, and I asked him what for? He said that was his own business." *London Advertiser*, January 26, 1881.

46 *London Advertiser*, January 26, 1881.

47 "There was a slight commotion in the court when Connor's name was called, and all eyes were turned towards the door of the witness room . . ." *Toronto Mail*, January 27, 1881.

48 *Toronto Mail*, January 27, 1881.

49 Butt, *The Donnellys: History, Legend, Literature*, p. 307.

50 Baptism Record of Jeremia (Johnny) O'Connor, St. Patrick's Church, from July 12, 1866, indicating his date of birth as June 22, 1866.

51 Aemilius Irving: "I'll go over the evidence with the boy, which the learned counsel did at some length referring to the great number of times the witness has been examined, having been brought up five times for examination, including the present court." *London Advertiser*, January 28, 1881.

52 "MacMahon, very adroitly, got Everett to say that he had suggested to both Chief Williams and Dr. Hossack, the coroner, that 'it would be well to take the boy O'Connor's evidence that

evening.' The coroner innocently asks MacMahon, 'What did the coroner say?' Irving tries to block this since the rules of evidence forbid hearsay, Hossack can himself tell what he said to Everett when he is called later on. But Judge Armour was tricked by MacMahon into allowing Everett then to assert that, 'No doubt the boy will give better evidence after Bill Donnelly has had two or three talks with him.'" Reaney, *The Donnelly Documents: An Ontario Vendetta*, p. 212. Reaney is quoting Samuel Everett's testimony from the first trial, Thursday, October 7, 1880: University of Western Ontario, Middlesex Court Records, Queen v. James Carroll, Murder of [Johannah] Donnelly, February 4, 1880. See also: "There was naturally suspicion that the son had been coached and instructed . . ." *Exeter Times*, February 4, 1881, and "Well, in the first place the boy Connor's evidence is no good. He has been stuffed . . ." Toronto *Globe*, February 20, 1880.

53 "He was dressed in a neat suit of dark gray clothes, and wore a watch chain." *London Advertiser*, January 27, 1881. See also, "He was dressed in a neat suit, with gold studs in his shirt-front and a gold chain stretching over his vest." *Toronto Mail*, January 27, 1881.

54 "Today he stepped into the stand twirling a fur hat on his hand, but not at all nervous." *Toronto Mail*, January 27, 1881.

55 "Mr. Meredith stood directly in front of the stands and about three feet from the witness, who rested his arm on the rail and leaned forward." *Toronto Mail*, January 27, 1881.

56 *London Advertiser*, January 31, 1881.

57 Reaney, *The Donnelly Documents: An Ontario Vendetta*, p. cxxxv.

58 "A gold watch had been lent to him for the occasion by John Lewis, proprietor of the Huron Hotel, married to a Kennedy, a Donnelly friend who went bail for Robert in 1877. The watch chain attracted the attention of the defence in rebuttal and MacMahon averred that O'Connor had been given the watch as a bribe at the Donnelly wake; the lad fought him off. Anything to discredit him." Reaney, James, *The Donnelly Documents: An Ontario Vendetta*, pp. 241–242, note 696.

59 *London Advertiser*, January 27, 1881.

60 Toronto *Globe*, January 26, 1881.

61 *Toronto Mail*, January 27, 1881.

62 *London Advertiser*, January 28, 1881.

63 *Toronto Mail*, January 27, 1881.

64 *London Advertiser*, January 27, 1881.

65 *Toronto Mail*, January 27, 1881.

66 *London Advertiser*, January 28, 1881.

67 Toronto *Globe*, January 28, 1881.

68 Toronto *Globe*, January 28, 1881.

69 *Toronto Mail*, February 3, 1881.

70 *Toronto Mail*, January 28, 1881.

71 *London Advertiser*, January 28, 1881.

72 Testimony of William and Mary Thompson. Aemilius Irving Papers, F 1027-3, File 82-8, Transcript of the Donnelly Murder Case, 1880 (MS 6500) Public Archives of Ontario.

73 Testimony from Police Chief William T. Williams. Public Archives of Ontario, Aemilius Irving Papers, F 1027-3, File 82-8, Transcript of the Donnelly Murder Case, 1880 (MS 6500).

74 J.J. Talman Regional Collection, University of Western Ontario Archives, Donnelly Family Papers, B4878, File 15, Charles Hutchinson Letter Book, ca. January 15, 1881.

75 D.B. Weldon Library, University of Western Ontario, Armitage-Stanley, Papers re Queen v. James Carroll, et al., Donnelly to Hutchinson, December 14, 1880.

76 Letterbooks from the Office of the Clerk of the Peace, Middlesex County, Hutchinson to Sheriff, Grey County, January 14, 1881.

77 Letterbooks from the Office of the Clerk of the Peace, Middlesex County, Hutchinson to Donnelly, February 15, 1881.

78 Letterbooks from the Office of the Clerk of the Peace, Middlesex County, William Donnelly to Hutchinson, February 1, and Patrick Donnelly to Hutchinson, January 27, 1881.

79 "I live at Grand Bend on Lake Huron. I used to live in Biddulph. I lived on Sixth Concession, half mile north of the railway. I know Thomas Ryder. I lived a quarter mile from Ryder, was working for

him splitting rails. I remember the night of the murders. I slept at home. I was out about 6 or 7 one day. I was at work in Thomas Ryder's swamp, my brother and I went out, my brother died 7th February, 1880. We went to Thomas Ryder's probably about seven. I had supper. I went to get a job splitting stove bolts, my house was east of his. . . . Mrs. Ryder and the children were there. I asked for Mr. Ryder and Mrs. Ryder went into the sitting room and stayed there about a quarter of an hour, there was no light. Mrs. Ryder was putting one of the little ones to bed. I waited till half past ten, no one came in while I was there. I heard no voices, my brother was with me, no one came in and I saw no man about the place. I got home about 20 minutes to 11." Testimony of Robert Cutt. Toronto *Globe*, February 2, 1881.

80 *London Advertiser*, January 29, 1881. See also letter from Charles Hutchinson: "Luke Nangle told Charles Nangle and John Grace, that on the morning after the murder he saw Toohey dressed in woman's clothes and taking them off in the stable. He can prove that there were several meetings on part of the Vigilance Committee at Toohey's house, between the night of the Ryder fire and the murders, when the windows were screened with bed quilts. Nangle has been served with a subpoena, but says he will leave the country." J.J. Talman Regional Collection, University of Western Ontario Archives, Donnelly Family Papers, B4878, File 15, Charles Hutchinson Letter Book, ca. January 15, 1881. Also, Reaney, *The Donnelly Documents: An Ontario Vendetta*, p. xc, note 217: "Patrick Nangle. . . . The morning after the murders in 1880, saw a Vigilante dressed as a woman with a black eye returning to 'her' farm."

81 Testimony of Martin Darcy: "If I give you my opinion, I would say that the Donnellys were to blame for nearly all [of the crime in Biddulph]." *London Advertiser*, January 29, 1881.

82 *London Advertiser*, February 3, 1881.

83 "Henry Fysh was appointed jailer for the County of Middlesex in 1880 and died a few years later." *History of the County of Middlesex, Canada*, p. 409. Toronto and London: W.A. & C.L. Goodspeed, Publishers, 1889.

84 *London Advertiser*, February 3, 1881.

85 *London Advertiser*, February 3, 1881.

86 *London Advertiser*, February 3, 1881.

87 *London Advertiser*, February 3, 1881.

88 *London Advertiser*, February 3, 1881.

89 "Still others said that they would not convict for fear that dozens of others would have to be hanged as well." *Toronto Mail*, February 1, 1881.

90 Hutchinson has this confirmed by a carriage driver several days after the verdict: "It cannot be that these murderers will escape altogether. It is only sympathy that has protected them hitherto, and they will be prosecuted with more effect on some future occasion. I have this from the best authority — the foreman of the jury, Francis of Strathroy, told a gentleman in the cabs on his way home, that no less than six of the jurymen asked him, if it was possible to find a verdict of guilty in such shape as not to involve the death penalty, and when he said it was impossible, they resolved to give the prisoner the benefit of the doubt suggested by the judge, although satisfied of the prisoner's guilt." J.J. Talman Regional Collection, University of Western Ontario Archives, Donnelly Family Papers, B4848, File 15, Charles Hutchinson Letter Book, p. 543, February 7, 1881.

91 *London Advertiser*, February 3, 1881.

CHAPTER TWENTY-FOUR: JUSTICE DENIED

1 *Toronto Mail*, February 3, 1881.

2 "The announcement was received by a tremendous burst of applause, which was kept up for some time . . ." *London Advertiser*, 3 February 1881.

3 ". . . as the reporter saw them the boys were bent over her [Jennie Currie's] form with tears running down their cheeks." *Toronto Mail*, February 3, 1881. See also: "A year ago on Wednesday, Wm. Donnelly took dinner with his father and mother, and that was the last time he saw his parents alive. He and his sister and his brother

Pat sat in the attorney's office waiting for the verdict. It is natural to suppose that they wished to see the murderers of the family punished. When the verdict was announced and the vulgar cheers of the crowd fell upon the ears of the little party, the young woman fainted away, and as the reporter saw them the boys were bending over her form with tears running down their cheeks. It was sad indeed to see the poor girl lying on the floor, while an unfeeling crowd cheered out of doors." *Guelph Daily Mercury*, February 4, 1881.

4   ". . . notwithstanding the thundering voice of the High Constable roaring 'Silence' Judge Cameron said that if the constables could point out anyone who applauded he would commit him, and this had the effect of somewhat restoring order." *London Advertiser*, February 3, 1881.

5   *Toronto Mail*, January 31, 1881.

6   *Toronto Mail*, January 31, 1881.

7   *London Advertiser*, February 3, 1881.

8   *London Advertiser*, February 3, 1881.

9   "Caroll was respected in Golden despite being a mass murderer," https://thegoldenstar.net/community/caroll-was-respected-in-golden-despite-being-a-mass-murderer/ (accessed April 16, 2020).

10   Given that some estimates put the number of people who murdered the Donnellys at forty, had they all been hanged it would have cleaned out a large number of those who dwelled on or near the Roman Line in Biddulph Township. See: "The acquittal of Carroll was virtually the acquittal of fifty or sixty persons in Biddulph." *Guelph Daily Mercury*, February 4, 1881.

11   *Guelph Daily Mercury*, February 4, 1881.

12   "Purtell still remains in the city. He told our reporter it was not his intention to remain in Biddulph, and he intended to look for a job of work elsewhere." *London Advertiser*, February 5, 1881. See also: "At 730 PM [sic] this evening all the prisoners except Purtell (who staid [sic] in London) arrived at Claudboye [sic] Station. And in half an hour after were at the Central Hotel in Lucan. Where after partaking of some refreshments started for their respective homes at 945 [sic] p.m." William Porte's diary, February 2, 1881.

13 Butt, *The Donnellys: History, Legend, Literature*, p. 310.

14 *Exeter Times*, February 9, 1893.

15 Charles Hutchinson had been born in Newcastle upon Tyne, England, June 22, 1826. Aemilius Irving was born in Leamington, England, on February 4, 1823.

16 *Toronto Mail* article quoted in "The Great Trial — Opinions of the Outside Press on the Verdict," *London Advertiser*, February 4, 1881.

17 *London Advertiser*, February 4, 1881. Toronto *Globe* article quoted.

18 *London Advertiser*, February 4, 1881. *Hamilton Times* article quoted.

19 *Guelph Daily Mercury*, February 4, 1881.

20 *Toronto Mail*, January 31, 1881. It is worth noting here the journalist's use of the pejorative "Cracker," which, despite its modern-day use as a racial epithet, is actually a very old term. Its use in the *Toronto Mail* newspaper article is in the sense indicated in the online article from which the following quote has been extracted: "A person of lower caste or criminal disposition (in some instances, was used in reference to bandits and other lawless folk)" and Celtic immigrants — Scots-Irish people who came to the Americas who were running from political circumstances in the old world. Those Scots-Irish folks started settling the Carolinas, and later moved deeper South and into Florida and Georgia. But the disparaging term followed these immigrants, who were thought by local officials to be unruly and ill-mannered." Gene Demby, "The Secret History of the Word Cracker." https://npr.org/sections/codeswitch/2013/07/01/197644761/word-watch-on-crackers (accessed March 21, 2021).

21 *Toronto Mail*, February 3, 1881.

22 *London Advertiser*, February 4, 1881. See also Toronto *Globe*, February 4, 1881.

23 Toronto *Globe*, February 4, 1881.

24 *London Advertiser*, February 5, 1881.

25 J.J. Talman Regional Collection, University of Western Ontario Archives, Donnelly Family Papers, B4878, File 15, Charles Hutchinson, Charles Hutchinson Letter Book, February 7, 1881.

26 *London Advertiser*, March 7, 1881.

27 Letterbooks from the Office of the Clerk of the Peace, Middlesex County, Hutchinson to Irving, March 7, 1881.

28 Letterbooks from the Office of the Clerk of the Peace, Middlesex County, Hutchinson to Irving, March 4, 1881.

29 Toronto *Globe*, February 4, 1881.

30 "Bob Donnelly. . . . met James Carroll on a Lucan street and punched Carroll on the nose." Miller, *The Donnellys Must Die*, p. 224.

31 "Carroll laid a charge against him [Bob Donnelly]. It was heard in magistrate's court on March 14 . . . and was thrown out." Miller, *The Donnellys Must Die*, p. 224. Corroborating evidence that this assault took place can be found in William Porte's diary entry for March 14, 1881: "Carroll vs. Bob Donnelly assault trial at Ferguson's today."

32 "A few days ago, Bob Donnelly tried to pick a quarrel with James Carroll in a store at Lucan. He jostled against Carroll several times." *Irish Canadian*, March 24, 1881. See also: "It is true that Donnelly did jostle against Carroll on the sidewalk; and it is the opinion of spectators at the time that Donnelly's intention was that it should be resented . . ." *Irish Canadian*, March 28, 1881.

33 *London Advertiser*, May 23, 1881.

34 *London Advertiser*, May 23, 1881.

35 *London Advertiser*, May 23, 1881.

36 *Glencoe Transcript*, April 14, 1881.

37 An article appearing in the *Glencoe Transcript* some five years later would make the claim that William Donnelly had done more for the horse interests of Middlesex than any other man. *Glencoe Transcript*, May 14, 1886. See also references to William Donnelly's horse breeding expertise in the *Exeter Times*, October 3, 1878; and the *Glencoe Transcript*, September 17, 1885.

38 D.B. Weldon Library, University of Western Ontario, Armitage-Stanley, Papers re Queen v. James Carroll, et al., Donnelly to Hutchinson, February 21, 1881.

39 "I hope you are not too sanguine as to what can be done with Purtell. We have been so often deceived; besides unless Purtell could give information enabling other more reliable evidence being discovered, his own testimony after twice perjuring himself in the witness box would not be of much value." Letterbooks from the Office of the Clerk of the Peace, Middlesex County, Hutchinson to Donnelly, February 21, 1881.

40 "I send you a letter which I received from William Donnelly this morning. I wrote him that I had no authority to expend more money in connection with the Donnelly murder cases, as the prosecutions were virtually at an end, & would not be renewed without the discovery of new evidence. At the same time I presumed that the offer of the reward still held good." Letterbooks from the Office of the Clerk of the Peace, Middlesex County, Hutchinson to Scott, February 12, 1881.

41 "I return you W. Donnelly's letter dated 11th February, forwarded by you to me on 12th instant for perusal. The answer you gave Donnelly is undoubtedly the correct one." (See footnote 40 for reference to Hutchinson's answer to Donnelly.) D.B. Weldon Library, University of Western Ontario, Correspondence, January–October 1881, Donnelly Papers, Box 2-4, Scott to Hutchinson, February 15, 1881.

42 "Purtell is still in the city, said to be drinking hard. I rather think Donnelly has him to some extent shadowed." Letterbooks from the Office of the Clerk of the Peace, Middlesex County, Hutchinson to Irving, March 4, 1881. See also: "My brother Pat and myself are going to hire the man I wrote you about — to follow Purtell. We are so sure of success, that is providing Mr. Mowat does not do it. Our man has succeeded in getting Purtell to say that he could make $4000.00 dollars if he liked." D.B. Weldon Library, University of Western Ontario, Correspondence, January–October 1881, Box 2-4, William Donnelly to Hutchinson, February 21, 1881.

43 Toronto *Globe*, January 31, 1881.

44 D.B. Weldon Library, University of Western Ontario, Armitage-Stanley, Papers re Queen v. James Carroll, et al., Donnelly to Hutchinson, April 8, 1881.

45 "The man I wanted hired has already in his devil-may-care way found out something very interesting, especially what he found out on last St. Patrick's night." Armitage-Stanley, Papers re Queen v. James Carroll, et al., Donnelly to Hutchinson, April 8, 1881.

46 "I says Bill [Feeheley] I always thought you knew something about it." Testimony of Patrick Donnelly. J.J. Talman Regional Collection, University of Western Ontario Archives, Donnelly Family Papers, B4877, File 61, Unknown, Statements Regarding the Feeheleys, July 10, 1881.

47 "After I had tea I started up the street toward the post office, and I saw William Feeheley taking his coat off asking Carroll to fight him telling him if he would fight him five minutes he would give him six dollars more. Called Carroll a murderer saying he could prove it." Written statement of Francis West, under the heading of "Information Picked Up Regarding The Donnelly Murders . . .", dated April 16, 1881, University of Western Ontario, Legal Papers: Information Picked Up Regarding the Donnelly Murder, February–April 1881. Donnelly Papers, Box 59.

48 *London Free Press*, October 12, 1881.

49 Testimony of Patrick Donnelly. J.J. Talman Regional Collection, University of Western Ontario Archives, Donnelly Family Papers, B4877, File 61, Unknown, Statements Regarding the Feeheleys, July 10, 1881.

50 Testimony of Patrick Donnelly. J.J. Talman Regional Collection, University of Western Ontario Archives, Donnelly Family Papers, B4877, File 63, Unknown, Statements About the Feeheleys, ca. April 31, 1881–July 31, 1881.

51 Signed statement of Thomas Shoebottom, May 5, 1881. University of Western Ontario Archives, Correspondence: January–October 1881, Donnelly Papers, Box 2-4.

52 Testimony of John H. McConnell. J.J. Talman Regional Collection, University of Western Ontario Archives, Donnelly Family Papers,

B4877, File 54, Various Authors, Information on Murders, 1881, ca. 1881.

53 "James Feeheley told me the following in connection with the Donnelly murder, on the morning the Feeheley family moved away to the States. . . . Feeheley counted thirty-one men that he said were at the murder and amongst them were Jim Carroll, Martin, McLaughlin, all the Ryders he said but the one that had his foot cut. John Kennedy, John Dewes [sp?] & Michael Heenan and his (Feeheley's) own two uncles James Maher & John Cain. I am Feeheley's first cousin and do firmly believe that he and his brother were concerned in the murder and also believe that if they were now visited by someone with whom they are on intimate terms or placed under arrest, they would tell all about the affair." Robert Keefe Sr's statement dictated to and witnessed by William Donnelly, Donnelly to Hutchinson, April 8, 1881. University of Western Ontario Archives, Correspondence: January–October 1881, Donnelly Papers, Box 2-4.

54 "I don't know for certain whether my brother William belonged to the Vigilance Committee or not. They say he does." Testimony of James Feeheley. Public Archives of Ontario, Irving Fonds, F1027, 82 80, MS6500, Unknown, "Deposition of James Feeheley," February 31, 1880.

55 Written statements of Francis West, under the heading of "Information Picked Up Regarding The Donnelly Murders . . .", dated February 14, 1881 and March 18, 1881, University of Western Ontario, Legal Papers: Information Picked Up Regarding the Donnelly Murder, February–April 1881. Donnelly Papers, Box 59.

56 "James Feeheley told me when sleeping with him in his house that he was now about to leave Biddulph and there was only thing he ever done that he was sorry for. I asked him what that was. He said he sold Tom, the best friend he ever had. I asked him how that was. He said he went to the house that night to see who was there for them Vigilants son of bitches but he said he did not think they were going to murder them." Patrick Donnelly to Hutchinson,

University of Western Ontario Archives, Correspondence: January–October 1881, Donnelly Papers, Box 2-4. April 23, 1881.

57 Hutchinson, Charles, Letters and Papers, Clerk of the Peace Correspondence, Patrick Donnelly testimony at the Preliminary Hearing for the Feeheley trial, July 10, 1881.

58 Testimony of Patrick Donnelly. J.J. Talman Regional Collection, University of Western Ontario Archives, Donnelly Family Papers, B4877, File 61, Unknown, Statements Regarding the Feeheleys, July 10, 1881.

59 Pat Donnelly testimony, J.J. Talman Regional Collection, University of Western Ontario Archives, Donnelly Family Papers, B4877, File 61, Unknown, Statements Regarding the Feeheleys, sworn at the courthouse, July 10, 1881.

60 "He [James Feeheley] said he was going to tell all. He said he would have told immediately after the murder, only for his father." Testimony of William Donnelly. J.J. Talman Regional Collection, University of Western Ontario Archives, Donnelly Family Papers, B4877, File 54, Various Authors, Information on Murders, 1881, ca. 1881.

61 Patrick Donnelly Testimony. D.B. Weldon Library, University of Western Ontario, Armitage-Stanley, Spencer, Papers re Queen v. James Carroll, et al., April 26, 1881.

62 "William Feeheley said he would go with witness [Patrick Donnelly] and get a warrant for the arrest of the parties implicated, but for the fact that it would not be safe to do so while his folks remained in the country." *Huron Signal-Star*, July 15, 1881.

63 John H. McConnell: "[James Feehely] told me not to open my mouth to a soul about that, until he got out of the country, that all he wanted was protection and he would tell the whole of it." J.J. Talman Regional Collection, University of Western Ontario Archives, Donnelly Family Papers, B4877, File 54, Various Authors, Information on Murders, 1881, ca. 1881.

64 [James Feeheley said] "Those other sons of bitches, I could hang them if I had protection." Testimony of John H. McConnell. D.B.

Weldon Library, University of Western Ontario, Armitage-Stanley, Papers re Queen v. James Carroll, et al., Preliminary Examination of Feeheleys, July 10, 1881.

65 Testimony of John H. McConnell. Armitage-Stanley, Papers re Queen v. James Carroll, et al., Preliminary Examination of Feeheleys, July 10, 1881.

> JOHN MCCONNELL: "Jim [Feeheley] says if he had protection he would hang the whole lot of them."
> THOMAS SHOEBOTTOM: "I would protect you."
> JAMES FEEHELEY: "If you will come over to Saginaw I will tell you all about the murders."

66 *London Advertiser*, Monday, May 23, 1881.

67 Patrick Donnelly statement quoted from J.J. Talman Regional Collection, University of Western Ontario Archives, Donnelly Family Papers, B4877, File 61, Unknown, Statements Regarding the Feeheleys, July 10, 1881.

68 All information on the death of Michael Feeheley, the sale of his farm and the problems that followed involving James Carroll, is taken from the *London Advertiser*, May 23, 1881.

69 "When Michael Feeheley, father of James and William Feeheley, died, he was in insolvent circumstances. His farm was encumbered by a mortgage of $4,200, and he owed other debts to the extent of about $2,500. Old Feeheley's personal property amounted to only $900, and the numerous creditors would have to rely upon the surplus of the real estate after the payment of the mortgage." *London Advertiser*, May 23, 1881.

70 "After we left the Queen's Hotel on the 27, & were walking towards my house in Lucan, Father Connolly walked down the opposite side of the street. Jim [Feeheley] said sarcastically, 'that was a fine fellow,' that & 'an awfully fine fellow — didn't he come down Saturday forenoon & give my mother $350 of his own money, out of his own pocket — & when the other sons of bitches came down with the $500, she walked back to Father

Connolly, & gave him his $350 back again.' I told him, a bigger fool she was for it. He said, damned if she was . . ." Statement of John H. McConnell, University of Western Ontario Archives, Legal Papers: Information Picked Up Regarding The Donnelly Murder, February–April 1881. Donnelly Papers, Box 59. See also: "The priest made Carroll pay the money, first offering to pay it himself, sooner than have any trouble about the murder." William Donnelly to Hutchinson, University of Western Ontario Archives, Correspondence, Undated, Donnelly Papers, Box 2-5.

71 Letterbooks from the Office of the Clerk of the Peace, Middlesex County, Hutchinson to Crooks, May 13, 1881.

72 University of Western Ontario Archives, Clerk of the Peace, Middlesex County, Correspondence: January–October 1881, Crooks to Hutchinson, May 17, 1881, Donnelly Papers, Box 2-4.

73 "Please meet me on Monday eleven o'clock at Bishop's residence." University of Western Ontario Archives, Clerk of the Peace, Middlesex County, Correspondence: January–October 1881, Telegram from Adam Crooks to Charles Hutchinson, May 14, 1881, Donnelly Papers, Box 2-4.

74 "Therefore, on Monday I went to East Saginaw. I saw the young men, and endeavored to induce them to come voluntarily to London, and I promised that if they would do so and tell the whole truth concerning the whole Donnelly murders that I would undertake they should not be prosecuted. I think they would have come but for their uncle Patrick who is on the East Saginaw police force, and who would not let them do so." Letterbooks from the Office of the Clerk of the Peace, Middlesex County, Hutchinson to Irving, May 23, 1881.

75 "I go [to Detroit] again tomorrow, & hope to take witnesses that will make the extradition of the Feeheleys sure." Letterbooks from the Office of the Clerk of the Peace, Middlesex County, Hutchinson to Scott, May 29, 1881.

76 "The Feeheleys were committed for trial, & are now in gaol here. They are in separate cells, & as far as I know have no communication with each other." Letterbooks from the Office of the Clerk of the Peace, Middlesex County, Hutchinson to Irving, July 27, 1881.

77 "If it were possible to get the venue changed in this case, it would add to our chances greatly. A trial here would be the merest farce, & should not be attempted." Letterbooks from the Office of the Clerk of the Peace, Middlesex County, Hutchinson to Scott, July 15, 1881.

78 "Old Pat & James Keefe have been with me frequently since you left, & I have allowed them to have private interviews with James Feeheley. They have both told me that James would speak out as soon as the bail question was settled. They have also told me that what we have charged James with is quite correct, & their anxiety is to save his neck, & to have the right men punished." Letterbooks from the Office of the Clerk of the Peace, Middlesex County, Hutchinson to Irving, October 2, 1881.

79 "The [Feeheley] brothers were admitted to bail yesterday & discharged from custody. Wm Thompson & Patrick Darcy are sureties for James Feeheley & Wm Thompson & Martin Darcy for William Feeheley. They are substantial freeholders in the township of Biddulph — all Vigilance men of high degree, & all suspected of having been to some extent implicated in the Donnelly murders." Letterbooks from the Office of the Clerk of the Peace, Middlesex County, Hutchinson to Scott, October 25, 1881.

80 Letterbooks from the Office of the Clerk of the Peace, Middlesex County, Hutchinson to Irving, October 2, 1881.

CHAPTER TWENTY-FIVE: THE DONNELLYS' LAST STAND

1 *London Advertiser*, October 14, 1881. See also *London Advertiser*, November 8, 1881.

2 *London Advertiser*, November 8, 1881.

3 *London Advertiser*, November 8, 1881. See also William Donnelly's comment: "He [West] can rattle the piano, I can tell, at a lively rate." London Advertiser, October 14, 1881.

4 *London Advertiser*, November 8, 1881.

5 *London Advertiser*, October 14, 1881.

6   *London Advertiser*, November 8, 1881.

7   *London Advertiser*, November 8, 1881.

8   *London Advertiser*, November 9, 1881.

> EDMUND MEREDITH: "What were you to get for
> working up the Feeheley case?"
> FRANCIS WEST: "I was to become a detective and get the
> $4,000."

9   *London Advertiser*, November 8, 1881.

> EDMUND MEREDITH: "What was the first theft you were
> connected with?"
> FRANCIS WEST: "Taking two rifles from the Lucan Armory."
> EDMUND MEREDITH: "When was that?"
> FRANCIS WEST: "On the 1 day of April."

10 John Kent had been friends with Tom Donnelly, and had been
    present at Mitchell Haskett's farm when James Carroll had bran-
    dished a revolver and arrested Tom in September of 1879. Kent's
    father, William, had been a long-time friend of William Donnelly.
    For Francis West attempting to sell the rifles to John Kent, see
    London Advertiser, October 18, 1881.

11 *London Advertiser*, November 8, 1881.

12 *London Advertiser*, November 8, 1881.

13 *London Advertiser*, October 14, 1881.

14 FRANCIS WEST: "I pawned my watch for $15 about the first of
    May." Also, under cross-examination from Meredith: "Do you
    recollect selling a coat?" West: "Yes, an oil cloth coat and a pair of
    boots to Robert Dagg." *London Advertiser*, November 9, 1881.

15 *London Advertiser*, November 8, 1881.

> MEREDITH: "Well, what about burning a barn in
> London township?"
> WEST: "Frank Kent and I talked over the matter, but I
> was to get six dollars from John Kent for the job."

MEREDITH later asks: "You and Howe plotted to burn a barn in London township?"

WEST: "We spoke together about burning the barn, and he promised to go."

16 *London Advertiser*, October 10, 1881.

17 "William was at his own house when put under arrest and Robert was at, or going to, his sister's, half a mile away from the mill, making preparations to move to Glencoe. In fact, his furniture was on the wagon, and remained there during the whole of last night and during the day." *London Advertiser*, October 11, 1881.

18 *London Advertiser*, October 11, 1881.

19 *London Advertiser*, October 11, 1881.

20 *London Advertiser*, October 11, 1881.

21 *London Advertiser*, October 11, 1881.

22 *London Free Press*, October 13, 1881. William's last comment is clearly in caustic reference to Thomas Ryder's alibi during the trials.

23 *London Advertiser*, October 11, 1881.

24 "Mr. Stanley then stated that they intended to proceed under an amended information from which the name of Kent was omitted, there being no evidence against him, which was very materially changed from the first one." *London Advertiser*, October 11, 1881.

25 "Of the original the representatives of the press present requested the privilege of making a copy, but Squire Stanley transferred it to his pocket and absolutely refused, declining to go into explanations or reasons." *London Advertiser*, October 11, 1881.

26 *London Advertiser*, October 11, 1881.

27 *London Advertiser*, October 11, 1881.

28 "I saw that I could not get the drop on them that night if the mill was burned. I said to William that I was blamed for burning the Hall place; I told him I understood there was to be an investigation of that matter the following week, and that I did not want too much hanging over my head at once. He agreed to put it off for a

week; he said the Stanleys swore hard against him at the Carroll trial." Francis West quoted from the Preliminary Examination, *London Advertiser*, October 14, 1881.

29 "As far as I know William and Patrick Donnelly, their idea throughout has been to bring the murderers to justice through and by the law, and I have frequently heard them repudiate the idea of having recourse to unlawful means for obtaining vengeance on the murderers of their family. They are both sensible men, possessing in my judgment many good and estimable qualities." Letterbooks from the Office of the Clerk of the Peace, Middlesex County, Hutchinson to Scott, October 22, 1881.

30 "As to the depositions, they disclose a strange story, containing many things to my mind highly improbable, especially considering the character of William Donnelly, who whatever faults he may have, has never been considered other than a remarkably shrewd man. It seems to me, that had he designed to burn Stanley's barn, he would have accomplished his object in a very different way, and without use of such an instrument as Mr. West." Letterbooks from the Office of the Clerk of the Peace, Middlesex County, Hutchinson to Scott, October 22, 1881.

31 *London Advertiser*, October 12, 1881.

32 "Bail offered yesterday for the Feeheleys: Patrick Whalen, John Cain, Martin Darcy and James Maher, all freeholders in Biddulph but heavily mortgaged. After consulting with Mr. Magee I rejected all except Martin Darcy. It seems doubtful whether they will be able to obtain bail." Letterbooks from the Office of the Clerk of the Peace, Middlesex County, Hutchinson to Irving, October 13, 1881.

33 *London Advertiser*, October 11, 1881.

34 Middlesex Sheriff's Daybook, November 3 and November 4, 1881.

35 Middlesex County, Clerk of the Peace, Criminal Records, Becher to Hutchinson, October 13, 1881.

36 Under cross-examination (*London Advertiser*, November 9, 1881):

MEREDITH: "You ran a bill at the City Hotel here, and did not pay it?"

WEST: "Yes, but I was advised not to pay it. I had some
trouble one night before."
MEREDITH: "So you expected to beat Mr. McMartin
out of it? Did not Barney Stanley pay that bill of $1.75
today for you?"
WEST: "No, he didn't. Barney Stanley never did."
MEREDITH: "Come now, don't fence. Answer straight.
Was it William Edward Stanley?"
WEST: "I understand he settled it."

37 West's new lawyer, Henry Corry Rowley Becher, would write to
    Hutchinson: "All the law-abiding and respectable people at Lucan
    and in the vicinity are in favour of West's evidence being received
    and are anti-Donnelly." Middlesex County, Clerk of the Peace,
    Criminal Records, 1881, Queen v. William and Robert Donnelly,
    Arson, Becher to Hutchinson, October 29, 1881.

38 *London Free Press*, September 9, 1880. Pointing the finger at
    the Stanleys' crimes was not a healthy thing to do, but again, the
    Donnelly tendency of paying one back in his own coin is at play
    here. William Donnelly brings to light (without mentioning him
    by name) the actions of Bernard Stanley, who is "well used to the
    cries of fire and robbery" and a "high flyer" in the town of Lucan,
    and specifically Stanley's role in having burned out and robbed the
    African-American settlers within the area in 1848, and also his
    attack on Andrew Keefe's tavern on Christmas Eve 1857.

39 That Porte's date for the attempted arson of the mill is in error
    is evidenced by both newspaper reports and court records from
    the time. Porte writes in his diary: "Oct. 1, 1881: [fire at] Hall's"
    (which is correct) and then writes: "October 8, 1881: [fire at]
    Stanley, Dight & Co." (which is incorrect). J.J. Talman Regional
    Collection, University of Western Ontario Archives, Donnelly
    Family Papers, B4878, File 24, William Porte, William Porte
    Diaries indicating fires for October 1, 1881, and October 8, 1881.
    The *London Advertiser* indicates that "Lucan, [Sunday] Oct. 9
    [1881] — Parties were captured in the act of firing Stanley, Dight &

Co's mills at eleven o'clock to-night." *London Advertiser*, October 10, 1881. See also: "There is still considerable talk around the city in reference to the attempt at incendiarism on Sunday [October 9, 1881] night at Lucan." *London Advertiser*, Wednesday, October 12, 1881. A court record reads, "Be it Remembered, that William Donnelly and Robert Donnelly being Prisoners in the Jail of the said County, committed for trial on a charge of having on the ninth day of October 1881 at the village of Lucan in the county of Middlesex, feloniously and maliciously attempted to set fire to a certain mill, the property of William Stanley and others and being brought before me, William Elliot Esquire, Judge of the County Court of the said County of Middlesex, on the fourteenth day of October 1881, and asked by me if he consented to be tried before me without the intervention of a Jury, consented to be so tried . . ." J.J. Talman Regional Collection, University of Western Ontario Archives, Donnelly Family Papers, B4877, File 65, Unknown, Queen v. William and Robert Donnelly, Attempted Arson of Stanley and Dight Grist Mill, October 9, 1881.

40 Under cross-examination from Meredith: "Did you tell Barney or Ned Stanley about burning the barn?" West: "No, I told Hall about it. He lives inside the corporation of Lucan." *London Advertiser*, November 9, 1881.

41 WEST: "On Friday night I slept at Tom Hall's, the man who was burned out." *London Advertiser*, October 14, 1881.

42 MEREDITH: "What's the reason you said you must see Tom Hall before you came back into the box?" West: "He had a bottle of medicine for me." *London Advertiser*, November 8, 1881.

43 "Mr. Street urged that the offence charged was of a trifling character and he tendered substantial bail — that of Mr. W.E. Stanley and Robert Hall, both responsible property owners." ["Robert" is the reporter's error, as he refers to Hall as Thomas earlier in the same article.] *London Advertiser*, November 11, 1881.

44 WILLIAM STANLEY: "Hodgins stayed at the mill on Monday night; I was there on Saturday night. Thomas Hall went with me." *London Advertiser*, November 8, 1881.

45   WILLIAM STANLEY: "West saw me several times in the week [before
     the fire]" and "West was at my house several times [after the fire]."
     London Advertiser, November 8, 1881.

46   *London Advertiser*, November 9, 1881.

47   *London Advertiser*, November 10, 1881.

48   *London Advertiser*, October 14, 1881.

49   *London Advertiser*, October 18, 1881.

50   "The alleged amateur detective immediately dropped out of
     sight, being next heard of in Port Huron." *London Advertiser*,
     November 7, 1881.

51   According to Reaney, "Red Bill" Stanley was William and Bernard
     Stanley's brother. (*The Donnelly Documents*, p. 256, note 797).

52   WILLIAM DONNELLY: "They were all feeling pretty good and
     wanted to raise a row if possible." All details and dialogue from
     this encounter are drawn from the *London Advertiser*, October 14,
     1881, and the *London Free Press*, 15 October 1881.

53   *London Advertiser*, October 14, 1881.

54   The interview with William Donnelly is taken from the newspaper
     article "Behind Bars!" *London Advertiser*, October 14, 1881.

55   *London Advertiser*, October 14, 1881.

56   *London Advertiser*, October 15, 1881.

57   *London Free Press*, February 12, 1975.

58   *London Free Press*, February 12, 1975, citing a letter to the editor
     that William Donnelly had written to the *London Free Press* in
     October 1881.

59   *London Free Press*, February 12, 1975, citing a letter to the editor
     that William Donnelly had written to the *London Free Press* in
     October 1881.

60   Hutchinson, Charles, Letters and Papers, Clerk of the Peace
     Correspondence, Donnelly to Hutchinson, April 9, 1881.

61   Hutchinson, Charles, Letters and Papers, Clerk of the Peace
     Correspondence, Donnelly to Hutchinson, March 8, 1881.

62   Letterbooks from the Office of the Clerk of the Peace, Middlesex
     County, Hutchinson to Scott, October 13, 1881.

63 "Having heard a rumour that Mr. Charles Hutchinson, the County
Crown Attorney, had been superseded in his office as County Crown
Attorney, so far as the prosecution of William and Robert Donnelly
for arson was concerned, our reporter interviewed that gentleman
on the subject. In reply to a question, Mr. Hutchinson stated that
finding he could not without embarrassment perform his duties
as County Crown Attorney in the prosecution of the Donnellys,
and his sympathies being rather with the prisoners than with the
prosecution in the case, he had deemed it judicious to inform
the Attorney-General of the fact, and ask that some other gentlemen
be appointed to conduct the prosecution. The Attorney-General,
doubtless appreciating the motives which prompted the desire,
gratified it by appointing Mr. Idington, of Stratford, County Crown
Attorney of Perth, to conduct the prosecution before the County
Judge on Tuesday next." *London Advertiser*, November 4, 1881.

64 "I am instructed by the Attorney General to advise you of your
being retained to act for the Crown on the trial of this case before
the Judge of the County Court of this county, on Tuesday the 8th
instant at 11 AM. This is owing to the strong view I take & have
expressed, adverse to the case for the Crown, & my consequent
desire to have other counsel assigned to appear for the Crown at
the approaching trial. I send herewith the depositions, & have
advised Messrs Street & Becher, counsel for the private prosecution, two communicate with you at once." Letterbooks from the
Office of the Clerk of the Peace, Middlesex County, Hutchinson to
Idington, November 3, 1881.

65 *London Advertiser*, October 18, 1881.

66 Clerk of the Peace Letterbook, Middlesex County, Hutchinson to
Scott, October 22, 1881. Weldon Library, University of Western
Ontario. London.

67 "It is also rumoured upon good authority that Francis Morrison
West, the amateur detective who was in Port Huron recently,
will now return at once, having received a guarantee from the
government of immunity from prosecution for the larceny of rifles

from the Lucan Volunteer Armory. This was probably given him in order that the fullest enquiry into the guilt or innocence of the accused might be made." *London Advertiser*, November 4, 1881.

68 *London Advertiser*, November 7, 1881.

69 *London Advertiser*, November 7, 1881.

70 Unless otherwise indicated, all information and dialogue from the trial are drawn from the account in the *London Advertiser*, November 8 and 9, 1881.

71 *London Advertiser*, October 14, 1881.

72 *London Advertiser*, November 9, 1881.

73 *London Advertiser*, November 9, 1881.

74 *London Advertiser*, November 10, 1881.

75 *London Advertiser*, November 10, 1881.

76 *London Advertiser*, November 11, 1881.

77 *Morning News*, January 1, 1884.

EPILOGUE

1 Author Peter McKeown quoting a "Glencoe man" who "told the following story to his grandson" about Bob Donnelly: "He'd be walkin' down the street and he'd take three or four steps and he'd look over his left shoulder and he'd take three or four more and look over his right. He wasn't letting anybody get in behind him." Peter McKeown, *A Donnelly Treatise: After the Massacre*, Kindle edition, p. 6686.

2 Letter from James William Donnelly to Dr. W.J. Robinson, London Insane Asylum, London, Ontario, September 29, 1908. Robert Donnelly's case files, London Psychiatric Hospital Records, Public Archives of Ontario, Toronto.

3 *London Free Press*, September 29, 1908.

4 "He did run away and hide in a straw stack some three miles in the country, he has returned home none the worse of his experience that I can see." Letter from James William Donnelly to Dr. W.J.

Robinson, London Insane Asylum, London, Ontario, September 29, 1908. Robert Donnelly's case files, London Psychiatric Hospital Records, Public Archives of Ontario, Toronto.

5   "He was just away 24 hours, to the minute." Letter from James William Donnelly to Dr. W.J. Robinson, September 29, 1908. Robert Donnelly's case files, London Psychiatric Hospital Records, Public Archives of Ontario, Toronto.

6   Province of Ontario Conference Report, October 5, 1908 (F.M.): "Mr. Donnelly was presented at Conference today by Dr. Forster as a case of Melancholia Vera. Dr. Harris mentioned some interesting circumstances of which he was personally acquainted, showing the criminal tendencies in this man's early life. Those present were Drs. Robinson, Clare, Forster, Harris and McMillen." Robert Donnelly's case files, London Psychiatric Hospital Records, Public Archives of Ontario, Toronto.

7   "This patient escaped from the walking party this morning. He was missed on the return to the building. Attendants were at once sent out to look for him but they did not succeed in finding him. We notified his friends of his elopement. The nephew went to Lucan, the patient's home, and telephoned us from there that Robert Donnelly was at his home and said that he would bring him back." April 26, 1909. Province of Ontario Clinical Record. Name: Robert Donnelly. Case Book No: 1162: September 29, 1908. Robert Donnelly's case files, London Psychiatric Hospital Records, Public Archives of Ontario, Toronto.

8   "We were asked today to send attendants for Robert Donnelly, and he was brought back this evening but objected strongly to coming. He is in his usual condition." April 28, 1909. Province of Ontario Clinical Record. Name: Robert Donnelly. Case Book No: 1162: September 29, 1908. Robert Donnelly's case files, London Psychiatric Hospital Records, Public Archives of Ontario, Toronto.

9   Robert Donnelly's case files, London Psychiatric Hospital Records, Public Archives of Ontario, Toronto. October 30, 1909:

Discharged from Asylum
Name: Robert Donnelly
Registered No: 5924
Correspondence File: 295
County: Middlesex, Township: Biddulph tp. P.O.
Address: Lucan
Admitted: June 15/08. Hour: 12: A.M. Nativity:
Canadian Age: 55. Male.
Public/Private: Private [funding] Rate: $275 Ward: 6
Profile 23
Occupation: Farmer
Religion: R.C.
Habits: Not Good. Homicidal: Yes Suicidal: Yes
Heredity: No
Cause: ? No. Attacks: 1st Duration: 6 months
Correspondent: Mrs. R. Donnelly, wife, Lucan, Ont.
Date Discharged: October 30/09
September 29, 1908.

10 "On Wednesday evening last a frame house on O'Mara Street owned and occupied by Philip McCallum, caught fire from a lamp dropped on the floor by one of the children in the absence of the parents. The flames spread quickly and had enveloped one end of the house by the time the fire engine was got to the scene, after which a half-hour's work was sufficient to extinguish the fire. The children who are all young, had a narrow escape. R. Donnelly, who lives in the next house, heard them screaming and made his way into the building and carried out the two youngest, while another escaped through a window. The house was pretty well used up and some of the furniture destroyed." Glencoe Transcript, December 17, 1891.

11 Glencoe Transcript, February 22, 1900.

12 Notes from Enid McIlhargey, dated June 27, 1960, courtesy of Enid's daughter, Ely Errey, email to the author on January 15, 2021.

13 Notes from John Joseph McIlhargey; courtesy of Ely Errey, email to the author on January 15, 2021.

14 *Glencoe Transcript*, January 26, 1905.

15 *Glencoe Transcript*, January 26, 1905.

16 Author Peter McKeown states that Carroll also once lost a fight to Tom Donnelly on Lucan's Main Street as a result of Carroll insulting one of the O'Connor girls, which, if true, would drop Carroll's pugilistic record in Biddulph to 0 and 4 (McKeown, *A Donnelly Treatise: After the Massacre*, Kindle edition, p. 3301). However, the author can find no source for this match having taken place.

17 *London Advertiser*, May 3, 1882.

18 "The Biddulph assault and trespass case came before Squire Peters yesterday. James Carroll admitted the charge, and was fined $10 for the assault and $2 for the trespass, which, together with costs made the sum of $20.75." *London Advertiser*, May 10, 1882.

19 Thomas Keefe's letter to the editor, *London Advertiser*, May 15, 1882.

20 According to Carroll: "So soon as the fight began, Mrs. Ryder ran screaming across to Maher's house crying 'murder, murder' and that the Maher boys coming in saw the scrimmage from a distance." *London Advertiser*, May 10, 1882.

21 William Porte's diary, May 26, 1883.

22 *Winnipeg Times* article quoted in the *Glencoe Transcript* September 25, 1884.

23 Miller, *The Donnellys Must Die*, p. 240.

24 Miller, *The Donnellys Must Die*, p. 241.

25 University of Western Ontario archives, Donnelly Family Papers, Collisson to Turner, September 2, 1952.

26 Lucan resident Leonard D. Stanley, speaking to a reporter of the *St. Marys Journal-Argus*, cited in Miller, *The Donnellys Must Die*, pp. 241–42.

27 *Glencoe Transcript*, July 3, 1884.

28 "Charles Burchell, who was assaulted by Bob Donnelly, on the night of the 2nd, has been lingering between life and death ever since." *Glencoe Transcript*, July 10, 1884.

29 *Glencoe Transcript*, July 10, 1884, and July 23, 1885. See also Hutchinson, Letter and Papers, Clerk of the Peace Correspondence,

William Donnelly to Hutchinson, July 3, 1884, and Leitch to Hutchinson, July 4, 1884, and Letterbooks from the Office of the Clerk of the Peace, Middlesex County, Hutchinson to Leitch, July 3 and 4, 1884.

30 Duncan McAlpine, Interview conducted with James Reaney, June 21, 1973. See also Regional History Collection, D.B. Weldon Library, University of Western Ontario, Donnelly Family Papers, C.A. MacFie to Miller, April 8, 1954.

31 University of Western Ontario, Donnelly Family Papers, Stafford Johnson to Miller, July 4, 1966.

32 Trevethick, Garnet. Interview with James Reaney, in St. Thomas, March 9, 1972, cited in Butt, *The Donnellys: History, Legend, Literature*, p. 375.

33 Mr. McCracken, Interview with Marjorie McCracken, March 14, 1971, cited in Butt, *The Donnellys: History, Legend, Literature*, p. 380.

34 *Glencoe Transcript*, November 29, 1883.

35 *Thorold Post*, June 1, 1888.

36 *Glencoe Transcript*, July 26, 1888, quoting an article that appeared in the *Bothwell Times* newspaper.

37 Ontario Death Registration for William Donnelly, Archives of Ontario.

38 *Glencoe Transcript*, April 14, 1881.

39 *Glencoe Transcript*, February 6, 1890.

40 *Glencoe Transcript*, February 13, 1890.

41 Interview with Robert Donnelly, May 26, 1908, in Lucan, Ontario, report of James Sutton, M.D., London Psychiatric Patient File for Robert Donnelly, Archives of Ontario.

42 Ontario Death Registration for Patrick Donnelly, Archives of Ontario.

43 McKeown, *A Donnelly Treatise: After the Massacre*, Kindle edition, p. 6117.

44 Ontario Death Registration for Rosemary Currie, Archives of Ontario.

45 Middlesex County Estate Files, Public Archives of Ontario (Toronto).

46 *Lucan Sun*, June 29, 1911.

47 See for example "Bill Donnelly Expects to See Those Who Survived Hanged Some Day," *Morning News*, January 1, 1884, and ". . . in thirteen years 32 persons, who were either directly or indirectly concerned in that slaughter, have met their just [deserts], and as none of them have been murdered, a direct visitation from Almighty God must have been the cause." William Donnelly quoted in the *Exeter Times*, February 9, 1893.

48 *London Advertiser*, July 31, 1881.

49 *London Free Press*, October 20, 1881.

BIBLIOGRAPHY

ARCHIVE SOURCES

Aemilius Irving Papers, Public Archives of Ontario, Toronto.
Archives of Ontario. Robert Donnelly, Casebook 1162: London
    Psychiatric Hospital patients' clinical case files, Robert Donnelly,
    File Number 295.
Assessment Rolls for Lucan and for Biddulph, 1873.
Bench Books, Justice Sir John Robinson, March–May 1858. Courthouse
    Vault, Goderich, Ontario, Criminal Proceedings.
Biddulph Township Assessment Roll, 1870, 1871 and 1872.
Canada Census, Biddulph Township, 1870, 1871.
Canada's Penitentiary Museum, Kingston, Ontario.
Correctional Service of Canada.
Huron County, Clerk of the Peace, Coroner's Inquests.
Huron County, Clerk of the Peace, Criminal Justice Accounts.
Huron County, Clerk of the Peace, Criminal Records.
Huron County Records, 1857–58.
Huron County Registry Records.

Huron District, Clerk of the Peace, Census Returns.

Huron Historical Notes, Huron Historical Society, 1993, Volume XXIX.

Library of the Law Society of Upper Canada, Judge's Note Books,
     Common Pleas, Book IV, 1881.

Middlesex County Court of General Quarter Sessions Minute Book,
     June 11, June 16 and June 17, 1874.

Middlesex Court Records.

Middlesex County Registry Office.

Middlesex County Sheriff's Day-Book, December 27, 1873.

Middlesex County Queen Bench and Common Pleas, Docket Book,
     1869–81.

Middlesex Special Commission, Biddulph Murders: Osler (Trial Notes of
     Justice Featherston Osler).

National Archives of Canada, Provincial Secretary's Correspondence.

Ontario Historical Society XVII (1919), Papers and Records.

Public Archives of Ontario.

University of Western Ontario Archives, J.J. Talman Regional
     Collection, Donnelly Family Papers.

University of Western Ontario Archives, J.J. Talman Regional
     Collection, Reaney Papers.

University of Western Ontario, Spencer-Stanley Papers.

University of Western Ontario, Orlo Miller Papers.

41st Congress, 3rd Session, *House Executive Documents*. No. 94, "State
     of Trade with British North American Provinces."

BOOKS

Adams, Bill. *The History of the London Fire Department of Heroes,
     Helmets and Hoses*. London Fire Department, 2002, first edition.

Berton, Pierre. *The National Dream: The Great Railway, 1871–1881*.
     Toronto: Anchor, 1970.

The Biddulph Tragedy. London, 1880.

Biggar, C.R.W. *Sir Oliver Mowat — A Biographical Sketch*. Toronto:
     Warwick Bros. and Rutter Ltd., 1905.

Carleton, William. *Traits and Stories of the Irish Peasantry, vol. II.* London, Wm. Tegg, 1867, seventh edition.

Culbert, Terry. *Lucan: Home of the Donnellys: Linger Longer in Lovely Lucan.* Renfrew: General Store Publishing House, 2006.

Doty, Christopher. *The Donnelly Trial: A new play based on the court transcripts of the only man brought to trial for the murders of the Donnelly family in 1880.* London: Christopher Doty, 2005.

Fazakas, Ray. *In Search of the Donnellys,* second revised edition, Trafford: Kindle Edition, 2012.

Fazakas, Ray. *The Donnelly Album: The Complete & Authentic Account of Canada's Famous Feuding Family.* Trafford, Kindle Edition, 2013.

Glass, Chester, Compiler. *Hon. David Glass — Some of His Writings and Speeches.* New York: Trow Press, 1909.

History of the County of Middlesex, Canada. Toronto and London: W.A. & C.L. Goodspeed, Publishers, 1889.

Hobson, W.B. *Old Stage Days in Oxford County.* Ontario Historical Society, Papers and Records, Vol. XVII (1919).

Kelley, Thomas P. *The Black Donnellys: The True Story of Canada's Most Barbaric Feud.* Darling Terrace Publishing. Kindle Edition, 2016.

Leverton, John. *Wilberforce Colony from Lucan.* 125 Souvenir Booklet, 18711996.

Marquis, Greg. *Policing Canada's Century: A History of the Canadian Association of Chiefs of Police.* Toronto: University of Toronto Press, 1993.

McEvoy, M. (Editor and Compiler). *The Province of Ontario Gazetteer and Directory, Containing Precise Descriptions of the Cities, Towns and Villages in the Province with the Names of Professional and Business Men and Principal Inhabitants Together with a Full List of Members of the Executive Governments, Senators, Members of the Commons and Local Legislatures, and Officials of the Dominion, And a Large Amount of Other General, Varied and Useful Information, Carefully Compiled*

from the Most Recent and Authentic Data. C.E. Anderson &
Co., Proprietors. Toronto: Robertson & Cook Publishers, Daily
Telegraph Printing House, 1869.

McKeown, Peter. *A Donnelly Treatise: After the Massacre*. Kindle
Edition. Self-Published, 2004.

Miller, Orlo. *The Donnellys Must Die*: Toronto: Prospero Books, 2001.

Morgan, Henry J. (Editor). *The Dominion Annual Register and Review
for the Fourteenth and Fifteenth Years of the Canadian Union,
1880–1881*. Montreal: John Lovell & Son, 1882.

Mozley, John and Charles. *The Monthly Packet of Evening Readings for
Members of the English Church*, Volume 3, 1852.

Oliver, Peter. *Terror to Evil-Doers: Prisons and Punishment in Nineteenth-
Century Ontario*. Toronto: University of Toronto Press, 1998.

Osler, William. *The Principles and Practice of Medicine*. 3rd ed. D.
Appleton and Co., New York, 1898.

Reaney, James, C. *The Donnelly Documents: An Ontario Vendetta*.
Toronto: The Champlain Society, 2004.

Salts, J. Robert, *You Are Never Alone: Our Life on the Donnelly
Homestead*, J. Robert Salts, Publisher, London, 1996.

Shearer, Herbert, A. *The Farm Workshop — With Information on Tools
and Buildings*. Read Books Ltd. Redditch, England, 2016.

Simcoe's Choice: Celebrating London's Bicentennial, 1793–1993.
Toronto, Dundurn, 1992.

Smart, Charles, ed. *The Medical and Surgical History of the War of the
Rebellion*. Washington, D.C., 1888, pt. 3, vol. 1.

Steward, Austin. *Twenty-Two Years a Slave, and Forty Years a Freeman;
Embracing a Correspondence of Several Years, While President of
Wilberforce Colony, London, Canada West* (electronic edition).
Originally published by William Alling, Rochester, 1856.

Wilson, Catharine Anne, *Tenants in Time: Family Strategies, Land, and
Liberalism in Upper Canada*, Montreal: McGill-Queen's University
Press, 2009; p. 160.

Wood, David. *Making Ontario*. Montreal: McGill-Queen's University
Press, 2000.

PH.D. THESES

Butt, William Davison, *The Donnellys: History, Legend, Literature*, Ph.D. thesis. Faculty of Graduate Studies, The University of Western Ontario, February 1977.

De Lint, Willem, Bart. *Shaping the Subject of Policing: Autonomy, Regulation, and the Constable.* A thesis submitted in conformity with the requirements for the degree Doctor of Philosophy, Centre of Criminology, University of Toronto, 1997.

NEWSPAPERS

Catholic Record
Daily Journal, Evansville, Indiana
Exeter Times
Glencoe Transcript
Guelph Daily Mercury
Hamilton Spectator
Hamilton Times
Huron Signal-Star
Listowel Banner
London Advertiser
London Free Press
London Times
Lucan Sun
Montreal Star
Morning News
New York Times
Norfolk Reformer
Oakland Daily Evening Tribune
Ottawa Free Press
Sarnia Observer
St. Marys Argus and Review
Stratford Weekly Herald

Toronto *Globe*
Toronto *Mail*
Toronto *Telegram*
Truro Daily News
Upper Canada Gazette

PERIODICALS

Maclean's magazine
Lancet (April 2001)

CORRESPONDENCE

Anthony Drohomyrecky, MD, email correspondence with the author, October 28, 2019.

Cameron Willis, Operations Supervisor for Canada's Penitentiary Museum, email correspondence with the author, November 22, 2019.

Doug McGuff, MD, email correspondence with the author, October 28, 2019.

Enid McIlhargey, email correspondence with the author, January–February 2021.

Notes from Enid McIlhargey, dated June 27, 1960, courtesy of Enid's daughter, Ely Errey.

Notes from John Joseph McIlhargey; courtesy of Ely Errey.

ONLINE SOURCES

http://ancestorsatrest.com/cemetery_records/stpats-int.shtml
http://biographi.ca/en/bio/mckinnon_hugh_13E.html
http://black-donnellys.com/the-story/
http://businessdictionary.com/definition/tampering.html
http://canadahistory.com/sections/eras/nation%20building/Scandal.html

http://contentdm.ucalgary.ca/digital/collection/p22007coll8/id/308402

http://historyplace.com/worldhistory/famine/coffin.htm

http://images.ourontario.ca/london/2369866/data?n=1

http://lostrivers.ca/points/porkpacking.htm

http://news.bbc.co.uk/2/hi/health/619259.stm

http://oldandinteresting.com/history-feather-beds.aspx

https://andersonfuneralservices.com/blogs/blog-entries/1/Articles/35/
The-History-of-a-Traditional-Irish-Wake.html

https://archive.macleans.ca/article/1955/11/12/the-tragical-death-of-the-
great-jumbo-a-macleans-flashback

https://blackpast.org/african-american-history/steward-austin-1793-1869/

https://blogto.com/city/2012/10/a_short_and_violent_history_of_
torontos_central_prison/

https://ca.practicallaw.thomsonreuters.com/6-556-9885?transitionType=
Default&contextData=(sc.Default)&firstPage=true&bhcp=1

https://canada-rail.com/ontario/railways/CASO.html

https://canadianmysteries.ca/sites/donnellys/home/indexen.html

https://catholicism.org/candles.html

https://celticlife.com/the-irish-wake/

https://civilwarmonitor.com/blog/the-most-fatal-of-all-acute-diseases-
pneumonia-and-the-death-of-stonewall-jackson

https://ckphysiciantribute.ca/doctors/christopher-william-flock/

https://collectionscanada.gc.ca/confederation/023001-3010.40-e.html

https://connollycove.com/insight-irish-wake-superstitions-associated/

https://cpha.ca/history-tuberculosis

https://crookedlakereview.com/articles/101_135/126winter2003/
126palmer3.html]

https://culbertfamilyhistory.blogspot.com/2018/11/the-donnellys-lucan-
biddulphs-most.html

https://dotydocs.theatreinlondon.ca/Archives/donnelly/auditions.htm#irving

https://electricscotland.com/history/canada/mckinnon_hugh.htm

https://en.wikipedia.org/wiki/1878_Canadian_federal_election

https://en.wikipedia.org/wiki/Canada_Southern_Railway_Station

https://en.wikipedia.org/wiki/Cat_o%27_nine_tails

https://en.wikipedia.org/wiki/Irish_Canadians

https://en.wikipedia.org/wiki/Middlesex_North

https://en.wikipedia.org/wiki/Oliver_Mowat

https://en.wikipedia.org/wiki/Pacific_Scandal

https://en.wikipedia.org/wiki/Splitting_maul

https://en.wikipedia.org/wiki/St._Thomas,_Ontario

https://en.wikipedia.org/wiki/Stagecoach

https://en.wikipedia.org/wiki/Template:Population_of_Michigan_cities_
and_counties_(1870_Census)

https://en.wikipedia.org/wiki/Toronto_Central_Prison

https://en.wikipedia.org/wiki/Wild_Bill_Hickok_–_Davis_Tutt_shootout

https://health.harvard.edu/newsletter_article/An_update_on_the_old_
mans_friend

https://historymuseum.ca/cmc/exhibitions/cpm/chrono/ch1798ae.html

https://in2013dollars.com/us/inflation/1880?amount=4000

https://irish-genealogy-toolkit.com/journey-to-Ellis-Island.html

https://lib.uwo.ca/archives/virtualexhibits/londonasylum/index.html

https://news-medical.net/health/Pneumonia-History.aspx

https://ontariossouthwest.com/listing/jumbo-the-elephant-monument/1646/

https://opentextbc.ca/postconfederation/chapter/1-2-historical-demography-
of-canada-1608-1921/#return-footnote-1350-14

https://ourworldindata.org/human-height.

https://patrick-donnelly.webs.com/patrickdonnelly.htm

https://pressreader.com

https://railwaycitytourism.com/about.html

https://railwaycitytourism.com/blog/the-railway-city-the-past

https://statista.com/statistics/568800/infant-mortality-rate-by-province-
or-territory-canada/

https://stthomaspubliclibrary.ca/wp-content/uploads/2018/04/
St.-Thomas-Timeline.pdf

https://thecanadianencyclopedia.ca/en/article/canada-company

https://thecanadianencyclopedia.ca/en/article/pacific-scandal

https://thecanadianencyclopedia.ca/en/article/toronto

https://theglobeandmail.com/news/national/kingston-penitentiary-
closes-its-doors-as-canadas-most-famous-prison/article14598900/?
page=all

https://theglobeandmail.com/report-on-business/economy/a-brief-history-of-the-canadian-dollar/article1366590/

https://thegoldenstar.net/community/caroll-was-respected-in-golden-despite-being-a-mass-murderer/

https://thoroldnews.com/local-news/donnellys-legend-lives-on-in-thorold-1226182

https://worthpoint.com/worthopedia/antique-1800s-large-heavy-solid-brass-427211127

https://xe.com/currencyconverter/convert/?Amount=101%2C165.10&From=USD&To=CAD

ACKNOWLEDGEMENTS

The author is beholden to all the Donnelly authors and researchers who came before him, each of whom has broadened our understanding of the Donnelly story. There exists a mountain of data — court transcripts; letters and diaries; newspaper articles from many different newspapers in many different towns, villages and cities; magazine articles; town histories; genealogical records and photographs — but these authors were the first to sift through these materials until a timeline of sorts was formed. The writers whose work was particularly thorough were Ray Fazakas, William Butt, James Reaney and Orlo Miller. Fazakas is worthy of particular praise, as he has engaged in decades of exhaustive research (including tracking down descendants of the Donnellys, which required him to travel over two continents) that has continued on long after his two books on the Donnellys were published. He also was the first to bring to light most of the photographs that may presently be seen in museum displays and online articles (and books such as the one you are reading presently).

Without his tireless efforts we may never have known what many of the characters in the drama looked like. I am particularly beholden to him for graciously allowing me to utilize photographs from his collection for my books and for sharing his insights with me during the creation of the maps that appear in both volumes. He remains the preeminent Donnelly authority in the world. I am also grateful to William Butt, PhD, who was the first to bring a great deal of the above indicated primary sources of information to print. His research was staggering, and his doctorate very well deserved. He was also very supportive to me during the writing and research of this book, encouraging me to develop ideas that came originally from his thesis. He further allowed me to use certain quotes and sources that appeared in his thesis for which I am grateful.

I also extend my deep appreciation to Anne Quirk and the wonderful staff at the University of Western Ontario's Archives and Research Collections Centre for sending me copies of all of the legal papers, correspondence, Letterbooks of Charles Hutchinson, researchers' notes, arts and entertainment and miscellaneous items relating to the Donnelly family, their murders and court cases, ranging from 1856–1973. As the Covid pandemic prevented me from going in person to the university for certain research, they were kind enough to bring the University archives to me. This material was hugely helpful in deciphering the behind-the-scenes activity that went on during the Coroner's Inquest, the Preliminary Hearings and the two trials. A special thank you is also due to the efforts of the good people and staff of the London Room within the London Public Library, who were inordinately patient with me and helpful in the extreme. Thomas Levesque, the museum supervisor of the Lucan Area Heritage & Donnelly Museum, went above and beyond in answering my questions and in providing access to specific materials I requested to further my research on the Donnellys. Tremendous assistance was also provided by the staff at the Ontario Archives, who allowed me to access rare documents that shed further light on the Donnelly story. I was also fortunate to make the acquaintance of Ely Errey, who provided notes from her mother and father (John and Enid McIlhargey) on their family's memories of the Donnellys, as well as the wonderful photograph of Bob and Tom Donnelly, which was given to her grandfather by no less a figure than Bob Donnelly himself.

Appreciation is also due to literary agent extraordinaire Beverley Slopen whom I was fortunate enough to hoodwink into taking on this project and who convinced me that I would need to write more than an overview to interest a Canadian publishing house (and she was correct, of course). Also owed a huge debt of gratitude is Jen Hale, without question the best and most entertaining copyeditor I've ever had the pleasure to work with. Her suggestions and amendments resulted in a far superior manuscript than the one I first submitted. I am further indebted to Jack David and the great staff of ECW Press, who insisted on my telling the full story of the Donnellys, rather than creating an abridged version, for which I am grateful, as I am for the great personal interest the publishing house has shown in my rendering of the Donnelly story.

A big thank-you is owed to professionals in law enforcement, such as Detective Vicki Hornick, who was willing to analyze the data (particularly with regard to matters of law and the courts and to advise on matters of procedure). I'm beholden as well to medical doctors such as Anthony Drohomyrecky and Doug McGuff, who offered me the benefit of their insights into pathology, particularly pneumonia and anti-anxiety medications used in asylums during the turn of the last century.

And then there are family and friends with whom I would speak about the manuscript at various stages of its progression, and who offered their input as to whether or not the story was as fascinating as I thought it was — people like my family members Terri, Riley, Taylor, Brandon and Ben Little (who also created the artwork used in the Preface of Volume II), and friends such as Kerri Stewart, Marcela Avendano, Tom Walking, Sue Morrison, John Vellinga, Jeremy Hymers and Anne and Rod Mundy. A special nod of appreciation is reserved for Ravel von Rose, better known as Jonathan Ross, whose constructive (and well warranted) literary criticism helped to shape the manuscript. All these people, and more, went into the creation of this book and to each is owed an enormous debt of gratitude.

ABOUT THE AUTHOR

John Little is the bestselling author of *Who Killed Tom Thomson?* (Skyhorse Publishing, New York). Little has authored over 40 books on subjects ranging from philosophy and history to exercise and martial arts, in addition to being an award-winning filmmaker. He is a contributor to Salon.com, the *Toronto Star* (Canada's largest daily newspaper) and has been interviewed by CNN, Canada AM, NPR, A&E, *People Magazine*, *Entertainment Weekly* and the Family Channel. He resides in Bracebridge, Ontario, with his wife, Terri, and children Riley, Taylor, Brandon and Ben.

INDEX

Page numbers in bold indicate photographs, illustrations or maps.

Creighton, Tom, 275–76
Crooks, Adam, 230–31
Cubbins, Thomas, 47, 48
Curtain, Richard, 37, 41, 319n47
Cutt, Robert, 203–4, 374n79

Darcy, John Sr., 66, 69, 325n28
Darcy, Martin, 204
defence: change of venue, 140–42,
   144–45; Johnny O'Connor's
   testimony, 104, 167, 175; and
   press, 154–55; strategy, 164–65,
   170. *See also* MacMahon, Hugh;
   Meredith, William; trial, first;
   trial, second
Delahay, John, 277–78
Doherty, John, 149, 203
Donnelly, Annie (née Currie), 127,
   128, 273, 275, 276, 284–85, 287
Donnelly, Bob (Robert), 271;
   assaults, then cares for, Charles
   Burchell, 281, 397n28; assaults
   Edward Brown, 274–75; assaults
   Hugh McKay, 282; assaults James
   Carroll, 219–21, 379nn30–32;
   beer keg incident, 275–76; buys
   and manages Western Hotel, 274,
   275–76; buys family farm, 271,
   274, 276, 285; cares for Mike
   Donnelly's children, 273; cartage
   business, 150, 273; Charles
   Hutchinson on, 257; compassion
   of, 280–81; confronts suspects,
   95–96; death of, 284–85; Everett
   shooting trial and conviction,
   48, 242; family's wake and
   funeral, 69, 74; Feeheley matter,
   223; financial success, 273; finds
   club, 104–5, 335n53; hatred of
   Vigilance Committee, 278–79;

and Kate Johnson, 113, 127–28,
   342nn24–26; later years and
   mental illness, 271–72, 394n1,
   394n4, 395nn6–9; neighbour's
   house fire, 273–74, 396n10;
   O'Connor house fire, 128,
   129–31, 132, 133, 175, 343n31,
   344nn40, 345n48, 345nn42–46;
   reaction to verdict and acquittal
   celebrations, 209, 211, 216–17;
   replaces fence, 125; threats
   against, 98; visits massacre
   site, 94–95, 187, 332n19;
   whereabouts, night of massacre,
   328n50. *See also* Stanley mill
   arson case
Donnelly, Bridget: brother's letter,
   124–25; ignored in press, 214;
   murdered, 10–11, 14–15;
   testimony about, second trial,
   188, 189
Donnelly, Ellen (née Hines), 273
Donnelly, James Michael (nephew
   of Bob), 272–73, 276
Donnelly, James Sr.: and Father
   Connolly, 80, 84; murdered,
   12, 312n9; night of massacre,
   5, 8–10; trial for shooting at
   Patrick Farrell, 242
Donnelly, Jennie (Jane), 299; after
   trials, 217; children of, 150, 217,
   273, 284; death of, 284; family's
   wake and funeral, 69, 72–73;
   later years and death, 273, 285;
   notified of massacre, 35; reacts
   to verdict, 208–9, 376n3
Donnelly, Jim (James), 284
Donnelly, Johannah: altercation
   with James Carroll, 62;
   characterization, xiii, 58; and

Father Connolly, 80, 83, 84;
murdered, 11–12, 16, 312n8;
night of massacre, 9
Donnelly, John: autopsy, 47,
49, 52–53, 321n4; and Father
Connolly, 86; inquest into
murder of, 111; murdered,
17–18, 19–20, 28, 29–30; in
press, 71–72; verdict on death,
111–12; whereabouts, 2, 3, 7, 8,
25–26, 27, 34, 310n2
Donnelly, Michael (cousin),
124–25
Donnelly, Mike (Michael): children
of, 273; trial for the murder of,
138–39; wake, 4, 194, 195
Donnelly, Nora (née Kennedy):
children, 151, 273; moves to
father's house, 99, 332n32; night
of massacre, 4, 7–8, 19–20,
29; pregnancy, 6, 7; testifies at
second trial, 194
Donnelly, Patrick, 208;
employment, 150; and Father
Connolly, 80–81, 83, 84, 86, 93;
Feeheley matter, 223–24, 227,
228–29, 232, 243, 248, 382n56;
godparent of, 94, 331n15;
later years, 273, 285; and
local farmers, 93–94, 331n14;
marriage and children, 273; and
press, 215, 330n12; settlement of
parents' debts, 93, 330n11; stabs
Joseph Roberts, 283; Stanley mill
arson case, 258, 261; stoicism,
53–54, 74; on suspects, 109;
threats against, 97; William
Lewis's trial, 138
Donnelly, Tom: Feeheley matter,
227, 232; fights mob, 10, 12,

312n10, 313n11; handcuffed,
10, 12, 14, 104, 114, 156, 163,
205, 218, 219; and James Carroll,
397n16; and James Feeheley,
226–27; murdered, 12–14, 16,
314n13, 314nn14–15; night of
massacre, 2–3, 5
Donnelly, William, 234; on
acquittal, 211–12; assaults
Randolph Parker, 283–84;
assists prosecution, 108, 148–50,
151, 353nn114–18, 354n119,
354nn123–24, 355n125,
356n126, 356nn128–29;
autopsies, 52–53; and Bernard
Stanley, 155–56; "Blackfeet" term,
122–23; and Charles Hutchinson,
150, 256–58; children of, 151,
273; compassion of, 281; as
constable, 273, 281; on crime
in Biddulph, 106–7; on deaths
among Vigilance Committee
and supporters, 267–70; debts
and reimbursement, 150–51,
356n133, 357nn134–35; on
divine retribution, 285; evidence
and observations, 28–32, 33–34,
34–35; as family leader, 105,
132; and Father Connolly,
60–61, 82, 83, 86–87, 89–90;
Feeheley matter, 223; and Francis
West, 221, 235, 253–54; horse
breeding, 3, 4, 31–32, 221,
379n37; house described, 6;
identifies perpetrators, 35, 49,
62; illnesses and death, 221, 284;
on jail, 252–53; John Donnelly's
autopsy, 49; on jurors for second
trial, 180–81; learns of parents'/
family's deaths, 35–36; mindset,

after massacre, 32–33, 34; night of massacre, 4, 7–8, 17–20; plans family's wake, 47; and press, 105–8, 215, 223, 223, 240–41, 243, 252–54; searches for new evidence, 221–22, 380n42; stoicism, 53–54, 74, 77; testimony, first trial, 162, 164; threats against, 97–99; on time, 287; and Vigilance Committee, 108; as witness, 101. *See also* Stanley mill arson case

Donnellys: anti-Donnelly sentiment, 100, 132, 154–55, 156, 204, 210, 243, 340n9; autopsies, 47, 49, 51–55, 321n4; compared to Vigilance Committee, 100–101; compassion of, 279–81, 282; dogs, 73, 277, 327n48; enduring story of, 285–87; family as group, xii; farmhouse, 1, 4–5, 219, 271, 311n3; and Father Connolly, 59–61; Feeheley brothers, history with, 226, 229; gravesite, 286–88; and inquest jury, 47–48; lease farmland to Feeheley family, 125; love for their birthplace, 285; name "Black Donnellys," xi–xii; payback attitude, 155–56, 359n155, 396on38; public opinion, outside Biddulph, xiv, 102, 216; reaction to verdict, 208–9, 211–12, 376n3; and Roman Catholic faction, 115; and Stanley brothers, xiv, 155–56, 242, 243, 390n38; and violence, 282–84; wake, 69–72, 74. *See also* funeral, of Donnellys; *See also* under individual family members' names

The Donnellys Must Die (Miller), 123

Dramatis Personae, 289–98

Elliot, William, 218, 254, 259, 265–66

Everett, Samuel, 48; death of, 269–70; hired/fired by prosecution, 153–54, 358n144; list of suspects, 161, 312nn8–9

Feeheley, Bridget, 229–30, 231, 244

Feeheley, James: regrets, 227, 314n13, 382n56; second trial, 182–84, 372nn44–45; as spy, 5–6, 7, 226, 311nn4–5. *See also* Feeheley matter

Feeheley, Michael, 229

Feeheley, William: and arrest of James Carroll, 64; and Vigilance Committee, 226; witnesses Tom Donnelly's murder, 13, 313n12, 314n13, 314nn14–15. *See also* Feeheley matter

Feeheley matter: brothers deny earlier statements, 228; brothers jailed and bailed, 232–33, 241, 385n76, 386nn78–79, 389n32; brothers leave for Michigan, 228; brothers' reluctance to testify, 227–28, 383n60, 383nn62–64, 384n65; charges and extradition efforts, 232–33, 385nn74–75; Charles Hutchinson's involvement, 228, 230, 232–33, 265; confrontation and disclosures, 224–25, 227, 382n56; dispute with James Carroll, 222–23, 381n47; and Father Connolly, 230,

O'Connor family's safety, 135–36; O'Connor house fire, 135, 346n63; and Oliver Mowat, 115; protection for Johnny O'Connor, 102–3, 127, 339n6, 342n22, 347n66, 368nn17–18, 368n20; regarding jury, second trial, 176; regarding Vigilance Committee fundraising, 218–19; and reward, 116–17, 337nn98–99, 338n102; Stanley mill arson case, 238, 239–40, 254–55, 256–58, 389nn29–30, 393nn63–64; and William Donnelly, 150, 256–58. *See also* prosecution; trial, first; trial, second

Idington, John, 246, 258, 259, 393n64
inquest, massacre: attempt to sabotage, 103, 120; autopsies, 47, 49, 51–55, 321n4; begins, 43; confessions, prospect of, 101; delayed, 108; disorder at, 110; Johnny O'Connor's testimony, 104; jury empannelled and described, 47–48; jury inspects site and hears witnesses, 48–49; jury's conduct, 110, 111; verdict, 111–12
inquest, O'Connor house fire, 134–35, 346n63
Irving, Aemilius, 170; on acquittal, 211–12; change of venue, 145; at first trial, 167; joins prosecution, 109; questions James Feeheley, 183–84; at second trial, 192, 193, 195, 209; treatment of suspects, 138

Johnson, Kate, 113, 127–28, 342nn23–26

Keefe, Andrew, 165
Keefe, James: and arrest of James Carroll, 65–66; delivers news of massacre, 43; leaves county, 121, 339n4; night of massacre, 3, 6, 7, 33, 34, 35
Keefe, James Sr., 60, 83, 162, 232
Keefe, Robert Sr., 163, 225, 232, 248–51, 382n53
Keefe, Thomas, 162, 276–77, 327n48, 362n11
Kelley, Thomas P., xii
Kennedy, John Jr.: alibi, 165; arrested, 66, 68; identified, 49; morning-after conversation with James Carroll, 40–41, 319n43; murder charges, 50; revolver, 148, 203; role in massacre, 18–19, 29, 33; threat against William Donnelly, 157; Vigilance Committee, 6–7
Kennedy, John Sr., 4, 6, 66, 325n30
Kent, John: arrested, charges dropped, 236, 238, 246; background, 387n10; in Francis West's testimony, 262, 263; hires Francis West, 235–36; stolen weapons, 235, 248, 258
Kerrick, George, 47, 48

Lamb, Joseph, 138, 146–48, 352nn110–12
Langmuir, John Woodburn, 146–47, 148
Larkin, John, 65, 68
Lawrason, Lawrence, 75

of witness, 41–42; William
Donnelly's actions, 28–36. *See
also* massacre; trial, first; trial,
second

Matthews, Charles Albert:
interviews Father Connolly,
59–60, 324nn19–20; testimony,
first trial, 163; and William
Donnelly, 60–61

Mayo, James, 47, 48

McConnell, John H., 225

McCosh, James, 238, 246

McGuire, John, 47–48, 246

McIlhargey, Enid, 274–75

McIlhargey, John, 275

McIlhargey, Patrick, 238, 246, 258

McKay, Hugh, 282

McKinnon, Hugh, 113, 242

McLaughlin, Martin: alibi,
165; arrested, 66–67, 68, 69;
identified, 35, 49; murder
charges, 50

McLaughlin, Temperance, 186–87

McRoberts, David, 131

Meredith, Edmund: background,
116, 336n69; hired by
Donnellys, 109; loyalties
questioned, 152–53; Stanley mill
arson case, 238–39, 245, 246,
255, 259, 259–60, 261–64, 265,
389n36, 391nn40–42

Meredith, William, 170;
background, 116, 173;
change of venue, 140, 145;
cross-examination of Johnny
O'Connor, 185, 186–92; and
Joseph Lamb, 147; on William
Donnelly, xi–xii, 167

Middlesex County Courthouse,
158

Miller, Orlo, 123

Moore, Silas Gilbert: arrests
suspects, 66, 69; collects John
Donnelly's body, 47; collects
remains, 53; testimony, first trial,
163

Morkin, Tom, 156

Morky, Frank, 130

Mowat, Oliver, 120; appoints
James Magee, 115; change of
venue, 120–21, 141, 144–45,
339n2; Feeheley matter, 231,
233; orders Special Commission,
171, 172–73; political situation,
114–15, 147; reluctance to
pursue case further, 221–22; and
reward, 117–19

Mowbray, Philip, 45–46

Murphy, Enoch, 34, 66, 68, 163

O'Connor, Johnny, 21; on
compensation, 136; cross-
examination of, 185–92;
describes massacre, 26,
313n11; describes site, 25,
38, 318n38; and Donnelly
family, 1–2; escapes fire, 15–17;
Feeheley matter, 232; identifies
perpetrators, 14, 26, 37–38,
43–44, 62, 94; informs parents
of massacre, 42–43; inquest
testimony, 104; Justice Cameron
on testimony, 205–6; name,
186–87, 372n50; night of
massacre, 2–3, 5–6, 311n4; and
press, 188–89; protected, 102–3,
135, 173–74, 347n66, 368n20,
368nn17–18; questioned by
constables, 44–45; testimony,
first trial, 160–61, 162, 163,

suspects, 144, 171, 340n7, 350n94, 351nn106–7, 366n3; and Vigilance Committee, 104, 106; on weapons theft, 248; and William Donnelly, 105–8, 215, 223, 240–41, 243; and William Stanley, 26–58, 243

prosecution: Aemilius Irving joins, 109; change of venue, 120–21, 126, 134, 140–42, 145–46, 172, 214, 348n84, 349nn87–88, 349nn90–91, 366n11; confessions as strategy, 101–2, 102, 110, 137–38, 146–47, 172, 351n107; declines to proceed, 209; hires/fires Samuel Everett, 153–54, 358n144; offers reward, 116–17, 337nn98–99, 338n102; reimburses William Donnelly, 151, 356n133, 357nn134–35; Special Commission announcement, 172–73, 367n14; William Donnelly aids, 108, 148–50, 151, 353nn114–18, 354n119, 354nn123–24, 355n125, 356n126, 356nn128–29. *See also* Hutchinson, Charles; trial, first; trial, second

Protestants, and politics, 181–82

Purtell, John: alibi, 164, 267; approached about confessing, 221–22, 380n39, 380n42; arrested, 94, 102; background, 94, 331n17; identified, 14, 38, 44; in jail, 94; murder charges, 50; role in massacre, 14

Quigley, Patrick, 13, 224, 314n13
Quigley, William, 47

Reaney, James, 94
"reign of terror," 106
reward, for information, 116–19, 194, 199, 200–201, 234, 235, 337nn98–99, 338n102
Roberts, Joseph, 283
Robinson, Thomas, 47, 48
role in massacre, 6
Roman Catholic faction: 'Blackfeet' and 'Whitefeet,' 123; celebrates verdict, 214; and Donnellys, 115; politics, 114–16, 172; population size, 114; and reward, 117, 119; supports suspects, 107, 116–17
Ryder, James "Buckshot," 276–77, 397n18
Ryder, James "Young Grouch": alibi, 164; arrested, 67, 69; identified, 35, 49; in jail, 137; murder charges, 50
Ryder, Jim "Sideroad," 249, 251–52, 269
Ryder, Patrick "Grouchy": altercation at Queen's Hotel, 248–51; arrest of sons, 67; arrested, 67, 69; Brimmacombe murder, 107–8, 250; collects funds for suspects, 218–19; godparent to Patrick Donnelly, 94, 331n15; Stanley mill arson case, 238
Ryder, Patrick Jr., 19, 67, 69, 162
Ryder, Thomas: alibi, 164, 203–4; arrested, 95; identified, 14, 38, 44; night of massacre, 374n79; role in massacre, 14, 313n11; Stanley mill arson case, 237–38
Ryder barn burning case, 6–7, 45–46, 318n41, 320n54

question of proof, 101, 334n42; St. Patrick's Church supports, 115; treatment of, 101–2, 109–10, 137–38, 145–46, 146–47, 348n76, 366n3; Vigilance Committee supports, 96–98, 108–9, 156, 218. *See also* Vigilance Committee

Sutherby, Edward, 6, 162

Thompson, Mary: about fire, 39; morning after massacre, 37, 316n20; testimony of, 201–3, 316n20

Thompson, William Jr.: morning after massacre, 37; testimony of, 201–3

Toohey, Catherine, 38, 39

Toohey, James: alibi, 204; night of massacre, 374n79, 375n80; role in massacre, 12, 13, 224, 312n10, 314n13, 314n16

Toronto, 142–44

trial, first: change of venue, 120–21, 126, 134, 140–42, 144–45, 339n2, 348n84, 349nn87–88, 349nn90–91; closing arguments, 166–67; defence's case, 164–66, 170; James Carroll at, 158–59; jury, 146, 169, 170, 171, 366nn7–8; prosecution's case, 160–61, 161–62, 170, 361n8; result, 169, 171–72; suspects plead not guilty, 159; and Vigilance Committee, 167–68, 171; Vigilance Committee control over, 157; witnesses and testimony, for defence, 165–66; witnesses and testimony, for

prosecution, 162–64. *See also* massacre; massacre, aftershock

trial, second: address to James Carroll, 209–10; charge to jury, 205–7; cross-examination of Johnny O'Connor, 185–92; defence strategy, 194–95, 201; James Feeheley's testimony, 182–84, 372nn44–45; Johnny O'Connor's testimony, 184–85; jury, 176–78, 180–82, 207, 371n40, 372n42, 376n90; Justice Cameron's involvement, 176, 192–94, 197, 204, 209–10; Mary O'Connor's testimony, 194–201; Police Chief Williams's testimony, 202–3; press, 184, 188–89, 190; prosecution's strategy, 182, 194, 201, 365n1; Thompsons' testimony, 201–3; verdict, 207; and Vigilance Committee, 184, 203, 204; witnesses and testimony for defence, 193, 204; witnesses and testimony for prosecution, 193, 194, 203; witnesses repeat testimony, 182

trials, aftermath: celebrations, 211, 212, 216–17; constables fired, 218; reaction to verdict, 208–9, 210–11, 376nn2–3, 377n4; Vigilance Committee fundraising, 218–19; whereabouts of Donnellys, 217–18. *See also* Feeheley matter

Vigilance Committee: and acquittal, 216; Bob Donnelly's enduring hatred of, 278–79; characterized by Hutchinson,

102; compared to Donnellys, 100–101; deaths among committee and supporters, 267–70; and Father Connolly, 59–60, 83–84, 87–90, 156, 333n38; fear of William Donnelly, 223; Feeheley matter, 224, 233, 241, 243–44, 386n79; and first trial, 161–62, 165, 167–68, 171; harassment of Donnellys and supporters, 121–23; intimidation campaign, 97–98, 121–22, 126, 127, 157; and James Carroll, 276; James Feeheley as spy, 5–6, 226, 311nn4–5; and Joseph Lamb, 148; justification of actions, 56–58; letter to Mary O'Connor, 174–75, 199–200, 369n23; makeup, xii, xiii; mindset toward William Donnelly, 46; O'Connor house fire, 132–33, 134; and Patrick Whalen, 112–13; and press, 104, 106; public opinion, 56–58; and Roman Catholic faction, 117; route taken, map of, vii; Ryder barn burning, 6; sabotage inquest, 103, 120; and second trial, 184, 203, 204; Stanley mill arson case, 237–38; supports suspects, 96–98, 108–9, 156, 218; threats against O'Connor family, 103; William Donnelly's information on, 108, 148–49. See also massacre; suspects

wake, Donnelly family, 69–72, 74
Walker, John, 34, 36, 149
Walker, William, 163

West, Francis: background, 235–36; death of, 269; Feeheley matter, 222–23, 226–27, 234, 263–64, 265, 381n47; Hall barn burning, 236; weapons theft, 234, 235, 248, 258, 261–62, 383n67, 387n9; and William Donnelly, 221, 235, 253–54. See also Stanley mill arson case
Whalen, Ann, 21–22, 26, 38
Whalen, John: on bodies, 38, 318n37; sees John Donnelly leave farm, 2, 310n2; testifies at inquest, 48, 49; witnesses Tom Donnelly's murder, 13, 17, 149; sees fire, 23–24, 24–25
Whalen, Joseph, 48, 49
Whalen, Patrick: altercation and arrangement with James Carroll, 26, 36, 40, 316n21, 319n45; death of, 268; fire at Donnelly farmhouse, 24–25, 26–27, 318n36; informs neighbours of massacre, 36–37, 40, 316n23, 317n26; night of massacre, 22–24; pressed by Casey about witness, 41–42, 319n46, 319n49; testifies at inquest, 48, 49; and Vigilance Committee, 112–13, 353n114
Whalen, William, 22, 149, 354n124
Williams, William Thomas Trounce: affidavit for change of venue, 140, 348n84, 349n87; arraignment of suspects, 75–76; arrests of suspects, 61–62, 66, 323n8, 325n25; complains about responsibilities, 110; describes massacre site, 46–47;

Printed on Rolland Enviro.
This paper contains 100% post-consumer fiber, is manufactured using renewable energy - Biogas and processed chlorine free.

 PCF
100%   BIOGAS ENERGY   PERMANENT